Coincidences in the Bible and in Biblical Hebrew

Also by the Author (English)

Radday, Y. T., Shore, H. *Genesis: An Authorship Study in Computer-Assisted Statistical Linguistics.* Analecta Biblica, 103. Series. Rome: Romae E Pontificio Instituto Biblico (Rome Biblical Institute Press), 1985.

Shore, H. *Response Modeling Methodology: Empirical Modeling for Engineering and Science.* Singapore: World Scientific Publishing Co. Pte Ltd., 2005.

Author Blog

haimshore.blog

Coincidences in the Bible and in Biblical Hebrew

Haim Shore

Coincidences in the Bible and in
Biblical Hebrew

ISBN: 978-965-598-628-0 (sc)

Preface to 2ⁿᵈ and 3ʳᵈ Editions

Third Edition: In this new edition, I have added several chapters, based on my blog (haimshore.blog), which have gained popularity amongst visitors to the site. These appear as an additional last (fifth) part of the book. Videos related to my research may be found on my personal YouTube channel. Some minor corrections were also applied.

Second Edition: On December, 4, 2009, the Israeli daily, the Jerusalem Post, published an interview with me about the findings of this book. The interview was posted on the Internet and translated to other languages. Following this interview, numerous communications were received and articles about the methodology used in the book published in various local newspapers. Some writers provided me with findings of their own. Concurrently, I continued with my own research and found some new relationships (not yet made public). In this second edition there are two new chapters: Chapter 21, which replaces the previous chapter and introduces a new methodology to statistically analyze some of the "Coincidences" in this book, and Chapter 23, which expounds on the new findings. Indeed, the latter introduce to the reader, in non-technical terms, the methodology of analysis pursued throughout the book. Since this chapter may be read as standalone (as most other chapters in the book), the reader is advised to read it prior to (or after) reading the introductory Chapters 1 and 2. Some minor corrections have been applied to other chapters of the book.

Preface

This book is about coincidences in the Bible and in the biblical Hebrew language.

The nature of these coincidences, what they are and what they are not, and the structure of this book will be expounded in the introductory chapter that follows this preface. For now, suffice it to say that the coincidences addressed here are those that I have become acquainted with from my long-standing familiarity with written Jewish sources, or coincidences that I have detected by personal observation over the many years since these coincidences first intrigued my curiosity.

From a personal perspective, I was reluctant to author this book. I am a tenured professor in an engineering department at an Israeli university, and coincidences are outside the reach of my area of expertise. Furthermore, writing about coincidences may not add points to my international academic standing. Yet for quite a few years now, I have observed peculiar coincidences in the Bible and in biblical Hebrew that were indeed troubling. As these amazing coincidences grew in number over time, a growing sense of uneasiness left me sleepless at night. I felt that my integrity as an academic researcher—whose mission in life, as I perceive it, it is to tell the truth—was starting to be undermined. I realized that the sheer number of these coincidences had reached a critical mass, where not making the coincidences public would compromise my personal ethical values. Furthermore, it would be incompatible with my values as a scientist and with the very scientific method, which I have applied throughout my academic career as a researcher. So I decided to put these coincidences in writing.

As the process of authoring this book progressed, I gradually have come to realize that my expertise in statistics may be useful in establishing in a more rigorous manner the true nature of some of the coincidences addressed in this book. Therefore, statistical analysis has been applied to some of the coincidences to ascertain whether they might be rightfully perceived as conveying concrete information. This endeavor brought forth about a dozen and a half statistical analyses, scattered throughout this book, where certain amazing relationships are explored, depicted, and statistically tested to establish their validity. These analyses, which can be traced by the list of figures given adjacent to the table of contents, are meaningful even as stand-alones. However, the analyses combined have implications that extend far beyond. In my judgment, the statistical analyses in this book compel one to perceive the other coincidences, which can not be subjected to statistical analysis, in a more serious fashion than would otherwise be justified—that is, if the statistical analyses were nonexistent.

We do hope that this book is, on the one hand, fun to read, and on the other hand be a trigger for further exploration of coincidences that the Bible and biblical Hebrew seem to have in store in abundance. Such explorations are expected to identify further amazing coincidences, not unlike the ones given in this book, that may, once found, be subjected to similar rigorous statistical analysis in order to remove their alleged coincidental nature.

Personal conclusions that one may derive from the coincidences displayed in this book are open for anyone to deliberate and shape up. These are considered by us to reside beyond the boundaries of the present composition.

HAIM SHORE
Beer-Sheva
October 2006

Contents

Part I
Coincidences in the Hebrew
Language: Messages of Design

Part II
Coincidences in the Hebrew Language: Hidden, Unexpected Information

Part III
Coincidences in the Bible

Part V

New Coincidences

Table of Figures

Introduction: About Coincidences, About This Book

What are coincidences, and how do they differ from other observations that appear to be random, meaningless, and yet, because they have been subjected to adequate scientific scrutiny, we treat them as conveying properly established information?

Science deals with observations that most often are random by nature. Given this quality of most observed phenomena, a certain approach developed within the science of statistics, and applied, throughout all disciplines of science and engineering, to observations where randomness, or noise, is integral and cannot be ignored. This approach has been realized in a methodology denoted "hypothesis testing." The major objective of the latter is to help the researcher separate, in a collection of noisy observations, the signal from the noise. What is implied by this is that if one has two competing hypotheses about the true State of Nature (namely, both hypotheses cannot be simultaneously true), then the decision as to which hypothesis is true cannot be taken with absolute certainty. Given the randomness of most observations of nature, all we can do is accept the hypothesis that is more likely to be true in light of the available evidence. Formulated in a more formal fashion, one assumes that there are two hypotheses about the true state of nature: the null hypothesis (H_0), which expresses the current state of our knowledge, and the alternative hypothesis (H_a), which expresses the claim that one wishes to examine for its validity, given the available data.

Since many observations of nature are random, performing hypothesis testing requires calculating the plausibility of H_0, given the data, and the plausibility of H_a, given the same data. Most commonly, these "plausibilities" are expressed in terms of probabilities to err, given the decision that has been selected and the data. In fact, the testing procedure is constructed in such a way that the error probabilities are minimal and specified prior to conducting the test. Thus, we commonly denote by α the probability of rejecting wrongly H_0 (this is also called an error of

Type I), and by β the probability to reject wrongly H_a (incorrectly accepting H_0, also called an error of Type II).

This description of the scientific approach to investigating nature, and the way it deals with the inherent random character of most observations of nature (when randomness cannot be ignored), lead one to conclude that the scientific discipline nearly always deals with coincidences. What these imply cannot be gauged in advance, but requires a formal statistical methodology that will ascertain, by the calculation of probabilities, which hypothesis is more plausible, given the sample of coincidences (read, "random observations"), and which is less plausible. It is the weight of the evidence, as quantitatively measured and estimated by statistical procedures, that leads one to decide which hypothesis should be accepted as probably true.

While the above description of the scientific methodology introduces one possible approach to dealing with coincidences, there are other cases less likely to be subject to the same routine.

Take as an example an eventuality that most of us have probably experienced one time or another: you think of a person, and shortly thereafter, you meet that person, or that person contacts you. One can formulate two hypotheses:

H_0: This is sheer coincidence.

H_a: When I think of a certain individual, I concurrently send a message to this person (via telepathy) to communicate with me.

How does one select a hypothesis as probably true? Surely, if the phenomenon of telepathy was invariably present, one would accept H_a to be true without any hesitation (the question of what is meant by "invariably" of course has also to be settled before a scientific claim is made). Most often, this is not the case. Telepathy has a nature of being extremely elusive; it is not always there. Therefore, the choice of the hypothesis which is more faithful to the true state of the world is not simple or self-evident. Alternatively, one can conduct a controlled experiment, where observations are generated and recorded. In this case, we have at our disposal a statistical methodology that would allow us to accept H_0 or H_a while controlling for the error probabilities. Indeed, such experiments have been conducted with regard to telepathy, and they are well documented in various books and published refereed papers.

But what if the number of available observations is limited to such an extent that no statistical analysis may be implemented—and, furthermore, one cannot generate controlled observations within a well-planned designed experiment, and all you have is a limited number of field observations that you have no control over (either in terms of their nature or their number)? In this case, formulating hypotheses for statistical testing may turn out to be futile; given the data, the size of the sample may be just too small to carry out statistical analysis with any acceptable degree of credibility. As a result, one would be at loss to convincingly persuade people trained in the scientific way of thinking that one hypothesis is true and the other is not. All one can do in such circumstances is call the observations "coincidences," and let each individual decide what the revealed coincidences really imply.

The objective of this book is just that: to present peculiar coincidences in the Bible and in the biblical Hebrew, and let the reader determine what the implications of these coincidences could be.

There is, however, one exception to the general qualification of the coincidences in this book, as just delineated: several statistical analyses have been performed with regard to some coincidences, and the results are displayed and explained in this book. We believe that these analyses would withstand any rigorous statistical scrutiny. It is doubtful that the results from these analyses fall in the category of "coincidences." Yet they are displayed, for the first time, in this book, out of the author's conviction that these statistical analyses have serious implications as to how the other coincidences introduced here should be appreciated.

The statistical analyses are scattered throughout this book. They are commonly accompanied by well-explained plots that render the implications of the analyses easily accessible, even to the non-technically oriented reader. These plots may be traced for their location by the table of figures placed adjacent to the table of contents. In these plots, note that the term "log" always refers to the natural logarithm—that is "log(x)" always means "$\log_e(x)$."

Prior to immersing ourselves in the arduous process of outlining a general characterization of the coincidences addressed in this book, it is imperative that we qualify what type of coincidences we are not dealing with. This book is not about Gematria, nor does it address what has become to be known as the Bible Code. Neither do we deal with possible fulfilling of biblical prophecies.

Jewish Gematria refers to a well-known practice, in Jewish mysticism, based on the assumption that two Hebrew words are somehow interrelated if the total numerical values of their constituent letters are equal. As explained in the first chapter of Part I of the book, each letter in the Hebrew language carries with it a certain numerical value. In "doing" Gematria, one assumes that there is some mystical implication to the fact that two given Hebrew words have equal numerical values. For example, in the Hebrew language, the word *Elohim* (God) has a numerical value of 86, the same as the Hebrew word for "the nature" (one word in Hebrew). Therefore, one would deduce that God is the source of all laws of nature, and that this fact is reflected by the numerical equivalence of the two words. We will not address such coincidences; neither do we express here our attitude about whether this practice—part and parcel of established Judaism since the time of the writing of the Talmud—has validity (the author does not feel qualified, nor of any authority, to render it meaningful conveying in public his attitude on such matters).

The Bible Code refers to the claim, made by respectable scientists and statisticians and supported by statistical analyses whose validity is debated to this day, that there are hidden messages in the Bible that are coded in a certain fashion. These messages can be exposed by treating the biblical text as an undivided string of letters and creating the words of the hidden message by equal skipping of letters (denoted equidistant letter sequence, or ELS).

For example, one could begin reading the first chapter of Genesis (in the original Hebrew language) and find the first *T* (*tav* in Hebrew). The first occurrence of this letter is as the last letter of the first word (*bereshit*). Then skip the next forty-nine letters to read the fiftieth letter as *vav* (the sixth letter in the Hebrew alphabet). You continue this way two more times to obtain the word "Torah," the Hebrew word for the first five books of the Bible (the Pentateuch). If more than one ELS exists that generate the same message (for example, skipping more than forty-nine letters or less), then experience has shown that the real message is hidden in the ELS with the shortest number of skipped letters (we will not elaborate here on how "real" is distinguished from "unreal," but there are various criteria that can be found in the related literature).

While the above example may seem simplistic, and is perhaps doing injustice to the whole approach (more interesting and intriguing instances have been found and made public), we again do not wish here to express our attitude toward the Bible Code, except to say that this book is not about the Bible Code and is not related to it in any way.

The interested reader may search for more information about the Bible Code via numerous published papers, books, and Internet sites (a Google search for "the Bible Code" produces, at the time of writing this chapter, 59,400 matches!).

Having delineated coincidences that are not addressed here, we may now qualify coincidences that are included, and explain the sense of uneasiness that has ultimately led to the writing of this book.

We start with coincidences in the Hebrew language. Unlike most other languages, which are based on conventions, the Hebrew words are all based on a root that contains three letters (and sometimes four letters, though rarely). Variations of this root produce words with different meanings. Occasionally, the same word serves to convey different meanings. Thus, the verbs "sin" and "miss" (as in "miss the target") are the same word in Hebrew, sharing one and the same root, although their meanings are far apart. One can perceive the fact that these two words share the same root as sheer coincidence.

Alternatively, one can assume that two words sharing the same root must be interrelated. The last assumption (or hypothesis, if you will) derives its credence from long-held Jewish tradition that goes back at least to the time of Rabbi Akiva (who lived during the time of the Jewish rebellion against the Romans, 135 CE, and probably executed by the Romans a year later, at 136 CE). According to this tradition, each letter in the Hebrew alphabet carries a certain meaning, and indeed the true meaning of any Hebrew word can be contrived from the total sum of the meanings of the root constituent letters. Furthermore, the position of a letter in the root affects the "weight" it contributes to the word meaning. We will relate to this in more depth in chapter 1.

If this assumption is adopted, then apparently "sin" and "miss" must be interrelated, and in fact being derived from the same root they probably carry a certain message. In this case, the message is not hard to fathom. Judaism, with its typical optimism not eroded by experience, treats any moral aberration, or sin, as the outcome of "missing the target"—the result of misjudgment and lack of knowledge, not as the result of innate evil.

Having two words with the same root thus appears to be compatible, in this case, with the total philosophy of Jewish tradition and in fact is explained by it. Furthermore, it attests to possible design in the composition of Hebrew words. No practical considerations of any sort would lead one to believe that over the years the word "to sin" would naturally evolve from the word "to miss." Can one prove this apparent premeditated design by any commonly accepted statistical testing? Clearly not. Therefore, we relate to this as a coincidence, leaving it for the reader to decide whether this is really so.

Other coincidences, of perhaps more overwhelming and less explainable nature, are scattered throughout this book with regard to the Bible and the Hebrew language. One example of such unexplainable nature is the fact that "ear" and "balance," in biblical Hebrew, derive from the same root. Yet it is a historic fact that only towards the end of the nineteenth century did researchers reveal that the mechanism responsible for the human-body balance resides inside the ear (for details, see section 10.3.2).

While we attempt no explanation of the coincidences expounded in the book, it is important to stress two assumptions that we do make. These assumptions are deeply rooted in Jewish tradition, and although one might be tempted to attribute to them signatures of Jewish mysticism, they really are not. The assumptions derive their validity from dozens of examples in which the trueness of these assumptions had been demonstrated. We will show some such examples in the opening chapters of this book.

The two assumptions are:

- Words sharing the same root must somehow be interrelated. In other words, numerous examples have demonstrably shown that words with a common root are not so due to coincidence. If the relationship among such root-sharing words is not immediately comprehensible, this implies that the relationship needs be further explored, not that it is nonexistent.
- The sum of the numerical values of the letters, comprising a given word, occasionally delivers relevant information. This is demonstrated by four simple examples right at the beginning of the book (refer to section 2.1), where the information concealed in the numerical values of the letters constituting a word is undeniably related to its apparent revealed meaning. Reading these examples, the reader may gain insight into the general validity of this assumption, and thus become more open to the less obvious, though more stunning, examples or coincidences introduced in later chapters.

It is to be reemphasized that these two assumptions are not related, in any way, to Jewish Gematria. The latter attempts to identify common grounds (or shared meaning) to two or more words having equal numerical values for the total sum of their constituent letters. Though we do not express our position regarding this practice, it is important to assert that no such is attempted here. The only qualification that we can deliver, as embodied by the above assumptions, is that (based on numerous examples) the above assumptions are valid to a highly credible degree.

Similarly unexplainable coincidences permeate biblical text, most often hidden in visibly simplistic statements of facts, occasionally in bizarre names, which make one wonder where all these coincidences truly originated.

The coincidences presented in this book are divided into four separate categories:

- Coincidences in the Hebrew language that show design intended to convey a message, often of a moral nature. The example just given with regard to "sin" belongs to this category of coincidences.

- Coincidences in the Hebrew language that show design intended to convey hidden information, occasionally such which cannot be expected to be known in biblical times.

- Coincidences in the Bible that convey, or assume, information or knowledge that cannot be expected to be known in biblical times.

- Other coincidences from Jewish tradition or Jewish history (as related earlier, no reference to possible present-day fulfillment of biblical prophecies is attempted).

Accordingly, the book is divided into four major parts, with the following four titles.

Part I: Coincidences in the Hebrew Language: Messages of Design

Part II: Coincidences in the Hebrew Language: Hidden, Unexpected Information

Part III: Coincidences in the Bible

Part IV: Supplementary Coincidences

The larger part of these coincidences have been the result of my own observation over the many years that these coincidences have intrigued me (and occasionally deprived me of my peace of mind). Coincidences that I have known from other sources—and the origins of which I was able to trace—are quoted in the most possible accurate terms. The Internet and some good friends have been a great help for me in pinpointing these sources, wherever they existed.

All coincidences related to the Bible refer to the Old Testament only. This is because I am convinced that my knowledge of the Old Testament and my acquaintance with it qualify me to an acceptable degree (though lacking formal education related to interpreting of biblical texts) to write about coincidences therein. No similar qualification can be extended to the New Testament.

The notation in the book includes both English and Hebrew. Because the text is displayed in English, Hebrew words, given within the text in English letters, are marked by raised numerals, and then given in the appendix, in the original Hebrew letters marked by similar numbering.

In all Hebrew words written with English letters, the letter combination *ch* stands for the eighth Hebrew letter, *chet*, and should be read as "K" (there is no English letter equivalent to the *chet*). The *ch* combination is also used for the eleventh Hebrew letter, *kaf*, when the latter is pronounced similarly to *chet*. Also, the combination *tz* always stands for the Hebrew letter *tzadi*.

Biblical English quotations used in the book are based on several available Bible translations, a list of which is given in a separate paragraph at the book's references section. A major source for these Bible quotations was the Jerusalem Bible (2000). The reason for using different translations for different verse quotations was my experience that, for certain verses, and not for others, some translations are more faithful to the true meaning of the Hebrew text, and to how traditional Jewish scholars have interpreted it.

If the author's acquaintance with how Jewish sources interpret a certain part of a verse indicated that there might be, in available translations, a major departure from the true sense of the verse, or if it was felt that a verse in the English translation departed from the real Hebrew meaning (Hebrew is my mother tongue), an alternative translation was offered in brackets within the quote, or subsequently, without omitting the original English translation.

A companion book that has been a great assistance throughout the process of authoring this book is *The New Concordance for the Bible* (Even-Shoshan 1988). Also, I infrequently used the *Biblical Encyclopedia* (Mazar *et al.* 1976) and *Lexicon Biblicum* (Soliali and Barkuz 1965). These were used for some validation of concepts when deemed necessary. Other sources are quoted throughout the text.

A major source for some details in the text is existing Web sites. They are quoted numerous times in the text. Though I only used sites that to my judgment are credible enough (and usually cross-referenced), I do not assume any responsibility for the accuracy of these sites and their contents.

Finally, the coincidences displayed in this composition are not equally persuasive one way or another. In other words, some coincidences are more extraordinary than others. Some may be perceived as directly derived from the biblical text, or from the obvious meanings of Hebrew words. Others may look contrived to the reader. Still others may be incredibly difficult to explain. We have not attempted any screening of these coincidences. Furthermore, we have also not attempted any rating (or ranking) according to their possibly psychological or rational (or irrational) impact. Therefore, as befits a book about coincidences, these are arranged in no particular order, coincidentally scattered throughout the book. It is left for the reader to shape up his/her reaction as to how a particular coincidence, or a group of coincidences bound by a common theme, should be perceived.

A concluding epilogue conveys some personal sentiments.

We regard the nineteen statistical analyses displayed in this book the most important contribution of this research composition.

All else—ornaments.

PART I

Coincidences in the Hebrew Language: Messages of Design

CHAPTER 1

The Structure of the Hebrew Language

1.1 The Structure of a Hebrew Word (Biblical Only)

The Hebrew language has a unique structure unmatched by other languages. While in other languages, words represent agreed-upon conventions that attach no special meaning to the constituent letters, in Hebrew each letter has a unique meaning, which is conferred upon the word, thus partaking in the buildup of the word's meaning. In that respect, the Hebrew language is comparable to the language of chemistry, where the name of a composite reflects its constituent elements—for example, water is denoted by H_2O. One may think of written Chinese as perhaps coming closest to the Hebrew language in that parts of the characters create a gestalt meaning.

The internal order of the letters in a Hebrew word is also a major player that, to a large extent, determines the meaning of the word. As in the language of chemistry, where the composite's unique characteristics are decided both by the atoms comprising its molecules and by their internal layout, so in Hebrew the position of a letter determines its influence, or weight, in shaping up the word's meaning. The earlier a letter appears, the more significant its contribution to the meaning of that word.

A list of the Hebrew letters, with the letters' names and their approximate English equivalents, is given in Table 1.1.

In their pure and authentic form, as used in the Bible, Hebrew words have a three-letter root (though some have two- or even four-letter roots). The root of the word determines its meaning. For example, the word "child" (*yeled*[1] in Hebrew) has a three-letter root, the Hebrew equivalent of the English letters *ILD*. This root serves to generate a variety of words associated with delivery (giving birth to), which is expectable. In other cases, the link between words sharing the same root and seemingly conveying disparate meanings is not straightforward,

11

and has to be contrived from the underlying tenets and philosophy of the Jewish faith. We related earlier (refer to the introduction) to the pair of words "sin" and "miss." These share the same root, yet they appear to share no common meaning. Likewise, the words "virtue" and "measure" are one and the same in Hebrew (*midah*).[2] Only a thorough probe of Jewish basic tenets can lead one to the understanding of why these words are one and the same. These sequences of words and others are explored in section 2.1.

Another peculiar feature of the Hebrew language is the numerical value attached to each of its letters. These values are assigned to the Hebrew letters in an ascending order, respectively with the letters' positions in the Hebrew alphabet (however, the numbers are not necessarily identical with the letters' ordinal positions).

The numerical values of the Hebrew letters are displayed in Table 1.1.

Table 1.1. The Hebrew letters (letters in brackets appear only at the end of the word).

Letter	Numerical value	Name (English)	Name (Hebrew)	Pronounced as
א	1	alef	אלף	A
ב	2	bet	בית	B or V
ג	3	gimmel	גימל	G
ד	4	dalet	דלת	D
ה	5	hei	הא	H
ו	6	vav	וו	V
ז	7	zayin	זין	Z
ח	8	chet	חית	German Ch
ט	9	tet	טית	T
י	10	yod	יוד	Y (I)
(ך) כ	20	kaf	כף	K or German Ch
ל	30	lamed	למד	L
(ם) מ	40	mem	מם	M
(ן) נ	50	nun	נון	N
ס	60	samech	סמך	S
ע	70	ayin	עין	A
(ף) פ	80	peh	פה	P, Ph or F
(ץ) צ	90	tzadi	צדי	Tz
ק	100	kof	קוף	K or Q
ר	200	resh	ריש	R
ש	300	shin	שין	Sh or S
ת	400	tav	תו	T

To build on a previous analogy, the numerical values of the Hebrew letters may be likened to those of the chemical elements in the periodic table of the elements (the pure substances), where the element's position in the table, given by its atomic number, signifies some of the unique chemical characteristics of the element (like its weight, though this is given in the periodic table by a separate atomic weight).

The significance attached to the numerical values of the letters in the Hebrew alphabet explains why the total numerical value of the root of a given Hebrew word is also considered meaningful, and why words with different roots, which nevertheless share the same numerical value, are expected in Gematria to be somehow interrelated.

1.2 Letters and Their Meanings

How do we know what each letter stands for?

One of the greatest ancient Jewish sages, Rabbi Akiva (died 136 CE), is traditionally believed to have produced numerous interpretations based on the Hebrew letters. Indeed, one of the most ancient Jewish documents about the Hebrew letters, "Midrash D'Rabbi Akiva" ("Commentary of Rabbi Akiva") is attributed, as the name insinuates, to this Jewish sage (for details about Rabbi Akiva, visit http://www.ou.org/about/judaism/rabbis/rakiva.htm).

A primary source for the meanings of Hebrew letters is the Gemara (part of the Jewish Talmud), Masechet Shabbat (Daf 104, 1). A modern source to learn of the history of the immense research effort that has gone into the learning and interpretation of the Hebrew letters, mostly by Jewish scholars, is Elias Lipiner's monumental composition "The Metaphysics of the Hebrew Alphabet" (1989, 2003, in Hebrew). Finally, the Web site of Arachim (a charitable not-for-profit organization) provides some good information: http://www.arachim.co.il/.

So how do we know what each Hebrew letter stands for?
According to Jewish tradition, the meaning of a letter may be studied (or inferred) from four sources:

- The letter's name;
- The meaning of the word in the Bible, where the letter makes its first appearance as the first letter in the word (this rule excludes the word's prefix, if any; refer to Gemara, Masechet Babba Kamma, Daf 55, 71);
- The letter's geometrical shape;
- The letter's numerical value.

To demonstrate how each letter acquires its unique meaning, let us explore two letters of the Hebrew alphabet: the *alef* (the first letter) and the *hei* (the fifth letter, corresponding to the English *H*). Later, we will examine a combination of two other letters (corresponding to the English *P* and *R*), and show how their individual meanings confer meanings upon various Hebrew words in whose roots they appear.

The first letter of the Hebrew alphabet (corresponding to the English *A*) is named *alef.* It has a numerical value of 1 and signifies (justifiably, given its ordinal position) "God." The numerical value attached to the *alef* (1) is also understandable, given the importance Judaism assigns to the *oneness* of God. Thus, the first of the Ten Commandments states, "You shall have no other gods before me" (Exod. 20:3 and Deut. 5:7). Furthermore, a Jew is expected to say in his or her prayer twice a day, "Hear, O Israel: The Lord our God, The Lord is One" (Deut. 6:4).

In the Bible, the first word in which *alef* appears as the first letter means God (*Elohim*).[3] Furthermore, the name of the letter, *alef,* resembles the word *Aluf*[4] (derived from the same root as *alef*), one of the names the Bible uses for God (for example, Jer. 3:4; Prov. 2:17, 16:28).

As preached by Rabbi Akiva, the structure of the *alef,* א, also indicates its meaning. The letter is seen as the two letters *yod* (the tenth letter in the Hebrew alphabet) connected by *vav* (the sixth letter in the Hebrew alphabet). The sum up of the numerical values of these three letters (10 + 10 + 6 = 26) is the same as that of the Divine Name, Jehovah.

Finally, it turns out that not only the value of the first letter in the Hebrew alphabet is one. Adding together the numerical values of all the letters in its name (*alef*), one obtains, duly:

$$111 = (80 = ף) + (30 = ל) + (1 = א)$$

The second letter we introduce as an example is the ה, named *hei*, and given the numerical value of 5 (this is also its ordinal position in the Hebrew alphabet; refer to Table 1.1). The *hei* stands in the Bible (and also in the Hebrew language) for "fertility," or "pregnancy," and this is the meaning that the letter confers upon various words in which it appears. This will now be demonstrated by a few examples.

Most nouns and adjectives in Hebrew are either masculine or feminine. If one wishes to transform the meaning of a word from masculine to feminine, this is frequently done by adding the letter *hei* to the noun (or adjective). Thus, a boy is *yeled*[1] and a girl is *yaldah.*[5] A man is *ish,*[6] and a woman *Ishah.*[7] A wise man is *chacham*,[8] a wise woman *chachamah*[9] (with an additional *hei* at the end of the word).

References to the letter *hei* as implying fertility abound in the book of Genesis. When God breaks the news to Abram (without *hei*) that he will have children, the Bible recounts: "And Abram fell on his face: and God talked with him, saying, As for me, behold, my covenant is with you, and you shall be a father of a multitude of nations. No longer shall your name be Abram but your name shall be Abraham … [with *hei*] … for a father of a multitude of nations have I made thee" (Gen. 17:3–5). Likewise, with regard to Abraham's wife, "And God said to Abraham, As for Sar'ai your wife, you shall not call her name Sar'ai, but Sarah shall be her name. I will bless her, and moreover I will give you a son by her …" (Gen. 17:15–16).

Finally, when Abraham sends his servant to find a wife for his son, Isaac, the Bible describes the future wife of Isaac: "The maiden was very fair to look upon, a virgin, whom no man had known" (Gen. 24:16). However, the word "maiden," *naarah*,[10] which in standard Hebrew ends with *hei* (refer, for example, to the book of Esther 2:4, 7, 9) is misspelled as *naara*[11] (with the last letter, *hei*, missing, though pronunciation of the word is unchanged). This is no coincidence, since the same "misspelled" format appears several times in the same chapter. Obviously, the narrator intended to emphasize that the girl was a virgin (fertility not yet demonstrated), and therefore omitted the *hei*. This interpretation is corroborated in Deuteronomy 22, which explicitly deals with the virginity of a newly wed wife. The word "maiden" appears therein both with the *hei* (22:19) and without (22:15, 16, 20, 21, 23–29), dependent on the relevant context.

Incidentally, does not the shape of the letter *hei* (ה) reflect its meaning (the apparent sign of fertility—namely, pregnancy)?

How does a combination of letters in a root generate the underlying meaning common to all words sharing these letters? We will take as an example two letters: The ר (named *resh*, the Hebrew equivalent of *R*), and the letter פ (named *peh*, the Hebrew equivalent of *P* and *F*). The first letter is pronounced nearly as the Hebrew word for "head" (*rosh*[12]), while the second is pronounced and written as the Hebrew word for "mouth" (*peh*[13]). Whether or not this association with parts of the body is coincidental, it is obvious, as judged by the formerly specified criteria (for example, *reshit* is the first word in the Bible, where *resh* heads a word) that *resh* is associated with features of wholeness, completeness, order, existence of meaning. Conversely, the *peh* represents segregation, division, partition, disarray, loss of meaning. Put metaphorically, the *resh* stands for products of the head, like a thought or a feeling, which are experienced as whole (as single indivisible units), while the second letter represents their outwardly expression (through the mouth) as a stream of separate words and sentences, which may be chaotic.

In accordance with this concept, we would expect a root combination of $P+R+X$ (where X stands for any third letter) to convey the idea of an entity that was whole and then disintegrated into many parts—something in order that was transformed into disarray, part of a whole that has become separate. Examining words that have the root *P.R.X* shows that indeed this is the case.

Let us examine some of the realizations of the above combination. These will be given in the Hebrew alphabet order of the X (not all possible realizations are detailed here).

The root *P.R.A* generates an adjective that implies "wild, savage, out of order." The root *P.R.D* generates words that mean "to separate" or "to depart." The root *P.R.H*[14] is the source of words meaning "to become fruitful or pregnant" ("one made into two that eventually separate"). The root *P.R.Z* means "excessive" and "overflowing," but also generates an adjective describing a city with no boundaries (no surrounding walls). The root *P.R.T* means "to give details," but also to change a banknote into small coins. The root *P.R.M* means "to take apart" (a cloth). The root *P.R.S* means "to slice into many parts" (like slicing bread). The root *P.R.XX*[15] (the third letter in the root stands for the Hebrew *ayin*, which has no English equivalent, yet is pronounced nearly like A) means "to inflict disorder, chaos." The root *P.R.Tz*[16] means "to break into" (like in a burglary), but also "to make a dent or a hole" (in a wall). The root *P.R.K* means "to dismantle." The root *P.R.S*[17] (the English S has two equivalents in Hebrew) means "to separate from" (as a person would from a company of people, or a business from a partnership). However, the root *R.P.A*, where the R heads the word (preceding the P), has the meaning of putting something which was out of order into order—the reverse of the meanings imparted by the previous examples. More explicitly, "to cure."

1.3 Precision of Biblical Language

The mathematical precision of biblical language is one of the most stunning, and perhaps alleviating, aspects of biblical text. One can hardly appreciate this precision until an in-depth exploration is conducted, perhaps assisted with some accessible complementary biblical interpretations, in order to experience this textual precision. In this section, we introduce some examples for the precision of biblical discourse. Seven examples are given in subsections 1.3.1-1.3.7.

There are two reasons why these examples are expounded already at this point.

First, a natural inclination of a naive reader would be to relate to the coincidences presented in this composition as just that—namely, coincidental anecdotes that bear no meaning. While a reader making such deductions may be correct (or may not be), it is our feeling that one should first have a good feeling for the precision with which the Bible presents its stories and claims. Experiencing this precision with some good examples would inevitably equip the reader with some sense of the seriousness of the coincidences presented later in the book. Whatever conclusions a reader may then derive from the coincidences, he or she would, at the very least, base his or her judgment on an educated understanding of the nonrandom use of words and phrases in biblical text.

A second reason for the introduction of these examples of biblical-text precision is to let the reader simply enjoy the implementation of a modern concept, hyperlinks, in biblical text. A hyperlink in a given text is an underlined word, or phrase, that appears on the computer screen, which, when activated by a click on the mouse, takes one to another place in the text (or to another Web site), where the selected phrase is explained, or some further relevant information is given. A network of hyperlinks of course needs to preserve a very high degree of consistency.

Such consistency is prevalent in biblical text to a surprisingly high degree. This implies that when a word, or a phrase, is used in one place in the Bible, it would most probably retain the exact same sense in all other places where it appears, irrespective of the general context where it is used. It is as though biblical phrases are interconnected by an underlying network of hyperlinks that ensures that consistency is well preserved.

1.3.1   *The Donkey (Ass) in the Bible*

The donkey in the Bible has a very special place. This sounds ridiculous, yet it is true. One can easily realize this by reading various entries in the Bible where a donkey is addressed. Mentioning of the donkey in all these cases appears so trivial, so insignificant and out of place, that one may be tempted to reach either of two possible conclusions: that the Bible contains third-rate text, or that the concept of "donkey" bears special symbolism that must be explored prior to dismissing biblical text as badly written narrative.

From a thorough scanning of all places where a donkey is addressed, one may not avoid the conclusion that the latter is the true interpretation of "donkey" in the Bible: this animal, and riding it, symbolizes something unique. But what symbol does it stand for?

The essential clue is provided by the name of a donkey in the Hebrew language. We may recall that in the book of Genesis, God has given an assignment to Adam: "And out of the ground the Lord God formed every beast of the field, and every bird of the air; and brought them to the man to see what he would call them: and whatever the man called every living creature, that was its name. And the man gave names to all cattle, and to the birds of the air, and to every beast of the field" (Gen. 2:19–20).

So what name was given to the donkey? *Chamor*.[18] The root of this name is *Ch.M.R*, and it is pronounced nearly identically to another Hebrew word: *chomer*,[19] meaning "material, substance." This word generates many related words that are similar to English words derived from "material"—*chomrani*[20] (materialistic), *chomranut*[21] (materialism), and so on.

This special feature of the donkey's character—namely, being tied up to "material things"—is addressed by the prophet Isaiah when he describes the people of Israel: "The ox knows his owner, and the ass his master's crib; but Israel does not know, my people does not consider" (Isa. 1:3). Read it again: the ox is loyal to his owner, the ass to its crib!

So what is the symbolism in riding a donkey?

Riding a donkey implies rising to such spiritual heights that all materialistic considerations are subdued and subjugated to the spiritual. This symbolism cannot be avoided, unless one wishes to accept trivialization of biblical text.

The following examples corroborate this argument.

Example 1: The Sacrifice of Isaac

The story of the sacrifice of Isaac starts with the following: "And Abraham rose up early in the morning, and saddled his ass, and took two of his young men with him, and Isaac his son" (Gen. 22:3). And later, "And Abraham said to his young men, sit here with the ass, and I and the lad will go yonder" (therein, 22:5). And later, after the encounter with the angel of God who had prevented Abraham from sacrificing Isaac: "And Abraham returned to his young men, and they rose up and went together to Beer-Sheba" (therein, 22:19). In the last quotation, there is no mentioning of the famous ass. The ass simply evaporated after being addressed twice a few sentences earlier. Obviously, all materialism had disappeared after Abraham's encounter with the angel of God. No human materialistic inclinations need further be controlled, because they all vanished.

Example 2: Moses Returns to Egypt from Exile

After God delivers Moses his lifelong mission (over forty years) of delivering Israel from the bondage of Egypt, the Bible is very short on detail. Here is how the story of Moses returning to Egypt is told in the Bible: "And the Lord said to Moses in Midyan, Go return to Egypt: For all men are dead who sought thy life. And Moses took his wife and his sons, and set them upon an ass, and he returned to the land of Egypt: and Moses took the rod of God in his hand" (Exod. 4:19–20).

What is so important about this marginal fact regarding the ass, which the Bible bothers to mention here and in other places too?

One is again hard-pressed to make sense of the importance of the fact that Moses had an ass unless the symbolism of that ass, as expounded earlier, is being appropriately accounted for.

Example 3: The King Messiah

All Jewish commentators, including the renowned Rashi (1040–1105), agree that the passage by the prophet Zechariah, 9:9–10, relates to the King Messiah as the latter is related to in Jewish scripture. The prophet Zechariah thus describes the end of times, when the people of Israel will be back to their ancestral Promised Land and the Messiah will come (or return, according to the Christian faith): "Rejoice greatly, O daughter of Zion; shout, O daughter of Jerusalem: behold, thy king comes to thee: he is just, and victorious; humble and riding upon an ass, and upon a colt, the foal of an ass" (Zech. 9:9).

If we accept Jewish interpreters' assumption that this passage relates to the Messiah, then the Bible here really transcends itself in trivializing the Messiah: his near-divine characteristics are that he is just, victorious, humble, and … riding an ass?

It becomes clear that the only way to read this passage in a proper context is to adopt it as an allegory, having the same meaning as in all earlier examples. Most importantly, this is a further demonstration of the highly consistent fabric of biblical discourse.

1.3.2   *"Which God had created to do" (Gen. 2:3)*

The detailed story of creation ends thus: "And God blessed the seventh day, and sanctified it: because in it he rested from all his work which God had created and performed" (Gen. 2:3). Regrettably, this translation, like most others, is extremely inaccurate. The ending phrase, in Hebrew, is, literally: "which God had created to do." This changes the whole sense of the sentence. It implies that God has created work that needs to be done. This interpretation is consistent both with how Jewish tradition perceives the role of the human race on this planet—namely, to complete the not-yet-done work associated with creation (refer also to chapter 6)—and with how the commandment to preserve the Sabbath is expounded in the Torah. Referring to the latter, let us read carefully how the Second Commandment is explained: "Remember the Sabbath day, to keep it holy. Six days shalt thou labor, and do all thy work: but the seventh day is a Sabbath to the Lord thy God: in it thou shalt not do any work … for in six days the Lord made heaven and earth, the sea, and all that is in them, and rested on the seventh day: therefore the Lord blessed the Sabbath day and hallowed it" (Exod. 20:8–10, 11). And further on: "Six days may work be done; but on the seventh is the Sabbath of rest, holy to the Lord … for in six days the Lord made heaven and earth, and on the seventh day he rested, and was refreshed." (Exod. 31:15, 17). No "creating" is alluded to, only "doing." And the deeds to be done were also created by God, as detailed in the above quote from Gen. 2:3.

The distinction between the worlds of *creating*, *forming*, and *doing* is central to Jewish philosophy and theology. According to the Malbim (1809–79), one of the greatest biblical commentators, "creating" refers to bringing forth into existence out of nonexistence, "forming" refers to bringing forth that which is potentially in the created, still hidden ("bringing out the incidences that are glued to the created"), and "doing" is the completion of the forming and the removing of that which is not inherently in the nature of the created (the act of *tikun*, or repair). Refer to the Malbim interpretation of Isaiah 45:7.

The distinction between *creating*, *forming*, and *doing* permeates the Bible. An example: "Every one that is called by my name: for I have created him for my glory; I have formed him; yea, I have made him" (Isa. 43:7). This same verse may be differently read as (author's translation from the literal text): "All that is called by my name and for my glory, I have created it (him), I have formed it (him), yea I have made it (him)" ("it" and "him" are indistinguishable in Hebrew unless by context).

This triple partition into creating, forming, and doing (or making) is also one of the cornerstones of Jewish mysticism (Kabbalah).

The precise meaning of the Hebrew verse "which God had created to do," which appears in the title of this subsection and regrettably seems to be overlooked in common English translations, is another testimony to the precision of biblical text.

1.3.3 *"Thou shalt not … put a stumbling block before the blind" (Lev. 19:14)*

It is common human experience that the blind at times need assistance. In particular, no one would argue the truism of the assertion that if a blind person encounters a stumbling block one should remove it, all the more so not place one there.

Alas, this in not what the Bible is saying. The Bible does not at all relate to these trivial scenarios; they are too obvious. The Bible takes such scenarios, and the expected human response to such, as self-evident to the point of being trivial. The Scripture sees no need to address such cases, where the expected human response is clear. The commonly accepted translation, as appearing in the title of this subsection, simply does not appear in the original Hebrew text. The Bible is precise—here as elsewhere—and Jewish interpretations, over the centuries, indeed followed the exact phrase, as given in Hebrew, and not its somewhat misplaced English translation.

The keyword to understanding what precisely this verse means by "blind" is the word "put." The latter does not appear in the original Hebrew text. Instead, the word "give" is used. This changes the whole sense of the verse. "To put" (a stumbling block) conveys a scenario of passive cruelty. A stumbling block was placed, and either the blind will stumble over it or not. "To give" is something else. You are *giving* a present—or, at least, something that looks like one. The "blind," then, are not the physically sight-challenged. Rather, he or she is one who does not realize that the present is in fact poisonous, harmful to the recipient. Furthermore, it might be beneficial to the "giver." There is an obvious active malicious intent in the action: one gives his fellow man (or woman) an obstacle in the form of a favorable object or act, yet the taker is unaware (blind) of the real nature of the present, or to its adverse ramifications. The Bible could not be more precise.

The Talmud and other Jewish sources classify "malicious presents to the blind," or acts committed that take advantage of a temporary situation of "blindness," into five well-specified categories. We will not detail these here, but nevertheless convey a sense of what is meant by "to *give* a stumbling block to the blind."

Examples:

- "Refrain from giving bad advice that is intended to benefit you on account of the unsuspecting receiver of the advice." For example, one should not advise another party to sell his or her field in order to buy a donkey, when the advisor wishes to buy the field for herself or himself (Midrash Sifra, Lev. 19:14)!

- "Avoid introducing a prohibited, or harmful, temptation." For example, do not present wine to a Nazirite—a man who takes a vow to refrain from wine, cutting hair, or ritually contaminating himself by coming into contact with the dead (Babylonian Talmud, Pesachim 22b).

- "Do not lend money without having witnesses present lest the borrower might be tempted to deny the loan, thus causing him/her self harm by sinning" (Babylonian Talmud, Baba Metzia 75b).

- Do not sell a used item (car), hiding its defects.

- Nechama Leibowitz, a renowned Bible scholar, offers this wide interpretation (Leibowitz 1983): "The Torah teaches us that even by sitting at home doing nothing, by complete passivity and divorcement from society, one cannot shake off responsibility for what is transpiring in the world at large, for the iniquity, violence and evil there. By not protesting … you become responsible for any harm arising therefrom, and thus have violated the prohibition of 'Lifnei Iver'" ("before the blind").

It is interesting to note a similar case of usage of words in the Bible that conveys the exact sense of what is really meant—a sense devoid of the trivial meaning that one would expect. In Exodus, we have "And the Lord spoke to Moses, saying, Speak to the children of Israel that they bring me an offering" (Exod. 25:2). This sounds innocent enough, until one examines more closely what is really said in the Hebrew text, literally: "speak to the children of Israel that they *took me* [*ve-yekchu li*[22]] an offering."

This sounds bizarre. The Bible does not talk about giving, or bringing, an offering, but rather about "taking." Not taking from fellow citizens, but "taking to God" (a bizarre form of speech, as you commonly "take from," not "take to"). Does this insinuate that although the final physical outcome is the "giving" of the offering, in fact the "giver" is at the same time "taking" from God, being blessed because of the offering?

1.3.4 *"And Thou shalt not favor a poor man in his cause" (Exod. 23:3)*

The Bible is replete with warnings that the poor, and the widow, and the orphan, and the foreigner must all receive justice and decent conduct from fellow men and women, and that their relative position in society must not be taken advantage of in immoral ways. The Jewish prophets, in particular, repeatedly warn, "Learn to do well, seek judgment, relieve the oppressed, judge the fatherless, plead for the widow … they judge not the fatherless, neither does the cause of the widow reach them" (Isa. 1:17, 23); "Oppress not the stranger, the fatherless, and the widow, and shed not innocent blood in this place … Thus said the Lord … deliver the robbed out of the hand of the oppressor: and do no wrong, do no violence to the stranger, the fatherless, nor the widow, neither shed innocent blood in this place" (Jer. 7:6, 22:3).

One would expect that when the law of God is first revealed to the children of Israel while still in the Sinai desert, the Bible would likewise emphasize that the less fortunate of society should get fair treatment in all walks of life. Although the Bible does do this occasionally (for example, Exod. 22:21, Deut. 24:17), when it comes to formal institutions, the Bible takes a very strange position: it simply does not relate to the obvious, to the trivial. One would expect that warnings against bias in favor of the strong, the wealthy, and the well-connected would be emphasized. But they are not. This is too trivial to mention. The precision of the Bible is revealed again: one must warn against the less expected eventualities that might violate justice. So, as in Leviticus 19:14, where warning against *placing* a stumbling block before the blind is never mentioned, here too the warning is against the more unexpected violations of justice and equality. Observe this:

- "Neither shalt thou speak in a cause to incline after a multitude to pervert justice: nor shalt thou favour a poor man in his cause" (Exod. 23:2, 3).

- "Thou shalt not pervert the judgment of thy poor in his cause" (Exod. 23:6). It is not clear whether this is a warning against bias in favor of or against the poor—perhaps it means both.

- "You shall do no unrighteousness in judgment: thou shall not respect the person of the poor, nor honour the person of the might: but in righteousness shalt thou judge thy neighbour" (Lev. 19:15).

Note, in the last example, that although a warning is added against bias in favor of the "person of the might," this is secondary. The first warning, which is the more important, is again leveled against bias towards the poor. Being biased in judgement in favor of the rich is not mentioned at all. Yet the Bible repeatedly emphasizes the equality between the poor and the rich—for example, when offering the commanded half-shekel to God: "The rich shall not give more, and the poor shall not give less than half a shekel, when they give the offering of the Lord …" (Exod. 30:15).

One is once again impressed by the precision with which the Bible conveys its prescriptions of what needs attention, avoiding the more trivial and the obvious.

1.3.5   *Eda and Kehila*

Witnesses are a recurring theme in the Bible. In fact, a search in a biblical concordance reveals that the noun "witness," with its various forms, appear no fewer than sixty-nine times, and as a verb additional forty times. Both God and the people of Israel are supposed to serve as witnesses. But witnesses to what, and why is this important?

Let us first observe some examples in the Bible where God asserts his role as a witness (or, alternatively, summons heaven and earth to serve as witnesses):

- "I call heaven and earth to witness against you this day …" (Deut. 4:26);

- "Here, O my people, and I will speak; O Israel, and I will testify against thee: I am God, thy God …" (Pss. 50:7);

- "Yet many years didst thou bear with them, and didst forewarn [literally, "testify against"] them by thy spirit in thy prophets …" (Neh. 9:30).

Yet the central theme in the Bible, and the most frequent one to appear, is not God's testimony, but rather the other way around: the "people of Israel" serving as a living testimony, witnesses to the nations of the existence of God. This recurring theme finds its most explicit expression in the repeated utterances of the prophet Isaiah:

- "Behold, I have made him a *witness* to the peoples, a leader and commander of nations" (Isa. 55:4).

- "You are my *witnesses*, says the Lord, and my servant whom I have chosen: that you may know and believe me, and understand that I am he: before me there was no God formed, neither shall there be after me. I, even I, am the Lord; and beside me there is no deliverer. I have declared, and have saved, and I have announced, and there was no strange god among you: therefore you are my *witnesses*, says the Lord, and I am God. Yea, from the first I am he; and there is none that can deliver out of my hand: I will work, and who shall reverse it?" (Isa. 43:10–13).

That the people of Israel are witnesses of God finds its way in many other forms and shapes. One notable example is the way the most well-known Jewish verse is written: "Here, O Israel: the Lord our God; the Lord is one" (Deut. 6:4). In Hebrew, it is written in the Bible thus:

שמע ישראל יהוה אלהינו יהוה אחד

The third and last letters (from right to left) are written in bold and in much larger fonts. Combined, these letters form the word *ed*,[23] Hebrew for "witness."

There is another word that carries with it a declaration of the special assignment destined for the Jewish people—that is, being a witness to God. This is the Hebrew word for congregation, or community. There are many words in Hebrew for community, like *kehilah*,[24] *tzibur*,[25] *kahal*,[26] *agudah*,[27] *hammon*,[28] and numerous others.

Yet there is another very specific word for community, outstanding in its specific meaning: *edah*.[29] Its root is the same as that which gives rise to *ed*[23] (witness). It is a lesson in precision to learn where the Bible uses the word *edah*[29] to refer to the children of Israel, and when *kahal*,[26] or *kehilah*,[24] the lesser terms, are judged appropriate to describe the community of Israel and their spiritual condition, faith-wise.

A good example is introduced in chapter 20 of Numbers. God calls upon Moses to take his rod (baton), to assemble with his brother, Aaron, the community (*edah*),[29] and then talk to the rock before Israel's eyes. God promises that the rock shall give forth water, and the complaining *edah*,[29] who do not have drinking water, would have ample water, for them and for their beasts. Moses, however, has lost faith, both in the possibility of the miracle and in the Israeli congregation. So instead of talking to the rock, as commanded, Moses first addresses the community, calling them rebels and asking them whether they believe water can be produced from the rock. Then "Moses lifted up his hand, and with his rod he smote the rock twice: and the water came out abundantly, and the congregation [*edah*][29] drank, and their beasts too" (Num. 20:11).

For their failure to obey God's command to talk to the rock (instead hitting it), Moses and Aaron are punished and forbidden from entering the Promised Land (Num. 20:12). However, let us trace how the biblical narrator discriminately uses the words *edah*[29] (implying that the congregation comprises willing witnesses of God) and just *kahal*.[26] To the unsuspecting eye, both words in this story obviously convey the same meaning of "community," or "congregation." But the Bible speech is more precise than that.

God had never lost his confidence in the people of Israel. Obviously, Moses had. So the narrator tells us that God commanded Moses to assemble the *edah*[29] and talk to the rock, and the water coming forth will serve for the *edah*[29] to drink—both them and their beasts. But then Moses assembles not the *edah*,[29] as commanded. Instead, he and Aaron assemble the *kahal*[26] (verse 10), obviously not believing that they have under their leadership *edah*.[29] The narrator has his or her own opinion: he or she keeps denoting the congregation *edah*:[29] "and the water came out abundantly, and the congregation [*edah*[29]] drank ..." (Num. 20:11).

Later, what Moses and Aaron have just done has an adverse effect on the congregation. So when God rebukes Moses and Aaron after the whole incident is over, the words used are, "Because you did not believe in me, to sanctify me in the eyes of the children of Israel, therefore you shall not bring this congregation [*kahal*[26]] in to the land which I have given them" (Num. 20:12). God's reference to the *edah*[29] just a few verses earlier, when he commands Moses, renders a reference to the *kahal*[26]—an obvious allusion to the effect of Moses' sin on the condition of the people of Israel, which the narrator wishes to convey.

This sort of analysis may be extended to the paragraph preceding this story (relate to Num. 20: 1–6).

1.3.6 *Why Was the Earth Punished? (Gen. 3:17)*

The divine command should be followed to the letter. No aberration is permitted.

There are at least four episodes in the Bible where both obeying God's command or slightly deviating from it are addressed—with grave consequences for the latter. Reading some of the biblical descriptions in these episodes is a lesson in speech precision—in refined understatements and in how assertions of fact can be concealed, yet slightly exposed, for anyone to find out with little effort.

We start with a case of positive, strict observance of the word of God. No show of creativity on the part of the commanded is attempted. The divine command is strictly pursued, and so is it emphasized, repeatedly, by the biblical narrator.

When God orders Moses to construct the Tabernacle (God's sanctuary while the children of Israel were still wandering in the Sinai desert), he turns to Bezaleel, the artist, "in whom the Lord put wisdom and understanding to know how to work all manner of work for the service of the sanctuary, did according to all that the Lord had commanded" (Exod. 36:1). The building of the Tabernacle, with all its different parts, is then described in great detail, and this goes on for five complete chapters (to the end of the book of Exodus). Yet, throughout the overwhelmingly detailed description of the construction work, one verse is endlessly repeated, in one version or another: "And they did … as the Lord commanded Moses." For example, chapter 39, with forty-three verses, repeats this no fewer than *ten* times—namely, about every fourth verse!

Two opposite cases demonstrate deviations from God's command, and what this may entail.

Moses and Aaron are ordered by God to talk to the rock, in front of the people of Israel, after the latter complain that drinking water is scarce. Yet Moses, instead, smites the rock with his baton. Water then comes forth from the rock. But the punishment for not obeying God's command is prompt: "And the Lord spoke to Moses and Aaron, because you did not believe in me, to sanctify me in the eyes of the children of Israel, therefore you shall not bring the congregation in to the land which I have given them" (Num. 20:12). The command was to speak; instead, there was a physical act. And the punishment was prompt.

Another episode of violation of God's command, with grave consequences for the transgressors, is related regarding the sons of the high priest Aaron (Moses' brother). The sons, Nadav and Avihu, serve with their father at sacrificing the offerings brought by the tribes of Israel to the Tabernacle. But then, "And Nadav and Avihu, the sons of Aaron, took each of them his censer, and put fire in it, and put incense on it, and offered strange fire before the Lord, which he commanded them not. And a fire went out from the Lord, and devoured them, and they died before the Lord" (Lev. 10:1–2). The Bible then goes on to describe, succinctly and respectfully, the brief dialogue between the comforting Moses and the grieving father, Aaron: "Then Moses said to Aaron, This is it that which the Lord spoke, saying, I will be sanctified in them that come near me, and before all the people I will be glorified. And Aaron held his peace" (Lev. 10:3).

The third case of punishment for not obeying God's command to the letter is told in the unfolding story of Adam, Eve, and the serpent in the Garden of Eden. God describes the punishment that would befall each for eating from the tree of knowledge. But then the curse is extended to the earth: "Cursed is the ground for thy sake; in sorrow shalt thou eat of it all the days of thy life" (Gen. 3:17).

Jewish sages asked why the ground was cursed. What was the sin? The reply: not obeying God command to the letter. For God commanded earth, "Let the earth bring forth … fruit tree yielding fruit" (Gen. 1:11). But what came forth instead was a "tree yielding fruit …" (therein, verse 12). The original intent of the command was that both the tree and its fruit would be edible. The earth, instead, brought forth just "a tree yielding fruit."

The rest of the verse describes the realization of exactly that which was commanded in the preceding verse, word for word.

This is once again a lesson in linguistic precision, with clues hidden within what looks to be innocent and uninformative text.

1.3.7 *"Please be fruitful and multiply," with Variations*

As a last example for precision in scripture textual descriptions, it is interesting to learn how Genesis describes God's command to the living to multiply.

On the fifth day of creation, "And God said, Let the waters swarm abundantly with moving creatures that have life, and let birds fly above the earth …" (Gen. 1:20). And then, "And God blessed them, saying [*le-emor*[30]], Be fruitful, and multiply, and fill the waters in the seas, and let birds multiply in the earth" (Gen. 1:22).

Yet the word "saying" is a wrong translation from Hebrew, which again distorts altogether the true meaning of the sentence. The exact meaning of the word *le-emor*[30] is "that is to say" or "meaning." It appears numerous other times in the Bible, with no "saying" involved. For example, observe Reuben speaking to his brothers in Egypt, in the presence of their estranged brother Joseph: "And Reuben answered them, saying [*le-emor*[30]], Did I not speak to you, saying [*le-emor*[30]],

Do not sin against the child; and you would not hear? therefore, behold, even his blood is required" (Gen. 42:22). One may wonder why the second *le-emor*[30] is required here; it is redundant altogether … unless it is perceived as a summary, or the meaning, that Reuben conveys of that which he had said earlier. In other words, *le-emor*[30] can only be perceived as intended to express "namely" and "meaning," but not "saying" the words that have actually been spoken.

Let us readdress the above quote from Genesis, this time with what is probably the correct translation: "And God blessed them, that is to say [*le-emor*[30]], be fruitful, and multiply" (Gen. 1:22). Now we realize that there is no direct talk from God. Only the narrator's pointing to a blessing from the Divine, and what it really meant.

A few verses later, the same command is directed towards the just-created first man and woman: "And God blessed them, and God *said to them*, Be fruitful, and multiply" (Gen. 1:28). The same words are used as earlier, "Be fruitful and multiply," yet *le-emor*[30] is not there. This changes the context altogether. The central message is embedded in the four words "God said to them." There is direct speech from the Divine to human mortals, right from the start of their existence on earth. This is not just some general blessing; a message is well conveyed.

This represents another lesson in precision and in delivering messages within what would otherwise seem like naive text.

1.3.8   Summary

The examples, introduced at some length in the previous subsections, have one objective: to acquaint the reader with the precision of biblical text, and to demonstrate that the Bible uses very structured and well-focused language. Pronouncements are not coincidental. No word is redundant. No phrase is put anywhere by random selection. Words or combinations of words all intend to convey a message, and they are not there by chance alone. The examples expounded in earlier subsections can lead one to a single logical conclusion: one should not take coincidences in biblical Hebrew or in the Bible too lightly. The mathematical precision in biblical texts needs to be properly addressed and taken into account. And when final conclusions are formed regarding possible implications and ramifications (or lack thereof) of the coincidences introduced herewith, the precision of the biblical Hebrew and its demonstrable design should not be ignored or forgotten.

1.4   Playing with Gematria: An Acceptable Practice (Not Here)

In section 1.1, the Hebrew alphabet was introduced, and the traditional numerical value attached to each letter in the Hebrew alphabet detailed. The numerical values of Hebrew letters are the basis and foundation on which the practice of Gematria has evolved over many generations in Jewish mysticism and beyond. The art of Gematria has been integrated into numerous Jewish books of scholarship and interpretations of scriptural texts, and it is considered to this day an acceptable and legitimate practice in all denominations of the Jewish faith.

What is Gematria? Gematria is the calculation of the numerical values of words or phrases in an attempt to find those with equal numerical values. It is assumed that words of numerical equivalence are somehow interrelated, even though the words do not seem to have anything in common. Numerical equivalence is thus not coincidental. The world, according to the Gematria logic, was created through God's utterances. Each letter in the Hebrew alphabet represents a different creative force. Since each letter carries a numerical value, the numerical equivalence of two words reveals an internal connection between the creative potentials of each one.

Therefore, revealing and studying words with equal numerical values may lead one to the common concept that binds the words together, thus delivering an insight into the meaning of this shared concept.

Let us expound by an example that we referred to earlier. One of the names of God is *Elohim*.[3] As explained elsewhere (chapter 7), this is the plural of the word "force" (*eloah* or *el*).[31] However, it is commonly related to in the singular to emphasize the oneness of God. Calculating the numerical values of this word's letters and summing up, we have

$$86 = (40 = \text{מ}) + (10 = \text{י}) + (5 = \text{ה}) + (30 = \text{ל}) + (1 = \text{א})$$

Take another word, *ha-teva*[32] (the nature). Its numerical value (summing up the numerical values of the letters) is

$$86 = (70 = \text{ע}) + (2 = \text{ב}) + (9 = \text{ט}) + (5 = \text{ה})$$

One realizes that the two words are numerically equivalent. From the point of view of Gematria, this numerical equivalence insinuates that God is the source of all laws of the universe—that which we call nature.

Gematria is to this day an acceptable form of gaining knowledge and insight, either from biblical texts or from Hebrew names or words. It is frequently addressed in the Talmud, and has been considered, in particular, a legitimate form of interpretation of Jewish scriptures—and, more generally, as an acceptable form of learning messages from the Hebrew language.

While we do not express here our attitude regarding this practice, for reasons detailed in the introduction, it should be unequivocally emphasized that this book is not about Gematria. We would never, in this book, deduce that two words are equivalent because they have same numerical values. On the other hand, our own experience with the coincidences described in this book, as well as the common attitude of Jewish rabbis and scholars over many generations, teach us that due to the special structure of the Hebrew language, as detailed earlier, the composition of the root of a word is meaningful, and if two words share the same root they must be somehow interrelated.

Furthermore, although we relate to the numerical values of words as possibly carrying information and demonstrate this with numerous examples, these examples are still referred to, in this book, as coincidences (unless statistical analysis is applied). In any case, the numerical equivalence of words (or phrases) would never be taken to imply that the words are somehow interconnected by a hidden concept.

This basic tenet of Gematria is not adopted here; neither is it addressed as a theme of discussion anywhere else in the book.

CHAPTER 2

Cases of Design in the Hebrew Language

2.1 Information in a Hebrew Word: Visible and Hidden

The notion that there are Hebrew words that carry hidden information seems like an outrageous proposition. This book is not about Gematria; nor does it address Jewish mysticism. So what is intended when we relate to Hebrew words as messengers of visible, and possibly also hidden, information?

The key word for the reply is in the title of the book: coincidences. On many occasions (perhaps, one may argue, too many to be perceived as coincidental), Hebrew words seem to carry visible or hidden information in addition to the obvious revealed meaning of the word. Whether the cases demonstrating this proposition and displayed throughout the book are coincidences or otherwise is left open (except when proper and rigorous statistical analysis is applied—for example, in chapters 8 and 12). Since many of the coincidences outlined throughout the book rely on the structure of the Hebrew words and the sum of the numerical values of the letters comprising them, it is perhaps appropriate that we provide, even this early in the book, some instances that demonstrate coincidental design in the Hebrew language. These examples seem to deliver evidence that Hebrew words can, on the one hand, convey the obvious (as revealed in the meaning of the word), and, on the other hand, provide additional hidden information tightly related to the exposed sense of the word.

In this section, we demonstrate several instances of revealed and hidden information in Hebrew words, some of which relates to time periods.

2.1.1   Designed Words with Visible Information (and Message)

In this subsection, we address some Hebrew words displaying structure, which may be perceived as indicative of preconceived design. By "design," we refer to the

31

fact that the structure of the word is not simple, but rather displays features that seem to store more than first meets the eye.

In subsequent subsections, we will relate to more complex examples, where numerical values of words seem to be related to the revealed content of the respective words by delivering additional relevant information.

Yadid (Friend)

Yadid[1] comprises two repetitions of a single syllable, written the same but pronounced differently. In Hebrew, the word *yadid*[1] is written as follows (read from right to left):

$$(ד + י) + (ד + י)$$

The word "hand" in Hebrew is *yad*,[2] written like

$$ד + י$$

Figure 2.1 shows a friend according to the Hebrew language.

Figure 2.1. A friend in Hebrew

Olam (World, Eternity)

This single word appears in the Bible, with variations, no fewer than 437 times. In the Hebrew language, *olam*[3] represents both the physical dimension and the time dimension—relating, specifically, to their "boundlessness" property. Thus, *olam*[3] means, simply, "world" (all that exists), but also "eternity" (relating to boundless future), or the elapsed time from the beginning of time to eternity.

The word *olam*[3] is derived from the root *A.L.M.* In the Hebrew language, this root is origin to many words, all of which have one common sense: to be hidden, concealed. Examples include *healem*[4] (oblivion, disappearance), *taaluma*[5] (mystery), *le-aalim*[6] (to conceal), and *le-italem*[7] (to ignore, to act as though something is nonexistent).

One may justifiably ask, What is the connection between "world" and "concealment"? The answer is hidden in the outcry of the prophet Isaiah to God: "Alas, thou are a God who hides himself, O God and Saviour of Israel" (Isa. 45:15).

The theme of the hiding God is repeated numerous times in the Bible. When Moses requests of God "Show me thy glory" (Exod. 33:18), the reply he gets is, "And the Lord said, Behold, there is a place by me, and thou shalt stand upon a rock: and it shall come to pass, while my glory passes by, that I will put thee in a cleft of the rock, and will cover thee with my hand, while I pass by: and I will take away my hand and thou shalt see my back: but my face shall not be seen" (Exod. 33:21—23). Jewish tradition interprets this to imply that while the presence of God can be evidenced by things that have occurred ("thou shalt see my back"), the very existence of God is concealed to the eye. This is often likened to how one can see a human body, in its various manifestations, yet not the soul that resides within. Furthermore, "Thou cannot see my face; for no man may see me, and live" (Exod. 33:20).

The source of the word *olam*[3] now becomes clear: the whole world is a manifestation of the hiddenness of God. God is in the world, but the whole world is testimony to the concealed God. The design in the Hebrew word for "world" now becomes obvious: into a single word, *olam,*[3] the whole philosophy of the Jewish religion—in fact, of any monotheistic religion—is poured and concentrated.

Chet (Sin)

The Hebrew language is rich with words describing moral transgressions and their results. Indeed, it describes these with the same abundance that the English language describes roads (or pathways, or alleys, or passageways, or highways, or lanes, or streets, or avenues, or courses, or motorways, or tracks, or routes, or walkways …).

Some examples for moral transgression in Hebrew follow:

averah[8] ; *pesha*[9] ; *chatah*[10] ; *chatat*[11] ; *avon*[12] ; *aven*[13] ; *chamas*[14] ; *avel*[15] ; *maal*[16] ; *oshek*[17] ; *avla*[18] ; *nevalah*[19] ; *raah*[20] ; *rishah*[21] ; *gezel*[22] ;

naming just a few …

For each of these morally unacceptable roads to travel, the Hebrew language assigns very specific meaning. These words are not exactly synonyms. In fact, some Jewish sages claim there are no synonyms in the Hebrew language. Yet, the richness of this vocabulary is testimony to the focus of the Hebrew language on the very finely tuned "variations of errors of judgment" that a person can make in choosing the road to travel. Furthermore, even when no harm is inflicted on anybody, not all roads are acceptable or permissible. In other words, *laissez faire*, or "everything goes"—so long as no apparent harm has been done—is not a Jewish prescription for how one should conduct his or her life. This is well documented in the book of Numbers: "And remember all the commandments of the Lord, and do them; and you should not seek [*lo taturu*[23]] after your own heart and your own eyes, after which you go astray" (Num. 15:39). The interesting thing in this is the use of the word *tour*, which has the same meaning in English. In other words, if you think that you are going into uncharted, morally wrong territories, just out of interest, just for a limited period of time, just for a brief glance, like a tourist exploring new land, with no intention of staying there forever … then think again!

While this is one respect of how the Bible relates to moral transgressions, harmful or otherwise, there is also an optimistic undertone, expressed in the Hebrew word for "sin." This word points to an obvious design in the Hebrew language, because its root is far removed from any insinuation of moral transgression or its results (namely, punishment).

The word *chet*[24] in Hebrew derives from the root *Ch.T.A.* However, the main usage of this root is in altogether different contexts. The main meaning is "to miss" (as in "missing a target"). Once it is remembered that the Bible refers to sin as an aberration, an error, lack of essential knowledge ("But of the tree of knowledge, of good and evil, you shall not eat," Gen. 2:17), it is understandable why these seemingly unrelated words share a common root. This speaks volumes about how optimistic the Hebrew language is with regard to the sources of evil in the world. The philosophy here is not, as related by God after Noah emerges from the ark, following the deluge: "I will not again curse the ground any more for man's sake; for the impulse of man's heart is evil from his youth" (Gen. 8:21). To the contrary, the philosophy here is hopeful, optimistic: all evil originates from "missing the target"; for whatever reasons one seems to miss the target, there is always hope; evil is not innate in one's heart; the problem with the sinner is only that his or her "sight" is somewhat impaired.

Figure 2.2 displays "sin" according to the Hebrew language.

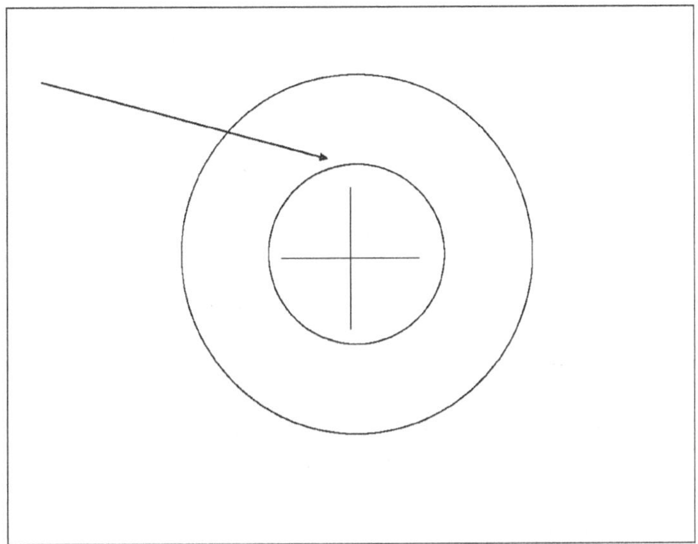

Figure 2.2. "To sin", in Hebrew.

Rachamim (Mercy, Compassion)

Mercy refers to a certain mode of conduct one living creature may pursue in relating to another. However, this is also one of the prominent thirteen attributes that Jewish tradition ascribes to the conduct of God. The source for this description of God's conduct is in Exodus (34). When Moses is commanded by God to go up Mount Sinai to receive the tablets with the Ten Commandments the second time (after the first ones have been broken by Moses), the latter gets the two tablets in his hands, and after God "descended in the cloud, and stood with him there," Moses proclaims, "The Lord, The Lord, mighty, merciful and gracious, longsuffering, and abundant in love and truth" (Exod. 34:6). The next sentence continues to describe qualities of God's conduct. We realize that being merciful is one such feature, and it is abundantly repeated throughout the Bible (for example, Deut. 4:31, Joel 2:13, Jon. 4:2).

How would one qualify the most essential components that need to exist for a living being to be merciful to another? We believe that it is safe to assert that there are at least two such ingredients. First, whoever shows mercy feels only compassion towards the subject of the mercy, so that only favorable acts and modes of conduct will ensue. Second, the recipient of mercy is in a state of helplessness, or some kind of hardship, that obviously calls for assistance. One cannot indeed think of a better example of a human being in a position of need for mercy than an embryo in the mother's womb. As the embryo is growing in the womb, completely helpless, mercy is the ultimate essential ingredient in the mother's feelings and conduct toward the yet unborn. The Hebrew language seems to adopt this depiction of the interrelationship between the mother and her yet-unborn offspring.

We repeatedly relate in this book to how the Hebrew language, or the Bible, generate epitomes for certain concepts, scenarios types, and modes of conduct or feelings. Two such examples are given elsewhere in the book: the concept of the ultimate *sham* (there) and the concept of the ultimate *ayin* (source of water)—see chapters 5 and 10, respectively.

For mercy, the Bible likewise reserves an ultimate object that embodies the concept.

In Hebrew, "a womb" and "mercy" are derived from the same root: *R.Ch.M.* A "womb" is *rechem*,[25] and to have mercy is *le-rachem*.[26] That the Bible refers to a woman's feelings toward her offspring as the ultimate embodiment of mercy and compassion can be realized by the following verse, from the prophet Isaiah, speaking in the name of God: "Can a woman forget her sucking child, that she should not have compassion [*me-rachem*[27]] on the son of her womb? Even these may forget, yet I will not forget thee" (Isa. 49:15).

These apparently unrelated common-root words provide another indication for design in the Hebrew language.

Ani, Anochi (I)

What does "I" mean? This concept is elusive, and has been the subject of much discussion throughout history, in almost all cultures and in various schools of philosophy. Any attempt to define "I" seems doomed to fail.

Yet some clues may be derived from the Bible, and from an exploration of Hebrew words derived from the same root as "I." We start with the ultimate "I," the source of all meaning: God. The Ten Commandments starts with "I": "I am the Lord thy God" (Exod. 20:2). Repeatedly, it is emphasized in the Bible, over and over again—in particular by Jewish prophets—that God is the absolute and ultimate "I." This focus on God as the ultimate "I" is carried out, with Jewish prophets speaking in the name of God, by repeating twice the word "I" as a major description of God in his relationship to humans.

Examples:

- "See now that I, even I, am he [Ani[28] Ani[28] Hoo[30]],/ and there is no God with me:/ I kill, and I make alive;/ I wound and I heal:/ neither is there any that can deliver out of my hand." (Deut. 32:39).

- "Hearken unto me, O Jacob and Israel, whom I called; I am [Ani[28]] he; I am [Ani[28]] the first, I am [Ani[28]] also the last." ... "I, even I [Ani Ani[28]], have spoken; yea I [Ani[28]] have called him: I [Ani[28]] have brought him, and he shall make his way prosperous" (Isa. 48:12,15).

- "I, even I [Anochi, Anochi[29]], am the Lord; and beside me there is no deliverer" ... "Yea, from the first I am [Anochi[29]] he; and there is none that can deliver out of my hand" (Isa. 43:11,13).

The root of "I" is *A.N.I.* It may be interesting to learn what other words are derived from close roots. Exploration of such words may be revealing with respectt o the true nature of "I," and perhaps provide guidelines as to the course of actiona human being should follow regarding his or her "I."

The first word we discuss is *anah*.[31] This word has close kinship to *A.N.I* (see also the first comment below). In the Hebrew language, *anah*[31] has double meaning: "where to," and, in the combination *ad-anah*, the meaning of "until when."

Thus, in a single Hebrew word, the essence of "I" is epitomized: "where" and "when."

A second meaning, derived from the close root *A.N.H*, is "to occur by accident." An example: "No evil shall happen [*yeuneh*[32]] to the just" (Proverb 12:21). Random occurrences are an essential ingredient of that which the "I" experiences.

Finally, a ship in Hebrew is *oniah*[33]—the relationship of which to "I" can easily be elaborated.

Comments

1. "I" in Aramaic is *Anah*.[31]

2. By an exchange of the letters in *Ani*[28] ("I"), it becomes *ain*,[34] which means "nothingness" (noun), or "there is not" (adverb). A fearsome reminder for the final destiny of the "I."

The Root *Ch.L.L*

This root gives rise to a variety of words. For a naive observer, the associations between these words look puzzling, at best, or altogether missing. Yet they all are interwoven together by an apparent logic that can hardly be ignored.

Consider a few examples for words derived from this root:

chalal[35] (space)

chalal[35] (a fatally wounded person; a dead person; a fallen person)

chiloni[36] (secular) *lechalel*[37] (to defile, profane, violate one's honor)

lechalel[37] (defame the name of God) *mitchalel*[38] (being desecrated);

These words, some of which seem unrelated, cannot acquire their true meanings unless premeditated design in the structure of Hebrew words is assumed. In other words, all these words become naturally related to one another if one takes into consideration Jewish philosophy, which regards absence of God, or denial of God, as, allegorically, "empty space" or "a body without a soul."

Midah (Virtue)

The Hebrew language has a unique position towards virtues. If virtues are perceived as desirable traits of human conduct, then all human traits are virtues, and no trait is absolutely and under all conditions unacceptable. This is expressed particularly well in the Talmudic proverb "He who shows compassion toward the cruel would end up being cruel to the compassionate." The lesson of this assertion is simple: all modes of conduct are permissible and acceptable as long as they are measured, adaptable to the circumstances, and consistent with good moral judgment.

A similar and related concept—which, we believe, exists only in the Hebrew language—is "villain with permission (or under the auspices) of the Torah." What this translates to, in simple terms, is that you can break no Torah law, yet remain a villain. In modern-day term, this implies that in addition to being a law-abiding citizen, one also has to exercise his or her own capacity to tell right from wrong—to exercise moral judgment.

The word "virtue" in the Hebrew language may be perceived as the ultimate embodiment of this attitude of Jewish philosophy.

Virtue, in Hebrew, is *midah*.[39] The same exact word also means "measure." For example, "to measure" is *limdod*.[40] To deliver something scarce to somebody would be expressed as, "I could give everything only *bi-mesura*[41] [with a strict measure]."

Thus, in Hebrew, a virtue means conduct with the right measure. The latter is an essential ingredient for any human mode of conduct to become a virtue. Conversely, a virtue ceases to be such if a certain behavior lacks the right measure.

Once again, we realize that the Hebrew language and biblical messages are intertwined in words of seemingly no relevance to one another—that is, unless one inserts design into the overall equation.

"Acknowledge," "Thank," "Confess"

"Acknowledge," "thank," and "confess" represent unrelated modes of activity of a human being.

- One acknowledges that a letter has arrived, that the signature on a document is hers—or, simply, that the world is beautiful and beyond imagination.

- One thanks for a present that he has received, for a rescue from disaster due to assistance of fellow men and women, or, more generally, for everything that he has.

- One confesses that she was indeed involved in this crime, that she is responsible for the error that was the source of all this trouble, and that her conduct indeed was inappropriate.

There are three modes for a human being to stand before God: by acknowledging ("O Lord, how manifold are thy works! In wisdom hast thou made them all," Pss. 104:24), by thanking ("to give thanks to the Lord because his steadfast love endures forever," 1 Chron. 16:41) and by confessing ("And it shall be, when he shall be guilty in one of these things, that he shall confess that he has sinned in that thing," Lev. 5:5).

By sheer coincidence, this triad of verbs (to acknowledge, to thank, to confess) share the same root in Hebrew. Indeed, they are all expressed by a single word: *le-hodot*.[42]

2.1.2   *Designed Words with Hidden Information*

Shanah (Year)

The word "year" in Hebrew is *shanah*.[43] The obvious revealed content of this word is clear. Both *shanah*[43] and *shnayim*[44] (two) derive from a common root: *S.N.H.* This root originates various words associated with the act of repetition. Thus, when one continuously repeats learning a lesson, we say that he *shanah*.[43]

Also, one of the two major parts of the Talmud, the basic source of Jewish law, is called Mishnah[45] (possibly relating to the fact that it is being repeatedly learned).

A similar term is indeed used in English. When a person wishes to offer sup port for a motion already proposed, we say that he or she is "seconding" this motion (namely, repeating it).

It is therefore no surprise that if one wished to coin a name for a cyclic phenomenon that repeats itself in a regular never-changing cycle, an obvious choice would be a word derived from the Hebrew root for repetition. Both the exposed meaning of the word "year" in Hebrew and its root source are quite obvious.

Let us now learn how the Hebrew calendar year is structured, but precede this by learning other commonly used calendars.

A calendar can be based either on the sun, on the moon, or on a combination thereof. The Christian calendar, also called the Gregorian calendar, is based on the sun, and the earth's yearly circling of it. The exact length of the year depends on the reference point. The most common is the tropical year, based on the equinoxes, and its length is 365.24219 days (Mitton 2000). Since the Gregorian year is 365 days long, this means that in order to keep pace with the exact solar cycle (365.242 days), a day is added to the month of February every four years.

The Islamic calendar, the Hijri calendar, is based on the moon. The time it takes for the moon to encircle the earth is, from most recent measurements by NASA satellites, 29.5305888 days. This means that the year, based on the lunar month (also known as the synodic month) is

$$12 \times 29.53059 = 354.36707 \text{ days}$$

The Islamic year is exactly 354 days long (refer to Table 2.1). This implies that the Islamic calendar is consistently shorter than a tropical year, and therefore shifts with respect to the Christian calendar (which is 365 days long). Furthermore, the Islamic year also lags behind the actual lunar year (based on the synodic month)

Table 2.1. Names of months in the Islamic calendar (their durations, days).

Month no.	Month name (no. of days)	Month no.	Month name (no. of days)
1.	Muharram (30)	7.	Rajab (30)
2.	Safar (29)	8.	Sha'ban (29)
3.	Rabi' al-awwal (Rabi' I) (30)	9.	Ramadan (30)
4.	Rabi' al-thani (Rabi' II) (29)	10.	Shawwal (29)
5.	Jumada al-awwal (Jumada I) (30)	11.	Dhu al-Qi'dah (30)
6.	Jumada al-thani (Jumada II) (29)	12.	Dhu al-Hijjah (29)

by 0.36707 days per year (about a third of a day per year). This "missing" time is added to the Islamic calendar by adding one day to the last month of the year (the month of Dhu al-Hijjah). This is done for eleven "leap years" in a cycle of thirty years. The leap years—when the year is 355 days long—are when *year mod 30* (the residual obtained by dividing the year by 30) is one of the following: 2, 5, 7, 10, 13, 16, 18, 21, 24, 26, and 29. For a cycle of thirty years, such a calendar would give average month duration of

$$[(354*19+355*11) / 30] / 12 = 29.53056 \text{ days}$$

This is quite close to the synodic month of 29.53059 days (the mean length of the month of the thirty-year tabular calendar is about 2.9 seconds less than the synodic period of the moon). So on average, this answer would be quite accurate, but in any given month, it is still just a rough estimate.

Note that in the Islamic calendar, even with leap years, there is still a difference between the solar year, which is 365.242 days, and the lunar year, which is 354.367 days. This is a difference of about eleven days per year, which causes Muslim festivities to keep pace with the yearly moon but not with the annual seasons, which are related to the tropical year (based on the sun).

The Jewish calendar is essentially based on the moon. Therefore, it is, on average, 354 days long. Every month starts (approximately) on the day of a new moon. The months of the Jewish calendar and their durations are given in Table 2.2.

There are three types of non-leap years in the Jewish calendar: "deficient" (353 days), "regular" (354 days) and "complete" (355 days). In a regular year, durations of the months alternate between 30 and 29 days, and the year is 354 days long. A complete year is created by adding a day to the month of Cheshvan, and a deficient year is created by removing a day from the month of Kislev. The alternation between 30 and 29 days ensures that when the year starts with a new moon, so does each month. Rules regarding whether a non-leap year is 353, 354, or 355 days long are somewhat complex, and will not be given here.

The interested reader may find these rules detailed at http://webexhibits.org/calendars/calendar-jewish.html.

An ordinary year has twelve months. A Jewish leap year has thirteen months, where an extra month, Adar I, is added to the calendar (in addition to the regular Adar, which then becomes Adar II). This extra month aims to "mind the gap" between the solar year and the lunar year. The month Adar I is only present in leap years. In non-leap years, Adar II is simply called "Adar."

What are leap years?

A year becomes a leap year if the number *year mod 19* is one of the following: 0, 3, 6, 8, 11, 14, or 17, where *year mod 19* refers to the residual number obtained on dividing the Hebrew year by 19. For example, on September 16, 2004, the Jewish year 5765 has started. Divide by 19:

$$5765 / 19 = 303 \text{ and } 8/19.$$

Since 8 is included in the set of numbers above, that year is a leap year. Let us now explain why leap years are needed in the Jewish calendar. Jewish festivities are tightly linked to the seasons (like Shavuot, the festivity of harvesting and bringing the prime of the land produce to the temple in Jerusalem). The added months in leap years ensure that the Jewish year also keeps pace with the tropical (solar) year.

The corrections to the Jewish year follow the following scheme.

The difference between the lunar year and the solar year is

$$365.242 - 354.367 = 10.875 \text{ days}$$

It can be easily realized that in a 19-year cycle the difference is $19 * 10.875 = 206.625$ days, which, in terms of the lunar synodic month of 29.53059 days, is

$$206.625 / 29.53059 = 6.99698 \approx 7 \text{ months.}$$

Table 2.2. The Hebrew calendar.

Name	Length in a deficient year	Length in a regular year	Length in a complete year
Tishri	30	30	30
Heshvan	29	29	30
Kislev	29	30	30
Tevet	29	29	29
Shevat	30	30	30
Adar I	30	30	30)
Adar II	29	29	29
Nisan	30	30	30
Iyar	29	29	29
Sivan	30	30	30
Tammuz	29	29	29
Av	30	30	30
Elul	29	29	29
Total	353 or 383	354 or 384	355 or 385

This implies that in a cycle of 19 years, seven months have to be added to the Jewish years. These are the leap years in the Jewish nineteen-year cycle. A "leap year," in Hebrew, is *shanah meuberet*[46] (same description as given to an impregnated woman). Chapter 18 addresses the secret of the related concept of Ibur.

It is interesting to note that the calendar used by the ancient Greeks was also based on the moon, and is known as the Metonic calendar. This calendar was based on the observations of Meton of Athens (440 BC), which showed that 235 lunar months made up almost exactly 19 solar years. This nineteen-year cycle became known as the Metonic cycle. Given a nominal twelve-month year, an additional

$$235 - 19*12 = 7 \text{ lunar months}$$

are required to synchronize the moon-based Greek calendar to the tropical year. The same conclusion is reflected in the Jewish calendar, which is similarly based on a 19-year cycle. The Jewish nineteen-year cycle calendar is believed to be invented by Rav Hillel II, an Amora of 4th Century CE.

Having learned the structure of the three major calendars used by millions of people the world over, we may now probe some interesting hidden information in the Hebrew word for year, *shanah*.[43]

Recall that the word *shanah*[43] is linguistically derived from the same root as "two" and "repetition." This may explain the visible structure of the word *shanah*.[43]

But no information seems to be conveyed about the year's duration. As we sum up the numerical values of the letters, some hidden information is suddenly exposed. We find out that

$$355 = (5 = ה) + (50 = נ) + (300 = ש)$$

This is identical to the basis for the Jewish calendar—namely, the lunar year of 354.4 days, or the "complete year" of 355 days!

It is worth noting that while other words for time periods in Hebrew convey in a precise fashion the nature of the respective time periods, the word *shanah*[43] is unique in that it does not. Thus, the word for "week" is *shavua*,[47] derived from "seven" (*sheva*).[48] "Month" has two synonyms in Hebrew: *chodesh*[49] and *yerach*.[50] The first shares the same root as the Hebrew word for "renewal," indicating thereby that the Hebrew calendar is based on the lunar month (in ancient Israel, the beginning of the month was declared by "testimony" given for renweal of the moon). The second word, *yerach*,[50] states more explicitly that the month is based on the moon, because the same word is also used for "moon" (written the same though pronounced slightly differently: "yareach").[50]

These three words for week and month are self-explanatory and openly convey the message about their root origin. The word for year is the only one in the Hebrew calendar that remains mute about its origin relative to the time period it represents. As we have just realized, the missing information is contained, hidden, within the numerical values of the letters comprising this word.

"Day," "Night," "Midday," "Midnight"

"Day" in Hebrew, *yom*:[51]

$$56 = (40 = \text{מ}) + (6 = \text{ו}) + (10 = \text{י})$$

"Night" in Hebrew, *lail*[52a] (*lailah*[52b] is also occasionally used):

$$70 = (30 = \text{ל}) + (10 = \text{י}) + (30 = \text{ל})$$

"Midday" in Hebrew, *tzohoraim*:[53]

$$345 = (40 = \text{מ}) + (10 = \text{י}) + (200 = \text{ר}) + (5 = \text{ה}) + (90 = \text{צ})$$

"Midnight" in Hebrew, *neshef*:[54]

$$430 = (80 = \text{ף}) + (300 = \text{ש}) + (50 = \text{נ})$$

As discussed in chapter 18, the division of the day into twenty-four hours was customary in biblical times, and served as the basis for the calculation of the duration of the synodic (lunar) month. However, the hour was divided into 1,080 parts, rather than into the minutes and seconds of today.

Is there indication, in the above Hebrew names for midnight and midday, of the time of their occurrence (namely, at the sixth hour of the respective night and day)?

We divide the numerical values of the Hebrew midnight (430) by that of night (70).

$$\text{"Midnight" / "Night"} = 430 / 70 = 6.1429 \text{ hours}$$

A coincidence?

Let us repeat the same for midday and day:

$$\text{"Midday" / "Day"} = 345 / 56 = 6.1607 \text{ hours}$$

The mean of these two coincidentally close figures (6.1429 and 6.1607) is 6.1518, implying that there is a delay of $60 \times 0.1518 = 9.1$ minutes in the mean transit time of the sun through the meridian. It is left for astronomers to figure out whether this number, with its deviation from 6, carries any significance.

Design in the Hebrew language?

Evening + Night versus Morning + Day

Modern-day usage of the concept "day" relates to a time period that spans twenty-four hours—namely, starts at midnight, 0:00 AM, and ends the next midnight, at 12:00 PM.

By contrast, in Jewish tradition, the "day" starts in the preceding evening, at sunset, or when three stars have been observed in the sky. This follows from the repeated phrase in Genesis (chapter 1): "And there was evening and there was morning [X] day," where X stands for one, second, …, sixth. (Refer for example to Gen. 1:5, 8, 13, 19, 23).

In another sense, "day" implies in everyday parlance daylight time as opposed to darkness time, which we call "night." These senses for the words "day" and "night" apply both in English and in Hebrew. In fact, they are supported by a verse in Genesis: "And God called the light Day, and the darkness he called Night" (Gen. 1:5).

In modern Hebrew, "evening" is *erev*[55] and "morning" is *boker*.[56] Both words have linguistic contents that can be easily explained. The former has the same root as "mixture." The root for mixing is *A.R.B* (to mix is *le-arev*).[57] A derivative of this word is used, for example, to describe the mixture of non-Israelite nationalities who escorted the Israelites, on their exodus from Egypt. They are called *erev rav*:[58] "And a mixed multitude [*erev rav*[58]] went up also with them" (Exod. 12:38). One can easily understand why evening is *erev*:[55] in darkness, everything seems mixed together.

In a similar vein, the word for morning, *boker*,[56] may well be linguistically explained, because this word has, as its root, the letters *B.K.R*, which in Hebrew gives rise to the verb "to control" (*le-vaker*).[59] This also makes sense: as one mixes everything together during dark hours (*erev*),[55] everything is under control during daytime (*boker*).[56] Both words seem to entertain the same logic, which confers justification on the selection of these words to describe, in Genesis and in the Hebrew language, the start of darkness time and the start of light time, respectively. However, these words, as well as *yom*[51] (day) and *lailah*[52b] (night), release no contents with respect to the time durations they represent. We may recall that a similar scenario was encountered with *shanah*[43] (year): Although the word implies, linguistically, "repetition," we know not a repetition of what. This information was hidden in the numerical values of the letters comprising the word, as we have just realized (previous section).

With *yom*[51] (day) and *lailah*[52b] (night), *erev*[55] (evening) and *boker*[56] (morning), the words are mute about their relative durations!

But is that so?

Consider the relative duration of daylight time (defined by the interval between sunrise and sunset) and darkness time (the rest of the twenty-four-hour cycle). We will denote, these, for short, "day" and "night." It is everyone's experience that day and night are, on average, of equal durations. Yet, they vary throughout the year. We define certain "threshold" days, where the relative durations of "day" and "night" reach unique points. Some of these days are used, in certain countries, to define the beginnings of certain seasons—in particular, the winter and the summer.

There are four such threshold days:

- The fall (autumnal) equinox: Day and night are of equal durations. This day occurs in the Northern Hemisphere on September 23 (±1 day). Thereafter, daylight duration becomes progressively shorter.

- The spring (vernal) equinox: Day and night are of equal durations. This day occurs in the Northern Hemisphere on March 21 (±1 day). Thereafter, daylight duration gradually becomes longer.

- Winter solstice: Daylight duration is the shortest in the year. This day occurs in the Northern Hemisphere on December 22 (±1 day).

- Summer solstice: Daylight duration is the longest of the year. This day occurs in the Northern Hemisphere on June 21 (±1 day).

Variation of the day duration, throughout the year, is caused, as is well-known, by the tilt of the earth by $23.45° = 23° 27'$, relative to the axis perpendicular to the orbital plane around the sun. One may naturally ask about the average annual daylight duration—or, equivalently, what percentage, on average, constitutes the day and what percentage constitutes the night in the twenty-four-hour cycle. An intuitive answer is 50%. But this is not the correct answer. Although daytime and nighttime each constitute, on average, about 50% of the twenty-four-hour cycle, the annual average deviates somewhat from this figure, for reasons that are not elaborated here.

Let us take, as an example, the registered sunrise and sunset times in the city of Chicago in 1999. Daylight duration varied from a minimum of 9:20 (on the winter solstice of December 22, 1999) to a maximum of 15:02 (on the summer solstice of June 21, 1999). The average of these extreme values is 12.183 hours, which implies that daylight duration comprises, on average, 50.76% of the twenty-four-hour day cycle. Yet, this is only an approximation. The exact average, based on actual daily data, should be computed.

Such an analysis was done for the city of Jerusalem. The data were collected using public-domain Internet sites that allow derivation of daily sunrise and sunset times anywhere on the globe (for example, the U.S. Navy site at http://aa.usno.navy.mil/data/docs/RS_OneYear.html).

These times were calculated for the city of Jerusalem, and then the (simple) annual average daylight duration was computed to be 12:11 (twelve hours and 11 minutes). This figure was derived by deducting, for each day of the year, sunrise time from sunset time (adding 1 minute to obtain the right duration), and then averaging for the whole year. The calculation was repeated three times, using two separate Web sites that allow such computations.

This result carries two implications:

- The average daylight duration in Jerusalem is longer than that of nighttime.

- The annually averaged daylight duration is about 51% (more precisely, **50.76%**) of the total day cycle.

Comments

1. Prior to arriving at the above figure (which is based on calculating an annual average for data given in the public domain, as explained earlier), we have contacted Dr. Eran Ofek of the School of Physics and Astronomy at Tel-Aviv University (we thank him for his cooperation and assistance). Ofek graciously made his own calculation and told us that he had "calculated the yearly mean daylight time from altitude 32, including the effect of refraction, and it is 11h50m" ("atmospheric refraction will shorten the nighttime by 4 or 5 minutes"). Altitude 32 is about that of Jerusalem (the latter has north altitude of 31.7830). Thus, according to Ofek's theoretical calculations, annually averaged daylight duration in Israel is shorter than nighttime duration, contrary to our calculations (which were based on public-domain data of daily sunrise

and sunset times). The discrepancy between the two results has never been resolved.

2. Taking refraction into consideration, our own data-based calculation would give a daylight duration of 12:16, which results in daylight duration comprising 51.1% of the total day cycle.

Let us sum up the numerical values of the letters that comprise each of the four words describing the four periods into which a twenty-four-hour cycle is divided:

"Day" in Hebrew, *yom*:[51]

$$56 = (40 = \text{מ}) + (6 = \text{ו}) + (10 = \text{י})$$

"Night" in Hebrew, *lailah*[52b] (*lail*[52a] is also occasionally used):

$$75 = (5 = \text{ה}) + (30 = \text{ל}) + (10 = \text{י}) + (30 = \text{ל})$$

"Morning" in Hebrew, *boker*:[56]

$$302 = (200 = \text{ר}) + (100 = \text{ק}) + (2 = \text{ב})$$

"Evening" in Hebrew, *erev*:[55]

$$272 = (2 = \text{ב}) + (200 = \text{ר}) + (70 = \text{ע})$$

Let's add them together:

$$\text{"Morning"} + \text{"Day"}: 302 + 56 = 358$$

$$\text{"Evening"} + \text{"Night"}: 272 + 75 = 347$$

The first amazing thing to observe about these figures is that they are so close together (as one would expect if significance were attached to these numbers). Calculating their *relative* weights in the sum-up of their numerical values (which is assumed to represent the whole twenty-four-hour day), we find

$$\text{"Morning"} + \text{"Day"}: 358 \, / \, (358 + 347) = 358 \, / \, 705 = 50.78\%$$

"Evening" + "Night": 347 / 705 = 49.22%

In other words, the numerical "linguistic weight" of morning + day implies that light-time periods in the twenty-four-hour daily cycle constitute, on average, **50.78%** of the complete daily cycle.

Does the figure **50.76%** looks familiar from the previous discussion?

Heraion (Human Pregnancy)

Human pregnancy is known to last about nine months. When this period is measured in days, there are two ways by which the medical profession measures the period of pregnancy. One method is to measure human pregnancy from fertilization time, which is commonly accepted to be, on average, 266 days. Another method is to measure human pregnancy from the last menstrual period, which is commonly accepted as 280 days.

The simple average (midpoint) between these two figures is 273 days (about nine months).

Human pregnancy is called *heraion*[60] in Hebrew. This word derives from the root *H.R.H*, the same root that gives rise to variations of the verb *le-harot*[61] (to become impregnated). The word appears once in the Bible, in Hoshea 9:11: "As for Efrayim, their glory shall fly away like a bird; No birth, and no pregnancy [*heraion*[60]] and no conception" (in our opinion, a bad translation). A variation of this word is *heron*,[62] which is not commonly used in modern Hebrew. It appears once in Genesis 3:16: "Unto the woman he said, I will greatly multiply your sorrow and your pregnancy [*heronech*[63]]."

Let's sum up the values of the letters comprising the Hebrew word for pregnancy (*heraion*):[60]

$$271 = (50 = ‏ן‎) + (6 = ‏ו‎) + (10 = ‏י‎) + (200 = ‏ר‎) + (5 = ‏ה‎)$$

This value is not far off from the simple average of the two modern-day commonly accepted durations of human pregnancy, which was calculated earlier (namely, 273 days).

Comments

1. As the writing of this book drew to completion, we realized that the relationship of the numeric value of the Hebrew word for pregnancy to the duration of human pregnancy had already been noted in an ancient Jewish source,

Midrash Rabbah (Genesis Parashah 20 [chapter 20]), in the name of Rabbi Shmuel.

2. There are at least two other places where ancient Jewish sources make predictions regarding conceiving and human pregnancy. First, from the combination of words conveyed by God to the woman: "*harbeh arbeh etz-vonech*"[64] (Gen. 3:16), meaning "I will greatly multiply your pain," Rabbi Shmuel deduces, since *harbeh* adds up to 212, that an embryo surviving 212 days (about seven months) will most probably survive the pregnancy (Midrash Rabbah, Gen. 20). A second prediction regards the peculiar verse "If a woman have conceived seed, and born a man child …" (Lev. 12:2). Why the emphasis on the *woman* conceiving seed and a *male* baby been born as a result? Midrash Tanchuma says, in the name of Rabbi Ibon Halevi, "If the man precedes—giving birth to female baby; If the woman precedes—giving birth to male baby" (Midrash Tanchuma, Parashat Ishah Ki Tazria, C).

We were unable to locate scientific research evidence supporting, or denying, these two medical observations (predictions) based on biblical text.

2.1.3   *Repeated Single Digit in the Value of a Hebrew Word*

There are at least four words in Hebrew where summing up the values of the letters comprising the word results in a figure that contains repeated appearances of a single digit. Although we will later in the book relate to each of these cases separately, these words are presented already at this point to demonstrate design in the Hebrew language.

Case 1: *alef*[65] (name of first letter in the Hebrew alphabet):

$$111 = (80 = ף) + (30 = ל) + (1 = א)$$

Case 2: *bechor*[66] (firstborn, root of which is *B.K.R*):

$$222 = (200 = ר) + (20 = כ) + (2 = ב)$$

Case 3: *sheleg*[67] (snow):

$$333 = (3 = ג) + (30 = ל) + (300 = ש)$$

Case 4: *dam*[68] (blood):

$$44 = (40 = \text{ם}) + (4 = \text{ד})$$

"So what?" the reader may ask. Why are these cases indicative of design in the Hebrew language?

Simply put, it's because the single-digit, which appears repeatedly in each of these cases (words), is tightly related to the revealed meaning of the word. Indeed, this single digit expresses a major feature of the object that the word stands for in each of these cases. We will elaborate on this further, relating to each case individually, in succeeding chapters.

2.2   Information in Interrelated Hebrew Words, Visible and Hidden

There are certain sequences of words representing objects that are interrelated in any language. Thus, if one relates to parents and children, father and son, one generation and the next, obviously the concepts represented by these words are interrelated. Similarly, the words "fountain," "river," "cloud," and "fog" are interrelated, since each denotes a water-carrying object. There are, however, sequences of words, where the interrelations are more explicit than in others. These are sequences that represent order precedence, expressed in temporal terms (time sequence), in terms of cause and effect, or in terms of one object being part of a greater whole, represented by another word in the sequence.

In the Hebrew language, such interrelationships would most probably be reflected in the structure of the respective words. Observing logically interrelated sequences of Hebrew words, one may consistently discover that interrelationships within sequences of related concepts or objects, examples of which have just being given, manifest themselves in corresponding words sharing letters that clearly explain the direction of the relationship (if such exists)—or just that there is a relationship.

The Bible repeatedly asserts the rule that if one entity is derived from another, or the two are interrelated in some logical order, they should be similarly named by sharing common letters. The design, to be demonstrated in this section by several examples, thus acquires its legitimacy in the Bible itself. For example, we have in Genesis

- "And the man said, This is now bone of my bones, and flesh of my flesh: She shall be called Woman [*ishah*[69]], because she was taken out of Man [*ish*[70]]" (Gen. 2:23);

- "In the sweat of thy face shalt thou eat bread, till thou return to the ground [*adamah*[71]]; for out of it wast thou taken" … "therefore the Lord God sent him out of the garden of Eden, to till the ground [*adamah*[71]] from whence he was taken" (Gen. 3:19, 23; "man," in Hebrew, is *adam*).[72]

The phenomenon of related words sharing common letters will now be demonstrated by several examples. We will then analyze these, attempting to find out whether regularities may be deduced. In later chapters, other examples will be displayed, where the same phenomenon is demonstrated with regard to sequences of words having an element of mystery in their mutual interrelationships, that which has been denoted here "coincidence."

We start with sequences of words that have clear and visible contents to their interrelationships.

2.2.1 *Successive Generations in the Family and in a … Tree*

Family Relationships

In the Hebrew language, family relationships manifest themselves by sharing a common letter in such a way that the *first* letter in a new generation is identical to the *last* letter of the preceding generation. Observe this:

- "Father" (*av*)[73] ends with the second letter in the Hebrew alphabet (*bet*, standing for *B*, though pronounced like *V*). This is also the first letter in the word Son (*ben*).[74]

- "Son" (*ben*)[74] ends with the letter *N* (*nun* in Hebrew). This is the first letter in the word "grandson" (*neched*).[75]

- "Grandson" (*neched*)[75] ends with the letter *D* (*dalet*). This is the first letter for "fourth generation," which is called just that in Hebrew (*dor reviei*).[76] For example: "But in the fourth generation will they return here" (Gen. 15:16).

- "Great grandson" (*dor reviei*)[76] starts with the same letter as the last letter of the previous generation.

All these cases are displayed now with their original Hebrew letters:

(אב) ← (בנ) ← (נכד) ← (דור רביעי)

Comments

1. Another word for son, *neen*,[77] is used in modern Hebrew to denote "great grandson." However, the biblical *neen*[77] invariably precedes *neched*[75] (grandson), thus probably strengthening the acceptable interpretation that it means son in the Bible (or, more generally, an offspring). Consider these examples: "For I will rise up against them, says the Lord of hosts, and cut off from Babylon name, and remnant, and son [*neen*[77]] and grandson [*neched*[75]], says the Lord" (Isa. 14:22); "that you will not deal falsely with me, nor with my son [*neen*[77]] nor with my son's son [*neched*[75]] ..." (Gen. 21:23); "He shall neither have son [*neen*[77]] nor grandson with his people" (Job 18:19).

2. The word "son" is displayed above in Hebrew with the last letter, *nun*, as it would appear anywhere in a Hebrew word but at the end position. In fact, *ben*[74] is written in Hebrew with a final *nun*, differently than given in the display above. We preferred to write the "son" in Hebrew as above to make it easy for the reader to follow the phenomenon that we demonstrate in this example.

Generations in the Structure of a Tree

A tree is always regarded as the epitome of successive generations in a human family. A genealogical hierarchy is routinely referred to as "the family tree." It may therefore come as no surprise that the same relationships observed earlier for successive generations in a human family is manifested also in the various parts of the tree, as each successive part emerges out of the preceding one (in a time succession). Furthermore, it depends on it for its survival.

Observe this:

- "Stem" (*geza*)[78] ends with the letter *ayin*. This is the first letter in "branch" (*anaf*).[79]

- "Branch" (*anaf*)[79] ends with the letter *peh* (*P* in English). This is the first letter in "flower" (*perach*).[80]

- Flower turns into fruit. Unlike the earlier examples, where the previous "generation" survives to cohabitate with the later generation, a fruit is a flower in a modified form. One replaces the other. Appropriately, the two words share the same *first two letters* of their root, and it is only the third letter that is different: the letter *yod*, the last in the Hebrew word for "fruit" (*pri*),[81] replaces the letter *chet*, the last in the Hebrew word for "flower" (*perach*)[80] (*yod*, coincidentally, also appears later in the Hebrew alphabet). A comparable phenomenon is observed in another case, given in section 10.2, where "knee" is the end part of a "thigh," and therefore the two words share the same last two letters.

This sequence of four family-related words regarding "tree" are now displayed in their Hebrew form:

$$\text{(גזע)} \leftarrow \text{(ענפ)} \leftarrow \text{(פרח)} \leftarrow \text{(פרי)}$$

There are several other interesting words relating to a tree. Examples:

- *Pura*,[82] or *pora*,[82] appears several times in the Bible, mostly in Ezekiel (17:6, 31:5, 6, 8, 12, 13). While the exact meaning of the word is not altogether clear, the description in Ezekiel gives the impression that this term refers to small branches that stretch out of the main branches (like in "And *peorotav* were made longer" [31:5]). The last letter of *anaf*[79] (branch) is the first letter of *pura*.[82]

- The word "shadow" appears in the Bible fifty-three times. Many of these instances relate to shade cast by a tree or by products of a tree, namely products made of wood. The words "tree" and "wood" in Hebrew are one and the same: *etz*.[83] The last letter of *etz*[83] (*tzadi*, roughly corresponding to *Z*) is the first letter of *tzel*[84] (shadow). Similarly, the first letter for the highest part of the tree, *tzameret*[85] (treetop), is again the last letter of "tree" (*etz*).[83]

The same rule that was demonstrated for interrelated parts of the tree also occasionally applies to parts of the human body. A special section (10.2) is dedicated to demonstrate this rule, among other coincidences regarding the human body.

2.2.2 The Route of Water in Nature

Another natural sequence of related words describes the route that water travels from deep underground all the way to the river. In the Hebrew language, this sequence of words shares the same typical pattern (namely, sharing of a single letter) as depicted earlier for the human family and for a tree.

Regard this:

- *Tehom*[86] is the Hebrew word relating to underground cavities where water is stored. For example: "Land of water rivers, fountains and underground water [*tehomot*[87]]" (Deut. 8:7). The last letter of the primordial source of water, *tehom*,[86] is *mem* (the English *M*).

- *Maayan*[88] in Hebrew means "fountain." This is the place where the underground water finds an outlet to go above ground. The last letter of *tehom*[86] is the first letter of *maayan*.[88]

- *Nahar*[89] means "river." A river receives water from fountains along its route. The first letter of *nahar*[89] (river) is the last letter of *maayan*[88] (fountain). A synonym for *nahar*[89] is *nachal*.[90] More precisely, *nachal*[90] in biblical language refers to the valley where water is flowing. Again, the last letter of "fountain" (*maayan*)[88] is the first letter of *nachal*.[90]

This sequence of words is now displayed in its Hebrew form:

$$\text{תהום} \leftarrow \text{מיימ} \leftarrow \text{מעיינ} \leftarrow \text{נחל (נהר)}$$

Nachal ← *Maayan* ← *Mayim* ← *Tehom*

Comments

1. The order, insinuated for the flow of water by the above sequence of words, appears explicitly more than once in the Bible, either in the "correct" (natural) order or in a reverse order.

   Examples:

   - "Land of water rivers, fountains and underground water" (Deut. 8:7)—a reverse order.

   - "He who dispatches fountains into rivers, among mountains will they travel" (Pss. 104:16)—the natural order.

2. In the first three Hebrew words above (read from right to left), the last letter of the word would in practice be written differently. The reason is that both the letters *mem* and *nun* are written differently when at the end position in a word. As related to earlier, we have opted to write word-end letters as they would appear anywhere else in a word, so that the reader may trace the relationships between these consecutive words.

2.2.3   Conclusions

What regularities may one deduce from these examples? Two rules seem to emerge.

First Rule: "Objects" that are related in time would share an extreme-position letter in the right sequence—namely, the latter object would start with the same letter as the last letter in the preceding object.

Second Rule: If one object evolves naturally from another, either one or two letters may be shared, dependent on how much the newly evolving object departs from the originating object. For example, since a "fruit" is a "flower" in a different form (they do not coexist, as do human generations), two letters are shared; similarly, since the knee is part of the thigh, also two letters are shared (not one—refer to section 10.2 for details).

2.3   Information in Unrelated Hebrew Words of a Common Root

In section 2.1.1, sets of Hebrew words sharing the same root, yet having different meanings, have been explored. How the words' meanings are nevertheless inter-related was easily explained based on the basic concepts of the Bible. For example, the pair "sin" and "miss" (a target) share the same root, with understandable inter-relationship. Or the root *Ch.L.L* produces several words, all of which indicate emptiness, which in the last analysis leads to the understanding that they all are traceable to the ultimate "emptiness"—namely, emptiness from God.

There are, however, cases where it is much harder to trace why sets of words share the same root. Subject to our basic assumption that there is design in the structure of the Hebrew language (its rules and its ingredients), such words, seemingly unrelated, require more exploration in order to fathom the underlying concept that binds them together with a common root. An example for such seemingly unrelated words is given in chapter 3, where two words with a shared root—meaning, essentially, "to happen by chance" and "cold"—are probed. These words are, in fact, the subject of the chapter. Another example is given in section 6.2. Yet another example is given in section 11.1, where an attempt is made to explain the relationship between "river" and "light," two obviously unrelated words sharing the same root.

Some other examples for seemingly unrelated sets of words sharing the same root are addressed in this section. The section is unique in that we do not attempt to give any explanations for these sets of words. Yet some clues at possible explanations are occasionally offered. The reader is encouraged to figure out why the Hebrew language had selected to interrelate these words by a common root.

Example 1: "Desert" and "Speaking"

The word "desert" in Hebrew is *midbar*.[91] To speak is *ledaber*.[92] Both are derived from the common root *D.B.R.* Why do these words share a common root? Possible hint: Mount Sinai!

Example 2: "Number," "Book," "Tale"

The Hebrew words for "number," "book," and "tale" all derive from the root *S.P.R.* "Number" is *mispar*,[93] "book" is *sepher*,[94] and "a tale" is *sippur*.[95] While the last two may somehow be related as two distinct forms of communication, it is hard to explain why "number" belongs in that category.

Sepher Yetzirah (*Book of Formation*) is an ancient Hebrew manuscript, "withoutq uestion the oldest and most mysterious of all Kabalistic texts" (Kaplan 1997). It is traditionally attributed to the Patriarch Abraham, but truly its ancient origins are unknown. This book starts with the following: "And He created His universe with three books [*sepharim*[96]]: with book [*sepher*[94]], with number (or counting) [*sephar*[97]] and with a tale [*sippur*[95]]." All these words originate in the same root, yet are seemingly unrelated.

Kaplan (1997) explains that this three-way partition (the "three books") represents, respectively, quality, quantity, and communication. In other words, "These three books correspond to the three divisions of creation defined by *Sepher Yetzirah*, namely, 'Universe, Year, Soul'" (therein, 19).

We wish not to delve, in this book, into Kabbalistic interpretations of the Hebrew language. Our aim in introducing this set of words is just to indicate that the mysterious interrelationship between these words is still a mystery in need of explanation.

Example 3: "To Know" and "Have Sexual Encounter"

Both these words are indeed one word in Hebrew, having the root *I.D.A.* Thus, the Bible, relating to Adam, says: "And the man knew [*yada*[98]] Eve his wife; and she conceived, and bore Cain ..." (Gen. 4:1). Yet the same root serves also in altogether different context: "Thus says the Lord, Let not the wise man glory in his wisdom, neither let the mighty man glory in his might, let not the rich man glory in his riches: but let him that glories glory in this, that he understands and knows [*yadoa*[99]] me, that I am the Lord who exercise faithful love, justice, and righteousness, in the earth" (Jer. 9: 22–23).

What basic underlying concept can possibly cause these two meanings to merge in a single root—in fact, the same word, with all its variations?

Chapter 17 is dedicated to a discussion of this subject, and offers one avenue of explanation.

Example 4: "Male" and "Memory, Remembrance"

Both words in Hebrew derive from a common root *Z.Ch.R.* A "male" is *zachar*[100] and "he remembered" is *zachar*.[100] A possible hint is provided in how the Bible explains the purpose of the Brit-Mila: "In the same day the Lord made a covenant with Abraham, saying, To thy seed have I given this land …" (Gen. 15:18). The covenant between God and Abraham's seed is then repeatedly recalled in the Torah, particularly by the prophets calling on Israel to *remember* the Brit (covenant). In fact, the Brit is mentioned in the Bible no fewer than 283 times.

Another explanation is that a man's children are his memory in the land of the living (after his death), so perhaps an association may be established.

Could there be another explanation for this strange association—perhaps of a medical sort?

Example 5: "Flesh," "Meat," "Tidings"

In Hebrew, "flesh" and "meat" are represented by one word: *bassar*.[101] This word, with variations, appears in the Bible 270 times. Its root is *B.S.R.*

To break the news that something is about to happen, to the better or to the worse, is *le-vaser*,[102] derived from the same root.

What could possibly be the connection between these words—"flesh" and "tidings" (*bessora*)?[103] What is the particular message that the Hebrew language attempts to convey? Is the latter ("tidings") the destination of the former ("flesh")?

Indeed, the Bible occasionally insinuates such an inter-association—for example, in

- "But whilst I am still in my flesh, though it is after my skin is torn from my body, I would see God" (Job 19:26).

- "And the glory of the Lord shall be revealed, and all flesh [*bassar*[97]] shall see it together: for the mouth of the Lord has spoken it" (Isa. 40:5).

Example 6: "Create," "Get Healthy," "Get Fat"

The Hebrew words for "create," "get healthy," and "get fat" derive from the root *B.R.A.* While one may possibly figure out why in ancient times to be fat and to be healthy were considered equivalent, it is by far harder to see a connection between the Hebrew words for "creation" (*briah*)[104] and "health" (*briut*),[105] both deriving from a common root.

We do not attempt any explanation and leave this question open.

Example 7: "Sign," "Omen," "Me," "Him"

The Hebrew for "sign," or "omen," is *ot*.[106] This word also means "letter" (in the alphabet), though the latter usage probably does not appear in the Bible.

The word *ot*[106] is the basis for various notations for the subject of speech, like "me" (*oti*),[107] "him" or "it" (*oto*),[108] "them" (*otam*,[109] masculine, or *otan*,[110] feminine), and so forth.

The relationship between the two usages of the same word is hard to work out. An immediate, uneducated logical guess is that perhaps the Hebrew language regards all that exist as meaningful, as conveying a message to the universe, just like the *ot*[106] (sign or letter).

2.4   Information in Hebrew Words Read in Reverse

Hebrew words are read from right to left. This may probably be attributed to how letters were carved in stone in ancient times: it is easy to progress from right to left (assuming that you are right-handed) than from left to right.

This chapter is about design in the Hebrew language. Design may be inferred also from the highly nonproportional number of Hebrew words that, when read from left to right, reveal hidden messages that are tightly linked to the exposed meaning of the word, when read (properly) from right to left.

Example 1: Laban

Laban[111] is the name of an evil biblical hero, to whom chapter 15 is dedicated. Read in reverse, it means "villain" (*naval*).[112]

Both words in Hebrew (*laban*[111] turned into *naval*)[112] are given below:

$$(ל) + (ב) + (נ) \; \leftarrow \; (נ) + (ב) + (ל)$$

Example 2: Moses

This is an exact opposite of *laban*.[111] Moses, read in reverse, yields *Hashem*,[113] one of the names of God (meaning, literally, "the Name").

Both *names* in Hebrew ("Moses" turned into *Hashem*)[113] are given below:

$$(מ) + (ש) + (ה) \; \leftarrow \; (ה) + (ש) + (מ)$$

Example 3: *Sneh*

The *sneh*[114] is a thorny bush, from which the angel of God miraculously revealed to Moses. The Bible describes it thus: "And the angel of the Lord appeared to him in a flame of fire out of the midst of a bush [*sneh*[114]]: and he looked and, behold, the bush burned with fire, but the bush was not consumed" (Exod. 3:2).

Sneh,[114] read in reverse, is *hannes*[115] (the miracle).

Both names in Hebrew (*sneh*[114] turned into *hannes*[115]) are given below:

$$(\text{ס}) + (\text{נ}) + (\text{ה}) \leftarrow (\text{ה}) + (\text{נ}) + (\text{ס})$$

Example 4: *Roa*

Roa[116] in Hebrew means "malice, wickedness" (noun). Earlier, we indicated how the Hebrew language relates to sin as missing a target. A similar position is revealed in reading the word *roa*[116] (evil) in reverse. The result is *iver*[117] (blind). No explanation needs be added.

Both words in Hebrew (*roa*[116] turned into *iver*[117]) are given below:

$$(\text{ר}) + (\text{ו}) + (\text{ע}) \leftarrow (\text{ע}) + (\text{ו}) + (\text{ר})$$

Example 5: *Osher*

Osher[118] in Hebrew means "riches." (Another Hebrew word, similarly pronounced but differently written, means "happiness"; we do not address this word). Read in reverse, *osher*[118] yields *resha,*[119] which means "iniquity, injustice." The association between these words may come as no surprise. Jewish prophets repeatedly warn rich people who have amassed their wealth by unjust ways. For example: "As the partridge sits on eggs, but hatches them not; so is he that gets riches [*osher*[118]], and not by right; he shall leave them in the midst of his days, and at his end shall be a fool" (Jer. 17:11).

Both words in Hebrew (*osher*[118] turned into *resha*[119]) are given below:

$$(\text{ע}) + (\text{ש}) + (\text{ר}) \leftarrow (\text{ר}) + (\text{ש}) + (\text{ע})$$

Example 6: *Mavet*

Mavet[120] in Hebrew means "death." Read in reverse, *mavet*[120] yields *tom,*[121] which means "innocence, wholeness, purity, or naivety," but also "end." The relationship between *mavet*[120] and *tom*[121] could be the subject of many books. Job makes explicit connection between the two concepts: "One dies in his full strength [*be-tumo*[122]], being wholly at ease and quiet" (Job 21:23).

Both words in Hebrew (*mavet*[120] turned into *tom*)[121] are given below:

$$(מ) + (ו) + (ת) \; \leftarrow \; (ת) + (ו) + (מ)$$

Example 7: *Aluf*

Aluf[123] in Hebrew means "leader, the head." However, it is often used in the Bible as one of the names of God. For example: "Wilt thou not from this time cry to me, My father, thou art the guide [*aluf*[123]] of my youth" (Jer. 3:4)—or, "A perverse man sows strife: and a whisperer separate close friends [*aluf*[123]]" (Prov. 16:28).

The last translated verse is one of the worst translations of a biblical verse we have ever encountered. Let us trace how Rashi (1040–1105, the most revered interpreter of biblical Jewish text) would have translated this verse (based on his explanation of the verse): "A perverse man sows strife: and a grumbler separates from the World Leader [*aluf*[123]]" (Prov. 16:28).

Read in reverse, *aluf*[123] yields *peleh*,[124] which means "wonder." God is related to in the Bible numerous times as "the one who is doing wonders." For example: "Who is like thee, O Lord, among the gods?/ who is like thee, glorious in holiness,/ fearful in praises, doing wonders?" (Exod. 15:11).

Both words in Hebrew (*aluf*[123] turned into *peleh*)[124] are given below:

$$(א) + (ל) + (פ) \; \leftarrow \; (פ) + (ל) + (א)$$

Comment

Aluf[123] appears in the Bible with the letter *vav* or without (as done above).

Example 8: Noah

Noah is the hero of the deluge, in Genesis (chapters 6–9). The name derives from the same root as "to rest," and in modern Hebrew, the name means also "comfortable." In section 15.5, we discuss the meaning of Noah's name and how Noah compares with Jonah, another biblical hero, regarding his moral conduct.

The unique feature about Noah's name is that with this name the Bible indeed confers legitimacy on the previous seven examples, at least with regard to the practice of reading *names* in reverse (as done earlier for Laban and Moses).

The Bible introduces Noah thus: "Noah found favor in the eyes of the Lord" (Gen. 6:8).

However, as often happens with biblical translation, a major message is lost. In the Hebrew Bible, the verse is "Noah found [*chen*[125]] in the eyes of the Lord" (Gen. 6:8).

In Hebrew, you ask a girl whether the boy she just met "found *chen*[125]" in her eyes, meaning whether she found him to her liking. But it is not coincidental that the Bible uses the word *chen*[125] at this particular spot, because this word is written like Noah, only in reverse:

$$(נ) + (ח) \leftarrow (ח) + (נ)$$

Thus one can deduce that by using the two words, "Noah" and *chen*,[125] in the same verse, the Bible insinuates that it is legitimate to identify information about a person's personality and moral conduct by reading the name in reverse, just as done earlier with Laban and Moses.

PART II

Coincidences in the Hebrew Language: Hidden, Unexpected Information

CHAPTER 3

"Randomness" and "Cold"

3.1 Introduction

Entropy is one of the most fundamental concepts in modern physics, in cosmology theories, information theory, statistics, and, more generally, in the way we perceive our world. As popularly perceived, entropy is a measurable quantity which conveys the amount of disorder that a physical system has. A related law in physics, the Second Law of Thermodynamics, states, in its simplest form, that as a result of processes that cause a complex system to emerge from a state of equilibrium, the total entropy either increases or remains the same, but never decreases. In modern cosmological theories, the universe as a whole is seen as a system that had minimal entropy at the moment of creation (the big bang), and the total entropy of the universe, according to the Second Law of Thermodynamics, has been increasing ever since, irrespective of the theorized future history of the universe (Greene 2004, 171–76, and Penrose 2004, 728).

The notion of entropy was first introduced in 1865 by Clausius, who had also stated the Second Law of Thermodynamics simply by saying that "It is not possible for heat to flow from a colder body to a warmer body without any work having being done to accomplish this flow." However, it was the Austrian Ludwig Boltzmann who, in 1877, gave entropy a more rigorous mathematical treatment and definition, which had since affected many branches of science and technology.

Both Clausius and Boltzmann referred to physical systems when they developed their notions of entropy.

In 1948, Claude Elwood Shannon introduced his concept of entropy from a totally innovative perspective. In a landmark paper (Shannon, 1948) which was published a year later in a book (Shannon and Weaver 1949, and also 1963), Shannon expounded his mathematical theory of communication. Unlike Boltzmann's entropy, which relates to complex *physical* systems, Shannon's entropy

65

relates to the statistical contents of information. As we will later discuss, although derivations of the two concepts of entropy were based on altogether different concepts and arguments, later developments (with some heated debates) have shown that the two concepts of entropy are in fact equivalent.

It is not our intention here to deliver a full account of the theory underlying entropy and how it is integrated in various scientific disciplines. Rather, we wish to demonstrate two realizations of this concept in seemingly unrelated areas—statistics (or information theory) and thermodynamics, respectively with Shannon's and Boltzmann's concepts of entropy. More explicitly, it is our intention to demonstrate how the same scientific construct, entropy, is related to randomness and to the Second Law of Thermodynamics, as the latter is realized in chemical or physical processes that involve transfer of heat.

By coincidence, both concepts of entropy seem to be associated with Hebrew words of a shared root.

3.2   Two Concepts of Entropy

3.2.1   Information (Shannon Entropy)

We start by explaining how Shannon entropy is associated with the concept of randomness. Suppose that we have a random phenomenon, which can be realized in N different nonoverlapping ways. For example, the outcome of throwing a dice is a set of six results (N = 6), conveniently displayed by the set {1, 2, 3, 4, 5, 6}. We denote the quantitative value attached to each possible result of a random phenomenon a random variable, r.v. Thus, the result shown by a thrown dice may be defined as an r.v.

Suppose that each possible value of an r.v. has associated with it a certain probability, and let us denote the probability of result i by p_i. The collection of values, $\{p_i\}$ (i = 1, 2, …, N), defines the distribution of the r.v. According to Shannon definition, entropy is the expected information content of the distribution, and it is defined by

$$H = -\sum_{i=1}^{N} p_i \log_2(p_i)$$

(The sign Σ means summing up over all possible values of i.)

This entropy is measured in bits. However, if the natural logarithm is used (log on the basis of e = 2.7182 …, rather than 2), then H is measured in nats.

To understand how this concept is associated with randomness, suppose that we have seven boxes, and one of these boxes contains a fortune. We wish to select one of the boxes in accordance with the available information. Let us distinguish three different scenarios.

Scenario A: We know that the fortune is in Box 4.
Translated into probabilities, this means that the probability that the fortune is in Box 4 is 1 (or 100%), while all the other probabilities are zero. The Shannon entropy associated with this decision, or with the distribution that led us to this decision, is given by

$$H = -(1)\log_2(1) = 0$$

This decision was taken in conditions of complete certainty; therefore, entropy is zero.

Scenario B: We do not know for certain where the fortune is hidden—however, we have some information that allows us to assign probabilities to the various boxes.
Suppose that these probabilities are (they have to sum up to 1):

$$p_1 = 0.05; p_2 = 0.1; p_3 = 0.4; p_4 = 0.05; p_5 = 0.2; p_6 = 0.15; p_7 = 0.05$$

Shannon entropy is

$$H = -[0.05*\log_2(0.05) + 0.1*\log_2(0.1) + 0.4*\log_2(0.4) + 0.05*\log_2(0.05) +$$
$$0.2*\log_2(0.2) + 0.15*\log_2(0.15) + 0.05*\log_2(0.05)] = 2.384 \text{ bits}$$

The decision as to which box contains the fortune has to be taken under conditions of uncertainty. Some randomness entered our decision. The amount of this randomness is expressed by the entropy that characterizes the distribution of probabilities that we face under this scenario. The size of this entropy is 2.384 bits.

The decision in Scenario B will be taken knowing that entropy is not zero (neither is it maximal, as we will learn from Scenario C).

Scenario C: We are completely ignorant about the fortune location.
Therefore, we have no alternative but assign equal probabilities to each box—
which, in this case, since the probabilities have to sum up to 1, means that each
box is assigned a probability of 1/7.

Shannon entropy is

$$H = -\Sigma \ (1/7) \ \log_2(1/7) = -\log_2(1/7) = 2.807 \ \text{bits.}$$

Shannon's entropy has increased to 2.807, which is the maximum entropy thatt
he defined random variable (the box number where the fortune is hidden) can
assume. The reason is that it can be easily shown that when the distribution of the
probabilities is uniform—the entropy reaches its maximum possible value.

The decision in Scenario C will be taken under conditions of ignorance, and it
will be completely random.

From this simple example, we realize that Shannon entropy is in fact a measure
of the amount of randomness that is inherent in the distribution of probabilities,
associated with the values of the random variable (in our case, the box number containing the fortune). That this indeed is the case may be demonstrated
by increasing the number of boxes for Scenario C, from 7 to 20. Intuitively, we
would assert that the amount of randomness associated with our decision has
increased. Shannon entropy reflects this:

$$H = -\Sigma \ (1/20) \ \log_2(1/20) = -\log_2(1/20) = 4.322 \ \text{bits}$$
$$\text{(compared to 2.807 for 7 boxes)}$$

3.2.2 *Thermodynamics (Boltzmann Entropy)*

Boltzmann provided a complete theory for his concept of entropy, which resulted
in a formula to calculate entropy of complex physical systems. A good demonstration for the derivation of Boltzmann's entropy is given in Penrose (2004, 690),
and the more scientifically and mathematically oriented reader may refer to this
source for clear derivation and explanation of Boltzmann's entropy. Here, we show
how a simple process of transfer of a quantity of heat, Q, from a hot object to a
cold object, changes the total entropy of the two objects so that this total increases
(in accordance with the Second Law of Thermodynamics).

Suppose that heat flows in response to a temperature gradient between two
objects that are in thermal contact. The temperatures of these objects are T_1 and
T_2 (assume that $T_1 > T_2$), and energy is transferred in the form of heat, Q. To

simplify the scenario, assume also that both objects are big enough so that at a small interval of time, dt, when the amount of heat flowing from the hot object to the cold object is dQ, no change in temperature occurs in either objects. Then, from Boltzmann's entropy formula, it may be shown that for an object with temperature T, the amount of entropy gained, dH, is equal to

$$dH = dQ/T$$

Note, that although we refer to this expression only with a simplified scenario that does not require the use of calculus, this expression for the entropy change, resulting from heat transfer between two objects, is much more general. In fact, one can say that this ratio measure is the "driving force" for every spontaneous chemical reaction in the universe. Gibbs's known equation, which describes how energy, formerly bound in reactants, is spread out in the products, can actually be put in terms of this equation.

Let us calculate the total change in entropy for the two objects in thermal contact. Conveniently denoting dQ as negative for outflow of heat and positive for inflow, one obtains from the above equation

$$dH_1 + dH_2 = dQ\,[1/T_2 - 1/T_1] = dQ(T_1 - T_2) \,/\, (T_1 T_2) \geq 0,$$

where nonnegativity for this expression is implied from the (arbitrary) assumption that $T_1 \geq T_2$.

This result implies that the total change in entropy is nonnegative, in accordance with the Second Law of Thermodynamics. The same would have been obtained if we calculated the total amount of entropy change throughout the whole process, assuming that the objects' temperatures are changing as a result of the heat flow (only then we would have to use calculus, which we avoid here in order to keep the level of the required mathematics to the possible minimum).

An interesting property of the above result, which can be proved also for the whole process of a heat transfer, is that the lower (relative to T_1) is the temperature T_2, the higher the increase in total entropy of the two objects as a result of the heat transfer. Mathematically, this can be seen from the above right-hand side of the formula: decreasing T_2 results both in an increase in the numerator and a decrease in the denominator. In other words, the *colder* T_2, the *higher* the increase in entropy.

A similar pattern can be traced for any transfer that is activated as a result of a gradient between two objects that are in a state of disequilibrium—for example, an electric discharge as a result of the potential (gradient) between two poles of a battery.

The example above for a realization of Boltzmann's entropy demonstrates that lower temperatures are associated with higher rates of generation of entropy. The same result is obtained (though from different considerations, also associated with the Second Law of Thermodynamics), in cosmology theories. The universe was at the highest temperature at the point of the big bang, while its entropy was at its lowest level (relate to the previously cited references). As the universe started to expand, and still is expanding, both the average temperature of the universe keeps falling, and its entropy is increasing.

3.2.3 *About the Equivalence of the Two Concepts of Entropy*

That the two concepts are indeed equivalent has been the subject of some heated debate for some time. Weaver, a coauthor with Shannon (Shannon and Weaver 1949), in fact claims that

> "the quantity which uniquely meets the natural requirements that one sets up for "information" turns up to be exactly that which is known in thermodynamics as entropy … That information be measured by entropy, is, after all, natural when we remember that information, in communication theory, is associated with the amount of freedom of choice we have in constructing messages" (therein, 12–13).

A more rigorous connection between information theory (Shannon's) and physics (Boltzmann's) was established by Jaynes (1957).

A demonstration for the debate that is still ongoing about the nature of the relationship between the two concepts of entropy may be found in "Shannon said information is physical entropy," an Internet exchange of messages between a group of scientists at http://webmail.unizar.es/pipermail/fis/2004-June/000661.html.

3.2.4 *Summary of Main Points*

- Two concepts of entropy have been developed in two seemingly unrelated branches of science and technology: Boltzmann's entropy, rooted in thermodynamics, and Shannon's entropy, rooted in the mathematical theory of communication and information.

- The first concept of entropy resulted from observations about the behavior of physical systems, and it has been applied in various branches of the physical world—like thermodynamics, cosmology and biology. It is associated with the Second Law of Thermodynamics (SLT), and in fact forms the foundation for this law. A typical feature of Boltzmann's entropy is its dealing with energy and matter in all its forms, where thermal energy (heat) provides some of the most common and widely observed realizations of the SLT.

- For Boltzmann's entropy, it has been demonstrated that objects with lower temperatures (cooler objects) generate larger entropy on absorbing heat than hotter objects.

- The second concept of entropy was developed by Shannon from mathematical theory in relation to the information contents of communication. Shannon's entropy is purely statistical in nature, and it provides a measure of the amount of randomness that is "contained" in a specified statistical distribution.

- For Shannon's entropy, it has been demonstrated that increasing randomness—that is, increasing the uniformity in the distribution of probabilities—results in higher entropy. More randomness implies increased entropy.

- A heated debate conducted among scientists whether the two concepts of entropy are equivalent has led to the conclusion that the two concepts are indeed one and the same.

If the two concepts of entropy (Shannon's and Boltzmann's), are equivalent, then "randomness" and "coldness" should be considered equivalent in some sense, with respect to their relationship to entropy and its generation.

3.3   "Randomness" in Biblical Hebrew and in the Bible

The Bible relates to any indication that randomness rules our universe as an abomination. God is the ruler of the world, not randomness. True, the actions, or the results of the actions, of the Divine are sometimes hidden. God occasionally hides, or conceals, his face, and sometimes also hides the hiding. But the truth is that the world is conducted by the Divine, and if this is ignored, then the wrath of the Divine will befall the blind, who believe in the god of randomness. Furthermore, the wrath itself will appear in the form of sheer randomness (or coincidences).

Consider a few examples for this general approach:

- When Moses turns to God and asks, "Show me thy glory" (Exod. 33:18), he is responded to by the Divine: "And it shall come to pass, while my glory passes by, ..., and I will take away my hand and thou shall see my back: but my face shall not be seen" (Exod. 33:22–23). Jewish sages interpreted this as implying that a human being can only see the deeds of God post-factum, after they have occurred, and not in advance. This gives a general sense of how randomness is perceived in the Bible: what may seem as random, when perceived in real time, may indeed be intentional and purposeful, and also look like this, when observed post-factum.

- Just before Moses is about to ascend Mount Nebo to depart from this world, God is warning Moses about the catastrophes that may befall the people of Israel if they violated the covenant that God had made with them: "Then my anger shall be kindled against them in that day ... and I will hide my face from them ... And I will surely hide my face [literally, "hide the hiding," *haster astir*[1]] on that day for all the evils which they shall have perpetrated" (Deut. 31:17–18). This sentence served to explain the name of another book of the Bible, the book of Esther (refer to section 16.2 and the next paragraph).

- In the book of Esther, the latter is the central figure, and the name of God is not mentioned, not even once. However, the root of the name Esther is "hide." When one reads the book of Esther, it is self-explanatory (and thus has it been traditionally interpreted by Jewish sages) that although the conduct of the Divine is hidden and not addressed explicitly in the book (and the name of Esther makes this clear), it is the intervention of the Divine that is obviously behind the miraculous story of the rescue of the Jews from the Holocaust that was ready for them, Nuremberg style: "And books were dispatched by runners to all of the king kingdoms to destroy to kill and to annihilate all the Jews ... and the king and Haman sat down to drink" (Esther 3:13–15).

- The hiding of the face of God is consistently related to in the Bible as the reason for evil and mishaps that befall the children of Israel, either as a people or as individuals. In fact, the verb "to hide" appears eighty-two times in the whole Bible, and most of these hidings relate to the Divine hiding his face. For example, "Your sins have been hiding my face from you" (Isa. 59:2); "And I will hide my face from them" (Ezek. 39:23, 24); "I was angry and stroke him, hiding and will be angry" (Isa. 57:17); "Do not please hide your face from your servant" (Pss. 69:18).

As the scriptures continuously remind us, the concealing of the face of the Divine starts with the humans who attempt to hide from God. However, the root used in not *S.T.R*, as in the earlier examples, but *Ch.B.A*, pronounced *le-hechavae*[2] (to hide). As the story is told in the book of Genesis, "And they heard the voice of the Lord God walking in the garden in the breeze of the day, and the man and his wife hid themselves from the presence of the Lord God amongst the trees of the garden" (Gen. 3:8). And later, the excuses came: "And he said I have heard your voice in the Garden, and I was afraid because …" (Gen. 3:10). And still later, when Cain is punished for murdering his brother, Abel, he says to God, "Behold, you have today expelled me from the face of the earth and from *your face* I will hide" (Gen. 4:14). Thus, both God hides his face, hiding which is invariably the outcome of human transgression, or man attempts to hide himself from the face of God (it is always the face—nothing else).

From these examples and others, God's hiding of his face obviously intends to convey a sense that the presence of the Divine, or the intervention of the Divine in what is happening, is concealed, and thus all look as a consequence of sheer randomness. In fact, the Hebrew word *olam*[3] (world) derives from a root that means "concealment."

The Bible reserves for the concept of randomness a very particular root in the Hebrew language. Furthermore, this root, with its manifold variations, always intends to convey extremely negative connotations. In fact, some translations of the Hebrew Bible refer to Hebrew words derived from "randomness" as "rebellion" (an example will be shortly given). The usage in a negative sense of the Hebrew root for "randomness" is consistent throughout the Bible. Although the latter does not always expressly emphasize this negative respect, it is always clear from the context that the usage of the root implies that somehow the existence of God, or the intervention of God in the affairs depicted, is denied. At times, the Bible does so in a cynical fashion, like implying "You, the reader, might think this was an accident, but you can easily deduce from the context that it was not" (examples will shortly be given).

The Hebrew-language root for randomness is *K.R.H*.
From this root, various words are derived, like "to occur," or "occurrences." The root may appear in the Bible in various forms and shapes. But it always means "occurred to happen," "occurrence," "happened to be meeting" (as in, "Joseph happened to meet John"), "occurring by sheer coincidence."

Examine a few examples for the usage of this root throughout the Bible.

Example 1: *Keri*

God warns the people of Israel to refrain from walking with God as though randomness, or coincidence, were the true profile of reality. The key word here is *keri*[4] (from the root *K.R.H*). This word appears several times in a single chapter int he Bible, and only there, at Leviticus 26:21, 23, 24, 27, 28, 40, 41. God warns the people of Israel that if they walk with him in *keri*,[4] then he will walk with them with the wrath of *keri*,[4] punishing them seven times over for their transgressions. This "wrath of *keri*"[4] may simply be interpreted to mean that if the childreno f Israel considered everything to be happening to them by coincidence, then God would inflict randomness upon them, punishing and at times torturing them" randomly" for their sins, thus depriving them even of the ability to associate, in any way, those punishments with their misconduct.

Note that *keri*[4] appears only in this chapter in Leviticus, so the interpretation of the word varies. In some Bible translations we find *keri*[4] to mean "rebellion." Although we are not aware of the source of this interpretation, it is apparently consistent with Jewish sages' attitude that to consider events as happening by chance constitutes rebellion against God.

Since *keri*[4] appears only at this chapter in Leviticus, it is perhaps appropriate that more supportive evidence be provided for the biblical perception of randomness as grave abomination—and, indeed, vilification of the name of God. Therefore, some further examples for the negative use of the root *K.R.H* in the Bible are now provided.

Example 2: Accidental Occurrences or Encounters

The Bible consistently employs the word "to meet," based on the root *K.R.H*, to imply that a seemingly coincidental meeting is in fact intentional, or that one of the participants to the meeting live in denial of God and therefore perceives the meeting to be coincidental. By the same vein, when one tells of what has happened to him or her and wishes to convey to the other party the impression that his or her story implies a coincidental chain of events (or so he or she believes), the root *K.R.H* is invariably inserted in the text.

Examples:

- The epitome for a culture based on randomness and denial of God, as will be realized by further examples later on, is the tribe of Amalek. When an Amalekite boy wishes to convey to David that he had just killed his adversary, King Saul, and his son, Jonathan, the endeared friend of David, he is afraid of the possible wrath of David for participating in the war of Amalek with Israel. Therefore, the Amalekite slave emphasizes the random nature of his encounter with Saul and Jonathan: "And the young man that told him ... [to David] ... said, As I happened by chance [*nikro nikreti*[5]] upon mount Gilboa, behold, Saul leaned upon his spear" (2 Samuel 1:6). The Hebrew word used by the Amalekite youngster for "I happened by chance" is doubled, thus doubling the focus on the random nature of this encounter.

- Moses leaves his instructions for the children of Israel: "Remember that which Amalek did to you on your way out of Egypt; When he occurred to you [expressed by the two words *asher karcha*[6]]" (Deut. 25:17–18, author's translation). Of course, Amalek has not the faintest idea that everything that occurs is an act of God, so the Bible in an ironic fashion conveys how Amalek relates to the encounter with the people of Israel ("when he occurred to you"). Also, Moses emphasizes that Israel at the time was also somewhat like Amalek, because its people were "tired and exhausted *and not God-fearing*." So the random encounter that occurred at the time is adequately described as "occurrence," both from the perspectives of Amalek and that of the people of Israel (at the time).

- Pharaoh, the omnipotent king of Egypt, denies any existence of God. So he says, "I own the Yeor [the Nile river] and I have made it" (Ezek. 29:3); Or: "And Pharaoh said, Who is the Lord that I should obey his voice to let Israel go? I know not the Lord and also Israel I will send not" (Exod. 5:2). Therefore, when God instructs Moses on how to talk to Pharaoh, he adequately uses a language fit for this king: "And you would come together with the elderly of Israel to the king of Egypt, and said unto him, The Lord God of the Hebrews has *occurred* [*nikrah*[7]] to us, and now let us go, we pray thee, for three days in the desert and put sacrifices to the Lord our God" (Exod. 3:18). Indeed, Moses uses this phrase (*nikrah*[7]) when he comes before Pharaoh (Exod. 5:3). Needless to add, this word, "occur," is not in Moses' vocabulary when he addresses his own fellow men and women, the children of Israel. Neither does God instruct him to use such language when breaking the news about the upcoming salvation from the bonds of Egypt (Exod. 3:13–17).

- The story of Balak, King of Moab, who has summoned the non-Israelite prophet Balaam to curse the people of Israel, while the latter were wandering in the vicinity of Moab on their way to the land of Israel, is saturated with "occurrences" words (Num. 23:3, 4, 15, 16). In fact, the *K.R.H* root is used as a basis for various derivatives four times in a single chapter (out of the twenty-three times that this root appears in the whole of the Bible). The Bible again emphasizes that the culture of these individuals—King Balak and the prophet Balaam—is a culture of randomness. This is shown in the advice of Balak to Balaam to change the location where the curse was to be delivered by the latter, after the king had realized that on an earlier occasion, Balaam had blessed the people of Israel instead of cursing them. Even the appearance of God to Balaam is described as, "And the Lord has occurred [*va-yikar*[8]] to Balaam" (Num., 23:16). This "occurrence" of God never reappears anywhere in the Bible—and obviously not when God conveys his messages to the Jewish prophets. The "occurrence" of God to a prophet appears only here, and for only one purpose: to reflect and emphasize the mode of thinking in the kingdom of Moab—where all, including Balak and Balaam, regard everything as occurring by sheer accident.

- It is worth noting that the book of Leviticus starts with, "And the Lord called to Moses" (Lev. 1:1). However, the last letter of "call," the *alef*, is smaller than the rest, and if omitted would mean *va-yikar*,[8] implying God accidentally encountered Moses. Of course, the *alef* bestows upon this word its true meaning here—namely, a real and intended call (see details in subsection 16.1.1).

- Recall the book of Esther, where God is hidden, not mentioned at all. Appropriately, "occurrences" appear in abundance in the book of Esther. Thus, when Esther sends one of her servants, Hathach, from the palace to meet her uncle, Mordecai, she orders him to learn "what is this and why is this" (Esther 4:5)—she never orders the servant to learn what has *occurred* to Mordecai. The latter, Mordecai, tells Hathach everything that has *occurred* to him, obviously attentive to the culture of the place (Esther 4:7). Similarly, when an unfortunate chain of events befalls
  Hamman (the central foe of the Jews, of Amalek seed, who had earlier designed a Holocaust for the Jews), he tells "his wife and all his lovers all that had *occurred* to him" (Esther 6:13). This is again in conformance with the prevailing culture of randomness, where all is coincidental.

- In the book of Ruth, the Bible wishes to convey, in an allegoric and ironic way, that things do not happen by chance. So, when the story of the first encounter of Ruth and Boaz is related (the latter would later become the great grandfather of king David; there were also Obed and then Yishai [Jesse] in between), the Bible, in a sense of defiant irony, describes, "And *an occurrence has occurred* to her [to Ruth] to be at the piece of land that belonged to Boaz" (Ruth 2:3). Unlike in most previous cases, where a single use of the word "occur" takes place, here the Bible ironically emphasizes the nonrandom nature of the encounter by relating to "random occurrence" twice, thus ensuring that no one doubts that in the mind of the storyteller this seemingly random "occurrence" is not random at all, neither should it be perceived as such.

From all these examples, it becomes clear that randomness is represented in the Bible by the root combination *K.R.H.*

3.4   "Randomness" and "Cold"

Section 3.2 introduced two concepts of entropy: the physical-systems entropy, developed by Boltzmann and related to the Second Law of Thermodynamics, and the statistical concept of entropy, developed by Shannon and related to information theory. It was emphasized that the first concept is tightly related to heat and temperature, while the second measures the amount of randomness in a distribution of probabilities.

In the previous section 3.3, the concept of randomness, as perceived by the scriptures and expressed in Hebrew by variations of a single basic root, *K.R.H*, was introduced and amply demonstrated.

"Randomness" and "cold" are interrelated concepts, emanating from two concepts of entropy that, although separately developed, are by now agreed upon by most scholars to be realizations of a single concept of entropy.

The answer to this question, however, is less obvious: How is it that the Hebrew language treats the two concepts, random and cold, as one and the same, using the same root to refer to these intuitively altogether different concepts?

- Why are "cold" (*karah,*[9] a noun) and "occurred" (*karah,*[9] a verb) read and pronounced the same, and also written by the same sequence of letters (*karah*)?[9]

- Why are *mikreh*[10] (occurrence) and *mekareh*[10] (a place with cool air—Judges 3:20, 24), written by the same sequence of letters?

- Why are *kareh*[9] (occurrence) and *karah*[9] (cold) written the same?

Comments

The modern Hebrew verb for "to cool" is *le-karer,* based on the root *K.R.R.* This root does not appear in the Bible, neither any other verb for "to cool." The modern adaptation of the Hebrew language is based on various nouns and adjectives that appear in the Bible, like the nouns *karah*[9] and *kor*[11] (both meaning "cold") or the adjective *kar*[12] (cold).

Summary

According to biblical Hebrew, "cold" and "random" have a common origin. This is not at odds with the two concepts of entropy in modern science. One can only wonder at this peculiar association: Why does biblical Hebrew use the same root for the two seemingly unrelated concepts of the biblically detested randomness (nonpresence of God, relate to section 3.3) and coldness?

In other words, how did such two different concepts become interrelated so many centuries ago, when no concept of entropy had yet been conceived?

These are all coincidences ... maybe.

CHAPTER 4

The Name of God (Jehovah)

4.1 The Divine in Hebrew and in English

God appears in the Bible in a multiplicity of names. Some examples are *Adon*[1] (for example, Josh. 3:11, 13), *El*[2] (Gen. 14:20, 22), *El Shadai*[3] (Gen. 43:14), *Elohim*[4] (Gen. 1:1), *Eheyeh*[5] (Exod. 3:14), *Hashem*[6] (literally, "the Name"—refer, for example, to Lev. 24:11, Deut. 28:58). A combination thereof is also not rare, for example: *Hashen Elohenu*[7] (Hashem our Elohim).

However, the most sacred in Hebrew is the four-letter Divine Name, also denoted as the tetragrammaton (or tetragram), and in Hebrew, literally, *Hashem Hamephorash*[8] (the Explicit Name).

This name is *Yehovah*[9] (*YHVH*), pronounced in English "Jehovah" or "Yahweh."

The most frequently appearing names of God in the Bible are probably *Elohim*[4] and Jehovah. *El,*[2] (or *Eloah),* from which *Elohim*[4] is derived, also means "force" in Hebrew. *Elohim*[4] is therefore perceived, in Jewish tradition, as "the one who has all the forces"—in short, the God of nature. This name for the Divine appears repeatedly in the first chapter of Genesis, where creation is detailed; furthermore, this is the only name for God used therein. Although plural in linguistic structure, *Elohim*[4] is always related to in the Bible in the singular, emphasizing the oneness of God (there is a single exception that we will discuss shortly).

The other name for God, Jehovah, makes its first appearance only in the second chapter of Genesis, when the story of the creation of Adam and Eve is retold in detail (a previous version is related in the first chapter of Genesis, verses 26–28).

In Jewish tradition, the two names, *Elohim*[4] and Jehovah, convey two "pictures" of the conduct of God. The former is God of absolute justice (*Din*), the latter of justice softened with grace and compassion, which results in a perception of the Divine as God of mercy. Jewish sages relate to the differences between the two perceptions of the conduct of the Divine: "Thus said the Lord: "If I create the world with a measure of mercy—sin increases; with a meaure of absolute justice—how could the world stand? Therefore I will create it with a measure of absolute justice *and* a measure of mercy, and hopefully the world would stand" (Midrash Rabbah, Bereshit, chapter 12).

The issue of the "true" name of God reappears repeatedly in the Bible. In the episode where God delivers Moses his mission to save the people of Israel from Egyptian bondage, the Bible tells us, "And Moses said to *Elohim*[4] [God], Behold, when I come to the children of Israel, and shall say to them, *Elohim*[4] [God] of your forefathers has sent me to you; and they shall say to me, What is his name? what shall I say to them? And *Elohim*[4] [God] said to Moses, "I will be that which I will be" [*Eheyeh asher Eheyeh*[10]]: and he said, Thus shalt thou say to the children of Israel, "I will be" [*Eheyeh*] has sent me to you" (Exod. 3:13, 14). And in the next verse, we read, "this is my name for ever and this is my memorial for all generations to come" (Exod. 3:15). Later the issue of the true name of God resurfaces when God says to Moses, "I was seen to Abraham, to Isaac, and to Jacob, by the name of God Almighty [*El Shadai*[3]], and by my name, Jehovah, I was not known to them" (Exod. 6:3).

Jewish prophets also make repeated reference to the name of God. For example, "I am Jehovah this is my name" (Isa. 32:8); "For the sake of my name I will restrain my anger" (Isa. 48:9); "And they would know that my name is Jehovah" (Jer. 16:21).

The various names of God, and God's various forms of conduct as revealed to humans, have been the subject of much discussion in Jewish scholarship, and the topic is too vast to address here in any detail. In this section, we discuss only the most sacred name, Jehovah.

This name is never explicitly pronounced by observant Jews either in the reading of Scripture or in recitation of prayers. In these cases, the Divine Name is pronounced as *Adonai*[1] (same vocalization as Jehovah, meaning "my master"), while in everyday speech, the name *Hashem*[6] (the Name) is used. Whenever the Divine Name is written in nonsacred documents, like in dictionaries, the double letter *I.I* (two *yod*s), a double repeat of the first letter in the Divine Name, stands for Jehovah.

Only the high priest of the temple is allowed to pronounce the Divine Name in the temple, and then only in the most sacred festivity of the year, at Yom Kippur[11] (Day of Repentance) and then only in the Holy of Holies.

The Divine Name, *Yehovah*,[9] is in Hebrew a compilation of mystery upon mystery. We will attempt to expose these mysteries in this chapter. However, prior to doing that, we repeat an alert already given in the preface: one may be inclined to relate to the pursuing coincidences as play tricks. The statistical analyses, scattered throughout the book, with their extremely significant results, may suggest otherwise.

4.2   Jehovah and God: Analysis

The root of the Divine Name originates in the Hebrew root *H.I.H.* This is the origin for various Hebrew words meaning "to be" in various linguistic forms. The Divine Name is therefore based on the most fundamental concept: being. However, the various time tenses of this root, when the latter appears as a verb, are *hayah*[12a] or *havah*[12b] (he was), *oveh*[13] ("he is," meaning also the present), and *yehiyeh*[14] (he will be).

Combining parts of these words together, one obtains the Divine Name going from the future tense, to the present tense to the past tense:

Yehovah:

yeh (Future) + ov (Present) + ah (Past)

Once one has become familiar with the source of the word and what it conveys to the "naked eye"—namely, a combination of "being" with "time"—a deeper probe may reveal some bizarre structures internal to this name.

First, let us detail the numerical values of the letters comprising the Divine Name Jehovah:

$$26 = (5 = ה) + (6 = ו) + (5 = ה) + (10 = י)$$

(*yod* = 10) + (*hei* = 5) + (*vav* = 6) + (*hei* = 5) = 26

Repeating the same for the numerical values representing ordinal positions of the English letters comprising "God," it is extraordinary that the same result is obtained:

$$\text{"God"} = (G = 7) + (O = 15) + (D = 4) = \mathbf{26}$$

Next we examine the composition of the *name* of the first letter in the Divine Name, the *yod*. This composition is indeed extraordinary. If one was required to convey in the *name* of the first letter that appears in the name of the Divine the concept of creation as depicted by the big bang—namely, as that of an expanding universe—one could hardly opt for a better way to do that than by an ordered sequence of three plots, as these are indeed conveyed by the three letters comprising the *name* of the letter *yod*:

$$(\daleth) + (\vav) + (\yod)$$

- **First** letter in the *name* of the first letter of Jehovah: $\yod$ = *yod*; virtually a point floating in space; a zero-dimensional coordinate system.

- **Second** letter in the *name* of the first letter of Jehovah: $\vav$= *vav*; virtually a line; a one-dimensional coordinate system.

- **Third** letter in the *name* of the first letter of Jehovah: $\daleth$ = *dalet*; virtually a plane; a two-dimensional coordinate system.

The name of the first letter in the Divine Name thus appears to be displaying the dynamics of creation: gradual transition, in this order, from zero dimension (point), to one dimension (a single line), to two dimensions (two perpendicular crossing lines). If one would be allowed to float in a fantasy world, one could say that for the letter *yod*, which is plotted as a point, when its *name* is dismantled into its three constituent letters, these three letters convey an impression that its hidden message has something to do with the dimensions that define our world—or at least, those that were evolving from the initial singularity point at the moment of creation.

Which is indeed becoming for the name of God, the Creator!
Next we examine the numerical values of these three letters, comprising the name of the first letter in the name of the Divine. Recall that we have previously demonstrated that the numerical value of a word can store information that is relevant to its revealed meaning. We have demonstrated this (subsection 2.1.2) with the Hebrew words for "year," "evening," "morning," "day," "night," "midday" and "midnight," and "human pregnancy." In view of this, one may justifiably be tempted to probe deeper into the numerical values of the various components of the Divine Name.

Observe the numerical values of the letters that comprise *the name* of the first letter of the Divine Name. Here, the bizarre nature of the *yod* becomes even more revealed:

$$Yod = \text{יוד} = (4 = \daleth) + (6 = \vav) + (10 = \yod)$$

In other words, the value of the *letter yod*, 10, which is also the value of the first letter in its name, is split, in the succeeding two letters, into two numbers, 6 and 4. Thus, the value of the first letter in the *name* is the sum of the last two letters. Furthermore, the 10 corresponds to a letter that represents zero-dimension, the six corresponds to the letter that is plotted as one-dimensional, and the four corresponds to the letter that represents two dimensions. It is as if someone has said, "Since the visible structures of the letters that comprise the letter-name *yod* indicate creation (depicted as an expansion in space with geometrical dimensions evolving from zero, to one, to two), then perhaps the numerical values associated with these letters also relate a story insinuating something to do with dimensions!"

In a fantasy world, one would claim that these numerical values convey a story:

In the beginning, at the moment of creation (when the world was just a dimensionless point), there were ten dimensions (the value of the first letter, *yod*). These were later split into six dimensions (unseen to us, represented by the letter *vav*) and into four dimensions (our world—namely, the three spatial dimensions and time, herewith represented by the letter *dalet*, plotted as a two-dimensional coordinate system).

Indeed a fantasy world!

Let us next rewrite the Divine Name, Jehovah (Hebrew) and God (English), with the numerical values of their constituent letters (as explained earlier).

Hebrew:

$$\text{Jehovah} = (yod = 10) + (hei = 5) + (vav = 6) + (hei = 5) = (6 + 4) + (5) + (6) + (5) =$$
$$(6) + (4) + (16) = 26$$

English:

$$\text{God} = (G = 7) + (O = 15) + (D = 4) =$$
$$(7) + (4) + (15) = 26$$

What does this all mean? How has such a bizarre coincidence taken place with two names for God, in two different words from two different languages, having the same total numerical value (26), and concurrently preserving a pattern for the numerical values of their constituent letters so alike (take, in the English "God," 1 from the 7 and add to the 15 to obtain the same "numerical arrangement" as in the Hebrew "Jehovah")?

Obviously one word (God or Jehovah) cannot be assumed to have originated, over the history of the development of the two languages, from the other word. The two names for the Divine are so at odds with one another, both in pronunciation and in structure, that a common source and a common designer can hardly be fathomed.

Let us move again to fantasy world. We remember that the sequence of the three letters of the word *yod* convey, by their very geometrical shapes, an impression of an evolving dynamic creation, moving from zero dimension, to one dimension, to two dimensions. Do the numbers 10, 6, 4, 16 and the total sum, 26, bear any meaning in view of modern cosmological theories, as far as dimensions are concerned?

In other words, are these seemingly senseless numbers important in any sense?

4.3   Higher Dimensions in Modern Cosmologies

The latest developments in cosmology theories, nowadays part and parcel of modern physics, can be studied from many books that have been published in recent years. In the following, we base our descriptions of these developments regarding higher dimensions on six sources: Kaku (1994, 2005, 2005a), Greene (2004), Helpern (2004), and Penrose (2004).

No attempt is made here to convey in detail the intricate arguments for the various claims, made by cosmology theories of recent years, regarding the possible existence of higher dimensions (additional to the four known dimensions of space and time). The concept "higher dimensions" has become an essential part in these theories. We will, however, provide a short introduction for the origin of the need to develop such concepts, and then provide several quotations from the above sources.

A major endeavor of physics, as it has been developing for the last hundred and fifty years or so, is to integrate all the forces of nature under a unifying single theory. At first, there were five major forces:

- The electric force
- The magnetic force
- The weak nuclear force
- The strong nuclear force
- Gravitation

Over the best part of the nineteenth century and in the twentieth century, attempts at unifying these forces (or those known at the time) by a single theory have been an ongoing major focus in physics. These efforts may be summarized by the following somewhat simplistic highlights of major efforts and turning points:

- The unification of the theory of the electric field (Faraday) and the theory of the magnetic field (Maxwell) via Maxwell theory of electro-magnetism (in the late 1860s).

- The unification of the theory of the weak force with the theory of the electromagnetic force into the electroweak theory by Weinberg and Salem (1967–68)—refer to Weinberg (1992, 118–28).

- The development of grand unified theories, starting in 1974. These theories unify the weak, strong, and electromagnetic interactions, without gravity (Guth 1997, 131, 333; Kaku 2005, 389).

- The establishment of quantum chromodynamics, a quantum field theory that describes the strong nuclear forces. This is the accepted unifying theory of the forces that bind quarks together to form protons, neutrons, and other strongly interacting particles (Weinberg 1992, 147 and 183; Guth 1997, 339; Kaku 2005, 82).

- The development of superunified theories—theories that, hopefully, unify all forces in "the theory of everything." Superstring theories seem to be the latest most promising group of such unifying theories.

The last subject, superstring theories, is currently the focus of most endeavors to arrive at a "theory of everything." It has been realized for quite some time now that a good approach (perhaps the only feasible approach) to unifying gravitation with all other forces (in other words, the combining together of the general theory of relativity, focusing on the macro scale of the universe, with quantum physics, dealing with forces on the micro nuclear scale) is by a theory that describes our world in higher dimensions. Various theories have been proposed, with varying numbers of dimensions. Without going into details regarding these theories, the following selection of quotations offers brief glimpses at the most popular super-unified string theories, as they have evolved in the last twenty-five years or so with regard to higher dimensions.

By sheer coincidence, these testimonials, from some of the greatest physicists of our time, address the same "magic numbers", alluded to earlier.

I. Quotations from Kaku (1994, 2005):

- In referring to the elliptic modular functions, basic mathematical tools for string theories, which have been developed by the Indian mathematician genius Srinivasa Ramanujan, Kaku writes, "When we add two more dimensions to Ramanujan's functions" [physicists add two extra dimensions to mathematical functions in order to construct a physical theory], "the 'magic numbers' of mathematics become 10 and 26, precisely the 'magic numbers' of string theory" (2005, 202–03).

- "The Big-Bang, as we shall see, perhaps originated in the breakdown of the original ten-dimensional universe into a four- and a six-dimensional universe" (1994, 195).

- "Beginning with the instant of Creation, we have the following stages in the evolution of our universe: 10^{-43} seconds: The ten-dimensional universe breaks down to a four- and a six-dimensional universe. The six-dimensional universe collapses down to 10^{-32} centimeter in size. The four-dimensional universe inflates rapidly." (1994, 213).

- "The laws of physics simplify in higher dimensions. In this case, the 26-dimensional space of the counterclockwise vibrations of the heteronic string has room enough to explain all the symmetries found in both Einstein's theory and quantum theory" (1994, 159).

- "One of the deepest secrets of string theory, which is still not well understood, is why it is defined in only ten and 26 dimensions. If the theory were three dimensional, it would not be able to unify the known laws of physics in any sensible manner" (1994, 172). In a modified statement reflecting advances in the pursuing ten years since 1994, Kaku writes, "Consider Type I and the heterotic SO(32) string theory ... The type I string is defined entirely in ten-dimensional space, while the SO(32) string is defined with one set of vibrations defined in the twenty-six dimensional space ... However ... the theories possess a powerful duality: if you let the strength of the interactions increase, type I strings change into SO(32) heterotic strings, as if by magic" (2005, 216).

- *"In other words, physicists have not the slightest understanding of why ten and 26 dimensions are singled out as the dimension of the string"* (1994, 173; italics in the source).

- "The heterotic string begins by compactifying 26-dimensional space down to 10-dimensional space, leaving us with 16 compactified dimensions, which yields the group E(8)xE(8). This is more than enough to accommodate the Standard Model" (1994, 345).

II. Quotations from Halpern (2004)

- "Supersymmetry charged into the picture of the early 1970s to help rescue an imperiled model of the strong nuclear force, called hardonic string theory." Claud Lovelace, "fascinated by the string model, sought a means of eliminating strange, faster-than-light entities called 'tachyonic cuts' that had poked their heads into the calculations. Lovelace found that the only way to ward off this conundrum would be to situate the strings in a twenty-six-dimensional manifold" (232–33).

- "In 1984, Green and Schwarz put their minds together and made one of the greatest breakthroughs in their careers" (251), by developing superstring theory. "Within a year after Green and Schwarz published their paper on anomaly-free superstrings, a number of other physicists discovered a host of additional viable models" among them the four discoverers of heterotic string theories—David Gross (a Nobel laureate for physics in 2004), Jeffrey Harvey, Emil Martinec, and Ryan Rohm— "… they found an ingenious way of blending separate string theories to form a greater harmony" (255). The developed theory is most "suitable for modeling nature's disparity between left- and right-handedness. This is like a country dance with two concentric rings: the men circling in one direction and the women in the other. Replace the men with super-symmetric strings living in 10 dimensions, and the women with bosonic strings living in twenty-six-dimensions, and one has a good picture" of the new theory. "In order for the 'dance partners' to be well matched, the bosonic strings must hide sixteen of their twenty-six dimensions. These extra dimensions must curl up into a compact space" (255).

III. Quotations from Penrose (2004)

- "It turns out that there are five quite distinct possible overall schemes for the detailed way in which the supersymmetry interrelates the 'bosonic' and 'fermionic' modes of vibration of the string. Thus, there are five dif-ferent string theories" … "The Heterotic strings are particularly strange in that the left- and right-moving disturbances seem to belong to two spacetimes of different dimensionality (26 and 10, respectively). This hardly makes good geometrical sense—certainly not to me(!)—but it appears to make the appropriate formal sense" (912).

- Relating to the recently developed M-theory: "How is it that a theory with an 11-dimensional 'space-time' [1 dimension for time and 10 for space] can be something that specializes, in certain low-energy or high-energy limits, to various theories, each (but one) of which has a 10-dimensional space-time? Again, this discrepancy in space-time dimensionality seems to be regarded as an 'energy effect,' and not particularly fundamental" (915).

Comments

1. That last quote seems to relate to the superstring theories that had been produced in the first superstring revolution, thus implying that the theories were not wrong, but rather special cases of the more general M-theory that emerged later.

2. Most of the quotations above refer to what is called the first superstring revolution. A later development, triggered by Edward Witten in the mid-nineties of the previous century, unified all five string theories of earlier years into M-theory. Witten's work is considered today to be the starting point of the second superstring revolution. M-theory links together all five string theories of the first revolution by showing that each is part of a grander theoretical synthesis. While M-theory is still in its developmental stages, with new insights gradually evolving, a major characteristic of this theory is the realization that space-time contains eleven dimensions: ten space dimensions and one for time (Greene 2004, 382; Penrose 2004, 915). Furthermore, "Witten showed that the five ten-dimensional frameworks that string theorists had developed for more than a decade were actually five approximate descriptions of a single, underlying eleven-dimensional theory" (Greene 2004, 383). In other words, the previous partition of the ten time-space dimensions into four dimensions (including time) and six unseen spatial dimensions (often referred to as the Calabi-Yau space) is reformulated into ten spatial dimensions and a single time dimension.

3. Current cosmological theories are evolving at an accelerated rate. These theories are now in a very fluid state. Some theories that are popular today may be discarded tomorrow, or some long-ago discarded theories may regain respectability tomorrow (like Einstein's revived cosmological constant). Kaku (2005a), while describing present-day attempts to submit experimental and observational evidence to various predictions derived from modern physics and from recent cosmology theories, concludes: "Some theorists believe that the final verdict on string theory will not come from experiments at all. Rather the answer may come from pure mathematics. The principal reason predictions of string theory are not well defined is that the theory is not finished … Even its greatest proponents agree that the final version has not yet been determined" (therein, 37).

4.4 Summary of Main Points

- The Divine Name in Hebrew, Jehovah, is numerically equivalent to 26.

- The Divine Name in English, God, is numerically equivalent to 26.

- The *first* letter in the Hebrew Divine Name, *yod*, is plotted as a floating point (zero dimension). Modern cosmological theories refer to the big bang as a singularity point, emphasizing its *spatial* zero-dimensional property.

- The *first* letter in the Hebrew Divine Name, *yod*, has a numerical value of 10. This is exactly the number of *spatial* dimensions required by modern cosmologies to describe the universe at the moment of creation.

- The written letters of the *name* of the letter *yod*, the first in Jehovah, appear as consecutive plots of a point, a line, and a coordinate two-dimensional system (in that sequence), conveying the impression of the dynamics of an expanding universe with changing dimensionality from zero (י), to one (ו) to two (ד), in that particular order (apparently, the latter dimensionality is the highest that may be conveyed by written letters).

- The first letter of Jehovah (*yod*) appears also in the *name* of that letter. This name comprises three letters: *yod*, *vav*, and *dalet*. The value of *yod*, 10, is split in the succeeding two letters into 6 (for the *vav*) and 4 (for the *dalet*); This partition of the 10 is identical to the splitting, at the moment of creation or soon thereafter, of the 10 "original" dimensions into a four-dimensional universe, in which we live, and another unobservable six dimensions that have "curled up." That the numerical values of the letters comprising the name of *yod* may be associated with dimensions is strongly insinuated by how the *name* of the letter *yod* is written.

- The splitting of 26 (the sum up of the numerical values of the letters comprising the Hebrew Jehovah) into the numerical values of the constituent letters, $(5 + 6 + 5) + (6 + 4)$, is nearly identical to that of "God": $15 + 7 + 4$.

- The patterns of splitting the 26 into 16 and 10, in the Hebrew Jehovah, like the resplitting in the name of the first letter, *yod*, into 6 and 4, is reminiscent of similar splitting of the "magic numbers," 26 and 10, proposed by modern cosmological theories (the latter refer to this splitting, reflecting the process of dimensions rolling up, as "compactification").

These are all coincidences … maybe.

CHAPTER 5

"Double" and a Message of Symmetry

5.1   Introduction

The concept of "double" plays unique role in the biblical Hebrew. It is hard to pinpoint the logic and underlying motivation for this particular reference to the concept of "two" (as contrasted with "plural" in general). But in Hebrew, "plural referring to two" gained special status. Perhaps the fact that "two," in many cases, goes hand in hand with symmetry, explains why the special reference to "double" extends, in the Hebrew language, to plurality of objects that are, in one sense or another, symmetrical.

A good departure point to describing "double" and the message of symmetry in the Hebrew language is to explain how "two" is pronounced. For most nouns in the plural, the plurality property is achieved in Hebrew via an added suffix of *-im*, pronounced "eam," for masculine nouns, and a suffix *-ot*, pronounced "ot," to a feminine noun. Thus, a man is *gever*,[1] and men are *gevarim*.[2] A sister is *achot*,[3] sisters are *achayot*[4] (at times, the last letter of the singular is also changed, like in the last example). A male child is *yeled*,[5] and children are *yeladim*.[6] A female child is *yaldah*;[7] the plural is *yeladot*.[8]

Generating plurality is altogether different where the plural signifies two. "Two" in Hebrew is *shnayim*[9] (masculine) and *shtayim*[10] (feminine). The suffix of *-ayim* is extended to all cases indicative of "two." This is the most common case. However, it occasionally extends naturally to cases of multiplicity beyond "two." Thus, all organs of the human body which come in symmetrical "double" are denoted in the plural by a suffix of *-ayim*. This extends to the case when the same object counts more than "two." For example, "a hand" is *yad*;[11] two hands (or more, as just explained) is *yadayim*.[12] "A leg" is *regel*;[13] two legs or more are *raglayim*.[14] The same rule applies to the eyes, the ears, the palms of the hands, the knees, and so forth.

90

A nearly equivalent rule is valid for nouns that have plurals that are not typically manifested in pairs (doubles), like "weeks." In this case, unlike in previous examples, the Hebrew word for the general plural of "weeks" is *shvuot*.[15] However, "*two* weeks" is *shvuayim*.[16] Just "days" is *yamim*[17] (the regular plural); however, two days is *yomayim*.[18]

To sum up, the affix *-ayim* is added to nouns in plural either to indicate two, or when the objects of the noun commonly appear in pairs.

The fact that pairs most often show symmetry (like pairs of human body organs) has been extended, in the Hebrew language, to special cases, where it is clear that the noun in plural is not typically realized in pairs, yet symmetry is still a most prominent feature of the objects the noun describes. For instance, though teeth do not commonly appear in pairs (the way hands do), their arrangement in symmetry within the mouth (for most people) indicates that the affix of *-ayim* would be adequate. This is indeed the case. While "tooth" is *shen*,[19] "teeth" is *shinayim*.[20] Thus, the *-ayim* has been extended, as this example demonstrates, to include objects associated with symmetry—not necessarily symmetry of the "two" sort.

Once we are familiar with the rules just laid down, it is perhaps instructive, and at times amazing, to learn of some comprehensible examples and some incomprehensible coincidences employing *-ayim* for symmetry or for duality.

5.2   "Jerusalem"

The Hebrew word for the city of Jerusalem is *Yerushalayim*. Being aware of rules expounded earlier, Jewish sages understood that there is something peculiar about calling Jerusalem, the most sacred city for the Jewish people and a sacred city for others, by a name indicative of "two." Jewish sages therefore explained that there are two Jerusalems: the heavenly Jerusalem (*Yerushalayim shel malah*[21]—literally, "Jerusalem of the above") and the earthly Jerusalem (*Yerushalayim shel matah*).[22]

The latter, the Jerusalem of the below, is a reflection of the former, Jerusalem of heaven, but both mutually influence one another.

5.3   "Sky"

5.3.1   Symmetries in Our Universe

The space, time, and matter of our universe are awash with symmetries. Modern cosmology has shown that symmetries permeate the universe that we inhabit. There are symmetries in the time-space dimensions; there are symmetries in the composition of matter, as revealed by quantum mechanics; and there are symmetries in the laws of nature. Symmetry is a most fundamental concept in how modern cosmologies perceive our universe.

A recent book by Lederman (a Nobel laureate) and Hill (2004) discuss all these symmetries and what they imply. We will refer here only to some basic ones, revealed in our universe in the time-space dimensions. The exposition herewith follows mainly the quoted source.

The concept of symmetry in space and time is tightly connected to another concept: that of continuum. Scientists call space a continuum, because so far, no experiments have indicated that space is not continuous. This implies that there is no smallest step through which a subatomic particle, like an electron or a quark, or an atom or a planet in space needs to move, in order for the laws of physics to be valid, because there is no such smallest step. Likewise, time is continuous, and so far, there have not been any experimental results to indicate that there is a smallest step of time beyond which one cannot cross.

The experimental fact that both space and time are, in essence, continuous allows certain symmetries that are the cornerstones of modern cosmology. What is implied here by symmetry is that the laws of nature, as we know them, and the fundamental constants of nature—like the speed of light or Newton's gravitational constant—remain the same irrespective of the state of motion of the observer, the point in space he or she occupies, or the time when observations are made. In fact, as asserted by Lederman and Hill (2004), the laws of physics themselves are essentially defined by symmetry principles (therein, 98).

Examples for such laws are given by Noether's very fundamental theorem, which states that "for every continuous symmetry of the laws of physics, there must exist a conservation law; For every conservation law, there must exist a continuous symmetry" (therein, 97). One example for the realization of this law is the law of the conservation of momentum, which is derivable from the experimental fact that the laws of physics are invariant under spatial continuous translation (moving in any direction in space would not change the observed laws of nature). In other words, from the point of view of the laws of nature, any point in space is equivalent to any other point in space. From this symmetry, the law of the conservation of momentum can be deduced in compliance with Noether's theorem.

Likewise, since the laws of physics are invariant under translations in time—namely, there in also continuous symmetry in time—the law of conservation of energy can be deduced based on Noether's theorem. Finally, the law of the conservation of angular momentum results from a third continuous symmetry in space—namely, that the laws of physics are rotationally invariant. The latter symmetry means that if an observer changes his or her angular position by simple rotation, he or she will still observe the same laws of nature.

To sum up, the space-time environment of our observed universe contains symmetries that make every point in space, every "there," equivalent to any other "there," as far as the laws of nature are concerned. And any movement within thiss pace, in whatever direction and in any time point specified, would still cause the observer to see the same laws of nature.

But there is another, no less profound symmetry, confirmed by recent observations. It relates to the cosmic microwave background radiation. More than four decades ago, scientists discovered that the universe is suffused with microwave radiation—long-wavelength light that is a cool relic of the initial conditions just after the big bang (refer to sections 11.2 and 14.2). As the story is toldi n Greene (2004, 227), the temperature of this radiation is just 2.7°K (Kelvin) above absolute zero (–273.15°C). An essential property of this radiation, revealed by precision satellite measurements over the past decade, is that it is extremely uniform throughout space. In fact, the temperature of the radiation in one part of the sky differs from that in another part by less than a thousandth of a degree. That means that anywhere in space where measurements are taken, these measurements will be in agreement by four significant digits. This uniformity of radiation not only implies that the young universe, at its earlier stages, had been homogenous, but also that the evolution of the universe since the big bang, on average, must have been nearly identical anywhere across the cosmos.

The last assertion implies that not only is the cosmos symmetrical with respect to space, as revealed by the constancy of the laws of nature and of the cosmological constants (irrespective of your place in the universe, the direction of your measurement devices, or the type of motion you are having—moving at constant speed, accelerating or decelerating, or in a rotational speed), symmetry is noticeable also with respect to the history of the evolving universe. Everywhere in the cosmos, the evolution is identical from a macro perspective, as shown by the extraordinary uniformity of the cosmic microwave background radiation. Note that an exploration of various specified segments of the sky would obviously reveal locally varied cosmos, as different planets, stars and galaxies reside in different segments of space. However, in macro perspective, the evolution to the present state essentially followed a history that is identical anywhere in the universe.

In summary, a most fundamental conclusion of present-day cosmologies, supported by most recent precise observations, is that any direction you point in the sky it is essentially the same. Space is symmetric and homogenous in any sense that you may think of. This conclusion obviously stands in sharp contrast to our intuitive everyday experience of the sky as a "screen" inhabiting a variety of different stories that are concurrently projected on it.

5.3.2 The Hebrew Message of "Sky Symmetry"

There are two words for sky (or space) in Hebrew: *rakia*[23] (Gen. 1:7, 8) and *shamayim*[24] (Gen. 1:7, 8). Genesis 1:8 explains that God separated the water under the sky from the water above the sky, and thence called the sky (*rakia*)[23] by the name *shamayim*.[24] Although both words are used in the sense of "there, where the stars are," the latter synonym entertains the more common usage to denote "sky," both in the Bible and in modern Hebrew. Thus, when God approaches Abraham and ask him to count the stars (if he could), he says: "Look towards the sky [*shamayim*[24]], and count the stars if you could count them ... so will be your offsprings" (Gen. 15:5). In fact, while *rakia*[23] appears 17 times in the whole of the Bible, variations of the word *shamayim*[24] appear 421 times! There is thus no doubt that *shamayim*[24] is the more used word for what one observes when he or she looks upward.

In modern Hebrew, there is a distinction between *shamayim*,[24] in the sense of the place where the *observed* stars are, and *chalal,* as a common word for space in general (in the modern sense of the word). It is obvious that this distinction could not have existed in ancient times, when only the *shamayim*,[24] as observed from Earth, could be a subject of discourse.

The structure of the word *shamayim*[24] is extremely peculiar. It is no different from that of *yadayim*[12] (hands). As *yadayim*[12] is the plural of *yad*[11] (a two-letter word for "hand"), so *shamayim*[24] could be interpreted as the plural of *sham*[25] (also a two-letter word). That the word *sham*[25] is the basis for the term "sky" looks appropriate, as *sham*[25] means "there" in Hebrew. Therefore, *shamayim*[24] implies the plural of "there." This seems appropriate. For our ancestors, the epitome of "there"—namely, the whereabouts which is the absolutely inaccessible, a "there" that can never be turned into a "here"—is the sky (or at least that would be expected in ancient times).

Yet there is mystery about this word, *shamayim*.[24] It is not just a plural for "there." It is the plural of "there" in a symmetrical way. As explained in detail earlier, this type of suffix, *-ayim*, added to a noun in order to turn it from singular to plural, is characteristic to plural noun that conveys symmetry. The suffix *-ayim*, let us recall, is identical to the last syllable of *shnayim*[9] (two). As shown in an earlier section, a suffix like this is characteristic to plural nouns that commonly appear in the plural as "two," but also to plural noun of objects that typically show symmetry, like teeth.

The word *shamayim*[24] no doubt delivers a message of "symmetry." In concrete terms, it tells you that anywhere you point your finger in the sky is the same as anywhere else. No point in the sky is any different from any other point; all directions are identical.

That this is the message conveyed by *shamayim*[24] is indeed a bizarre coincidence. Why should the sky be conceived by the Hebrew language to be symmetrical? The sky shows extreme asymmetry. No two parts of the observable sky looks alike. Denoting the sky by a term that carries a message of symmetry is counterintuitive. It contradicts any experience that an earthly-bound observer of the sky could have had, in ancient times as well as in ours: in that segment of the sky, and not another, we expect to see the sun during daytime; during dark hours, different groups of stars occupy different segments of the sky, creating patterns (well-known to our ancestors) that were supposed to influence the fates of everything that happens on Earth. The asymmetry in the patterns observed in the sky in fact served the platform for personal predictions in the art known by the name astrology (if we remember correctly, this term from a long-gone culture …).

The word *shamayim*,[24] by contrast, offers no distinction with respect to which direction in the sky one points his or her finger. *Shamayim*[24] implies that the sky is perfectly symmetrical. Rabbi Ovadia Seforno (1470–1550) was probably the first to offer this interpretation of *shamayim*.[24] In his interpretation for Genesis 1, he explains, "The word 'Shamayim[24]' indicates an object, far-away relative to us in two equal distances on each side, and this would not occur unless in a wheel turning around in a perfect circle." From this, Seforno deduces that the earth is in the center of a perfect wheel (consistent with the geocentric cosmology of Ptolemy (100-170 AD), prevalent at Seforno's time). Though Seforno does not explicitly say this in so many words, obviously the concept of symmetry was behind his interpretation for the word *shamayim*.[24] Yet, he had not heard of fundamental symmetries of the universe or any cosmology theories. In fact, the latter did not even exist at that time.

Shamayim,[24] as even fifteenth-century Rabbi Seforno had felt, conveys symmetry. That is compatible with all modern cosmologies, and is in concert with a profound single principle—namely, that our time-space universe is saturated with fundamental symmetries.

Whatever direction one chooses to point one's finger in the sky, wishing to call it *sham*,[25] the Hebrew language teaches us that it is indeed *shamayim*[24]—symmetrical in every conceivable way, and profoundly counterintuitive.

5.4   Water

5.4.1   "Water" in Hebrew

Unlike "water" in English, which is singular, in Hebrew *mayim*[26] (water) is plural. There is no singular for water. This is just the start of the peculiar nature of the word *mayim*.[26] As we have learned earlier in this chapter, the structure of *mayim*[26]i nsinuates that this substance is associated somehow with "two," or at least with some kind of symmetry.

This guesswork is reinforced when observing the structure of the word "water." It is

מ + י + מ

M.I.M (*mem, yod, mem*)

Thus, both the way that the word *mayim*[26] is pronounced and its letter composition point at some profound symmetry, or, perhaps, at the existence of symmetrical "double," which is associated with "water" (the same way that "hands" or "legs," in Hebrew, are associated with symmetrical "double").

How can both the structure of the *plural* "water," the composition of the word(*M.I.M*) and the way it is pronounced (*mayim*[26]), all point to a symmetrical "double"? What is it in "water" that would associate it with a symmetrical double?

What could this possibly be?

Of course, for a modern-era human being, these are all rhetorical questions. For the uninitiated, here is some description of the particular properties of water and its molecules, taken from various sources (mostly, from sources on the Internet that are in the public domain).

5.4.2 *Water Molecular Structure and History of Discovery*

The water molecule contains an atom of oxygen (O) and two of hydrogen (H). This molecule is usually denoted by chemists as H_2O. The atoms in a water molecule are arranged at the corners of an isosceles triangle, with the oxygen atom located at the point where the two equal sides meet. The angle between these sides is about 105°.

Figure 5.1 displays the structure of the water molecule. This structure is symmetrical in that it is left unchanged by a rotation of 180° about the vertical axis through the oxygen atom, and by planes parallel and perpendicular to the molecule. This symmetry is described mathematically by the point group C_{2v}.

Early chemists confused hydrogen with other gases until British physicist and chemist Henry Cavendish described the properties of the hydrogen gas in the mid-1700s. Many scientists before Cavendish had made the "flammable gas" by mixing metals with acids. Cavendish called the gas "flammable air" and studied

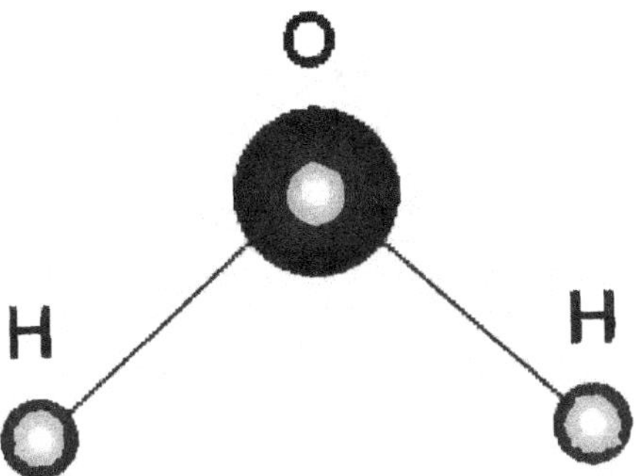

Figure 5.1. The water molecule.

it. He demonstrated in 1766 that sulfuric acid reacted with metals to produce flammable air. Later, Cavendish burned his flammable air in regular air to produce water, and only water. Many historians consider Cavendish to be the principal discoverer of the hydrogen gas and its role in water, although Scottish engineer James Watt reported that he had produced water at about the same time as Cavendish (and determined—a most unusual determination for the time—that water was composed of two gases). The first decomposition of water, via electrolysis, into its consituent hydrogen and oxygen, was done in 1800 by William Nicholson (1765–1844), an English chemist.

5.4.3   *Mayim Summary*

- The word *mayim*,[26] given in the plural as a symmetrical double (like *yadayim*,[12] "hands"), indicates that something about water is double in a symmetrical way.

- Both the composition of the letters in the Hebrew word for "water" and the letters' sequential arrangement mimics the structure of a molecule of water.

- The water molecule includes double hydrogen atoms, arranged around a single oxygen atom in a symmetrical way.

5.5   Life

Life in Hebrew is *haim* (like the author's first name). It is pronounced in Hebrew *chayim*.[27] Like with *mayim*,[26] this word is loaded with mysteries. We elaborate here on some.

First, unlike "water," which does not have a singular form in Hebrew, "life" is plural, but its root also appears in the singular. The latter, however, is used in a somewhat different sense than the common usage of "life." In Hebrew, the singular is either *chai*[28] (masculine) or *chaiyah*[29] (feminine). However, their meanings are different. The former is in fact an adjective, meaning "living". It is changed into a noun by preceding it with the word "all" (*kol*).[30] *Kol chai*[31] is used to mean assembly of all living creatures. By contrast, *chaiyah*[29] is a noun, meaning, simply, "animal" or "beast."

Examples:

- "And Adam called his wife's name Eve; because she was the mother of all living" (*em kol chai*,[34] Gen. 3:20).

- "From all the living" (*mi-kol ha-chai*,[32] Gen. 6:19);

- "and all the animals" (*ve-kol ha-chaiyah*,[33] Gen. 7:14);

The plural of *chaiyah*[29] is *chaiot*,[35] while *chai*,[28] as alluded to earlier, never appears as a noun on its own, only as an adjective (meaning "living").

Let us investigate *chayim*[27] (life) as a noun.

The structure of the word is reminiscent of (and in fact not different from) that of *yadayim*[12] (hands), which has a singular form of *yad*.[11] Thus, *chayim*[27] in Hebrew implies "double" in a symmetrical way. From a biblical standpoint, this is not so far-fetched as it first sounds. There are several incidents in the Bible in which God calls upon a biblical hero, calling him by name twice, and then answered by "Here I am [*hineni*[36]]," occasionally also twice.

Consider a few examples (later we will relate to how these verses are interpreted in Jewish tradition):

- **Abraham:** "And the Angel of the Lord called upon him from heaven, and said, Abraham, Abraham: and he said, 'Here I am [*hineni*[36]]'" (Gen. 22:11).

- **Jacob:** "And God spoke to Israel in the visions of the night, and said, Jacob, Jacob. And he said, 'Here I am [*hineni*[36]]'" (Gen. 46:2).

- **Moses:** "God called unto him out of the midst of the Bush [*hasneh*[37]], and said, Moses, Moses. And he said, 'Here I am [*hineni*[36]]'" (Exod. 3:4).

- **Samuel:** "And the Lord came, and stood, and called as at other times, Samuel, Samuel. Then Samuel answered, Speak; for thy servant is listening" (1 Sam. 3:10). Note that as it is related in the Bible, God had called Samuel three previous times, on each occasion calling the name of Samuel only once. Only at the fourth time, after Samuel has finally realized that God is calling on him (and not the high priest, Eli, as he previously thought), the name of Samuel is called twice—indicating, perhaps, that now "all of Samuel" is clearly ready for the call of God.

This latter interpretation is compatible with how Jewish sages explain God's double calling of the names of the most revered of biblical figures. For example, the Malbim (1809–79), in his interpretation for the above quote from 1 Samuel, explains that God calls twice in order to awaken the two parts, the bodily and the spiritual, so that the recipient is ready for the word of God.

Life-after-death advocates may have their own different interpretations why "life" in Hebrew conveys a meaning of "double," in a symmetrical way. We do not attempt any here. The only purpose of this subsection was to indicate a peculiar phenomenon that a most central word in Hebrew, that which characterizes all the living, is given in a symmetrical double, not unlike all names of symmetrically double organs of the human body.

These are all coincidences … maybe.

CHAPTER 6

The Purpose of Life

Encountering in the Hebrew language sets of words of common roots, which nevertheless convey meanings that widely differ, one has a good cause for an in-depth exploration of what is hidden behind these unexplainable sets of words, and what their message is.

Some such word sets were explored earlier, in section 2.3.
Other seemingly unrelated sets of words, sharing a common root, which may be intended to convey a message about the purpose of life, are studied in this chapter.

6.1   The Letter *L*

The Hebrew letter *lamed* corresponds to the English *L* (we will below occasionally call the *lamed* "the Hebrew *L*"). It conveys multiple meanings in the Hebrew language.

On the one hand, it implies "for the purpose of." Thus, in the first chapter of Genesis, verses 14–18, the narrator repeatedly uses the letter *L* in that sense. For example: "And God said, Let there be lights in the firmament of heaven *to* [use of Hebrew *L*] divide the day from the night; and let them be *for* [use of Hebrew *L*] signs, and *for* [Hebrew *L*] seasons, and *for* [Hebrew *L*] days, and years: and let them be *for* [Hebrew *L*] lights in the firmament of heaven *to* [Hebrew *L*] project light upon the earth" (Gen. 1:14–15). And later: "And God set them in the firmament of heaven *to* [Hebrew *L*] project light upon the earth, and *to* [Hebrew *L*] rule in the day and in the night, and *to* [Hebrew *L*] divide the light from the darkness" (Gen. 1:17–18).

All these examples, and others, uniformly convey one possible meaning for the use of the Hebrew *L* as a prefix to words.

100

Another meaning of the *lamed* is the equivalent of the Hebrew word *el*[1] (the latter, by coincidence, coincides with the *name* of the English letter *L*).

El[1] in Hebrew means, simply, "to," "toward," or "in the direction of." This word, with its various derivatives, appears no fewer than 5,464 times in the Bible. It already appears in the first chapters of Genesis.

Examples:

- "And God said, Let the waters under the heaven be gathered towards [*el*[1]] one place, and let the dry land appear" (Gen. 1:9).
- "And out of the ground the Lord God formed every beast of the field, and every bird of the air; and brought to [*el*[1]] the man to see what he would call them" (Gen. 2:19).

In fact, the word *el*[1] is used in the Hebrew language interchangeably with the Hebrew *L*, when the latter precedes the word as a prefix, meaning "to." For example, the prophet Zechariah, speaking for God: "Therefore thus said the Lord; I have returned to [Hebrew *L*] Jerusalem with mercies: My house shall be rebuilt in it, says the Lord of hosts ..." (Zech. 1:16).

Yet, the word *el*[1] has some other meanings in Hebrew. It means "force" and "God." We will address the implications of these additional meanings in a later section (7.2).

Once the different usages and meanings of the Hebrew *L* are learned, it is natural to expect its name in Hebrew to convey a related meaning, like the *name* of the English letter *L*, which is compatible with the Hebrew meaning just delineated (*el*).[1]

Surprisingly, the Hebrew name does not convey such a meaning. The name of the letter is seemingly devoid of any relationship to its meanings, as employed in Hebrew sentences and as just expounded. The Hebrew name for the Hebrew *L* is comprised of the root of a verb that means ... "to learn": *L.M.D.* The Hebrew *L* is called in Hebrew *lamed*, written *LMD*. This seems a bizarre coincidence that requires some investigation.

Let us start by saying that the biblical meaning of "to learn" somewhat departs from that of modern Hebrew. In the latter, *li-lmod*[2] means "to learn": learning in school, at a university, and so on. This learning is related to, in the Bible, as "acquiring knowledge" ("purchasing of knowledge," *kniyat daat*).[3] In the biblical sense, and as related by the Malbim (1892), one of the most revered Jewish sages, to learn (in the sense of *limud*)[4] means practicing and training—that is, one is repeatedly learning until what is learned "gets into his or her heart" and becomes like second nature. Thus, the prophet Isaiah prophesizes: "And they shall beat their swords into plowshares, and their spears into pruning hooks: Nation shall not lift up sword against nation, neither shall they *learn* war any more" (Isa. 2:4). The learning here obviously does not relate to "acquiring knowledge" about war but rather to practicing war, to training for war, in other words, to "repeated learning until what one has learned becomes part of his nature."

In view of this interpretation, it is only natural to find in the Bible that the root *L.M.D* is mostly used in the sense of "learn the ways of the Lord until his ways become to you (the learner) like second nature."

This interpretation is strengthened by reading how Moses conveys God's statutes and laws to the children of Israel. Consider the book of Deuteronomy. Moses does not convey "thou should," as in earlier books of the Pentateuch, but rather, "thou could not do otherwise," implying that as a result of learning, in the sense expounded above, the children of Israel will not be able to deviate from these laws, as they would have become, for them, second nature.

Consider these examples:

- "Thou *may* not eat within thy gates the tithe of thy corn, or of thy wine ..." (Deut. 12:17).

- "Thou *may* not sacrifice the passover within any of thy gates, which the Lord thy God gives thee: But only at the place which the Lord thy God shall choose to place his name in ..." (Deut. 16:5–6).

- "In like manner shalt thou do with his ass; and so shalt thou do with his garment; and with every lost thing of thy brother's, which he has lost and thou hast found, shalt thou do likewise; Thou *may* not hide thyself" (Deut. 22:3).

In all these cases, and others, the "thou shalt," or "thou shalt not," of previous books of the Pentateuch, are replaced in Deuteronomy, quite often, with "thou may," or, "thou may not." The Hebrew original text indeed emphasizes the change of heart even more strongly (than the English translation insinuates): "you can" or "you would not be able to [*lo tuchal*]." Like second nature.

What then is the connection of "repeated learning until what you learn changes your nature," implied by the root *L.M.D* in the *name* of the letter *L*, and the meanings associated with common usages of that letter?

For lack of an alternative interpretation, one is led to apply the same mode of interpretation that has allowed us to understand why the name of the first letter of the alphabet, which has a value of 1, is called *alef* (derived from *Aluf*, one of the names of God).

Let us specify how one can interpret the message of the Hebrew *L*.

With the letter *L* and its bizarre name, the Hebrew language directs one to what it "perceives" to be the real purpose of life, the *direction* that one should take—namely, learning new righteous ways until they become second nature.

Stated differently, the Hebrew language conveys the following message:

> "We have come here, to this world, in order to learn. But learning we must in such a fashion that the learned modify our very nature and becomes part of it."

This same theme is summarized in the verse from Isaiah: "Thus says the Lord God, thy redeemer, the Holy One of Israel; I am the Lord thy God, who teaches thee [*melamdecha*[6]] for thy profit [literally, "to be useful"], who leads you by the way that thou shalt go" (Isa. 48:17).

In other words, the letter used in the Bible for direction (or for purpose) also has a name which means "learning," implying that "this is the direction that you need to take in conducting and molding your lives"!

Comments

1. The reader may perceive the above as preaching. It is not; nor is it intended to be. What we wished to demonstrate here is that Hebrew letters, and their linguistic properties, have hidden messages that the Hebrew language conveys. In this case, the common usages of the letter *lamed* (the Hebrew *L*), and its name, are so at odds with one another, that one is led, nearly in spite of herself or himself, to receive a very powerful message that biblical Hebrew is attempting to convey.

2. The source of the root *L.M.D* (used in the sense of learning) is unknown. However, it is known that in ancient times the *malmad*, a pointed rod, was used to hurry up livestock. Perhaps this somehow explains the use of the Hebrew letter *lamed* for direction. The association with learning is still vague, until the above message is considered.

6.2   "Work," "Angle," "Messenger"

6.2.1   Melachah (Work)

"Work" in Hebrew is *melachah*.[7] This word has a special position in the Hebrew language. There are altogether thirty-nine basic types of "work"s (*melachot*)[8] that a Jew is forbidden doing on Shabbat and on holy Jewish festivities. The reason is that each of these "work"s have, about them, an element of creation, introducing something new that was not there before. Creation on Shabbat is not allowed, since on the seventh day of creation, God "ceased all his work that God had created *to do*" (Gen. 2:3; author's translation).

The classification of all sorts of forbidden "work"s into thirty-nine basic categories originates in the description of the construction of the tabernacle by Bezaleel, as the story is being narrated, in great detail, in Exodus, chapters 35–39. Postbiblical eras have seen an explosion in the number of derivative "work"s not allowed on Shabbat by religious authorities. However, all these "work"s originate—some quite straightforwardly, others less so—in this common source: the description of the construction of the tabernacle while the children of Israel wandered in the Sinai desert on their way from Egypt to the Promised Land.

6.2.2 Malach (Angel, Messenger)

Malach,[9] in Hebrew, has two meanings that seem far apart. On the one hand, *malach*[9] means "a messenger"—namely, one who carries messages from one place to another. Occurrences of *malach*[9] abound in the Bible.
Examples:

- "Then Izevel sent a messenger [*malach*[9]] to Elijah" (1 Kings 19:2).

- "But there came a messenger [*malach*[9]] to Saul, saying, Make haste and come, for the Philistines are raiding the land" (1 Samuel 23:27).

- "And there came a messenger [*malach*[9]] to Job and said ..." (Job 1:14).

A second meaning of *malach*,[9] a more common usage in modern Hebrew, is "an angel."
Examples:

- "And an angel [*malach*[9]] of the Lord called him out of heaven and said, Abraham, Abraham: and he said, Here I am" (Gen. 22:11).

- "The angel [*malach*[9]] who redeems me from all evil, bless the lads;" (Gen. 48:16).

- "And God sent an angel [*malach*[9]] to Jerusalem to destroy it: and as he was about to destroy, the Lord beheld ..." (1 Chron. 21:15).

6.2.3   "Work," "Angle," "Messenger": Integration

As in the previous example (section 6.1), we encounter once again a bizarre coincidence that needs some elaboration. While it is explainable why "a messenger" and "an angel" are the same word in Hebrew (given the biblical mission of angels as messengers), the interrelationship with "work" (*melachah*)[7] seems out of place. Let us be reminded that specifying forbidden "work"s for Shabbat implies that these are our duty on other days of the week, as explicitly stated at the end of the story of the creation: "And God blessed the seventh day, and sanctified it, because in it he ceased all his work [*melachah*[7]] that God had created *to do*" (Gen. 2:3; author's translation).

Read it again carefully. Here the Bible describes not the creation of the world, but the creation of work. Furthermore, this work has been created for the purposeo f executing it ("created to do"). The mathematical precision in biblical language is at its peak. How can this phrase be explained?

We have earlier related to the fact that in the Hebrew language, as well as in Jewish mysticism, there is distinction between the worlds of creating, forming, and doing (or making). This is particularly outstanding in the story of creation, in the first two chapters of Genesis. God has created "*the* Heaven and *the* Earth," then he has *done* "the sky" and "the dry land"—which he called, respectively, just "Heaven" and "Earth" (without "the"). However, with respect to man and woman, he either created (Gen. 1:27), or formed (Gen. 2:7) them. And then, "And by the seventh day God ended his work which he had *done*" (Gen. 2:2), and "These are the generations of *the* heaven and of *the* earth when they were *created*, in the day that the Lord God *made* earth and heaven" (Gen. 2:4; author's translation). In the same verse, there appear "the Heaven" and "the Earth," which were created, and "Earth" and "Heaven," which were made. And on the seventh day God has ended his work, which he had done. No word about ending creation. These differences would have been taken lightly, were it not for the high mathematical precision of biblical discourse, as this was demonstrated in an earlier section (section 1.3).

The prophet Isaiah makes the distinction between the three worlds of creating, forming, and doing very explicit: "Everyone that is called by my name: for I have created him for my glory; I have formed him; yea, I have made him" (Isa. 43:7).

The relationship between "work," "messenger," and "angel" (according to the biblical Hebrew) now seems clear:

> "We have come here, to this world, as messengers, in order to do certain work. This work *to be done* is part of creation. In that sense, we are no different from angels, who also have each a certain mission—certain work to be done!"

6.3   *L,* "Work," "Angle," "Messenger": The Overall Message

Sections 6.1 and 6.2 may now be summarized as follows, according to the message of the Bible and of biblical Hebrew:

There are two purposes for our being sent, like "messengers" or "angels," into this world:

- To learn, in such a fashion that as a result of the learning process our very nature be remolded;

- To carry out certain work that is part of our mission as "messengers," and which is indeed the purpose of creation (Gen. 2:3).

CHAPTER 7

Unity, Unity, All Around

7.1　Introduction

This chapter addresses some aspects of the physical world, as "perceived" by the Hebrew language and reflected in respective Hebrew words, their structures, and their interrelationships. Corresponding (coincidental) references in modern physics and in cosmology theories are then indicated.

There are four main topics to this chapter:

- The unity of all forces (section 7.2)
- The unity of energy and space (section 7.3)
- The unity of all time tenses (section 7.4)
- The unity of time and space (section 7.5)

For all these cases, the Hebrew language treats seemingly separate entities as though they are one and the same, with the obvious intent of demonstrating the ever-present underlying unity, the central credo of monotheism: the oneness of God.

7.2　The Unity of All Forces

If a Jew were required to choose one slogan to be recognized by, it would undoubtedly be

"Hear, O Israel: The Lord our God; the Lord is one" (Deut. 6:4).

By a bizarre coincidental twist, this phrase may be somewhat modified to describe the main focus of research in mainstream physics for the last century and a half. The second and third parts of this phrase are "Jehovah [the Lord] *Elohenu*[1] [our God], Jehovah is one."

The word *Elohim*,[2] as related elsewhere in this book (for example, chapter 4), is in Hebrew also the plural of force. This means that literally *Elohenu*[1] can be translated "our forces." A physicist of our time could easily modify this sentence to represent the core of physics in modern times, spanning an era from the mid-nineteenth century up to the present:

"Hear, O dear colleagues: the forces of nature, our forces (since we investigate them); they are all one."

In what follows, we first deliver a succinct account of the main stages of the ongoing effort, carried out by physicists for the last century and a half, to unify all forces of nature under a single theory, hopefully described by the "theory of everything." Later, we will explore whether indications of a similar position, with regard to the unity of all forces, are conveyed by the Hebrew language.

A very long time has elapsed since forces of nature were perceived as expressions of the wills and emotions (and at times also intrigues) of the gods, who dominate our world, and the relatively recent history when those forces have become legitimate subjects of scientific enquiry. The science of physics has, for some centuries now (at least from Newton's era of the seventeenth century), focused mainly on the investigation of the forces of nature. Today, there is an ongoing scientific collaboration of physicists the world over to integrate the known forces of nature, particularly the elusive force of gravity, into a unifying theory where all forces be grasped as manifestations of a single unified force.

What are these forces of nature? At first, there were five distinguishable and separate forces.

- The electric force
- The magnetic force
- The weak nuclear force
- The strong nuclear force
- Gravitation

Efforts to integrate all these into all-encompassing theories may be pinpointed by certain defining moments and stages in the history of modern physics. These highlights have been expounded in section 4.3.

The heroic attempts by physicists to combine all phenomena of nature into a unifying theory can hardly be distinguished from the basic philosophy of monotheism. Although one may doubt that most physicists would agree with this contention, it seems as inescapable conclusion that scientists of physics, for the last century and a half (unwillingly or unnoticeably, combining mathematics with experimental observations) have done their best to provide scientific evidence for monotheism—with a good degree of success.

How is the unity of all forces reflected in the Hebrew language?
Devoid of any aspiration for a scientific statement, the Hebrew language nonetheless insinuates unity for all forces of nature by using the plural of "force" as the name of God, yet relating to this plural-tense word in the singular, as befit a monotheistic faith. The Hebrew language relates to God by the name *Elohim*.[2] This word is linguistically the plural of *el*[3] or *eloah*[3] (both meaning force). Justifiably, it is the only name for God used throughout the story of creation, in the first chapter of Genesis. Yet the Bible always relates to this plural word in the singular—as, for example, in "In the beginning God [*Elohim*[2]] created [*bara*,[4] in the singular] the heaven and the earth" (Gen. 1:1).

It is as though the Bible, via the Hebrew language, conveys a message: "All these forces appear in the plural, as the linguistic structure of the word implies, yet they are indeed manifestations of one."

Interestingly, the only time in the Bible where *Elohim*[2] is referenced in the plural is in the verse "And he received the gold at their hand, and fashioned it with a graving tool and made it a molten calf: and they said, These *are* thy gods [*elohecha*[5]], O Israel, which brought thee up out of the land of Egypt." "And the Lord said to Moses … they have made them a molten calf, and have worshipped it, and have sacrificed to it, and said, These *are* thy gods [*elohecha*[5]], O Israel, which have brought thee up out of the land of Egypt" (Exod. 32: 4, 7, 8).

This incidence insinuates that, Bible-wise, the only time when "the forces" (*Elohim*)[2] start to look not as one but as separate ("these are") is when the monotheistic faith, the perception of the oneness of God, is weakened.

Or when scientists have not yet succeeded proving the oneness of all forces …

Comments

All of modern-physics attempts to unify the forces of nature rely on the basic mathematically unprovable concept of the existence of laws of nature. That such laws do exist, or that the world is governed by unbreakable regularities "promised by God," is a repeated theme in the Bible. For example: "I will not again curse the ground any more for man's sake … neither will I again smite any more everything living, as I have done. While the earth remains, seed time and harvest, and cold and heat, and summer and winter, and day and night shall not cease" (Gen. 8:21–22; refer also to Gen. 1:14, 18; Jer. 31:34–35 and 33:25; and to Job 38:33).

7.3   The Unity of Energy and Space

While physics and related cosmology theories are complex and still evolving, there is no doubt that the basic characterization of "force," as already articulated at the time of Newton, still holds today: all forces need to be defined in terms of *size* and *direction*.

A convenient and commonly accepted way to realize this characterization is by expressing any force as a vector. In physics and engineering, the word "vector" typically refers to a quantity that has close relationship to spatial coordinates; a vector is informally described as an object having both "magnitude" and "direction." In other words, a vector is a "directed number" (or a set of directed numbers)!

Though this characterization of force was already used by Newton, the term "vector," as nowadays used in all branches of science and engineering, was first introduced, according to *The Oxford English Dictionary*, in 1864, by W. R. Hamilton (1805–65).

Let us observe how the Hebrew language relates to the concept of force. There are many words for force, like *koach*,[6] *oz*,[7] *otzmah*,[8] and others. However, among such words that describe "force," one has a unique position. The reason for this is that this word alone is intended, in both its singular and in its plural forms, to imply "God" (or "gods"). We introduced this word earlier: *El*[3] (or *Elohim*,[2] in the plural form). The connection between the two concepts, "God" and "force," is self-evident: We perceive God (or the "gods," as in ancient times, premonotheism) to have all forces under his control. Naturally, God is identified with "forces," just as the ancient Greeks have done (for example, Prometheus had control over the force of fire).

A less obvious aspect of the Hebrew word for force, *el*,[3] is that the same word also means "toward" or "in the direction of" (see reference to this word also in section 6.1).

In other words, for the Hebrew language, just as mandated by the field concept of modern physics, "force" has meaning only when direction is also intended:

$$\text{"force"} <= el^3 => \text{"toward, to" (direction)}$$

Thus, energy (force) and space (spatial coordinates realized by direction), are united by a single short *el*.[3]

The unifying of energy ("force") and spatial dimensions ("toward") in a single Hebrew word, *el*,[3] bizarre though as it may look, seems to constitute yet another example of design in the Hebrew language.

7.4   The Unity of All Time Tenses

Biblical Hebrew has a special mode for describing events that have occurred, and those that have not yet. This unique biblical pattern of speech would look extremely bizarre to a naive reader. In fact, not knowing that this pattern exists would, to the ignorant reader, distort the sense of the read.

The Bible's special way of conveying the time tense of verbs employed to describe events has no parallel in any other language. The secret and key for this special pattern of recounting time tense is the letter used for conjunction, namely, the letter *vav* (pronounced "waw" in English). The regular function of this letter, when used as a prefix for a given word, is to serve as the conjunction "and" in English. However, in the Bible it serves a double purpose: To connect words and sentences, but also to connect future with past, and past with future. In other words, the letter converts the time direction of a verb, and as such it is named: the "conversive *vav*." A verb in the past tense, preceded by the conversive *vav*, implies the future, and vice versa.

To understand this particular function, let us first describe what the letter *vav* stands for.

Vav is the sixth letter in the Hebrew alphabet, having the numerical value of six. The letter name is written by two *vav*s, and pronounced "vav." However, the word *vav*[9] has an additional meaning, which is its most common use: "hook." The *vav*[9] is simply that which connects. It is written ו as just that: a hook. Faithful to this function, the letter *vav* is used as a conjunctive *vav*. A Hebrew speaker just has to add the letter *vav* in front of a word to mean "and"—life could not be simpler.

Yet, as explained earlier, this letter also connects future to past and past to future. This is the special pattern of speech used throughout the Bible. Explanations for this special pattern are scarce, although it is possible to formulate one. Before doing that, let us observe how the conversive *vav* works.

To describe future events, the Bible uses verbs in the past tense, preceded by the conversive *vav*. The latter converts these verbs into a future tense. The opposite direction is also utilized: to a verb in the future tense a conversive *vav* is attached as prefix to imply an event in the past.

We demonstrate with a well-known verse from Isaiah: "And it shall come to pass in the last days, that the mountain of the Lord's house shall be established on the top of the mountains, and shall be exalted above the hills" (Isa. 2:2).

Analyzing how this verse is given in Hebrew, the sentence "And it shall come to pass" is expressed by a single word: *ve-hayah*.[10] *Hayah*[11] means, simply, "it was." The conversive *vav* attached to the word (pronounced "ve"), reverses the direction into the future to mean "it shall be" (or "it shall come to pass," as it appears in most English translations). The same rule virtually applies to all other verbs in the same verse: "and shall be exlated" is in Hebrew *ve-nissa*[12]—meaning, literally, "and it was exalted." However, knowing that the *vav* is the conversive *vav*, the *ve-nissa*[12] means "it *shall* be exalted."

Regrettably, many biblical English translations ignore the function of the conversive *vav* in cases when it functions only as that, and add the word "and" in front of a word, thus confusing the conversive *vav* with the conjunctive *vav*. For example, one may doubt that Isaiah vision should start with "and," or should it more correctly be read, without the "and," as: "It shall come to pass in the last days …" (Isa. 2:2).

Similar examples may be given for verbs in future tense that, with the conversive *vav*, acquire the meaning of a past tense. Let us take the most well-known first chapter of Genesis. The only verbs therein that are given in the right past tense relate to creation or describing the just created. First, there are the first two verses: "In the beginning God *created* the heaven and the earth. And the earth was without form and void … And a wind from God moved over the surface of the waters" (Gen. 1:1–2). The "created" is given in the right past tense: *bara*.[4] So are all other verbs in these two verses. Later, describing the creation of the first human beings, male and female, the right past tense is again used, but only once, in part of the verse (verse 27). But that is it. All other verbs revert to the regular biblical pattern, where a verb in the past tense, preceded by *ve*, implies a future tense, and vice versa.

Consider this example: "And God said, Let there be light: and there was light" (Gen. 1:3). Both descriptive verbs, "said" and "there was," are in future tense, preceded by *ve* (or *va*). The first is, in Hebrew, *va-yomer*.[13] *Yomer*[13] means "he will say." But the *va* reverses the direction from future to past. The second verse is *va-yehi*[14] (and there was). *Yehi*[14] alone means "it will be", but the conversive *va* renders it past tense.

It is interesting to note that in the second chapter of Genesis, verses 5 and 6, there is a mixing together of all time tenses, with and without the conversive *vav*. Yet they all refer to the past tense. Thus, "And no plant of the field *was* yet in the earth" (5), is literally, in Hebrew: "And no plant *will yet* be in the earth" (5). No conversive *vav*, yet a future tense conveys a past tense.

Why does the Bible use verbs in future tense to describe events in the past and verbs in past tense to describe the future? The answer to that question is anyone's guess. An explanation, based on no prior knowledge of previous explanations, is now attempted.

The word "Jehovah" in Hebrew is linguistically analyzed in Chapter 4. As elaborated there in some detail, the structure of the word implies a procession from future to present to past. Although the root of the word "Jehovah" means "being," the structure includes three syllabi: *ye, ho, vah*. Each is a syllable in wordsr elating to time—namely, "will be" (*yehiyeh*),[15] "is" (*hoveh*),[16] and "was" (*havah* or *hayah*).[17] The flow of time is, as we read the word, from future to present to past. But all these different time directions are united in one name: the name of God, Jehovah.

An explanation for the conversive *vav* may likewise be offered, based on what the name Jehovah insinuates. In sacred scriptures, one may expect to find time erased, nonexistent: "The word of God is timeless." The value of that which is described is not limited by time. Past is future and future is past. The text is eternal, and therefore must be expressed in a timeless frame of discourse. Were you ignorant of the function of the conversive *vav*, you might have read the text with time reversal: All past is future, all future is past. Conversely, if you know the function of the conversive *vav*, then you know what time era you are in while reading. But you never forget that a right determination of the direction of time depends on you understanding of the function of the letter *vav*, which serves to connect things in the physical dimensions as well as in the time dimension.

In summary, the oneness of God in the physical dimensions, as detailed in the previous section, is extended to the oneness of God in the time dimension.

How would one explain the bizarre exception that only the first two verses in the Bible (the two opening sentences in the book of Genesis, which describe the creation of the world) are yet in their correct time tense (past)? This is perhaps because at the time described in these two verses, time was not yet. The description, in the second verse, of the just-born universe as *tohu va-vohu* (without form and void) may corroborate that explanation and is consistent with it (refer to a thorough analysis of these words in chapter 14, and to some explanation about the precision of biblical discourse in section 1.3). Similar explanation may be extended to the verse depicting the creation of humankind.

7.5   The Unity of Time and Space

Time and space are differently referenced in most languages. Thus, in the English language, when one wishes to obtain information about physical dimensions, the question is "Where?" When the time dimension is involved, the question is "When?"

The Hebrew language, strangely enough, unites time and space by using a single word to ask both questions.

The Hebrew words *anah*[18] or *an*[19] both probably originate in the root *A.I.N.* For example, "*Me-ain?*" means "Where from?" and "*Le-ain?*" (though not biblical) means, like *anah*[18] or *an*,[19] "Where to?" Note that *anah*[18] may be interchangeably written also *le-an*[19] (to an), since the *L* (*le*) attached to a word as a prefix can be added at the end of the word in the form of a suffix *-ah*. Thus, one may say that he or she is traveling "*le-Yerushalayim*" (to Jerusalem) or, simply, *Yerushalaimah*. However, *le an*[19] is not biblical.

The word *an*[19], or *anah*[18], appears in the Bible, in its various forms, forty-two times. Yet it is used interchangeably to show direction, or bounds, for dimensions that are either geometrical (space) or time-related. Indeed, anyone reading biblical text may feel confused by this concept of mixing together time and space (confusion pre-Einstein, that is). A unique feature of *anah*,[18] when it relates to time, is that it always appears as "until when" (*ad anah*[20] or *ad an*).[21] But it still relates to "when."

Examples ("where to" and "until when" are author's translations):

- "And the Lord said to Moses, Until when [*ad-anah*[20]] will you refuse to keep my commandments and my laws?" (Exod. 16:28).

- "And the Lord said to Moses, Until when [*ad-anah*[20]] will this people provoke me? And until when [*ad-anah*[20]] will they not believe in me, for all the signs that I have performed among them?" (Num., 14:11).

- "and the old man said, Where to [*anah*[18]] do thou go, and where have thou come from?" (Judges 19:17).

- "To the chief musician, a Psalm of David. Until when [*ad-anah*[20]] wilt thou forget me O Lord? forever? Until when [*ad-anah*[20]] wilt thou hide thy face from me?" (Psal. 13:1–2).

- "Where to [*anah*[18]] is thy beloved gone, O thou fairest among women? Where to [*anah*[18]] has thy beloved turned aside? That we may seek him with thee" (Song of Songs 6:1).

- "And the king sent and called for Shim'i, and said to him, Did I not make thee to swear by the Lord, and did I not forewarn thee, saying, Know for certain, on the day thou goest out, and walkest abroad anywhere [*anah ve-anah*,[22] like "to and fro"], that thou shalt surely die?" (1 Kings 2:42).

"When" and "where" are used interchangeably by the same word, as though time and space are bound together in a single time-space coordinate system. How up-to-date.

If one may wish to regard the above as sheer coincidence, consider another word that expresses the same idea about the unity of time and space: *olam*.[23] The latter is discussed in section 2.1.1 in one of its senses—namely, "world." However, its most common sense in the Bible is "eternity." For example: "upon the throne of David, and upon his kingdom, to order it, and to establish it with judgment and with justice from henceforth for ever [*le-olam*[23]] ..." "... thy people also shall be all righteous, they shall inherit the land for eternity [*le-olam*[23]]" (Isa. 9:6, 59:21).

One word, *olam*,[23] expresses boundlessness, either in time or in space. No distinction is made.

Finally, the most sacred name of God in Judaism, Jehovah, expresses, in one word, the unity of that which exists ("being," being the root of the name) with time, future, present and past (refer to chapter 4 for details).

Vav,[9] *an*,[19] *olam*,[23] and "Jehovah" all express the underlying notion of unity: that of time and space (geometrical dimensions), or that of time and the universe (space and all that it includes)—not unlike Einstein's time-space universe, where time and the three spatial dimensions are united under a shared framework.

These are all coincidences ... maybe.

CHAPTER 8

Earth, Moon, Sun, Planets

8.1 "Earth," "Moon," "Sun" in Biblical Hebrew

The earth, the moon and the sun have all synonyms in the Hebrew language—
some more known than others.

"Earth" has, in Hebrew, a nearly identical word: *Eretz*.[1] This leads one to
suspect that the two words perhaps derive from a common source, or that the
historically more recent word evolved from the more ancient one.

The moon and the sun are related to already in the story of creation, where
the "assignments" given to these two celestial objects are clearly delineated:
"The greater light to rule the day ... and the lesser light to rule the night" (Gen.
1:16).

"Moon" has in Hebrew multiple synonyms to select from. These include

- *Yareach*,[2] the most commonly used name for "moon," which is the same
  word as used for "month," though the latter is pronounced differently, as
  yerach;[3]

- *Sahar*,[4] which in the Bible probably meant a circle (it appears only once,
  in Song of Songs 7:3), but in modern Hebrew means also "moon";

- *Levanah*,[5] which in Hebrew is close to *lavan*,[6] meaning "white."

"Sun" has three synonyms too:

- *Shemesh*,[7] which is the most common word, both in biblical and modern Hebrew; its origin is assumed by scholars to be in Mesopotamia,

where *shamash* was a (male) god of the sun and of justice; but refer to section 8.3;

- *Cheres*[8]—for example: "And the men of the city said to him on the seventh day before the sun came down [*beterem bo charsah*[9]]" (Judges 14:18); or, "Which commands the sun [*cheres*[8]] and it rises not; and seals up the stars" (Job 9:7). This name for sun is hardly used in modern Hebrew, and its appearances in the Bible are rare, relative to *shemesh*;[7]

- *Chamah*,[10] which is also the word for "hot" (feminine adjective).

Analyzing these words and their possible interrelationships, we start with the more controversial and rare name for sun, *cheres*.[8]

This name surprisingly is used also for "clay." This is a strange association, unless one assumes that the sun and clay have some common traits. However, the term *cheres*[8] is extremely interesting in its relationship to Samson. The name Samson in Hebrew is *Shimshon*, which obviously originated in the Hebrew word *shemesh*[7] (sun). The question is why Samson was named after the sun. Because this biblical hero had extraordinary physical capabilities, scholars believe that perhaps there was some legend prevailing, among ancient Israelites, that Samson was born out of sexual contacts between Samson's mother and "the man of God," who had come to tell her of the expected pregnancy. The way the Bible describes this encounter probably points to the source of the story in that legend and reflects it: "And the angel of God came again to the woman as she was sitting in the field: *and Manoah her husband was not with her*" (Judges 13:9). We recall that legends about sexual encounters between humans and sons of pagan Gods were common in ancient times. This is clearly indicated already in Genesis, just before the story of Noah (and the deluge) begins to unfold: "The Nefilim [giants] were on the earth in those days: and also after that, when the sons of God came in to the daughters of men, and they bore children to them" (Gen. 6:4).

Given the unique physical strength of Samson, the prevailing legend was probably that he was born out of the sexual encounter of his mother with the son of the god of sun. The Bible narrator, probably aware of this legend, wishes to uproot any such insinuation, and therefore is hinting at the "true" source of the name of Samson in the fact that the solution to the riddle that Samson had submitted to the Philistines was revealed before sunset. Thus, the legend about Samson as the offspring of the god of sun is in one strike obliterated (refer to Zakovitch and Shinan, 2004, for further details about this interesting explanation for the name of Samson).

The root of the name "Earth" was the subject of much debate as reported in Jewish written sources. The reason for these debates was the fact that the name "Earth" resembles the Hebrew word for "to run"—namely, "to move fast" ("Earth" is *Eretz*,[1] and "run" is *ratz*). Jewish scholars were puzzled about this resemblance and explained that the reason for it is probably that all stars and the moon and the sun are "running" around the earth. Rabbi Don Yitzchak Abarbanel (1437–1508), a well-known commentator of the Bible, did not accept this interpretation. In his commentary to Genesis (1), he explains that "since the earth is a still center, it would have been appropriate that the wheel [meaning sun] should be called 'Eretz,'[1] and not the still center around which it revolves." Obviously, living prior to Copernicus, Jewish sages have tried to fit their interpretations to the scientific knowledge of their time. Abrabanel rejected their explanations based on pure logic, unaware that not many years later, Copernicus (1473–1543), in his book published not long prior to his death, would introduce findings that resolved this quandary.

The source of other synonyms, the sun as *chammah*[10] (hot) and the moon as *levanah*[5] (white) are self-explanatory.

8.2 "And God made the two great lights; The great light ... and the small light ..." (Gen. 1:16)

A reader of this verse will indeed be baffled. How can such contradictory statements be given in the same chapter, let alone in consecutive sentences, let alone in the opening chapter of the whole Bible? Either the lights (obviously meaning the sun and the moon) are both great (large) or they are both small. Stating first that they are of equal size (great) and then the opposite (one is smaller than the other) leaves one pondering whether some error had gone undetected in the first most well-known chapter of Genesis. As one recalls how precise and consistent is biblical discourse (amply demonstrated in chapter 1), this puzzlement tends to grow.

The seemingly contradictory statements in the above verse from Genesis become compatible with one another as one recalls that biblical text is often given layer underneath layer. Such cases are introduced in chapter 16, where various words in the Bible are introduced, which are differently read than written. It is then explained that the written word represents the inner meaning of the word, while the read word represents the visible superficial appearance of the object that the word stands for.

It is clear that a similar scenario is encountered in this bizarre verse, which needs clarification. The explanation is straightforward.

The sun and the moon do appear, to an earthly observer, as of equal size. For an innocent observer of the moon and the sun (when the latter is observed, hopefully, with some eye protection), there is no way of knowing, unaided by a telescope, that the sun is indeed larger than the moon. The reason for this peculiar phenomenon is made clear by Figure 8.1: the observation *angles* of the circumferential edges of the moon and the sun are equal.

This peculiar coincidence is caused by the sun's diameter being about 400 times larger than that of the moon; however, the sun is also about 390 times further away. The exact ratios are given below.

Ratio of diameters (sun to moon, km):

$$1.391 \times 10^6 \,/\, 3474.8 = 400.3$$

Ratio of distances ("sun to earth" vs. "moon to earth," km):

$$149{,}597{,}890 \,/\, 384{,}401 = 389.17$$

(Source: the NASA Web site, http://www.nasa.gov/worldbook, and also http://www.windows.ucar.edu/tour/link=/the_universe/uts/intro.html.)

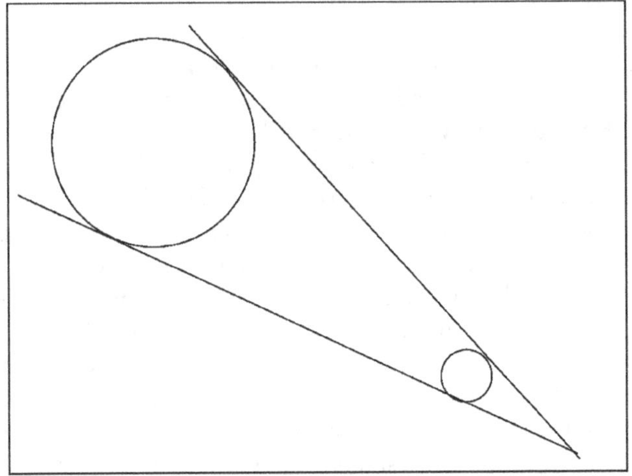

Figure 8.1. Observation angle of the moon and the sun (from Earth).

Thus, the combination of the moon's size and its distance from the earth (both relative to the sun's) causes the moon to appear the same size in the sky as the sun. This is one reason we can have total solar eclipses.

The two seemingly contradictory sentences in the first chapter of the Bible now make sense. The first sentence talks about reality as observed by mortals on earth in ancient times (namely, prior to the invention of the telescope). The second sentence addresses reality as it is: the sun *is* larger than the moon.

The only question left open: How was it known in ancient times to earth-bound observers which "light" is bigger and which "light" is smaller?

8.3   Predicting Diameters

8.3.1   What a Linear Regression Model Implies (Here)

A statistical analysis has been conducted to find out whether the size of the moon, the earth, and the sun can be predicted from the numerical values of their respective most common Hebrew names—namely, *yareach*[2] (moon), *Eretz*[1] (Earth) and *shemesh*[7] (sun).

Linear regression analysis was applied to the data. However, before we detail the analysis and its results, some general explanation is needed regarding the implication of obtaining, from the analyses implemented in this book, statistically significant linear regression models.

There are altogether over fifteen statistical analyses in the book (for their locations refer to the list of figures, adjacent to the table of contents). All analyses share two properties in common. First, they all use a linear regression model, with a single independent variable (regressor). Secondly, all models use as the regressor (the predicting variable) numerical values of the relevant Hebrew words, where these values are the total sum of the numerical values of the respective constituent letters.

What does a statistically valid linear model imply?
For a statistically significant linear regression model with one independent variable, a linear relationship implies that the response (the dependent variable) is a linear transformation of the regressor. This implies that both variables represent the same "entity"—yet they differ by location and scale. In other words, the two variables are one and the same, differing only in their measurement scale.

To demonstrate what is meant by difference in location and scale, suppose that at a speed of V kilometers per hour, a driver travels in his of her car from city A to city B. The distance between these cities is D_{AB}. After time T, the driver wishes to inform of his or her location. He or she may do that by saying how far he or she is from city A, in which case the position, P_A, is specified as

$$P_A = (V)(T) \text{ (kilometers)}$$

Alternatively, the driver may wish to inform the position in meters, in which case the scale is changed by multiplying by 1,000:

$$P_A' = (1,000)(V)(T) \text{ (meters)} = (1,000)P_A$$

Now suppose that the position is measured not from city A but from city B. The position would now be specified as (D_{AB} is the distance between the cities, in meters)

$$P_B = D_{AB} - (1,000)(V)(T) \text{ (meters)} =$$
$$D_{AB} - P_A' = D_{AB} - (1,000)P_A.$$

We realize that although the same "entity" is measured, namely, the distance from a certain "zero point," changes in scale (from kilometers to meters) and in location (selecting city B, instead of A, as the zero point) translate into a linear transformation: P_B is a linear transformation of P_A. The underlying meaning of P, however, is not altered.

Extending this interpretation to the linear regression analyses expounded in this book, the reader should bear in mind that whenever a statistically significant linear regression model is obtained, it implies that the independent variable (the regressor) is the same as the response (the dependent variable). The only difference is that the latter is measured on a different measurement scale than the former.

8.3.2   *The Statistical Analysis and Its Results*

The dependent variable (the response) was the celestial object's diameter (in kilometers), given on a natural-log scale, and the independent variable (the regressor) was the object numerical value (ONV), calculated from the numerical values of the letters comprising the corresponding Hebrew word.

Values for the diameters of the moon, the Earth, and the sun were taken from NASA Web site (given earlier, section 8.2).

Values for the ONVs were calculated as follows:

Moon (*yareach*):[2]

$$218 = (8 = ח) + (200 = ר) + (10 = י)$$

Earth (*Eretz*):[1]

$$291 = (90 = צ) + (200 = ר) + (1 = א)$$

Sun (*shemesh*):[7]

$$640 = (300 = ש) + (40 = מ) + (300 = ש)$$

The data are given in Table 8.1.
(Source for equatorial diameters: http://solarsystem.jpl.nasa.gov/planets/
profile.cfm?Object=Moon&Display=Overview)

Linear regression analysis was applied, with log-diameter as the response (the dependent variable). For a sample size n = 3, a correlation of 0.99898 was obtained, with R^2-adjusted of 0.9959. The model F-ratio is 487.9, which is significant at the 5% significance level (p = 0.0288).

Figure 8.2 displays the observations with the fitted regression line. The figure atop each observation is the response value (log-diameter), displayed for easy identification of the observations.

The final model is (diameter is in km):

$$\text{Diameter} = \exp\,[5.237150 + 0.013961\,\text{ONV}]$$

("exp" means "the exponential of"; taking the natural logarithm of both sides would give the log-diameter, on the left, as a function of the linear equation, on the right)

The predicted values are also given in Table 8.1. Based on the numerical values of the most commonly used Hebrew names for the moon, the Earth, and the sun, the respective diameters of these celestial objects could be predicted from

Table 8.1. Actual and predicted diameters of the moon, the Earth and the sun (based on ONV, the numerical value of the Hebrew names).

Name	Diameter (actual, km)	Log-diameter	ONV (Object Numercal Value)	Diameter (predicted)	Error (%)
Moon	3474.8	8.153292	218	3946.75	13.6
Earth	12756.28	9.453779	291	10935.84	−14.3
Sun	1 391 000	14.14553	640	1 428 577.8	2.70

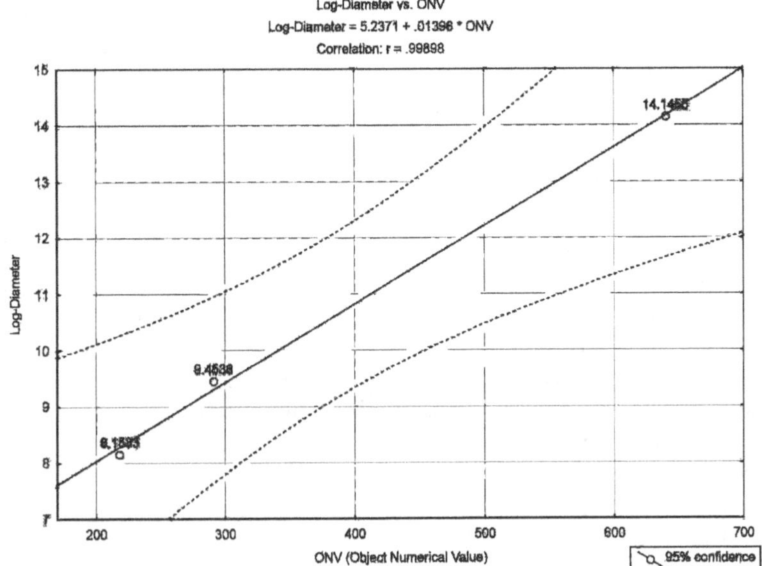

Figure 8.2. Plot of log-diameter of moon, Earth, and sun,
as a function of their celestial object numerical values (ONV).

the above statistically significant model with relative errors of about ±14% for the moon and the Earth, and with a relative error of less than 3% for the sun.

Much smaller absolute values for the absolute errors would have been obtained if nonlinear regression were applied to the celestial diameters in the original scale using the above model.

8.3.3   *The Planets*

May other planets in the solar system obey a law similar to that in Figure 8.2?

A search in the Bible reveals that apart from the Earth, the moon, and the sun, all other stars are never individually related to. For example: "the sun ... the moon and the stars" (Eccles. 12:2). There is reference to names that are traditionally conceived to denote *groups* of stars, like *ksil* (possibly the group called Orion) and *kimah* (referring to Amos and Job), or *ash* (occasionally *aish*), in reference to Isaiah. Subsection 8.3.5 casts doubt on this perception of the names as those of constellations of stars.

Although nonbiblical, there are Hebrew names for various known planets. Out of curiosity, though reluctantly, we have decided this single time to deviate from the stated restriction conveyed in the title of this book, and we have prepared a list of planets that have known Hebrew names, even though these are not biblical. For each name, the numerical values were calculated and diameter values taken from NASA Web site:

http://ssd.jpl.nasa.gov/?planet_phys_par

The planets included in the prepared list are: Mercury (*Kochav*),[11] Jupiter (*Tzedek*),[12] Saturn (*Shabtai*),[13] Venus (*Nogah*),[14] and Mars (*Maadim*).[15] From the Hebrew names, given in the appendix, the reader may work out the corresponding ONV values.

The data are given in Table 8.2.

The plot of the fitted linear regression equation is given in Figure 8.3. Excluded from the analysis is the sun (since it is not a planet). Also excluded is the large planet Jupiter (*Tzedek*),[12] the Hebrew nonbiblical name of which deviates considerably from the general pattern displayed by the other n = 5 observations. We will readdress Jupiter in section 8.3.5.

Figure 8.3 shows that all observations are within the 95% confidence interval limits. The linear correlation is 0.955 (for n = 5) and all observations lie within the 95% confidence interval limits.

8.3.4 Venus is Mazar[19]

The observation of Venus in Figure 8.3 deviates from the general pattern displayed in the plot (though this observation is within the 95% confidence interval limits). This initiated an exploration for the possibly true name of Venus in biblical Hebrew. The results of this inquiry are detailed in this subsection.

The Bible refers to all the planets by two forms of a single term: *mazalot*[16] or *mazarot*.[17] Both are in the plural form. Based on basic Hebrew grammatical rules, it is apparent that the singular form are *mazal*[18] and *mazar*,[19] respectively.

Table 8.2. Data for planets and the sun.

Name	Hebrew name (biblical starred)	ONV	Equatorial diameter (km)	Log-diameter
Earth	*Eretz**	291	12756.28	9.4538
Sun	*Shemesh**	640	1391000	14.1455
Mercury	*Kochav*	48	4879.4	8.4928
Jupiter	*Tzedek*	194	142984	11.8705
Saturn	*Shabtai*	712	120536	11.6997
Venus	*Nogah*	64	12103.8	9.4013
	Mazar	247	12103.8	9.4013
Mars	*Maadim*	95	6794.0	8.8238

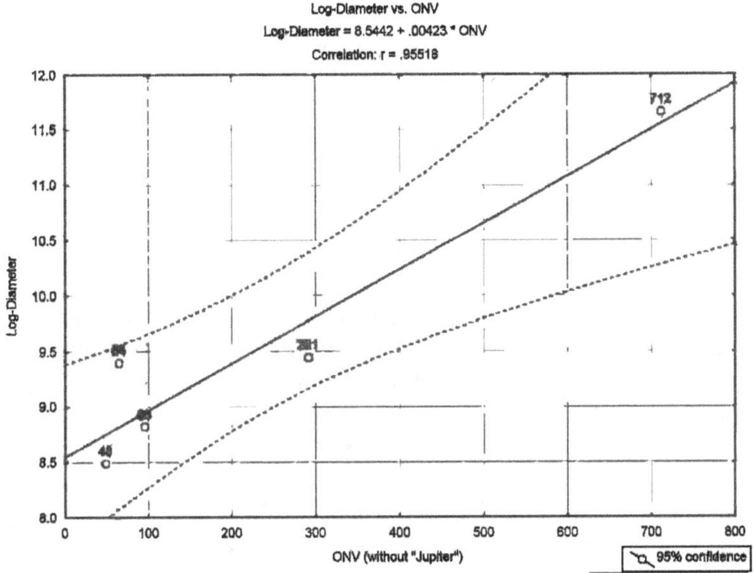

Figure 8.3. Plot of log-diameter of the planets (excluding Jupiter) as a function of their celestial object numerical values (ONV). All names (except Earth) are nonbiblical.

The former appears only once: "them also that burned incense to Ba'al, to the sun, and to the moon, and to the planets [*mazalot*[16]] and to all the host of heaven" (2 Kings 23:5). The latter also appears only once: "Can you bring forth the [*mazarot*[17]] in their seasons?" (Job 38:32).

The word *mazalot*[16] is common in modern Hebrew, and the singular form means, simply, luck. One can easily trace how this concept has evolved. The root of *mazal*[18] is *N.Z.L* (in *mazal,*[18] the *N* is "swallowed" in the *Z*, as often happens in Hebrew, and its concealed presence is then indicated by a point (a linguistic *mapik*)[20] in the Hebrew equivalent of *Z* (the letter *zayin*).[21] In the Hebrew language, the root *N.Z.L* is source to various words, all of which imply "to leak," "to drip," or to "flow (run) down." One can easily understand why the source of the Hebrew general name for planets is *mazalot,*[16] and why *mazal*[18] also means "luck." Planets are supposed to affect our lives, and their influence drips down to "make a difference" in our lives (this is basic astrological know-how, which needs no further elaboration if one is educated enough …).

But why does *mazar*[19] also mean "planet," and is this name intended for a particular planet?

An interesting theory is offered by Agnes M. Clerke (transcribed by Joseph P. Thomas), and expounded in detail at the Catholic Encylopedia web-site, at http://www.newadvent.org/cathen/02029a.htm#mazzaroth

The following quote is from this source, relating to *mazarot*[17] in Job:

> "Professor Schiaparelli then recurs to the Vulgate rendering of this passage. He recognizes in Mazzaroth the planet Venus in her double aspect of morning and evening star, pointing out that the luminary designated in the Book of Kings, with the sun and moon, and the "host of heaven" must evidently be next in brightness to the chief light-givers. Further, the sun, moon, and Venus constitute the great astronomical triad of Babylonia, the sculptured representations of which frequently include the "host of heaven" typified by a crowd of fantastic animal-divinities. And since the astral worship anathematized by the prophets of Israel was unquestionably of Euphratean origin, the designation of Mazzaroth as the third member of the Babylonian triad is a valuable link in the evidence. Still, the case remains one of extreme difficulty."

Obviously, the author was unaware that *mazarot*[17] is the plural of *mazar*,[19] but the basic argument makes sense. Since the allusion in Job to *mazarot*[17] is to their cyclic appearance in heaven "in their seasons" (or, in literal Hebrew, "in their times"), and since Venus is the most luminary star after the sun and the moon, it is highly likely that Venus was called *Mazar*,[19] and then this concept was generalized to include all planets (*mazarot*).[17] This interpretation is strengthened if one observes the root of the word *Mazar*.[19] It is *N.Z.R* (similarly to *N.Z.L of mazal*.)[18] The *N.Z.R* root is the source for the Hebrew word *nezer*,[22] which means "crown" (of a king). An example: "and I took the crown [*nezer*[22]] that was upon his head, and the bracelet that was on his arm, and have brought them here to my lord" (2 Samuel 1:10).

One can hardly conceive of a better term than *Mazar*[19] to denote the most luminary star in heaven (after the sun and the moon). This is particularly warranted if one remembers how the latter are described in Genesis: "And God made the two great lights; the greater light *to rule* the day, and the lesser light *to rule* the night" (Gen. 1:16).

It is our educated conjecture that *Mazar*[19] was the original word for Venus, the third "royalty" after the sun and the moon, and then it was generalized to all planets, as insinuated in Job (similar things happen all the time; for example, refer to the term "to xerox"). Since the Hebrew *R* and *L* are both "tongue letters," *Mazar*[19] probably evolved in ancient times into *mazal*,[18] so as to be consistent with the common belief (in ancient times—or, some would argue, even in modern times) that luck flows down from the planets to influence fates of human beings.

How well is this conjecture (that Venus was originally called *Mazar*)[19] aligned with the statistical results of the previous subsection?

In fact, incredibly well!

The numerical value of the word *Mazar*[19] is

$$247 = (200 = \text{ר}) + (7 = \text{ז}) + (40 = \text{מ})$$

With this value for the ONV of Venus, the linear regression analysis of the previous subsection was rerun to produce the results shown in Figure 8.4.

The improvement over Figure 8.3, where the observation relating to Venus (*Nogah*)[14] nearly touches the upper confidence-interval limit, is considerable. This also shows in the resulting statistics.

The correlation of 0.9552 in the earlier analysis (Figure 8.3) has now "jumped" to 0.9961. The model F-ratio is 386.4, which, for n = 5, is highly significant (p<0.000288). In other words, the probability that the five points in the figure would align themselves on a straight line, the way they did, by chance alone, is less than 0.029%!

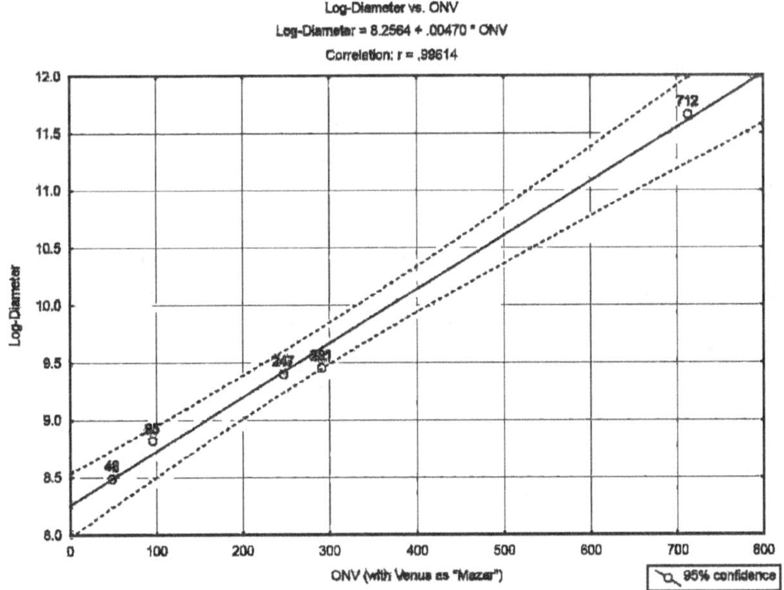

Figure 8.4. Plot of log-diameter of the planets (excluding Jupiter) as a function of their celestial object numerical values (ONV). All names (except Earth and possibly Venus) are nonbiblical. Hebrew for Venus is *Mazar*.

8.3.5   *Jupiter is Shachar*[23]

Jupiter is the largest planet in the solar system, with a mass that is more than twice that of all the other planets combined (the mass of Jupiter is 318 times that of Earth). Jupiter is also the fourth brightest object in the sky after the sun, the moon, and Venus. No wonder, therefore, that throughout history, planet Jupiter has been assigned a unique status by various peoples. Thus, the Greeks and the Romans named this planet after the most important deity in their pantheons (Zeus and Jupiter, respectively).

Both Venus and Jupiter are sometimes also called morning stars. This is due to the fact that both planets are often visible with the morning twilight. Thus, in they ear 2006, Venus may be seen in morning twilight from January 19 to September 19. Likewise, Jupiter may be seen in the period of January 1–May 4, and also in most of December (December 5–31).

Shachar[23] in modern Hebrew is "dawn." This is also how this word is regularly interpreted in English translations of the Bible. However, the correct biblicalt ranslation is "morning twilight," and this is indeed how *shachar*[23] is regularly interpreted by most Jewish scholars (observe, for example, Isa. 58:8, and how *shachar*[23] is interpreted therein by both Rashi and the Malbim).

The claim made here is that the planet Jupiter is referred to in the Bible as *Shachar.*[23] Furthermore, only in later years had the name of this planet evolved into the nonbiblical *Tzedek* (also meaning, in Hebrew, "justice"), for a possible reason that will be expounded shortly.

There are several arguments to support this claim. First, Jewish scholars occasionally relate to *shachar*[23] as the "morning star." Thus, in Song of Songs, we have, "Who is she that appears like the dawn [*shachar*[23]], fair as the moon, bright as the sun, majestic as the stars in procession?" (Song of Songs 6:10). One can wonder what "dawn" is doing amongst all these celestial objects. Indeed, "Metzudat David" and "Metzudat Zion" (pseudonyms for the eighteenth-century famous commentators Rabbi David Altschuler and his son Yechiel) interpret *shachar*[23] here as "morning star." One can easily interpret this as referring to Jupiter. Secondly, referring to the predicted fall of the king of Babylon, Isaiah refers to his destiny thus: "How art thou fallen from heaven, O bright star [*hillel*], son of dawn [*shachar*[23]]" (Isa. 14:11). While *hillel* obviously can be interpreted as a bright celestial object, one wonders at the use of the phrase "son of dawn." This hardly makes sense. Conversely, if one believes that Isaiah is conveying the word of God, then recalling that there are over sixty-three satellite moons orbiting Jupiter, then calling the future fallen king as the son of planet Jupiter does make sense. Similar analyses can be extended with regard to other uses of *shachar*[23] where interpreting it as a "morning star" makes more sense than simply "dawn" (for example, refer to Job 38:12).

So how has *shachar*[23] evolved from a "morning star" (probably Jupiter) into *tzedek* ("justice" in Hebrew)? We believe that this has to do with a certain verse in Isaiah: "Then your light will break forth like the dawn [*shachar*[23]], and your healing will quickly appear; then your righteousness [your *tzedek*] will go before you, and the glory of the Lord will be your guard" (Isa. 58:8). Recall that *mazar* evolved into *mazal*, possibly to signify how the influence of the planets "leak" unto "humans." So possibly the most "influential" star in heaven, the king of the deities in Greek and Roman pantheons (namely, Jupiter), had come to signify that "justice" also is determined in heaven. Jupiter as *Shachar*[23] thus rendered into the nonbiblical name *Tzedek*.

To examine this conjecture, namely, that Jupiter was originally called *Shachar*,[23] we step into so far uncharted territory, and attempt to assign meanings to names of celestial objects that appear in the Bible, yet their true meanings are obscure. Earlier (section 8.3.3) we related to some of these names, however we emphasized therein that these names are traditionally interpreted as representing groups of stars with noticeable constellations in the sky. We now discard this assumption, and relate to these names as those of planets. There are four such names: *Kimah*[24] (Amos 5:8; Job 9:9, 38:31), *Ksil*[25] (Isa.13:10; Amos 5:8; Job 9:9, 38:31), *Ash*[26a] (occasionally also *Aish*[26b]) and *Teman*[27] (Job 9:9). The latter means in biblical Hebrew also south. An additional biblical name for a celestial object is *Kochav*,[11] which, in biblical Hebrew, simply means star. We include this word to imply also one of the planets (in Table 8.2 it stands for Mercury).

Which planets do these names possibly represent?

Sorting the ONVs of these five names, plus *Mazar*[19] and *Shachar*,[23] in an ascending order, and doing likewise for the seven planets' equatorial diameters (excluding Earth), Table 8.3 is obtained (corresponding to Table 8.2).

Table 8.3. Data for celestial planets with biblical names.

Name	Hebrew name	ONV	Equatorial diameter (km)	Log-diameter
Pluto	*Kochav*[11]	48	2302	7.7415
Mercury	*Kimah*[24]	75	4879.4	8.4928
Mars	*Ksil*[25]	120	6794.0	8.8238
Venus	*Mazar*[19]	247	12103.8	9.4013
Neptune	*Ash*[26a]	370	49528	10.8103
Saturn	*Teman*[27]	490	120536	11.6997
Jupiter	*Shachar*[23]	508	142984	11.8705

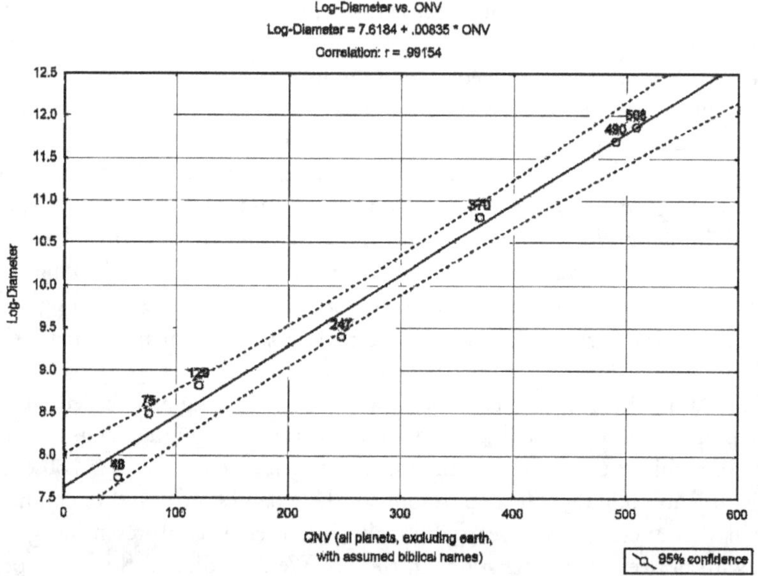

Figure 8.5. Plot of log-diameter of the planets as a function of their celestial object numerical values (ONV). All planets' names are biblical.

Linear regression analysis was applied to the entire sample of seven biblical names (note that planet Earth is not included since it is not mentioned in the bible as a celestial object). For the present analysis, we obtain adjusted R-squared of 0.9797. The model F-ratio is 291.9, which, for n = 7, is highly significant (p<0.00001). In other words, the probability that the seven points in this analysis would align themselves on a straight line, the way they did, by chance alone, is less than 0.001% (*vs.* 0.029% for the previous analysis)!

Figure 8.5 displays the results of this analysis. Since Venus (*Mazar*[19]) and Pluto (*Kochav*[28]) are close to the 95% confidence interval limits, the previous analysis was rerun without these observations. For this analysis, the adjusted R-squared is 0.9998. The model F-ratio has jumped to 22421, which, for n = 5, is highly significant (p<0.00000). In other words, the probability that the five points in this analysis would align themselves on a straight line, the way they did, by chance alone, is less than 0.0001% (vs. 0.001% for the previous analysis)!

Figure 8.6 shows the observations of the last analysis with 95% confidence interval limits (hardly distinguishable from the regression line).

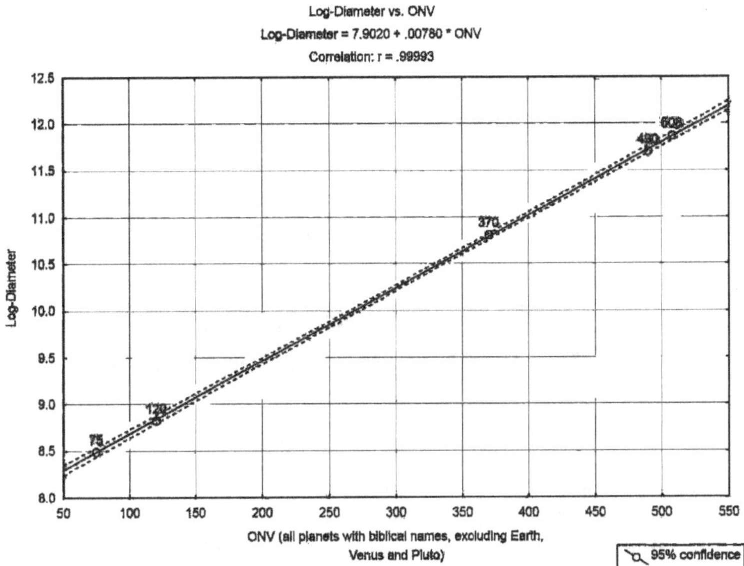

Figure 8.6. Plot of log-diameter of the planets as a function of their ONV, excluding Earth, Venus and Pluto.

These are all coincidences … or maybe not.

CHAPTER 9

"Water," "Clouds," "Fog," and Other Water-Related Words

Water in all its shapes and forms abound in nature. Naturally, it enters as a main constituent in many Hebrew words, with design revealed in unexpected patterns and relationships between words. In this chapter, we address bizarre coincidences, or signs of design, that one can detect in water-related words and phrases. Some of the material in this chapter has been introduced in detail in earlier chapters, and therefore will be displayed here only briefly.

There are four sections in this chapter:

9.1 Water and its properties

9.2 Water-carrying "substances"

9.3 The water cycle and the water path from underground to the river

9.4 Water heat capacity

9.1 Water in Hebrew (*Mayim*)

A first distinction that one can make between "water" in Hebrew (*mayim*)[1] and in English refers to how water is related to in the two languages: it is singular in English and plural in Hebrew. It is hard to pinpoint any logical reason for this bizarre difference until one learns the very special structure of the Hebrew *mayim*,[1] and why this structure leads to the logical acceptance of this word as plural.

A second feature of the Hebrew word *mayim*,[1] not unrelated to the previous one, is its association with symmetry in more ways than one. This was discussed at some length in section 5.3, and the reader is referred to that section for further detail.

132

In this section, the focus is on another property of water, which is revealed as hidden information in the structure of a Hebrew word related to water.

In section 2.1.3, we referred to the bizarre phenomenon that the numerical values of certain Hebrew words comprise repeated appearance of a single digit, which is strongly linked to an essential property of the object that the word represents. The example given was the root of the word for "firstborn" (*bechor*[2] in Hebrew; refer to section 2.1.3). The root of *bechor*,[2] B.K.R, yields: 2+20+200 = 222. We elaborated on why 2 is so significantly associated with a firstborn. In section 10.3.4, we relate to another Hebrew word that demonstrates the same phenomenon.

Can the same be identified with respect to a Hebrew word related to water?

Bizarrely enough, yes.

Take the Hebrew word for snow: *sheleg*.[3] Since water is associated with three phases of existence (solid, liquid, and vapor), all of which coexist in regular environmental conditions (no laboratory is needed to produce any of these phases), one would expect a word for water to be associated with 3, just as human blood is associated with 4 (since there are four human blood groups).

With *sheleg*,[3] the "significant" digit, 3, repeatedly appears in the numerical value of the word (though in reverse order relative to *bechor*):[2] 300+30+3 = 333. We realize that each succeeding letter in the word *sheleg*[3] has a smaller numerical value, but each of these values is a multiple of 3, and the total sum is 333. This is shown below:

$$333 = (3 = \text{ג}) + (30 = \text{ל}) + (300 = \text{ש})$$

Thus, a word which stands for one of the three possible states of water in nature convey by the numerical values of its constituent letters, as well as by their total sum, a basic property of water—namely, that it naturally exists in either of three different basic phases (solid, liquid, and vapor).

Finally, it is interesting to note that other Hebrew words that stand for water in its other modes of existence (nonliquid water) carry very close numerical values. Thus, ice is *kerach*,[4] with a numerical value of 308, and steam is *kitor*,[5] with a numerical value of 325. Section 9.4 shows that this is probably not a coincidence.

9.2 Water-Carrying Substances

The word *ayin*[6] in Hebrew conveys at least three different meanings: it can mean "a source of water" (a fountain) or "eye," and it is the name of the seventeenth letter in the Hebrew alphabet, with a numerical value of 70. (A fourth meaning, "color," is the subject of statistical analysis in section 10.3.3.)

Being "source of water" common to all these different senses of the word *ayin*[6] (the name of the letter simply means "an eye"), it is only natural to expect that design, visible in the structure of various Hebrew words, would also manifest itself, in words related to water production, by having the letter *ayin* appear in their roots.

Indeed, examining various Hebrew words, the common denominator of which is that they all relate to objects carrying water, one finds that these words invariably start with the letter *ayin*.

Examples:

- A cloud is *anan*;[7] *ayin* is its first letter.
- A cloud is *av*[8] (often, a small cloud); *ain* is its first letter.
- Fog is *arafel*;[9] *ayin* is its first letter.
- Clouds, in proverbial speech, are *arifim*[10] (a rare word, which can be found, for example, in Isa. 5:30); *ayin* is the first letter.

Comments

1. The word *av*,[8] for cloud, is interesting. It has as its root *A.B.H.* This root gives rise to words implying "thick" (*aveh*).[11] Thus, *av*[8] conveys the concept of condensation (thickening) of water vapor into droplets that form the cloud. The process by which a cloud is formed is thus conveyed.

2. The above four words describe a source of water, and they all start with *ayin*. However, the latter is the Hebrew name of the two epitomes for water-producing sources—namely, "fountain" and "eye," both named *ayin*.[6]

9.3 The Water Cycle

The continuous circular process in which water evaporates from the oceans (mainly), condenses, falls to earth (as rain, snow, or hail), and eventually returns to the oceans (through runoff in rivers or streams) is called the natural water cycle, also known as the hydrologic cycle. A major player in this cycle is the environment temperature. The earth water first vaporizes through low pressure but (mostly) high temperature. Rising from the surface of the earth into the atmosphere, it encounters a decrease in temperature, condenses to form clouds, which subsequently, when the temperature and atmospheric pressure are right, form large enough raindrops to cause precipitation. Some water is absorbed by plants and returned directly to the atmosphere as vapor.

The natural water cycle has been known for quite some time. Yet, taking into account that biblical texts relate to the water cycle, and that they are at least two and a half thousand years old, this may be an interesting coincidence. There are three places where the Bible relates to the hydrological cycle:

- "But there went up a mist [*ed*,[12] meaning, in modern Hebrew, "vapor" or "mist"] from the earth, and watered the whole face of the ground" (Gen. 2:6).

- "He draws up the drops of water, which distill as rain to the streams; the clouds pour down their moisture and abundant showers fall on mankind. Who can understand how he spreads out the clouds, how he thunders from his pavilion?" (Job 36:27–29).

- "who calls for the waters of the sea and pours them out over the face of the land——the Lord is his name" (Amos 5:8).

Job is estimated to have lived 950 BC or earlier, and the prophet Amos is estimated to have lived around 755 BC.

The following section is taken from the Web site:

http://www.pytlik.com/observe/deliverus/signature-02.html:

"This reference to evaporation is startling in its clarity and detail, and centuries ahead of its time. God revealed the existence of a hydrological cycle—water evaporating from the sea into the form of clouds and being dropped onto land as rain—about 3500 years before these concepts became known to scientific man. In fact, even after people understood the hydrological cycle, they believed that rain, being fresh water, came from rivers and lakes. The discovery that rain comes mostly from seawater as described in the Bible is fairly recent. In the 1600's it was finally realized that water could evaporate as a gaseous substance. In 1676, Pierre Perrault and Edme Marriotte made a scientific breakthrough by describing the hydrologic cycle in detail."

Find further details therein.

9.4 Water Heat Capacity

Heat capacity, or thermal capacity, is the ability of matter to store heat. The heat capacity of a certain amount of matter is the quantity of heat (measured in joules) required to raise its temperature by one Kelvin. SI denotes the International System of Units. The SI unit for heat capacity is J/K (joule per Kelvin).

Heat capacity can be measured using calorimetry.
The specific heat capacity (SHC) of a substance is defined as heat capacity per unit mass. It is commonly denoted by symbols like c or s, and occasionally called just specific heat.

The SI unit for SHC is joule per kilogram Kelvin, $J{\cdot}kg^{-1}{\cdot}K^{-1}$, or $J/(kg{\cdot}K)$. This is the amount of energy (heat) required to raise the temperature of one kilogram of the substance by one degree Kelvin. The equivalent definition using CGS (centimeter, gram, second) units is the amount of energy (measured in ergs) required to raise the temperature of one gram of the substance by one degree Celsius ($erg/(g{\cdot}°C)$). Other units of SHC include calories per gram degree Celsius ($cal/(g{\cdot}°C)$ or $cal/(g{\cdot}K)$), and Btu per pound degree Fahrenheit ($Btu/(lb{\cdot}°F)$)

The symbol c_p is often used to denote SHC at constant pressure.
Substances with low SHC, such as metals, require less input energy to increase their temperature. Substances with high specific heat, such as water, require much more energy to increase their temperature. The specific heat can also be interpreted as a measure of how well a substance preserves its temperature (i.e., "stores" heat—hence the term "heat capacity").

Water is often used as a basic standard relative to which SHC values are compared. However, the water's SHC depends on which state it is in. Frozen water (that is, ice), liquid water, and gaseous water (that is, steam) have different SHCs.

Table 9.1 displays SHC for all three states of water, measured in $J/(kg{\cdot}K)$.

The Hebrew words for these three water phases—namely, *kerach*[12] (ice), *mayim*[1] (water), and *kitor*[13] (steam), have the following numerical values, respectively (spelled consistently with how these words appear in the Bible):

$$308 = (8 = \text{ח}) + (200 = \text{ר}) + (100 = \text{ק})$$

$$90 = (40 = \text{ם}) + (10 = \text{י}) + (40 = \text{מ})$$

$$325 = (200 = \text{ר}) + (6 = \text{ו}) + (9 = \text{ט}) + (10 = \text{י}) + (100 = \text{ק})$$

These water numerical values (WNV) are displayed in Table 9.1.

Table 9.1. Specific heat capacity, C_p (at constant atmospheric pressure) for water in its various phases (in joule per kilogram per 1 degree Kelvin) with respective numerical values of the biblical Hebrew names, WNV (water numerical values). Source: http://www.engineeringtoolbox.com/

| | Heat capacity | |
Phase	J / (kg-Kelvin)	WNV
Ice ("Kerach") at 0C°	2050	308
Water ("Mayim") at 25C°	4181	90
Steam ("Kitor") at 100C°	1970	325

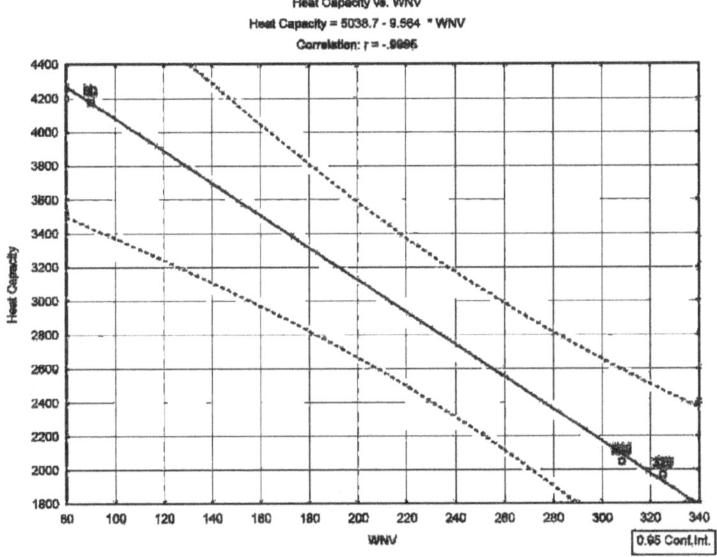

Figure 9.1. Specific heat capacity for the three phases of water (water, ice, steam) as a function of their Hebrew names' WNV (water numerical values).

Linear regression analysis was applied with water's SHC values as the response (the dependent variable) and the WNV values as the regressor (the independent variable).

For sample size n = 3, the linear correlation coefficient is -0.9999, with R^2-adjusted value of 0.9997. The model F-ratio is 3704, which at the 5% level is significant (p = 0.01046). In other words, the likelihood of the three points to be aligned on a straight line, as was obtained, by chance alone, is about 1%.

The original observations with the fitted regression equation and 95% confidence limits are shown in Figure 9.1. For easy identification, the WNV value is given atop each observation. Predicted values may be easily calculated from the regression equation included in the plot's caption.

These are all coincidences ... maybe.

CHAPTER 10

The Human Body

There are several features that characterize Hebrew words relating to parts of the human body. They may generally be typified by the following:

- Hebrew letters are often named after parts of the human body.
- Hebrew names of parts of the human body are often informative of their mutual relationships with one another.
- Hebrew names of parts of the human body are often informative of main visible, or hidden, functions, some of which could hardly be known in ancient times.

In this chapter, we discuss these properties and demonstrate them.

10.1 Hebrew Letters as Parts of the Human Body

It is indeed unusual to find so many of the Hebrew letters named after parts of the human body, either by carrying identical names or close ones. As explained in chapter 1, each letter's name is indicative of its major function within a Hebrew word. It may therefore come as no surprise that this function frequently bears resemblance to the main function of the part of the human body, after which the letter is named.

Following is a list of all Hebrew letters, arranged in alphabetical order, which are given names identical to those of parts of the human body, or closely resemble these names (there are six such letters, with their numerical values in parentheses):

- *yod* (10)—like *yad*,[1] meaning "hand";
- *kaf*[2] (20)—meaning "palm" (of a hand or a leg); sometimes also used for "hand"; this letter comes right after the *yod*;
- *ayin*[3] (70)—meaning "eye";
- *peh*[4] (80)—meaning "mouth"; this letter comes right after the *ayin*;[3]
- *resh* (200)—like *rosh*,[5] meaning "head"; in Aramaic, *resh* means "head";
- *shin* (300)—like *shen*,[6] meaning "tooth"; this letter comes right after *resh*.

Out of the twenty-two letters of the Hebrew alphabet (not including "final letters"), over a quarter are named after parts of the human body, which epitomize modes of interaction of the human body with the outer world. Furthermore, for each of these functions, there are strict laws in the Bible about what is permitted and what is not.

Examples:

- The letter *ayin* (meaning eye): "And you shall not tour after your heart and after your eyes" (Num. 15:39);
- The letter *peh*[4] (meaning mouth): "You shall not slander" (Lev. 19:16);
- The letter *resh* (resembling *rosh*,[5] "head"), in the Tenth Commandment: "Thou shalt not covet thy neighbor's house, thou shalt not covet thy neighbor's wife, nor his ..." (Exod. 20:14).

A recent book by Jeff A. Benner (2004) refers to the history of the ancient Hebrew pictographic alphabet—attempting to explain, among other things, the high frequency of human body parts in the names and structure of Hebrew letters.

10.2 Human Body Parts with Names Indicative of Mutual Relationships

Earlier in the book, several examples were introduced that demonstrated that letters in certain positions, shared by different words, were indicative of these words' mutual relationships (section 2.2). The most prominent example given was familial genealogy, where the last letter of an earlier generation is the first letter of the next. Similar patterns may be traced in how human organs relate to one another.

Examples:

- The Hebrew word for the upper part of the leg is *yerech*[7] (thigh); the knee, which connects the leg's upper part to the lower part, is *berech*;[8] the two words share the same last two letters (*resh* and *kaf*, as appropriate since *berech*[8] is part of *yerech*:[7]

ירך ← ברך

- *Rosh*[5] (head) ends with *S* (*shin*). This is the first letter of *se'ar*[9] (hair); conversely, the last letter of "hair" (*se'ar*[9]) is the first letter of "head" (*rosh*);[5] *safa*[10] (lip) is part of the *rosh*[5] (head); therefore, the last letter of the latter (*shin*) is the first letter of the former:

ראש ← שיער

ראש ← שפה

- *Metzach*[11] means forehead; being part of the *panim*[12] (face), the first letter of *mezach*[11] is the last letter of *panim*[12] (face); *peh*[4] (namely, "mouth"), being part of the *panim*[12] (face), shares the same first letter with the latter; *safa*[10] (lip), being part of the *peh*[4] (mouth), shares the same last two letters with the latter (as in the first example above):

פנים ← מצח

פנים ← פה

פה ← שפה

- *Leshad*[13] means "fat" or "fattish" or "juicy" (for example, Num. 11:8). Breast is *shad*.[14] The two words share the last two letters; *dad*[15] means nipple. The last letter of *shad*[12] (breast) is the first letter of *dad*:[15]

שד ← לשד

שד ← דד

In summary, dependent on how closely related two organs are, they share either the first letter or the last letter or the last two letters. If the Hebrew language judges one part to be indeed a component of the other—two letters are shared (like in the two examples given). More remote relationships may result in sharing of only one letter (at the head or at the end of the word).

10.3 Hebrew Names with Revealed (Hidden) Information

10.3.1 Face

The Hebrew word for face is *panim*.[16] It has several interesting features. While "face" in English is singular, it is given in plural form in Hebrew (*-im* indicates the plural for masculine gender). In modern Hebrew, the singular *pan* conveys the meaning of "respect" or "aspect" (as in "this statement has several aspects to it"). One may ponder the good justification for denoting "face" as plural.

The same letters comprising *panim*,[16] though with different vocalization, is *pnim*,[16] which means also "inside." (The biblical Hebrew does not have letters serving as vowels; this function is reserved for the *nikud,* the signs above and below the letters, which deliver the vocalization of the word.) One may again ponder the appropriateness of calling a "face" by the same word as "inside": there is no other human organ more appropriate than the *panim*[16] to surrender one's *pnim*,[16] the internal feelings and thoughts (a dog's tail serves the same function, nearly …)

10.3.2 Ear

A major function of the human ear is to hear. This is anyone's experience. However, an additional major function, perhaps somewhat less widely recognized, is that the ear is residence for a complex mechanism that keeps the body balanced. That the inner ear is responsible for this major function was not recognized until the mid-nineteenth century. As conveyed to us by the Howard Hughes Medical Institute's "Ask a Scientist" service (http://www.hhmi.org/askascientist/index.html; Our appreciation for this service), one cannot indicate a particular individual for the discovery of the balance mechanism within the ear. Many contributed to its gradual discovery over the nineteenth century and the beginning of the twentieth century.

In 1914, Robert Bárány was awarded the Nobel Prize for his work, among other things, on the vestibular apparatus, the balance mechanism in the human ear. In his Nobel lecture (September 11, 1916), Bárány gave an account of the history of the research that led to the discovery of the function of the vestibular apparatus. The edited lecture is accessible at http://nobelprize.org/nobel_prizes/medicine/laureates/1914/press.html.

We provide here some highlights from this source, in the form of quotations (clarifying details are added when deemed necessary):

"Up until the nineteenth century, there was a complete lack of knowledge of the function of the vestibulosemicircular apparatus. The first to begin experimental investigations in this field was the celebrated French physiologist Flourens" (Marie-Jean-Pierre Flourens, 1794–1867). "His investigations were published in 1825. Flourens thought that it would be possible to get an insight into the function of the semi-circular canal apparatus by destroying it. In fact, these experiments which were undertaken with pigeons, rabbits, and other animals produced quite remarkable constant and previously unknown disturbances." Yet, Flourens "did not have the faintest idea that the animals were suffering from vertigo" because "well-known symptoms of vertigo in humans are too different from those in animals for Flourens to be able to see this connection." Neither was aware of the significance of the phenomenon another physiologist in Prague, Purkinje, who, unknown to Flourens, investigated vertigo in humans. "As neither of these two great research scientists was able to find the solution to the mystery, it is small wonder that none of their contemporaries were able to do so either."

Science stood still for nearly forty years. Only in the year 1861 was a Frenchman, Ménière, able to take a bold step forward: "Vertigo, it was thought at the time, could only be caused by a disease of the cerebellum. Ménière observed this kind of patients for years and saw no symptoms of brain disease. Apart from Flourens's experiments, the semicircular canal apparatus, which is connected to the cochlea"—responsible for hearing—"was at that time thought to have no function."

Ménière now had the idea that the vertigo phenomena were symptoms of disease in the semicircular canal apparatus, and he now succeeded, where Flourens and Purkinje had failed, in seeing through the confusing diversity of the vertigo manifestations in humans and in animals, and recognizing that those animals, whose semicircular canals had been operated upon by Flourens, had vertigo. This was the principal great achievement of the man—who, unfortunately, did not survive to enjoy the fame of his discovery. "Ménière did not express himself as regards the importance of the semicircular canal apparatus in normal life. The first to produce a theory on this was the German physiologist, Goltz, in 1870. He thought approximately as follows: if the destruction of the semicircular canal apparatus gives rise to vertigo and imbalance, then the normal function of this apparatus must be to maintain equilibrium. And he formulated a theory as to how this might be so," which "subsequently proved to be incorrect."

"Only a few years later, in 1874, three men arrived, all at the same time, at a theory concerning the semicircular canal apparatus, which is even today, broadly speaking, is correct. These were a general practitioner who is still alive, Dr. Joseph Breuer in Vienna, Ernst Mach, who died last year, and the American, Crum Brown, in Philadelphia … these are the founders of the theory of the semicircular canal apparatus."

Thus far from Bárány's lecture of September 1916.

What does the Hebrew language consider as the ear's major function?

- **The Hebrew word for "ear" is *ozen*.**[17]
- ***Ozen*[17] derives from the same root as "balance": *A.Z.N.***

There are numerous Hebrew words in the Bible that derive from this root and relate to balance. Two examples are

- *moznaim*:[18] balance, scales for measuring weight; this word appears, with variations, fifteen times in the Bible (for example, in Lev. 19:36);
- *veizen*:[19] "and he weighed" (or "balanced," Eccles. 12:9).

In other words, according to the ancient biblical Hebrew, and in contemporary Hebrew as well, the main function of the ear is not *hearing* but *balancing* (the human body), a function that was finally exposed, with much surprise, in the late years of the nineteenth century!

10.3.3 Eye

The Hebrew word for "eye," *ayin*,[3] has several additional meanings in Hebrew. One was related earlier: the letter *ayin* is the seventeenth letter in the Hebrew alphabet. However, the most common alternative meaning is "a fountain." In fact, as shown in chapter 9, many Hebrew nouns that imply "source of water" start with the same letter, *ayin*. These include "cloud" (*anan*),[20] "fog" (*arafel*),[21] and various other synonyms (like *av*).[22]

The major function of the eye is to see. As we realized earlier (with ear), the Hebrew language occasionally "prefers" to name a body part by its supplementary invisible function (like "balance" for ear). Thus, according to Hebrew, a major function of the eye is to be a source of fluid, where water is a main component. This is indeed bizarre. Any individual can deduce that there is some source in the eye that allows tears to be formed when a person is in an emotional agitation. But is there a source in the eye that *constantly* "produces" and gives away fluid, like a fountain?

The various parts of the eye anatomy can be divided into front end and back end. The front end comprises eight different parts:

trabecular meshwork

ciliary body

lens

iris

pupil

cornea

aqueous humor

canal of Schlemm

Four of these functions (half) are associated with an "irrigation system" that constantly pumps fluid into the eye, like a fountain (*ayin*)[3], with no relevance to the sight function. Here are the descriptions of these functions:

- Aqueous humor: the watery fluid that fills the chambers at the front of the eye, produced by the ciliary body.

- Ciliary body: the thickened part of the vascular portion of the eye that lies between the iris and the choroid (the vascular membrane that covers the eye between the retina and the sclera). It is responsible for producing the aqueous humor that circulates in the chambers of the eye.

- Trabecular meshwork: a network of fibers responsible for draining the aqueous humor from the eye.

- Canal of Schlemm: a circular canal between the cornea and the iris that provides an exit for the aqueous humor from the eye into the bloodstream.

Interestingly, the latter organ, named after Friedrich Schlemm (1795–1859), is also named Fontana's canal, after the eighteenth century Italian chemist Felice Fontana (1730–1805), who had described the new canal in the eye in a publication from 1787.

The name Fontana seems like a proper name for an investigator of a human organ called in Hebrew "a fountain."

Comments

The meaning of *ayin* in Hebrew is also "color." As we detail in the chapter dedicated to colors (chapter 12), the human eye has three receptors for colors, which perceive red, green and blue (RGB), one color each. By mixing these colors in various intensities, the human eye produces all other colors. Correspondingly, all man-made devices that are intended to produce visible colors (like printers or color screens) do it by mixing these three primary colors (refer for details to Wikipedia, the free encyclopedia, at http://en.wikipedia.org/wiki/Colour_vision).

Assuming that the three letters comprising *ayin*, the Hebrew "eye," represent the three primary colors for which receptors exist in the human eye, linear regression analysis was applied. In this analysis, the RGB wave frequencies served as response values (midvalue frequencies, as given in Table 12.3 for each of the RGB colors, were used). The numerical values of the letters comprising *ayin*, sorted in an ascending order (like RGB), served as the regressor (the color numerical value, CNV, is employed as the independent variable).

A correlation of 0.9962 is obtained, with F-ratio value of 130.57. For n = 3, the significance value obtained is bordering the limit value, set for all analyses in this book (p = 0.05557, while the upper bound set for p values of all analyses is 0.050).

This close-to-significance result implies that the word *ayin*—commonly used in Hebrew to mean "eye" but bizarrely means also "color"—conveys information about wave frequencies of colors that dedicated receptors in the human eye were designed to receive and detect!

Figure 10.1 displays a scatter plot, along with the fitted regression line. Observations are identifiable by the CNV value atop each observation. Interestingly, the three human receptors for the red, green, and blue colors attain their peak sensitivity at 517.2, 551.5, and 681.8 THz (refer to the previously cited Web site), and not at midvalues of the ranges that define each of the RGB colors. When regression analysis is applied to these peak-sensitivity values, the good statistical fit, attained with the true RGB midvalues, is lost and highly statistically nonsignificant results are obtained.

10.3.4 Human Blood

Human blood comprises four blood groups: A, B, AB, and O (null). That different groups of human blood existed was unknown in ancient times. It had been discovered by Karl Landsteiner (1868–1943), who received in 1930 the Nobel Prize in physiology or medicine "for the discovery of human blood groups."

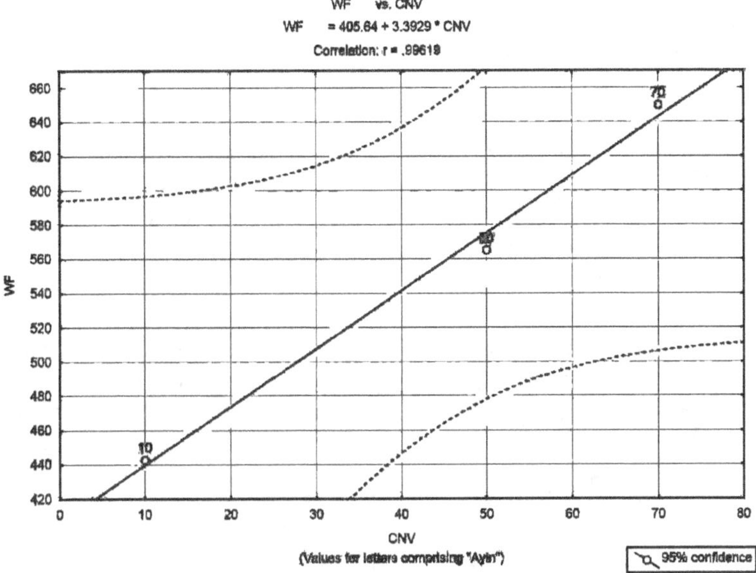

Figure 10.1. Wave frequency (WF) of the colors perceived by receptors in the human eye (red, green, blue) as a function of the letters comprising *ayin*: *yod* (10), *nun* (50), and *ayin* (70), respectively.

In 1901–03, Landsteiner pointed out that a pathological reaction, seen when a man is given transfusion of the blood from other animals, can also be seen when the blood of one human individual is transfused with that of another human being. His findings received little attention until, in 1909, he classified the blood of human beings into the now well-known blood groups and showed that transfusions between individuals of same groups A or B do not result in the destruction of new blood cells, and that this catastrophe occurs only when a person is transfused with the blood of a person belonging to a different group.

More details about blood groups and their discovery by Landsteiner may be found at the Nobel Foundation site: http://search.nobelprize.org.

Earlier, we demonstrated how adding the numerical values of letters comprising a certain word may result in a number that comprises repeated appearances of a single digit (section 2.1.3). Thus, the name of the first letter in the Hebrew alphabet, *alef*, which stands for God, submits a total sum of 111, emphasizing the oneness of God (the heart and soul of monotheism). Similarly, we realized that the root of the word for firstborn (*bechor*), B.K.R, results in the number 222. This signifies the main distinguishing feature of a firstborn—namely, that according to biblical law, the firstborn is legally entitled to inherit double the portion of each of the other children in the family (Deut. 21:17). Furthermore, each letter in the root *B.K.R* has numerical value double that of the preceding letter (in the alphabet), thus emphasizing the property which the word is intended to convey (this interpretation of the word *bechor* is attributed to the Gaon of Vilna, a Jewish sage living in 1720–97).

This strange phenomenon of obtaining words that have total value consisting of a single repeated digit seems to convey an intention of wishing to alert the word-user to the prime significance and implication of the word. In other words, because it may convey important relevant information, proper attention should be given to the total sum of the numerical values of the letters in the word (or its root, if the word is a verbal noun).

In Hebrew, the numerical value of the Hebrew word for blood conveys a message about the four varieties of human blood, just as "snow" does regarding the three "varieties" of water:

$$\text{Blood} = dam^{23} = D.M. = 4 + 40 = 44$$

$$44 = (40 = \text{מ}) + (4 = \text{ד})$$

Each letter is related to 4. The total sum of the values of the letters is also a repeat of 4. Note that the latter does not necessarily and logically follows from the former. An example: *dalet* (4) + *tav* (400) = 404.

(*Dat*,[24] written *DT*, means "law, regulation" in biblical Hebrew. In nonbiblical Hebrew, as in today's most common usage, it means "religion.")

10.3.5   Kidney

The kidney is the part of the human body that destroy poisons that circulate in the blood, and excrete them in the form of urine out of the body.

"Kidney" in Hebrew is *kiliah*.[25] This word derives from the root *K.L.H.* This root generates a myriad of words, all of which imply "putting an end to": destroy, annihilate, finish off, finish, complete, "run out of." For example, *le-chalot*[26] means "to destroy"; *chalah*[27] means "he finished"; and *chalu ha-mayim*[28] means "run out of water."

10.3.6   The Human Hand

The human hand has a complex structure that qualifies it to do the many functions that it is supposed to execute. These functions require much flexibility in order to allow the human hand a large number of degrees of freedom in carrying out its movements.

The flexibility of the human hand in performing these many functions is reflected in the comparatively large number of bones in a human hand. The hand has at least twenty-seven bones, which may be divided into three groups:

- The wrist (carpus), which accounts for eight bones (arranged in two rows of four; these bones fit into a shallow socket formed by the bones o f the forearm).

- The palm (metacarpus) contains five bones, one to each of the five fingers (digits).

- The hand (see comment), consisting of five fingers, has fourteen digital bones. These are also called phalanx bones. A human hand contains two bones in the thumb and three in each of the four fingers (2+3*4 = 14). The name "phalanges" is commonly given to the bones that form fingers and toes. In primates such as humans and monkeys, the thumb and big toe have two phalanges, while the other fingers and toes consist of three.

Comments

Collins Dictionary (Hanks *et al.*, 1988) defines "hand" as "the prehensile part of the body at the end of the arm, consisting of a thumb, four fingers and a palm." It is difficult to judge which exact part of the arm biblical Hebrew refers to in the corresponding term for "hand." But it seems that according to the Hebrew language, the most important feature of the hand is its fingers, as proved by the calculation that follows.

In the Hebrew language, "hand" is *yad*.[1] The sum total of the letters comprising this word adds up to exactly fourteen, the number of bones in a human hand:

$$14 \leftarrow (4 = \text{ד}) + (10 = \text{י})$$

10.3.7 Summary of Main Points

In the Hebrew language:

Face = "the inside" (in plural, "multifaceted")

Ear = "balance" (unrelated to "hearing")

Eye = "fountain," "color" (unrelated to "seeing");
Blood ⇒ 4
Kidney = "extermination" (of poisons)
Hand ⇒ 14

And a statistical analysis showed that the numerical values of Hebrew letters comprising *ayin* (Hebrew for eye *and* color) stand for wave frequencies of colors perceived by dedicated receptors in the human eye.

These are all coincidences ... maybe.

CHAPTER 11

Light, Darkness, Black (Holes)

Words and phrases related to light abound in biblical Hebrew and in modern Hebrew. In this chapter, light, lack of light (black), and some related bizarre concepts, like "created darkness" and black holes, are explored.

The related subject of "colors" is addressed in chapters 10, 12, and 15. This chapter has three sections, corresponding to the three parts in the title. In section 11.1, we detail how the Hebrew language regards essential properties of light by comparing two Hebrew words that share the same root but have altogether different meanings. In section 11.2, we address how the root of "darkness" is related to in different Hebrew words in the Bible. The last section, 11.3, pinpoints an interesting, coincidental relationship between black and black holes in the Hebrew language (whatever black holes may mean). That section will also discuss "created darkness," as it is bizarrely alluded to in the Bible.

11.1 "River" and "Light"

"River" and "light" do not seem, at first glance, to have anything in common. Yet a more in-depth analysis may reveal that in view of the modern perception of light the two may resemble one another more than initially believed.

We begin this analysis by detailing essential and defining features of "river" and "light," concentrating on those that the two seem to share in common.

River

- **"It displays a dual behavior of both wave and a stream of particles."** Explanation: A river is a stream of water molecules that move in a certain direction, confined by the riverbed. Although showing properties of

a stream, a river also appears in waveform, and exhibit wavelike properties, as are all streams of water.

- **"Its path is determined by the curvature of space in which it travels."**
Explanation: The path of a river is curved according to the landscape in
which it passes. Thus, a river flowing near a mountain would tend to
change its course, adapting it in accordance with the "space curvature"
created by the mountain.

- **"It carries energy."** Explanation: Water in a river carries with it kinetic
energy, which can be converted into useful work—for example, in the
form of electric energy produced by hydraulic power plants.

Light (according to modern physics)

- **"It displays a dual behavior of both wave and a stream of particles."**
Light is known to exhibit properties of waves. Newton, in particular, was among the first scientists to learn the properties of light and
its wavelike behavior. However, it is only with modern physics (from
the beginning of the twentieth century) that the behavior of light, as a
stream of massless but energy-carrying particles, has been thoroughly
studied. These massless particles of energy are called photons, and they
are affected by curvature created in space by gravitation, just like any
object that does have defined mass (this phenomenon results from
Einstein's general relativity, and will be addressed in the next paragraph).
The particle-like properties of photons were finally confirmed by Arthur
Compton in 1923 via a series of experiments involving the elastic scat-
tering of electrons and protons. On the dual particle-like and wavelike
properties of photons, refer, for example, to Greene (2004, 85–86, 90).

- **"Its path is determined by the curvature of space in which it travels."**
Curvature in space, produced by a gravitation field, may divert the
course of light. This was one of the earliest predictions of Einstein's general theory of relativity. That prediction was first verified in a dramatic
way by a delegation, headed by Arthur Eddington—who, on May 29,
1919, at the time of a total eclipse of the sun, measured the deflection
of light from stars near the sun's corona (the stars were still visible at the
time of the eclipse). These measurements were found to be consistent
with Einstein's prediction (within the known measurement error). For
the first time, it was experimentally established that deflection of light is
caused by gravity (in this case, gravity of the sun) and, furthermore, that
gravity itself causes space to be curved. Einstein's general relativity has

thus shown that "light's path is determined by the curvature of space in which it travels." Not unlike a river.

- **"It carries energy."** Light, being considered as a stream of photons, is known to carry energy, as are all electromagnetic fields. The mathematical expression for the energy, carried by the basic elements of light, is given by Planck's formula, which expresses the photon's energy as

$$E = h\nu = 2\pi\hbar\nu$$

where ν is the light frequency, and h is Planck's constant.

Does biblical Hebrew recognize this basic correspondence between "light", as we know it today, and "river"? Strangely enough, the answer is yes.
In the Hebrew language:

"river" is *nahar*:[1]

$$(ר) + (ה) + (נ)$$

"Light" is naharah[2] (though *or* is the more common word):

$$(ה) + (ר) + (ה) + (נ)$$

Both these nouns derive from a common root: *N.H.R.* This root gives rise to verbs that preserves the original meanings of the corresponding nouns.
Examples for light:

- "Then thou wilt see, and be filled with light [*ve-nahart*[3]]" (Isa. 60:5).
- "They looked to him and are radiant [*ve-naharu*[4]] and their faces shall not be ashamed" (Pss. 34:6).
- "Let that day be darkness; Let not God inquire after it from above, nor let the light [*naharah*[2]] shine upon it" (Job 3:4).

The Hebrew word for river, *nahar*,[1] with its variants, appear in the Bible no fewer than 117 times in Hebrew, and 15 additional times in Aramaic (in which case it appears as *naharah*).[2] Additionally, a combination of "fire" (though not exactly light) and "river" appears once in the Bible, in the book of Daniel: "A fiery stream issued and came forth from before him" (Dan. 7:10).

Why should the Hebrew language, by a bizarre coincidence, combine in a single root such disparate concepts as "river" and "light"? How could "light," about which nothing was known in ancient times (not even its wavelike behavior), be equated with "river"?

11.2 Darkness

Darkness appears in the Bible numerous times. It makes first appearance already in the second sentence of Genesis: "and darkness was on the face of the deep" (Gen. 1:2). Only later was light created: "And God said, Let there be light: and there was light" (Gen. 1:3).

Genesis description of this sequence of events is interestingly consistent with how the formation of light, and darkness, with the gradual cooling down of the universe, is described according to the big bang model. The following description is largely based on Singh (2004) and Aczel (1999).

At the moment of creation, the universe was so hot that matter existed only in the form of plasma. This state implies that atoms could not exist, because atom nuclei could not hold on to their electrons. There were no atoms as we know them today. The universe was a plasma soup of simple nuclei and free electrons. However, there was one additional ingredient in the universe: there was a sea of light. But the light was not visible. Light interacted with charged particles, like electrons, and then scattered off in all directions. Since there were electrons but no atoms, the universe looked like fog; nothing specific could be seen. The universe was opaque, not transparent.

If lack of light, as we know it today, could be described as "darkness," then darkness permeated the universe. In other words, "darkness was on the face of the deep." Only about 380,000 years after the big bang, the expansion of the universe caused it to cool down to 3,000 degrees (Kaku 2005, 58), at which temperature electrons could be attached to nuclei and form stable neutral atoms of hydrogen and helium. A transition from plasma to atoms took place. In cosmology, this transition is called "recombination." Only at that epoch could light start to be seen. As Singh (2004) describes this, "recombination dramatically changed the behavior of the light that filled the universe" … "the moment of recombination was the first time in the history of the universe that rays of light could start to sail through space unhindered. It was as though the cosmic fog had suddenly lifted" … "the light that was present at the moment of recombination should still be beaming its way around the universe today" … "creating the cosmic microwave background (CMB) radiation, discovered in 1964 by Penzias and Wilson" (refer to Singh 2004 for details).

The Hebrew word for darkness is *choshech*.[5] This word derives from the root *Ch.S.K*, which essentially means "deprivation," "avoiding of," and "sparing." Thus, the Bible relates to a father who does not spank his child: "He that spares [*chosech*[5]] his rod hates his son" (Prov. 13:24). A person who has no cure is described in Hebrew as *chasuch marpae*[6] (cureless).

Both the Hebrew root for darkness and how darkness is described in the second verse of Genesis seem to be consistent with the description of the universe, prior to the recombination, as "deprived of light", when it was filled with "darkness" that looked like fog.

The prophet Joel, by bizarre coincidence, uses similar analogy, when he describes the final day of judgment: "For the day of the Lord comes, for it is near at hand; A day of darkness [*choshech*[5]] and of deep darkness [*aphela*[7]], a day of cloud and fog ..." (Joel 2:1, 2). Similarly, Moses, reminiscing about the giving of the Ten Commandments, speaks to the children of Israel: "And you came near and stood under the mountain; and the mountain burned with fire to the heart of heaven, darkness cloud and fog" (Deut. 4:11).

11.3   "Black" and Black Holes

"Black" in Hebrew is *shachor*.[8] The root of this word is *S.Ch.R*. That "black" in Hebrew is associated with this root is strange, since that same root is source for many other words that convey meanings nearly opposite to that of black. For example, *sachar*[9] means the first rays of light in the morning (or, figuratively, the early morning, dawn). The same word also means "sense." Thus, one may ask: "What is the sense [*shachar*[9]] in doing that?"

Verbs that originate in this root mean "to seek," "to ask for," "to request," "to aspire for." All these verbs apparently relay a sense opposite to that of black.

One realizes that on the one hand, *shachor*[8] means lack of light; but on the other hand, its root implies the clarification (the making of sense) that comes with the first rays of morning light. In still other words, it embodies seeking a desirable thing like the first morning rays—desirable because they scatter the darkness of the night.

The most bizarre nature of the word *shachor*[8] (black), however, is its inclusion of the word for hole (*chor*).[10] In fact, adding one letter to the word for hole would yield *shachor*[8] (black). Furthermore, if that first letter (the letter *shin*) were used in its regular sense (when added as prefix to Hebrew words), meaning "because of," *shachor*[8] would be read, simply, as "because of the hole."

So why should "hole" be included as part of the word "black" in Hebrew? This is anyone's guess. One can explain that holes found in the ground (like deep wells) are expected to be black. However, more adventure-seeking people may offer other explanations for the Hebrew "black hole."

Addressing the "hole," the second syllable in the two-syllable Hebrew word for "black," as possibly significant in any way might seem outrageous and as forcing the desired in a twisted way. That might be so until one explores further some other words derived from the same sequence of letters, and in the same order, as "hole" (*chor*).[10] It turns out that the same word, occasionally pronounced differently, is the source for many other words in Hebrew, with different meanings, all implying ... "white."

Note these examples:

- *Chavar*[11] (a verb, same letters as "hole") means "he became white," as in: "Therefore thus says the Lord ... Jacob shall not now be ashamed, neither shall his face now grow white [*yachaviru*[12]]" (Isa. 29:22; see also Dan. 7:9).
- *Chur*[13] (a noun, same letters, different pronunciation), means "white material" (for example, Est. 1:6, 8:15).

In our modern world, we would easily understand associations between black, white, and (black) holes. How is it that the same associations are so prominently observed in corresponding Hebrew words that express the same concepts?

In other words, how is it that white (representing light with all its colors), black (absence of light) and hole have, in the Hebrew language, nearly identical sequence of letters, in the same order?

A final observation with respect to "darkness" is the way this concept is alluded to in Isaiah: "*Forming* light and *creating* darkness: *doing* peace and *creating* evil: I the Lord am doing all these" (Isa. 45:7; author's translation, italics added for emphasis). Let us recall the worlds according to Jewish tradition, which we alluded to earlier (subsection 1.3.2). There are four such worlds, structured in a hierarchical fashion: the world of *atzilut*[14] (the uppermost), the world of creation, the world of forming, and the world of doing (or making). Humans live in the lower two worlds: we can give form, and we are capable of doing. However, we are unable to create, since the latter, in biblical discourse, implies making something "jump" into existence out of nonexistence.

Given what we now know of the root of the Hebrew word for darkness, *choshech*[5]—namely, that it implies deprivation (in this case, lack of light)—one may wonder how is it that the prophet Isaiah refers to darkness as "created." This is particularly bizarre since, in an earlier verse, he shows in no uncertain terms that he is well aware of Jewish distinction between the different worlds: "All that is called by my name and for my glory, I have created him [or it]; I have formed him [or it]; yea, I have made him [or it]" (Isa. 43:7; author's translation). The same question of course extends to evil (see above quote form Isaiah). Evil is always presented in the Bible as the result of human's thoughts and actions, the outcome of which is God "hiding" his face (refer, for example, to Deut. 31:18 or Pss. 30:8). Furthermore, God sometimes even hides the hiding, causing things to look random and not the result of humans' actions (see, for example, discussion of *keri*[15] in section 3.5).

So why are darkness (the apparent result of lack of light), and evil (the apparent result of humans detaching themselves from God, causing God to "hide his face") both presented here as God's acts of "creation"?

While the answer to this question, with respect to evil, may lay in the realms of ethics, theology, and philosophy ("Why do bad things happen to good people?"), the answer regarding *created* darkness may lie with modern cosmologies (dark matter).

That is, if one does not refer to Isaiah's verse as a slip of a tongue. Given biblical precision language (section 1.3), this is an open question.

11.4 Summary of Main Points

- River and light share in Hebrew the same root; their similarity can be worked out only by modern physics (section 11.1).

- "Darkness" in Hebrew derives from "deprivation" (of light), making Genesis's "and darkness was on the face of the deep" consistent with modern cosmologies (section 11.2).

- By a bizarre coincidence, the sequence of the last three of the four letters comprising "black" in Hebrew (*shachor*[8]) means "hole" (*chor*[10]), but also "white" (section 11.3). All these terms are interrelated in modern physics: if black represents absence of light, and white represents existence of light, then a black hole represents the confinement of light (no light escapes a black hole).

- Isaiah refers to both darkness and evil as "created" by God. This is inconsistent with biblical Hebrew and other verses in the Bible, where darkness is the *result* of "deprivation of light," and evil is of human doing, causing the "hiding of God's face" and occasionally also "hiding of the hiding" (section 11.3).

CHAPTER 12

The Colors

12.1 Color and Its Human Perception

White, black, darkness, and light have been the focus of chapter 11. Section 10.3.3 addressed the human eye and its color vision. We may now step into yet more unexplored territory and attempt to find strange coincidences associated with *names* given to colors in biblical Hebrew.

The colors of the visible spectrum, called *the elementary colors*, are red, orange, yellow, green, cyan (green-blue), blue, and violet (seven colors, in an increasing order of wave frequency).

Table 12.1 presents approximate intervals for the wavelength and wave frequency of these colors.

In the table, wavelength is given in nanometer (1 nm = 10^{-9} meter), and wave frequency is given in terahertz (1 Hz equals one cycle per second, and a terahertz, or THz, is equal 10^{12} Hz).

The conversion formula from one scale to the other is simple, and is characteristic to any wave.

$$(\text{Wavelength}) \times (\text{Wave frequency}) = \text{Wave velocity}$$

All electromagnetic radiation advances at the speed of light (about 300,000 kilometers per second). Therefore, we have for conversion from wavelength to wave frequency:

$$\text{Wave frequency (THz)} = [3 \, / \, (\text{Wavelength, nm})] \times 10^5$$

All colors in Table 12.1 are visible colors. Therefore, only an approximate interval can be given for each color. Later, we will take midvalues of these intervals as representative values in order to conduct some statistical calculations, which store coincidences.

How does the human eye perceive color?
As a sensation experienced by humans and some animals, color perception is a complex neurophysiological process. In the human eye, there are three types of neuroreceptors, each sensitive to only one spectral color: red, green, or blue (RGB). All colors perceived by the human eye are built by a mixture of these three basic colors, and the same color sensation can be produced by different physical stimuli. To be precise, each type of light-sensitive cell, or "color receptor," is in fact sensing a *band* of colors—one band centered in the wavelength interval recognized as red, one in the green interval, and one in the blue interval. Any color that we see—including brown, olive green, and others absent in the rainbow—is an impression our brain produces when it combines signals from these three color bands. Thus, a mixture of red and green light of the proper intensities appears exactly the same as spectral yellow, although it does not contain light of the wavelengths corresponding to yellow.

Comments

This comment delivers some further details about the physiology of the color vision of the human eye. The comment is largely based on a description of the human vision taken from Wikipedia, the free encyclopedia, at http://en.wikipedia.org/wiki/Color_vision.

The retina of the human eye contains three different types of color receptor cells, or *cones*. One type, relatively distinct from the other two, is most responsive to light that we perceive as violet, with wavelengths around 420 nm (nm is nanometer and was defined earlier). Cones of this type are sometimes called short-wavelength

Table 12.1. Seven elementary colors in the human visible spectrum.

Elementary color	Wavelength interval	Frequency interval
red	~ 625–740 nm	~ 480–405 THz
orange	~ 590–625 nm	~ 510–480 THz
yellow	~ 565–590 nm	~ 530–510 THz
green	~ 500–565 nm	~ 600–530 THz
cyan	~ 485–500 nm	~ 620–600 THz
blue	~ 440–485 nm	~ 680–620 THz
violet	~ 380–440 nm	~ 790–680 THz

cones, S cones, or—most commonly, but misleadingly, blue cones. The other two types of cones are closely related genetically, and in chemistry and response, and each type is most responsive to light that we perceive as green or greenish. One of these types comprises cones called long-wavelength cones, L-cones, or, misleadingly, red cones. While L-cones are often referred to as red receptors, because the perception of red depends on this receptor, microspectrophotometry has shown that its peak sensitivity is in the yellow region of the spectrum, and it is most sensitive to light we perceive as yellowish-green, with wavelengths around 564 nm. Another type of cone is the middle-wavelength cone, also denoted the M-cone, or green cone. It is most sensitive to light perceived as green, with wavelengths around 534 nm.

A particular frequency of light stimulates each of these receptor types to varying degrees. Yellow light, for example, stimulates L-cones strongly and M-cones to a moderate extent, but only stimulates S-cones weakly. Red light, on the other hand, stimulates only L-cones, and violet light only S-cones. The visual system combines the information from each type of receptor to give rise to perceptions of different wavelengths of light. The sensitivity curves of the cones are roughly bell-shaped, and overlap considerably. The incoming signal spectrum is thus reduced by the eye to three values, sometimes called tristimulus values, representing the intensity of the response of each of the cone types. Refer also to Figure 10.1.

The special structure of the human eye, and how it perceives colors, explains why color TV and color printers can be based on the three so-called "primary colors"—red, green, and blue (RGB). These devices do not in any way reproduce the true spectral color of the objects they show, but they are still capable of representing any color our eyes can see.

That part of the electromagnetic spectrum that is visible to the human eye (namely, the visible light) have wavelength in the range between 380 to 740 nanometers (1 nm = 10^{-9} meter).

Consider these examples for mixtures of red (R), green (G) and blue (B), and the color they produce in the human eye:

$$R + G = \text{yellow}$$

$$G + B = \text{cyan}$$

$$R + B = \text{magenta (purplish red)}$$

$$100\% \ R + 50\% \ G + 0\% \ B = \text{orange}$$

$$75\% \ R + 75\% \ G + 23\% \ B = \text{gray}$$

(Note that the percentages do not add up to 100%; they are intended only to deliver the relative intensities of the different component colors. Also, the same name can be used for different hues obtained by slightly different mixtures of the primary colors. This is the reason for different mixtures given identical names in Table 12.2).

Since any color sensation that the human eye perceives can be duplicated by mixing varying quantities of red, green, and blue (RGB), these colors are known as the "additive primary colors." If light of all these primary colors is added together in equal intensities, the sensation of white light is produced. A number of pairs of pure spectral colors, called complementary colors, also exist.

Complementary colors are any two colors of the spectrum that, combined

Table 12.2. Perceived colors, and their RGB mixture

Primary RGB intensities (Scale 0-255)			
Color	R(ed)	G(reen)	B(lue)
Black	0	0	0
Blue	0	0	255
Brown	150	75	0
Carrot	237	145	33
Copper	184	115	51
Crimson	220	20	60
Cyan	0	255	255
Gold	255	215	0
Gray	128	128	128
Green	0	255	0
Lime	204	255	0
Magenta	255	0	255
Mauve	153	51	102
Navy Blue	0	0	128
Olive	128	128	0
Orange	255	165	0
Pink	255	192	203
Purple	102	0	153
Red	255	0	0
Violet	139	0	255
White	255	255	255
Yellow	255	255	0

in the right intensities, produce white or nearly white. Among these pairs are certain yellows and blues, greens and blues, reds and greens, and greens and violets.

Table 12.2 reproduces the mixture of the additive primary colors (RGB) needed to produce some perceived colors. This table is a short version of the table given by Wikipedia, the free encyclopedia, at: http://en.wikipedia.org/wiki/Color_list. The system used in the table is based on the RGB color model, which utilizes an additive model according to which red, green, and blue light are combined in various ways to create other colors. In the RGB system, each of the component colors is given a value (of intensity) on a scale between 0 to 255 (this scale is based on the fact that in the computer memory each of the RGB components has 8 bits associated, giving 2^8 or 256 intensities for each of the three primary colors).

To understand what the entries in the table mean, let us take, for example, mauve. It is obtained from 153 red, 51 green, and 102 blue. If we wished to convert these intensities into contributing proportions, we would have

$$\text{mauve} = [153(R)+51(G)+102(B)] / (153+51+102) =$$
$$= (1/2)(R) + (1/6)(G) + (2/6)(B)$$

12.2 Hebrew Names for Colors

How does biblical Hebrew relate to color names?

We start by first enumerating what we believe is an exhaustive list of Hebrew names of colors, most of them as they appear in the biblical text (when color names do not appear in biblical text but are used in modern Hebrew, we will note this). Names of colors are given in no particular order.

- *lavan*[1] (white)
- *chivar*[2] (white)—source Aramaic
- *shesh*[3] (white)—frequently interpreted as "white material," yet it gives rise to numerous white-related words such as *yashish*[4] (male elderly), shoshan[5] ("Lilium," a white garden flower) and *shaish*[6] (marble, made of crystal lime)
- *shachor*[7] (black)
- *kachol*[8] (blue)—nonbiblical, but inferred from a related verb
- *tchelet*[9] (blue)—perhaps also pale blue, and also the name of material so painted
- *adom*[10] (red)—the color of *dam*[11] (blood)

- *admoni*[12] (reddish)
- *adamdam*[13] (pale red—or, conversely, strong red)
- *shashar*[14] (red)
- *chachlili*[15] (reddish)
- *sharok*[16] (sorrel, light brown to brownish orange)
- *argaman*[17] (purple)
- *shani*[18] (scarlet, crimson)
- *chum*[19] (brown)
- *tzhaov*[20] (yellow, golden, derived from *zahav*,[21] or "gold" in Hebrew)
- *zahov*[22] (golden)—not biblical
- *sagol*[23] (violet)—not biblical
- *yerakon*[24] (green)—in modern Hebrew, *yarok*[25]
- *yerakrak*[26] (pale green, or, conversely, strong green—controversy exists)
- *barud*[27] (grizzled, grayish)—appears in Zechariah 6:3, 6; and Genesis 31: 10, 12, with debatable interpretations; some interpret it to mean "spotted," "pied"
- *chamutz*[28] (reddish brown, crimson)
- *afel*[29] (dark)
- *kasuf*[30] (silvery)—not biblical

Comments

1. Biblical scholars have differed on whether a repeated syllable at the end of a color name means stronger color or paler color (like in *yerakrak*, *adamdam*, and so on). Since in most other Hebrew words, a repeated syllable intends to convey an intensified impression, the former interpretation is probably the correct one.

2. "Red" has many other names that are less frequently used in biblical text, and therefore were not given here. Probably due to its close relationship to *dam*[11] (blood), *adom*[10] is by far the most commonly used name for "red," both in the Bible and in modern speech.

Is there any relationship between the sum of the numerical values of the letters comprising names of colors in the Hebrew language (henceforth denoted "color's numerical value," CNV) and the corresponding scientifically validated color wave frequencies?

This outrageous proposition from fantasy world is now being statistically examined.

12.3 Hebrew Color Names: A Hypothesis and Its Statistical Testing

12.3.1 The Hypothesis and an Outline of the Analysis

To test the above proposition, applying appropriate statistical procedures with all required scientific care, the following three stages are pursued.

Stage 1: Formulating the Hypotheses

We formulate two hypotheses that will be statistically tested.

> **Null Hypothesis:** There is no relationship between the numerical value of a Hebrew color name (CNV) and the color's wave frequency (WF). The latter is defined as the midvalue of the corresponding interval given in Table 12.1; refer to Table 12.3.

> **Alternative Hypothesis:** CNV and WF are *linearly* related.

Stage 2: Preparing the Samples

Since many of the biblical color names just given are open to different interpretations, we base our analysis only on color names of nondebatable clear meanings. We call this set of observations the basic set. Consistent with this book's title, only names that appear in the Bible are considered for inclusion in the basic set.

An extended set is also constructed that is used for some other analyses, as will be expounded shortly.

Stage 3: Analysis

Linear regression analysis is applied to the data, aiming to derive a model capable of predicting a color's spectral wave frequency (WF) from the numerical value of its Hebrew name (CNV). This statistical analysis comprises three separate analyses.

Analysis I: Statistical Analysis Based on the Extended Set

Assuming that the outrageous alternative hypothesis is true, we calculate expected CNVs for colors that are included in the analysis (the extended set) but not in the basic set. These are colors that belong to the group of elementary colors, yet do not have clear Hebrew names in the Bible. To obtain the expected CNV values for these colors, linear interpolation or linear extrapolation are applied, as required (these will be detailed later).

It should be noted that if there is no relationship between the CNV and the corresponding WF, or the relationship is nonlinear (that is, the null hypothesis is true), this operation of including linearly interpolated (or extrapolated) observations would add noise and thus cause the null hypothesis to be accepted with higher probability.

Conversely, if the alternative hypothesis is true, and there is a linear relationship between CNV and WF, generating observations via linear interpolation or extrapolation (to be added to the basic set) would increase the probability of rejecting the null hypothesis. In either cases, the added observations would rendert he conclusions derived from the analysis more powerful.

Analysis II: Statistical Analysis Based on the Basic Set

Only observations in the basic set are included in the analysis. Justification for this set is in subsection 12.3.2.

Analysis III: Further Analyses

Since, unlike all other observations in the basic set, the "red" observation is on the extreme margin of the visible spectrum (the upper margin of wavelength), the definition of its representative WF, to be used in the regression analysis, is open to debate. Therefore, in this third statistical analysis, only observations (in the basic set) internal to the visible spectrum are used.

Some other analyses that are executed at this part of the analysis will be detailed later (section 12.3.3).

The various stages of the analysis will now be detailed. The reader is kindly requested to persevere with reading the pursuing analyses, irrespective of how bizarre they may look. The validity of these analyses is established via implementation of rigorous statistical principles.

12.3.2 Preparation of the Samples (Stage 2)

Selecting the Basic Set of Observations

Based on a thorough search of a Bible concordance, only the following biblical color names, corresponding to the elementary colors in Table 12.1, were deemed as having clear, undebatable Hebrew meanings.

- *Adom*[10] (red). This color has CNV of

$$51 = (40 = ם = מ) + (6 = ו) + (4 = ד) + (1 = א)$$

- *Tzhaov*[20] (yellow):

$$97 = (2 = ב) + (5 = ה) + (90 = צ)$$

- *Yerakon*[24] (green):

$$366 = (50 = ן) + (6 = ו) + (100 = ק) + (200 = ר) + (10 = י)$$

- *Tchelet*[9] (blue):

$$850 = (400 = ת) + (30 = ל) + (20 = כ) + (400 = ת)$$

The basic set thus includes four observations. These observations are shown underlined in Table 12.3. The corresponding representative wave frequencies (WFs) are also shown. These were chosen as the midvalues of the WF intervals, given in Table 12.1.

Some explanation for the selection of these observations (and not others) is necessary, and will be given by the pursuing comments.

Comments

1. The judgment about which color names have irrefutable meaning was based only on how these names are used in the Bible. Thus, in Exodus (and other books of the Torah) the color name *tchelet*[9] is used extensively to describe the color of garments that are known to be blue, as in, for example: "And thou shalt make the robe of the efod all blue" (Exod. 28:31).

2. The word *chachol*[8] is commonly used in modern Hebrew to mean "blue." Yet it never appears in the Bible. The word *chachol*[8] may be *inferred* to imply "blue" from the one-word verb *chachalt*[31] ("you painted blue"), which appears only once, in Ezekiel: "for whom thou did wash thyself, did paint thy eyes blue [*chachalt*[31]], and did deck thyself with ornament" (Ezek. 23:40). By contrast, the word *tchelet*[9] for "blue" appears in the Bible no fewer than forty-nine times. Therefore, the latter was selected to represent "blue."

3. Just like *chachol*,[8] the word *yarok*,[25] for "green," is commonly used in modern Hebrew, yet it does not appear in the Bible as such. *Yarok*[25] appears only once in the Bible (in Job 39:8), but it appears as a noun, and it obviously has the same meaning as *yerek*[32]—namely, "greenery" or "green vegetation." The closest to mean the *color* green in the Bible is *yerakon*,[24] and its meaning is irrefutably "green" due to its proximity to the biblical *yerek*.[32] Furthermore, its meaning as a name of color is inferred by the way it is used in the Bible: "Why then do I see every man with his hands on his loins, as a woman in travail, and all faces turned [*yerakon*[24]]?" (Jer. 39:8). Note that "green" is similarly used in English to describe a person who is unhealthily pale in appearance. Finally, the structure of the word *yerakon*[24] is definitely consistent with other Hebrew words that describe colors like *chivaron*[33] (whiteness) or *admon*[34] (reddish).

4. One may write the first two colors in the basic set (red and yellow) either *with* the letter *vav* (waw) or without. *Tzahov*[20] (yellow) always appears in the Bible without the *vav*. We likewise followed this rule. For red (*adom*),[10] the Bible occasionally uses this word with *vav*. Therefore, we opted to write it with the *vav* too. Due to the small numerical value of the letter *vav* (6), deleting it from colors' names (or, conversely, including it) would not essentially alter the basic results from the statistical analyses.

Interpolation and Extrapolation

To fill in the missing CNV entries in Table 12.3 (elementary colors not in the basic set), an extended set of observations for all elementary colors was constructed using interpolation and extrapolation. In applying these procedures, we assume that the alternative hypothesis is true—namely, *linear* interpolation or extrapolation are applicable and therefore applied. Only the two nearest points with known CNVs

Table 12.3. Observations in the basic set (underlined), observations with interpolated (or extrapolated) CNVs, and *argaman* (magenta, not an elemenary color)

Color	Hebrew word (for basic set)	Color numerical value (basic set underlined)	Wavelength (interval midvalue)	Wave frequency (interval midvalue)
Red	*Adom*	51	682	443
Orange		82.06	608	495
Yellow	*Tzahov*	97	578	520
Green	*Yerakon*	366	533	565
Cyan		622.2	493	610
Blue	*Tchelet*	850	462	650
Violet		1334 (extrap.)	410	735
Magenta	*Argaman*	295		546 (Cal.)

(namely, those in the basic set) are employed for each interpolation or extrapolation. We reemphasize that if the assumption of linearity is invalid (that is, the null hypothesis is true), then CNV and WF values are completely unrelated, and the interpolated and extrapolated new entries in Table 12.3 (those added to the basic set) would just add noise (they are not expected to align themselves on a straight line). Adding noise would strengthen the tendency of observations to support the null hypothesis.

The final complete set of observations used, either in toto or by a subsample, for any of the linear regression analyses that follow, is displayed in Table 12.3. Observations belonging to the basic set are underlined.

The added entry for *argaman* will be addressed later on. This color has a known CNV, yet it is not included in the set of elementary colors of Table 12.1. Therefore, it will be added to the basic set later on, in a separate analysis, which will be based on an extended basic set.

To calculate by interpolation CNV values for colors in the set of elementary colors but not in the basic set, the following formulae were used (these may be easily derived from trigonometric considerations):

Interpolation (always based on the adjacent two basic-set observations, N_0 is the unknown CNV):

$$N_0 = \{N_1(f_2 - f_0) + N_2(f_0 - f_1)\} / (f_2 - f_1)$$

Where:

N_i–CNV value for point i (i = 1, 0, 2, where "0" index the point with unknown CNV (the interpolated middle point); 1 relates to the adjacent point with known CNV and the *smaller* WF (first interpolating point); and 2 relates to the adjacent point with known CNV and the *higher* WF (the second interpolating point);

f_i–WF for point i (i = 1, 0, 2); all values of f_i are known, and used for the interpolation.

Extrapolation (same notation as before; extrapolation was used only to obtain the CNV of violet, and was obtained based on CNV and WF values of the two colors preceding it, with known CNVs—namely, basic-set observations; N_2 denote here the *unknown* CNV):

$$N_2 = \{N_0 (f_2 - f_1) - N_1 (f_2 - f_0) \} / (f_0 - f_1)$$

12.3.3   Linear Regression Analysis: Description and Results (Stage 3)

Analysis I: Based on the Extended Set (basic set plus interpolated and extrapolated observations)

Implementing simple linear regression, with CNV as the regressor (the independent variable) and WF as the response (the dependent variable), the following equation is obtained:

$$WF = 475.95 + 0.20175*CNV$$
$$(p<10^{-6})   (p = 0.000197)$$

(Numbers in brackets indicate the significance levels of the model's coefficients.)

The associated linear correlation is $R = 0.9754$, with adjusted-$R^2 = 0.9745$. A normal probability plot shows the residuals to properly behave within the confines of the normal scenario (the latter is needed for linear regression analysis to be valid; refer to any basic text in statistics for definition of the normal scenario—for example, Shore 2005).

For $n = 7$ (the sample size), the model's F-ratio value is 97.85, which, with 1 and 5 degrees of freedom, has significance value of $p = 0.00020$. This implies likelihood of less than 0.02% of obtaining an F value that high (or higher) by chance alone. In other words, if the null hypothesis were true, this would be the probability of getting that high F value.

A scatter plot of the observations, with the fitted linear regression equation and 95% confidence limits, is given in Figure 12.1. To allow easy identification of each observation, the WF value is marked for each point in the plot.

The reader is encouraged to find out whether similar results would have obtained if one changed the CNV value of one of the observations in the basic set. For example, for yellow, let CNV = 600 (instead of the current 97!). Note, that for these further scenario analyses to be valid, the interpolated and extrapolated values need also be recomputed.

Analysis II: Based on the Basic Set (Four Observations)

Applying simple linear regression, with CNV as the regressor (the independent variable) and WF as the response (the dependent variable), the following equation is obtained:

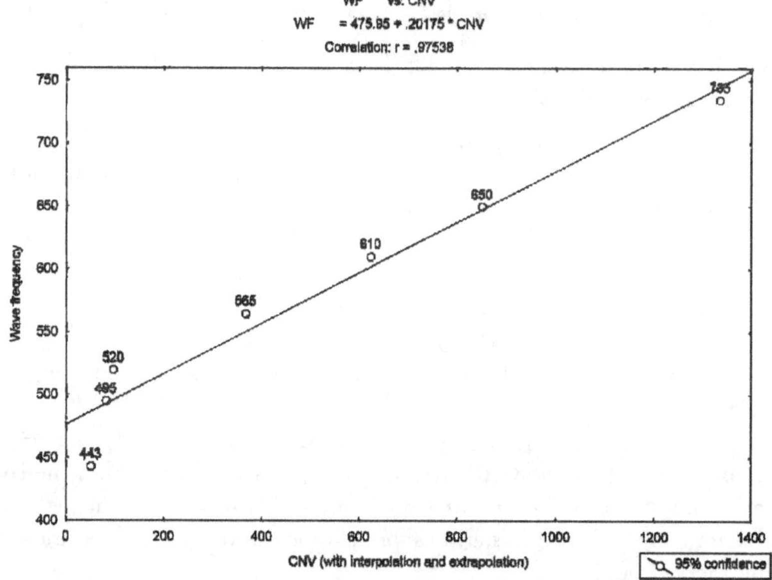

Figure 12.1. The extended set of colors (including interpolated and extrapolated points).

$$WF = 468.73 + 0.2222 * CNV$$
$$(p = .00309) \quad (p = 0.0582)$$

(Numbers in brackets indicate the significance levels of the model's estimated coefficients.)

The associated linear correlation is R = 0.9418, with adjusted-R^2 = 0.8305. For n = 4 (the sample size), the model's F-ratio value is 15.69, which, with 1 and 2 degrees of freedom, has significance value of p = 0.0582.

A scatter plot of the observations, with the fitted linear regression equation and 95% confidence limits, is given in Figure 12.2.

Analysis III: Based on the Basic Set (with "Red" Excluded)

The reason for performing this analysis is detailed earlier (section 12.3.1, stage 3, analysis III). Running simple linear regression, with CNV as the regressor (the independent variable) and WF as the response (the dependent variable), the following equation is obtained:

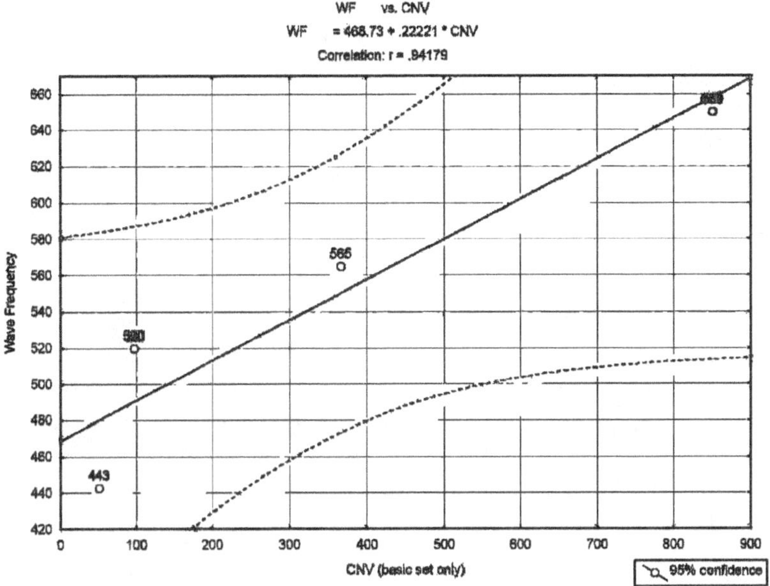

Figure 12.2. The Basic Set of colors.

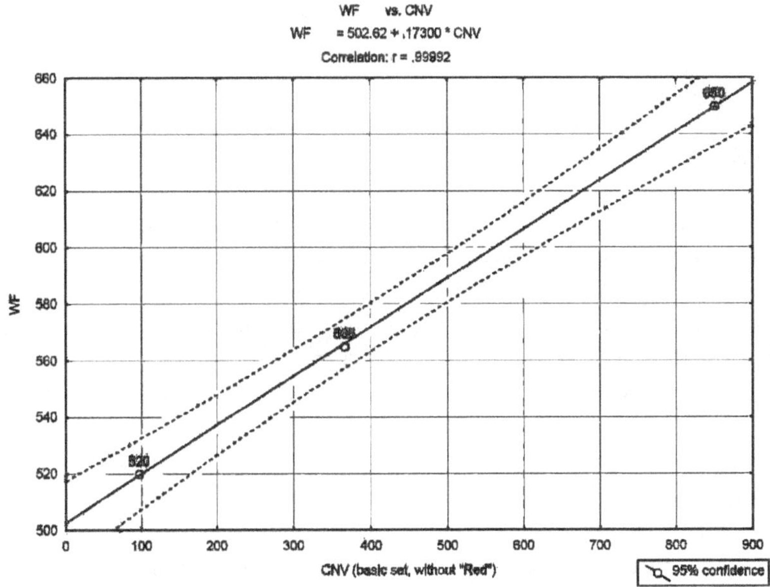

Figure 12.3. The Basic Set of colors (excluding red).

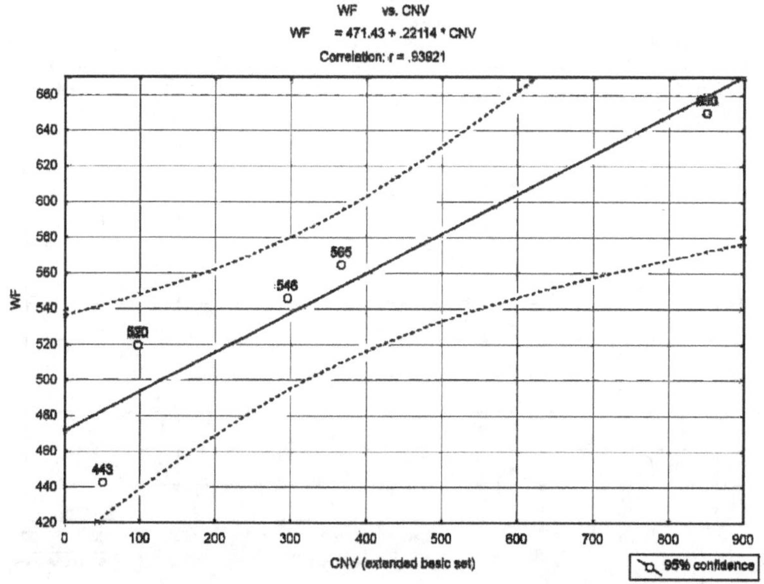

Figure 12.4. The extended Basic Set of colors (including *argaman*).[17]

$$WF = 502.62 + 0.1730 \cdot CNV$$
$$(p = .001464) \quad (p = 0.007916)$$

(Numbers in brackets indicate the significance levels of the model's estimated coefficients.)

The associated linear correlation is R = 0.9999, with adjusted-R^2 = 0.9997. For n = 3 (the sample size), the model's F-ratio value is 6468, which, with 1 and 1 degrees of freedom, has significance value of p = 0.007916. In other words, the probability of the three observations aligning on a straight line, the way they did, if the null hypothesis were true (that is, by chance) is less than 1%.

A scatter plot of the observations, with the fitted linear regression equation and 95% confidence limits, is given in Figure 12.3.

Comments

1. An alternative statistical testing procedure, simpler but also less powerful, may be suggested for the basic set, based on the following argument. Consider the four observations red, yellow, green, blue. One may ask whether the probability of the event that "the ordered (sorted) observations, according to their

CNVs, is consistent with the sorted WF" (an event that has occurred) is small enough, under the null hypothesis, to justify rejecting this hypothesis. The number of possible permutations of four observations is 1x2x3x4 = 24. Only one of these permutations gives CNV ordering consistent with that according to the respective WFs. Thus, the probability of randomly having values of colors' names sorted in the same order as the respective WFs (an event that will lead one to reject the null hypothesis and accept that there is a real relationship between the two), is 1/24 = 4.2%. Were one to select the significance level of the commonly accepted α = 5%, then, based on the data, this test would reject the null hypothesis in favor of the alternative hypothesis—namely, we conclude that there is a real relationship between CNV and WF.

2. The color name *argaman*[17] often appears in the Bible together with *tchelet*[9] (blue). The meaning of this word in modern Hebrew is purple (a non-elementary color), and that is probably how it was also used in biblical times. In this comment, we explore how this color name compares with the rest of the colors in the basic set, and how consistent it is with the model based on the observations in the basic set.

The purple color is obtained from red and blue in the ratio of about 2:3, respectively (see Table 12.2). Since light energy is known to be linearly related to the wave frequency, one could calculate the equivalent monochrome wave frequency—namely, the equivalent wave frequency that would result in the eye seeing purple from a monochrome spectral color.

Calculating an equivalent WF for purple, based on the RGB proportions for purple, given in Table 12.2, and on the WF of red and blue, one obtains

$$\text{purple WF} = [102(443) + 153(650)] / (102+153) = 567.2 \text{ THz}$$

The color name value (CNV) for *argaman*[17] is

$$294 = (50 = ‫ן‬) + (40 = ‫מ‬) + (3 = ‫ג‬) + (200 = ‫ר‬) + (1 = ‫א‬)$$

Introducing this value into the most accurate prediction model (Figure 12.3), we obtain

$$\text{predicted WF for } \textit{argaman}^{17} = 502.62 + 0.1730(294) = 553.5 \text{ THz}$$

This value is not far off from the true value for purple of 567.2, calculated earlier (a deviation of 2.4%). This result implies that including *argaman* in the basic set of observations would have increased the significance of the statistical results obtained in previous analyses.

If the true meaning of *argaman*[17] is the close relative of purple—namely, the color known as magenta (defined by the 1998 *Collins Dictionary* as "deep purplish red," and formed by blue and red mixed in equal proportions), then the equivalent WF for magenta would be 546.5 THz, even closer to the predicted WF for *argaman*[17] of 553.5 THz (deviation of 1.3%).

It seems more likely that in reality (that is, in ancient biblical times) purple would have been produced by equal shares of blue and red rather than by unequal proportions (since the former is simpler). In that case, magenta is probably the right color indicated by *argaman*[17] (there is no equivalent Hebrew for magenta).

The values associated with *argaman*[17] are therefore added to Table 12.2, assuming magenta is the real color. The basic set is now *enlarged* to comprise five observations.

Figure 12.4 shows the results for this enlarged basic set, with the associated fitted linear-regression equation. The adjusted R-squared is 0.8428, and for n = 5 the model F-ratio is 22.4, with significance level of p = 0.01783.

Note that the enlarged basic set of five observations still preserves the right order dictated by the corresponding wave frequencies. The number of possible permutations of a set of five observations is: 1x2x3x4x5 = 120. This implies that the likelihood of the five observations in the enlarged basic set preserving, by chance only, the right order of the allied wave frequencies is 1/120 = 0.0083 … that is, less than 1%!

Due to the unconventional character of the statistical analysis introduced in this chapter, we have opted, in the earlier statistical analyses, to pursue a more cautious conservative approach. This implies that we have excluded *argaman*[17] (namely, purple or magenta) from the basic set of observations used in the analyses.

3. A curious coincidence is noteworthy regarding the first letters in the Hebrew names for the additive primary colors R(ed), G(reen) and B(lue) (RGB, the colors originating all hues within the human visible spectrum). With respect to the visible spectrum (expressed in wave frequency), these three colors represent the lower end (red, with a representative wave frequency of 443 THz), about a middle point in the spectrum (green, with representative WF about 565 THz) and the upper end (blue, with representative WF about 650 THz). Correspondingly, first letters in the Hebrew names for these colors are, respectively, the first letter in the Hebrew alphabet (*aleph*, first letter of *adom*,[10] or

red), a near-middle letter in the Hebrew alphabet (*yod*, the tenth letter in the Hebrew alphabet, first letter of *yerakon*,[24] or green), and the last letter in the Hebrew alphabet (*tav*, first letter of *techelet*,[9] blue).

4. In Isaiah 44:13, a strange word appears, *sered*.[35] It shows up nowhere else in the Bible. In most English translations, the word is translated as "marker." However, Jewish interpreters (including the Malbim, 1809–79) refer to this word as an unknown color. To find out what this name implies, let us apply the color model derived in this chapter. The CNV of *sered*[35] is

$$504 = (4 = \daleth) + (200 = \resh) + (300 = \shin)$$

This value is recognized to be well within the range of CNV values for the visible colors, thereby implying that the interpretation of the Jewish sages, referring to *sered*[35] as a certain unknown color, was probably correct.

Introducing into the most accurate prediction equation (Figure 12.3), we obtain for the expected wave frequency, corresponding to this CNV:

$$WF = 502.62 + 0.173(504) = 589.8.$$

This locates *sered*[35] near the midvalue for the green zone (565).

5. An additional analysis associated with colors perceived by receptors in the human eye (that is, the RGB colors) is given in subsection 10.3.3.

12.3.4 *Wavelength as the Response*

In the earlier statistical analyses, we used wave frequency (WF) as the response (the dependent variable) for our analyses. Since wave frequency is a reciprocal number of wavelength (refer to the formula given at the beginning of this chapter), one may suspect that applying the same statistical analysis for wavelength would result in a nonlinear curve.

This is not the case. An example for a repeat of the analysis referring to the basic set (without red), where wavelength is the response, is displayed in Figure 12.5. We realize that the linear relationship is unexpectedly preserved.

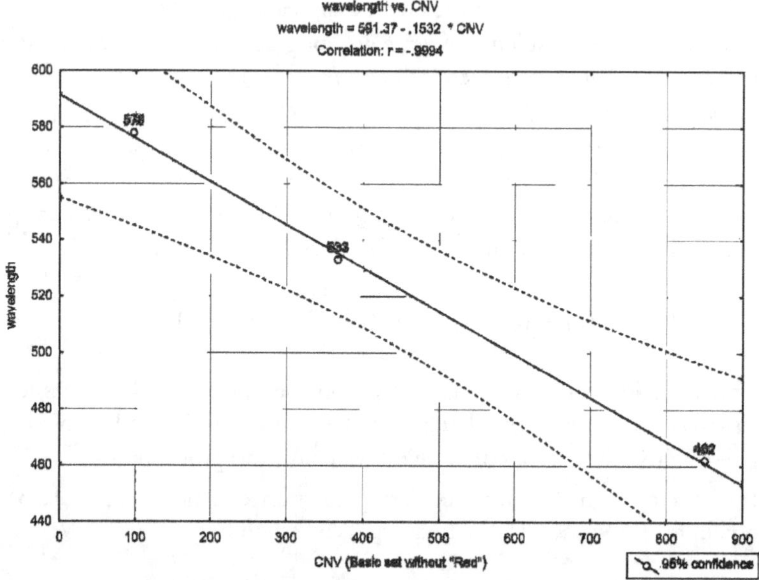

Figure 12.5. Wavelength as the response (Basic Set, without red).

12.4 Analysis of Other Frequencies

This chapter engages in the analysis of the relationship between the numerical values of Hebrew names for colors and the actual physical properties of colors, in terms of either wave frequencies or wavelengths.

One may wonder whether frequencies displayed in other cyclic phenomena of nature would also reveal such relationships. In this subsection, we provide two such analyses.

The first one analyzes the relationship between frequencies of day, month, and year, and their Hebrew names' numerical values.

The second analysis shows that analyzing frequencies does not have to be confined to phenomena of similar nature.

12.4.1 Day, Month, Year

Table 12.4 shows the data for the analysis of the relationship between the frequencies, in cycles per second (Hz), of the day, the month and the year, and the respective duration numerical values (DNVs), the numerical values of their Hebrew names.

Table 12.4. Data for analysis of frequencies
(in Hz, cycle per second) of day, month, year

Name	DNV	Frequency	Log frequency
Yom (day)	56	1.1574E-05	–11.3667
Yerach (month)	218	3.9194E-07	–14.7521
Shanah (year)	355	3.2661E-08	–17.2371

We first explain how frequencies were calculated.

Day

A day has 24 hours, each hour has 60*60 = 3600 seconds. Therefore, the frequency of a day, expressed in cycles per second (Hz), is

$$\text{day frequency (Hz)} = 1 / (24*60*60) = 1 / (86400) = 1.1574(10)^{-5}$$

Month

A month has, according to lunar (Hebrew) calendar, 29.53 days (refer to subsection 2.1.2). Therefore, the frequency (in Hz) of the month is that of the day divided by this number:

$$\text{month frequency (Hz)} = (\text{day frequency}) / 29.53 = 1.1574(10)^{-5} / 29.53 = 3.9194(10)^{-7}$$

Year

A year has twelve months. Therefore, the frequency (in Hz) of the year is that of the month divided by this number:

$$\text{year frequency (Hz)} = (\text{month frequency}) / 12 = 3.2661(10)^{-8}.$$

Next, values of the DNV of the respective Hebrew names are calculated

Yom[36] (day):   :

$$56 = (40 = \text{מ}) + (6 = \text{ו}) + (10 = \text{י})$$

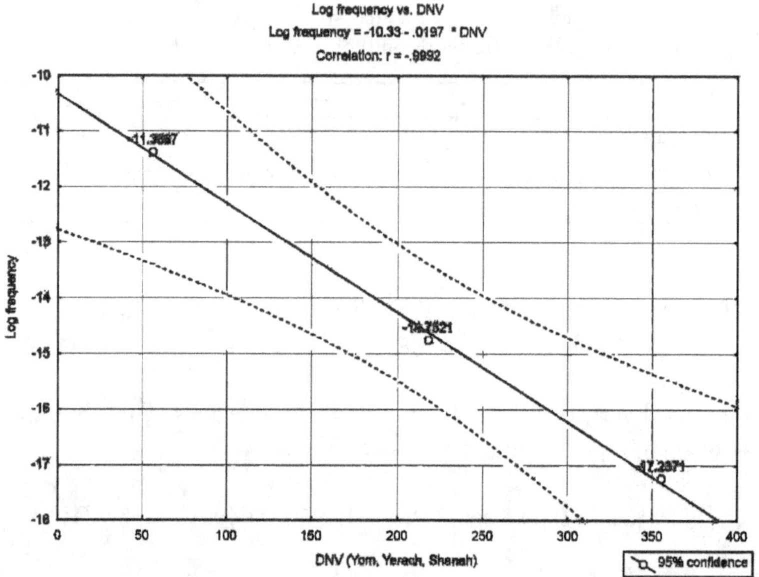

Figure 12.6. Frequencies of time-units durations, with log-frequency as the response.

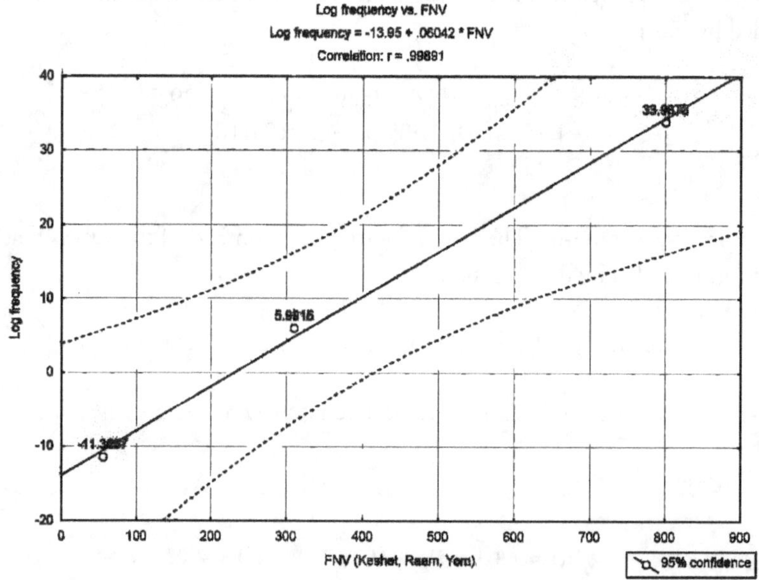

Figure 12.7. Various cyclic phenomena, with log-frequency as the response.

Yerach[37] (**month**):

$$218 = (8 = ח) + (200 = ר) + (10 = י)$$

Shanah[38] (**year**):

$$355 = (5 = ה) + (50 = נ) + (300 = ש)$$

The results of applying linear regression, with log frequencies as the response (the dependent variable) and DNV as the regressor (the independent variable) are shown in Figure 12.6.

The model F-ratio is 621.3, with significance level of p = 0.02553. The R^2-adjusted is 0.9968.

12.4.2   *Frequencies in Nonrelated "Entities"*

Does a linear relationship exist, between the log-frequencies and the respective numerical values of Hebrew names, for cyclic phenomena that, indeed, do not share anything in common except that they are all cyclic?

To examine this outrageous proposition, we have selected three "entities," some of which have had their cyclic nature proven only by modern science: light, sound, and day.

Selection of Frequencies

While for "day," the frequency is easily established (refer to the previous subsection), it is open to debate how the frequencies of sound and light should be determined (since each spans a whole spectrum). Because all three phenomena (light, sound, day) have frequencies that span different orders of magnitude, the exact values selected for sound and light are relatively immaterial, as long as the true order of magnitude is preserved.

Accordingly, for light we have selected as a representative value a midvalue of the visible spectrum, 565 THz, which is $5.65 (10)^{14}$ Hz. For sound, we have selected "A440," which is the 440 Hz tone that serves as the internationally recognized standard for musical pitch. A440 is the musical note A above middle C (find details at Wikipedia, the free encyclopedia, at http://en.wikipedia.org/wiki/A440).

Selection of Hebrew Words

As representative words for sound and light, we have selected words that are associated with the weather. For light, the Hebrew name for rainbow, *keshet*,[39] which is supposed to represent all colors of the visible spectrum, was selected. For sound, the Hebrew name for thunder, *raam*,[40] was selected.

The respective frequency numerical values (FNV) are

Keshet[39] **(rainbow):**

$$800 = (400 = ת) + (300 = שׁ) + (100 = ק)$$

Raam[40] **(thunder):**

$$310 = (40 = ם) + (70 = ע) + (200 = ר)$$

Yom[36] **(day):** see section 12.4.1.

With log-frequency as the response, Figure 12.7 displays the highly significant results (model F-ratio of 457.5, p = 0.02974).

Comments

While the Hebrew words *keshet*[39] (for light) and *yom*[36] (for day) are unique and cannot be replaced by other Hebrew words, it is not so with the Hebrew word that represents sound. One may question the selection of *raam*[40] and offer other terms. Therefore, we have selected another word for sound, *shaon*[41] (noise), which appears eighteen times in the Bible. Introducing the FNV of *shaon*[41] into the linear regression equation results in a predicted value of about 2000 Hz, which is well within the human audible spectrum.

These are all coincidences ... or maybe not.

CHAPTER 13

Metals and Other Substances

13. 1 Introduction

An analysis similar to that conducted with regard to colors (chapters 10 and 12) has been applied to Hebrew names of metals and other substances.

Like in the earlier endeavor (chapter 12), basic sets were established of metals and other substances that appear in the Bible with undisputable meanings. For a few cases where meanings are debatable, a thorough explanation for the selection of the final name (taken from the Bible) is given. A modern-day general physical property, characteristic to any material, is defined, with its value calculated for each material in the samples. The relationships between values of the selected physical property and the corresponding numerical values of the Hebrew names (metal numeric value, MNV, and material numeric value, MaNV) are then explored via rigorous statistical analysis.

A description of the considerations involved in preparing the samples and the final samples selected is given in section 13.2, for metals, and in section 13.3, for other materials. Descriptions of the statistical analyses and their results are given in section 13.4, for metals, and in section 13.5, for other substances.

13.2 Selecting and Preparing the Sample: Metals

13.2.1 Selecting the Sample (Metals)

A basic set of metals that appear in the Bible is defined. This set includes the three metals mentioned in the construction of the tabernacle (Exod. 35:32)—namely gold, silver, and copper (or brass), and, additionally, tin (or stannum), iron, and lead. The prophet Ezekiel refers to all these metals (excluding gold) in one verse: "As they gather silver, and brass, and iron, and lead, and tin, into the midst of the furnace ... so will I gather you in my anger and in my fury" (Ezek. 22:20). Another verse from Numbers counts all six metals: "Only the gold, and the silver, the brass, the iron, the tin, and the lead, everything that passes through the fire, you shall make it go through the fire, and it shall be clean ..." (Num. 31:22–23).

The above six metals differ in terms of their chemical attribution groups. Gold, silver, copper, and iron are all pure elements that appear in the periodic table of the elements as belonging to the group of transition metals. Tin and lead belong to the group of basic metals.

Brass is an alloy that seems to share, in the Bible, a common or similar name with copper (an element). Both will be discussed shortly.

13.2.2 Determining Hebrew Names and Their Numerical Values (Metals)

Selecting the biblical Hebrew names for the various metals was not easy.

While for some metals there are unique names, which survived to modern-day Hebrew, others are obscure, or have seemingly multiple names that need clarification. The latter will be aided by how most revered Jewish scholars have interpreted these debatable names.

We start with the simplest and the obvious, and calculate the corresponding numerical values.

Zahav[1] (gold):

$$14 = (2 = ב) + (5 = ה) + (7 = ז)$$

Kessef[2] (silver):

$$160 = (80 = ף) + (60 = ס) + (20 = כ)$$

Bdil[3] (tin):

$$46 = (30 = ל) + (10 = י) + (4 = ד) + (2 = ב)$$

Oferet[4] (lead):

$$756 = (400 = ת) + (200 = ר) + (80 = פ) + (6 = ו) + (70 = ע)$$

Two metals are missing from the list of six, mentioned earlier: copper (or brass) and iron. Each seemingly has two different Hebrew names in the Bible.

Copper (or Brass)

The first is the couple of names *nechoshet*[5] and *nechushah*.[6] The former appears 133 times in the Bible, the latter only 10 times. Most biblical translations invariably refer to both names as brass, or bronze. The former is an alloy of copper and zinc, the latter an alloy of copper and tin (plus other substances, like zinc and lead). We were for some time confused by the existence of two names with such parity in their Hebrew names' numerical values. To our surprise, we have found that regarding *nechoshet*[5] as an alloy (we considered it to be brass, as commonly alluded to in biblical translations), and *nechushah*[6] to be the pure copper element, is *extremely* consistent with the statistical models developed to describe the other eleven substances analyzed in this chapter. Furthermore, the selection of *nechoshet*[5] to represent brass is corroborated by how this name is used in the Bible, which cannot possibly mean just pure copper. This qualification does not extend to the other name. For example, in describing Goliath's armaments, the word *nechoshet*[5] is invariably mentioned, never the other name (1 Samuel 17:5–6). Conversely, *nechushah*[6] is occasionally referred to as raw material, like in "I will make your skies like iron and your earth like [*nechushah*[6]]" (Lev. 26:19).

For all these reasons, allusion to the two names follows this distinction.

The numerical values of *nechoshet*[5] and *nechushah*[6] are:

Nechoshet[5] (brass):

$$758 = (400 = ת) + (300 = ש) + (8 = ח) + (50 = נ)$$

Nechushah[6] (copper):

$$363 = (5 = ה) + (300 = ש) + (8 = ח) + (50 = נ)$$

Comments

Both names may be written with *vav* (the sixth letter in the Hebrew alphabet) or without. We opted to delete this letter from the calculation of the Hebrew name numerical values (MNV) in both cases. As alluded to in the previous chapter, due to its small numerical value, the inclusion of the letter *vav* only marginally affects the statistical results.

Iron

The other couple of names that appear in the Bible, seemingly relating to the same substance, are *barzel*[7] and *pladot*,[8] both probably relating to iron. The most common name for iron is *barzel*,[7] which appears in the Bible, with its various inflections, seventy-six times. There is however another name, probably alluding to iron, that appears only once: "The shield of his mighty men is made red, the valiant men are in scarlet: the chariots glitter with steel [*pladot*[8]] in the day of his preparation, and the spears of cypress wood are brandished" (Nahum 2:4, thus translated in the Jerusalem Bible, 2000).

The key word here is *pladot*,[8] written without the usual *vav* that is supposed to denote plural feminine. So *pladot*[8] is probably singular. In all other English translations regarding this verse that we are familiar with, *pladot*[8] is interpreted to be "torch." However, the Jerusalem Bible is consistent with how most revered Jewish interpreters, like Rashi (1040–1105) and Radak (1160–1235), interpret *pladot*[8]—namely, to mean iron. Rashi writes, "I would not know what "Pladot[8]" was, but I would say, quoting, that it is "Nice Iron" (no reference to the source of the quote is given).

In modern Hebrew, steel is *pladah*.[9] One can only assume that this notation for steel originally derived from *pladot*.[8]

So now we have two words for iron, *barzel*[7] and *pladot*.[8] How do they differ? We have no definite answer for that. In the pursuing statistical analysis (section 13.3), we refer to iron as *pladot*,[8] since this word is extremely consistent with the statistical models developed for the other metals in the sample. *Barzel*[7] is not. We assume that *barzel*[7] probably refers to the processed iron, which is an alloy containing other components (as with *nechoshet*[5]). The word *barzel*[7] does not participate in any of the following statistical analyses.

It is emphasized, though, that due to the relatively large sample size employed in the statistical analyses, excluding iron altogether from the analysis (due to its debatable MNV) would only marginally affect the significance of the results obtained.

The numerical values (MNV) of *barzel*[7] and *pladot*[8] are:

Barzel[7] (probably processed iron):

$$239 = (30 = ל) + (7 = ז) + (200 = ר) + (2 = ב)$$

Pladot[8] (denoting iron or processed iron):

$$514 = (400 = ת) + (4 = ד) + (30 = ל) + (80 = פ)$$

Comments

The Hebrew word *oferet*[4] is the most suitable to represent elemental iron, as obtained from the statistical analyses of the transition metals. For some time, we entertained the idea of using this to represent the pure substance iron. We finally abandoned this idea, but we still believe that it has merits for considerations that are now expounded.

The Hebrew name *oferet*[4] and the Hebrew word *afar*[9] (soil) are very similar, and probably derive from the same root. Perhaps *oferet*[4] was initially used in ancient Hebrew to denote ore that contains iron, and then it was generalized to imply soil in general.

A similar development may be traced in the English language. The word "ore" (corresponding to "soil" in the above case) is derived from "era." In ancient Rome, "aera" were disks or tokens made of brass, and used for counting (Ayto 1990). Thus, brass (era) was generalized to denote the general term "ore," the same as *oferet*[4] (seemingly raw iron, as dug from the earth) was probably generalized to denote soil (*afar*).[9] Also, *oferet*[4] is mentioned nine times in the Bible. In five of those instances, it is mentioned together with *barzel*.[7]

As alluded to earlier, statistical analysis of the available set of observations shows that the metal name *oferet*,[4] when referred to as the pure substance "iron," integrates smoothly with the other observations in the sample. However, to remove any doubts regarding the validity of the statistical analyses, we have not pursued this idea, with respect to the possible original meaning of *oferet*,[4] any further. In other words, *oferet*[4] is used in the statistical analyses to mean "lead," as in modern Hebrew.

13.2.3   *Values of the Analyzed Physical Property (Metals)*

The next step in the preparation of the sample for statistical analysis relates to the selection of the physical property to be analyzed. The most natural choice is to use as the response (the dependent variable) the metal's atomic weight (AW), as the latter is given in the periodic table of the elements (the pure substances).

The first researcher to construct a periodic table was the Russian Dmitri Mendeleev, and the table was first published in 1869. Medeleev had shown that when the elements were ordered according to atomic weight, a pattern resulted in which similar properties for elements recurred periodically. Based on the work of physicist Henry Moseley, the periodic table was reorganized later on the basis of increasing atomic number rather than on atomic weight. The revised table could be used to predict the properties of elements that had yet to be discovered. Many of these predictions were later substantiated through experimentation. This led to the formulation of the periodic law, which states that the chemical properties of the elements are dependent on their atomic numbers.

The reciprocal values of atomic weights (AWs) are used as response values in the pursuing statistical analyses (we will later elaborate on why the reciprocal values rather than the original values were used). This requires understanding what an AW means, and for that purpose we first define a mole. The latter is a chemical mass unit, defined to be 6.022×10^{23} molecules, atoms, or some other unit. This number is known as *Avogadro's number*. The mass of a mole is the gram mass of a substance having Avogadro's number of mass units.

The AW of an element is the average mass of its atoms contained in one mole. This is a weighted average of the naturally occurring isotopes. For example, the AW of hydrogen is 1.0079 grams per mole, a weighted average of the isotopes that appear in nature. Also, 1 mole of NH_3 has 6.022×10^{23} molecules and weighs about 17.03 grams (the sum of the AW of nitrogen, which is 14.0067, and three times the AW of hydrogen, which is 3[1.0079]). Similarly, the AW of copper (Cu) is 63.55, and therefore one mole of copper has 6.022×10^{23} atoms and weighs about 63.55 grams.

As with the case of colors (chapter 12), we have opted to base our analysis on a measure that represents a count, rather than one that is dependent on the measuring unit, used in a ratio scale. Thus, for color, we based our analysis on wave frequencies (a count of frequency), rather than on wavelengths. In a similar vein, the response ("the dependent variable") for the pursuing analyses is the reciprocal of the atomic weight. This response represents the *number* of moles per unit of mass (grams) (rather than grams per mole), and it will be denoted RMAW (reciprocal metal atomic weight).

The atomic weights for all metals that take part in the pursuing statistical analyses are given in Table 13.1. Table 13.2 provides details about other materials (section 13.3).

13.3 Selecting and Preparing the Sample: Other Substances

13.3.1 Selecting the Sample (Substances)

Other materials that will be analyzed, in terms of their relationships to corresponding numerical values of Hebrew names, are

- Limestone (the major ingredient of which is calcium, belonging to the group of alkaline metals);
- Burned lime (quicklime);

- Silica (of which glass is made—with silicon, the element that belongs to the group of semi-metals, being the major constituent);
- Sodium (natrium, an element that belongs to the group of alkali metals); two names with disputed interpretations appear in the Bible (see comment below);
- Sulfur, an element in the group of nonmetals;
- Lead, a nontransition elemental metal (a basic metal);
- Brass, an alloy composed of cupper and zinc.

Table 13.1. The sample for the statistical analysis of metals.

Metal name	Gold	Tin	Silver	Iron	Copper	Lead
Notation (Latin)	Au (Aurum)	Sn (Stannum)	Ar (Argentum)	Fe (Ferrum)	Cu (Cuprum)	Pb (Plumbum)
Atomic number	79	50	47	26	29	82
Num. val. (MNV)	14	46	160	239 or: 514	363	756
Ato. weight (AW)	196.97	118.69	107.87	55.847	63.546	207.2
Reciprocal AW (RAW)	0.005077	0.008425	0.009271	0.01791	0.01574	0.004826

Table 13.2. The sample for statistical analysis of other substances.

Material name	Calcium carbonate (chalk, lime)	Calcium oxide (burned lime)	Silica	Sodium	Sulfur	Lead	Brass
Notation (Latin)	$CaCO_3$	CaO	SiO_2	Na (Natrium)	S (Sulpur)	Pb (Plumbum)	Alloy (Copper & Zinc)
Atomic number				7	16	82	
Num. val. (MaNV)	213	314	516	612 or: 650	693	756	758
Ato. weight (AW)	100.087	56.0774	60.0843	22.98977	32.066	207.2	107.7197
Reciprocal AW (RAW)	0.009991	0.01782	0.03561	0.043498	0.03119	0.004826	0.009283

Together with the metals (related to in the previous section, with lead appearing in both sets for reasons to be explained later), twelve materials, the names of which appear in the Bible, will be analyzed in this chapter.

13.3.2 Determining Hebrew Names and Their Numerical Values (Substances)

Geer[11] (limestone, with calcium as the main ingredient):

$$213 = (200 = ר) + (10 = י) + (3 = ג)$$

Seed[12] (burned limestone, quicklime):

$$314 = (4 = ד) + (10 = י) + (300 = ש)$$

Sechuchit[13a] (silica):

$$516 = (400 = ת) + (10 = י) + (20 = כ) + (6 = ו) + (20 = כ) + (60 = ס)$$

Neter[14] or *borit*[15] (sodium):

$$650 = (200 = ר) + (400 = ת) + (50 = נ)$$

$$612 = (400 = ת) + (10 = י) + (200 = ר) + (2 = ב)$$

Gofrit[16] (sulfur):

$$693 = (400 = ת) + (10 = י) + (200 = ר) + (80 = פ) + (3 = ג)$$

Oferet[4] (lead):

$$756 = (400 = ת) + (200 = ר) + (80 = פ) + (6 = ו) + (70 = ע)$$

Nechoshet[5] (brass):

$$758 = (400 = ת) + (300 = ש) + (8 = ח) + (50 = נ)$$

Comments

1. A possible reference to limestone (and therefore to the element calcium) is
    made only once in the Bible, in Isaiah 27:9, where lime stone is called *geer*.[11]
    The same word is used in modern Hebrew. It is interesting to note that a
    bone, in Hebrew, that carries calcium in large proportion, is *etzem*,[17] with a
    numerical value of 200—very close to that of *geer*[11] (213).

2. Burned limestone—or quicklime, obtained in a limekiln, where chalk (cal-
    cium carbonate) is calcined to produce quicklime—is addressed three times
    in the Bible, twice with reference to burning (Isa. 23:12, Amos 2:1).

3. *Zechuchit*[13b] in modern Hebrew is "glass." This Hebrew name is mentioned
    in the Bible only once, in Job 28:17. It is written therein with the first letter
    zayin (the seventh letter in the Hebrew alphabet, corrersponding to the
    English *Z*). However, this word can be written in Hebrew also with a first
    letter *samech* (corresponding to the English *S*). As with the possible trans-
    formation of *Mazar* into *Mazal*, to denote Venus and later all planets (refer
    to section 8.3.4 for details), we believe that a comparable development has
    occurred in relation to the Hebrew word for "glass."

    The root of the word *sechuchit*[13a] (written with *samech*) is *S.Ch.Ch.* This is
    the root that gives rise to such words as "screen" (*masach*),[18] "to cover" (*le-sa-
    chech*),[19] and also, by a close root, "transparent" (*sachui*).[20] Since the root
    Z.Ch.Ch originates such words as to purify (*le-zachech*),[21] or "transparent"
    (*zachuch*[22] or *zach*),[23] it is understandable why both roots have originated
    words for glass, the difference being only in their different first letters. In the
    analysis that follows, we use for glass the word *sechuchit*,[13a] which seems to
    be the original word for glass (since it conveys the true function of glass—
    namely, to serve as cover, *masach*).[18] Most importantly, the numerical value
    of *sechuchit*[13a] obeys the same statistical rule that all other materials are con-
    sistent with.

4. The Bible does not relate explicitly to sodium. However, there is an allusion
    to a material named *neter*.[14] It appears twice (Prov. 25:20 and Jer. 2:22). Most
    Jewish interpreters (like Rashi and Malbim) agree that *neter*[14] is some kind of
    soil that in ancient times was used to rub into clothes in order to remove stains.
    This explanation is still unrelated to sodium. However, the Latin name for
    the latter—and this is how it appears in the periodic table of the elements—is
    natrium. This is the same word as used in the Bible (taking into account
    structural linguistic differences between the Hebrew language and Latin).
    We were unable to pinpoint the origin of this strange association of
    neter[14] and natrium. Given the active properties of sodium in water, which is

essential for removing stains, we concluded that probably the *neter*[14] of the Bible is sodium (natrium), the most abundant of the alkali metals. Finally, Proverbs 25:20 relates to *chometz*[24] (vinegar) as something that neutralizes *neter*.[14] This strengthens interpretation of the latter as sodium. (Some biblical translations refer to *neter*[14] as lye, caustic soda, which is a concentrated solution of sodium hydroxide.)

Another word that probably is related to sodium is *borit*.[15] It is mentioned twice in the Bible (Jer. 2:22 and Mal. 3:2). Most interpreters agree that this is also some kind of material for cleaning, and they interpret *borit*[15] as "soap." Since the latter is also based on sodium, we will assume in the following analysis that either *neter*[14] or *borit*[15] refer to the element sodium.

5. *Gofrit*[14] is sulfur both in ancient Jewish sources (like interpretations given for this word in the Bible) and in modern Hebrew.

13.3.3 *Values of the Analyzed Physical Property (Substances)*

Since some of the substances analyzed are composites (they are not pure substances), their AWs have to be carefully decided.

Limestone

Geer[11] (limestone) appears as sedimentary rock in nature. It consists mainly of calcium carbonate—C_aCO_3, which has AW of

$$\text{(AW of calcium} = 40.078) + \text{(AW of carbon} = 12.0107) + 3\text{(AW of oxygen} = 15.9994) = 100.0869 \text{ gram/mole (g/m)}.$$

Quicklime

Seed[12] (burned limestone, quicklime) consists of calcium oxide, C_aO, the AW of which is

$$\text{(AW of calcium} = 40.078) + \text{(AW of oxygen} = 15.9994) = 56.0774 \text{ g/m}.$$

Silica

Sechuchit[13a] is mainly made of silica—S_iO_2. Its AW is

$$\text{(AW of silicon} = 28.0855) + 2\text{(AW of oxygen} = 15.9994) = 60.0843 \text{ g/m}.$$

Sodium, Sulfur, Lead

All three are pure substances (elements). *Neter*[14] or *borit*[15] is assumed to be made mainly of sodium (N_a), the AW of which is 22.9898. *Gofrit*[16] (sulfur) has an AW of 32.066. Finally, *oferet*[4] (lead) has an AW of 207.2.

Brass

For brass, the calculation of the AW is somewhat more complex. To calculate the required AW, we refer to the sort of brass produced in ancient times. Since purification of substances was not developed as in modern times, the brass used in ancient times was Calamine brass. In the following explanations, we were assisted by Wikipedia, the free encyclopedia (http://en.wikipedia.org/wiki/Calamine).

Calamine brass is brass produced by a particular alloying technique using calamine, a zinc ore, rather than metallic zinc. Calamine brass was produced in ancinet times using proportions of two-sevenths fine copper, four-sevenths calamine, and one-seventh shruff (old plate brass). Calamine brass was the first type of brass produced, probably starting during the first millennium BC, and was not replaced in Europe by other brass manufacturers until the eighteenth century (it is likely that Chinese and Indian brass manufacturers had developed more advanced techniques some centuries earlier).

"Calamine" is the common name for an ore of zinc. Calamine brass is obtained by mixing copper with calamine. During the late eighteenth century, it was discovered that what had been thought to be one zinc ore was actually two distinct minerals:

- Zinc carbonate: $ZnCO_3$;
- Zinc silicate: $Zn_4Si_2O_7(OH)_2.H_2O$.

(Zn is zinc, Si is silicon, C is carbon, H is hydrogen, and O is oxygen.)

The two minerals are usually very similar in appearance and can only be distinguished through chemical analysis. The first to separate the minerals was the British chemist and mineralogist James Smithson in 1803. In the mining industry, the term "calamine" is still used to refer to both minerals indiscriminately, but the zinc carbonate is the more abundant mineral in nature and was probably used in ancient times to produce calamine brass.

To obtain the AW (for brass), that will be used in the pursuing statistical analysis, the AW of zinc carbonate was first calculated:

$$AW \text{ of zinc carbonate} = 65.38 \ (= AW \text{ of } Zn) + 12.011 \ (= AW \text{ of carbon})$$
$$+ \ 3*15.9994 \ (= AW \text{ of three oxygen}) = 125.3892 \ g/m$$

$$AW \text{ of calamine brass} = (2/7)*63.546 \ (= AW \text{ of copper})$$
$$+ \ (5/7)(125.3892) = 107.7197 \ g/m$$

This AW is used for *nechoshet*,[5] related to as "brass."

Comments

The above calculation should be regarded as approximate due to the nonprecise weights given to the copper and calamine ingredients that comprise the calamine-brass alloy.

For the six materials addressed in this section, Table 13.2 displays the numerical values of Hebrew names (material numeric value, MaNV), together with the AWs and their RAWs (reciprocal atomic weights).

13.4 Statistical Analysis

13.4.1 Metals

In this section, we apply linear regression for all metals—namely, the four transition metals (gold, silver, iron, and copper) and the two basic metals, tin and lead. The data for this analysis are displayed in Table 13.1. The response used is RAW, the reciprocal of the metal AW, and the regressor (the independent variable) is the Hebrew name's numerical value (metal numeric value, MNV).

Linear regression analysis was implemented. It was realized that lead, a basic metal, does not belong in this analysis, and it was removed from this set of (mostly) transition metals to the more general set of "substances" (to be analyzed in the following subsection). Tin, the other basic metal, also deviates slightly from the general pattern displayed by the transition metals. However, since the tin observation still falls within the 95% confidence limits (after the removal of lead from the analysis), we decided to include it in the analysis of metals.

The results are displayed in Figure 13.1. The MNV values are given atop each observation for easy identification (refer to Table 13.1).

For n = 5, the model F-ratio is 67.78, which is highly significant (p = 0.003752).

As alluded to earlier, the tin observation in Figure 13.1 is somewhat deviant (probably since it is the only nontransition metal). However, it still resides within the 95% confidence interval limits.

A further analysis, which excluded tin, is displayed in Figure 13.2. The regression correlation jumped from 0.97858 in the previous analysis to 0.99113, though the significance of the results is somewhat weaker (for n = 4, the model F-ratio is 111.2, with p = 0.00875).

In both analyses, the likelihood of obtaining by chance F-ratio values these high (or higher) is smaller than 1%.

13.4.2 Substances

This analysis comprised all observations detailed in section 13.3. A first regression run stored a surprise. The results of this analysis are displayed in Figure 13.3. Apparently, there are two distinct groups here: one group that comprises lime, quicklime, silica, and sodium (where the latter is represented by *borit*),[15] and another subset that includes all the other observations (with sodium representable either by *neter*[14] or *borit*[15]—the former was included in the analysis).

We will shortly allude to a possible explanation for that bizarre partition of observations, which still exhibits an interesting pattern.

Analyzing separately the first group, we obtain the results displayed in Figure 13.4. The regression correlation is 0.9998, and for n = 4, the model F-ratio is 4372, which is highly significant (p = 0.00023).

Analyzing the second group, we obtain the results displayed in Figure 13.5. The regression correlation is -0.9915, and for n = 4, the model F-ratio is 115.6, which is highly significant (p = 0.008542).

Why the partition of the two groups? One possible explanation is that the two groups contain elements from different chemical groups, as these are defined in the periodic table. Thus, for the first group, we have composites of calcium (alkaline metal), silicon (semi-metal), and sodium (alkali metal). For the second set of substances, we have sodium (alkali metal), sulfur (nonmetal) and lead (basic metal).

A linguistic explanation may be provided based on the size of the MaNV values in the two groups. All substances in the second group have extremely high values of MaNV, which have put these substances in a set of their own. The high values of the MaNVs still needs elaboration.

Both explanations are not satisfactory, and some more in-depth exploration is needed. The high statistical significance is undebatable.

194

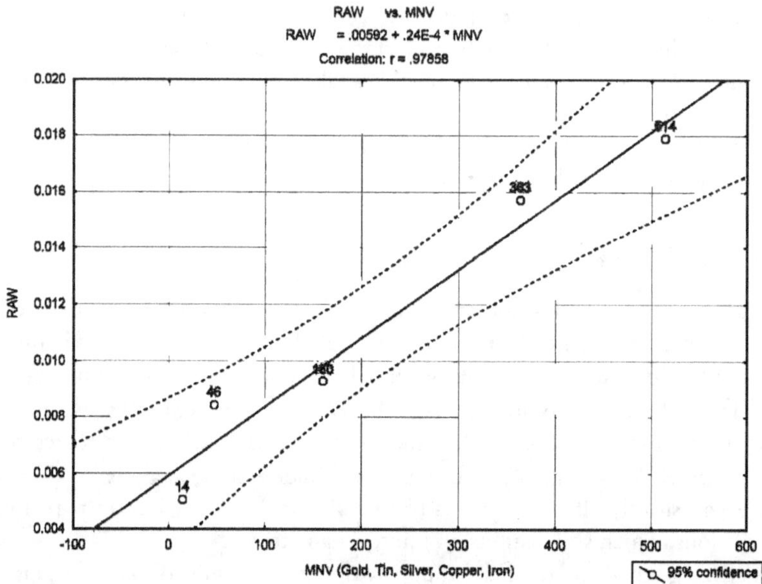

Figure 13.1. Plot for all metals. MNV values are given atop each observation.

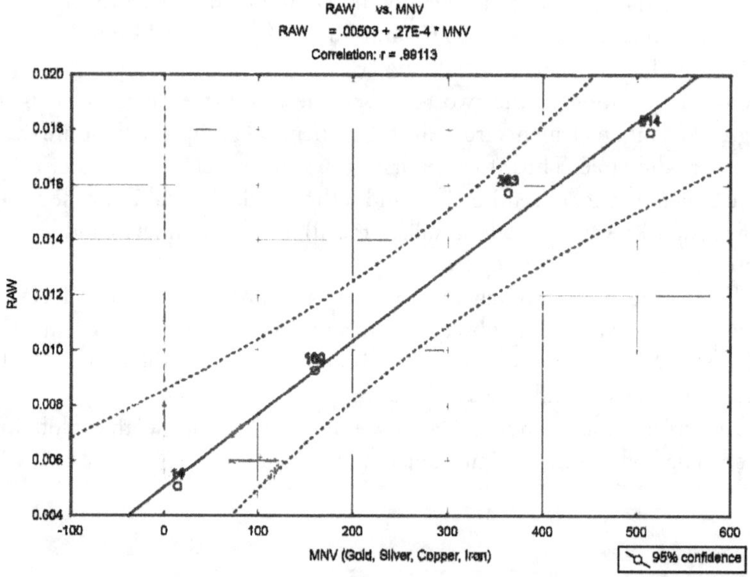

Figure 13.2. Plot for metals (without Tin).

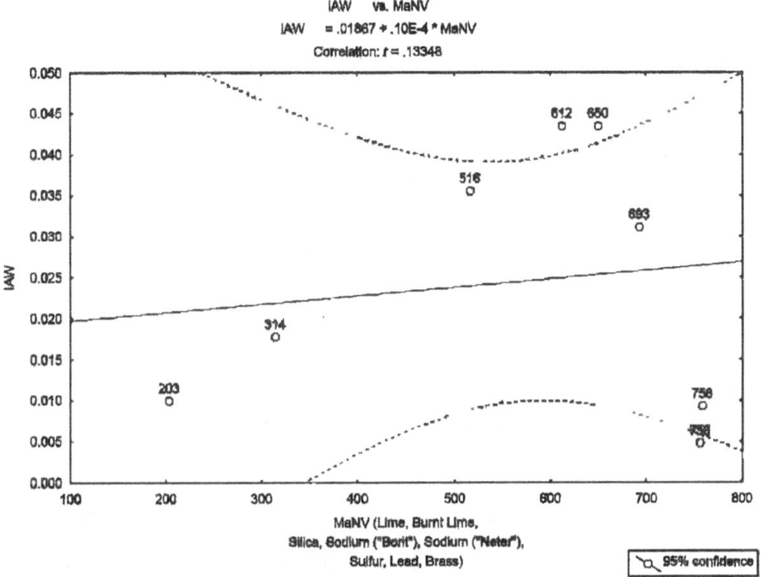

Figure 13.3. All other materials.

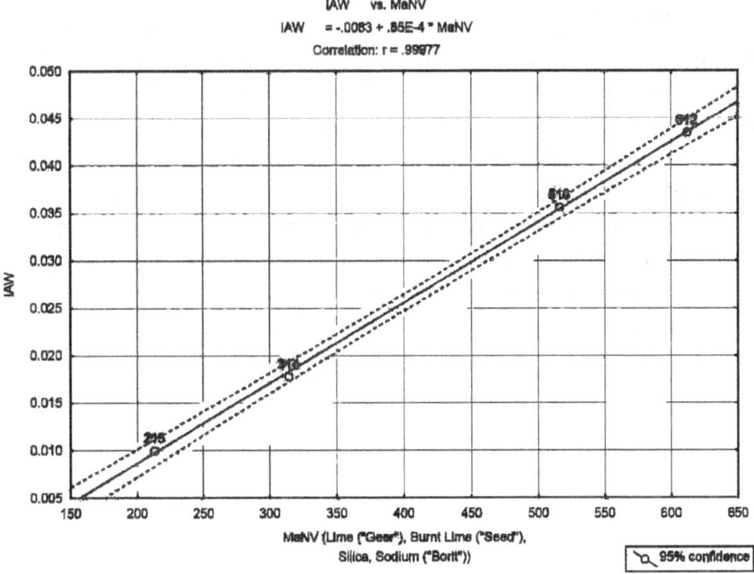

Figure 13.4. Plot of other materials (Group I).

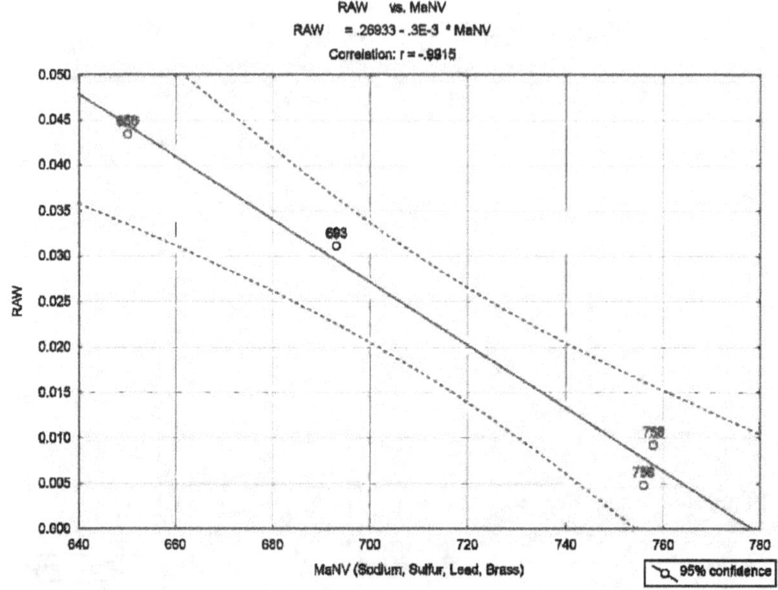

Figure 13.5. Plot of other materials (Group II).

13.5 Summary

Statistical analysis has been applied to the numeric values of biblical Hebrew names, and the corresponding reciprocal atomic weights, of twelve substances, eight elements (gold, silver, tin, lead, copper, iron, sodium, and sulfur), three composites (calcium carbonate, calcium oxide, and silica) and one alloy (brass).

The results of this analysis reveal that the values of the Hebrew names are equivalent to the reciprocal AW of the materials analyzed—namely, they represent linearly transformed number of molecules per unit of mass (irrespective of how this unit is defined), or, equivalently (up to a change in location and scale) the number of moles per gram.

These are all coincidences ... or maybe not.

PART III

Coincidences in the Bible

CHAPTER 14

"In the beginning ...
the earth was without form and void" (?)

14.1 Biblical Description of the Beginning and Its Hebrew Context

The book of Genesis starts with the story of creation:

> "In the beginning God created the heaven and the earth. And the earth was without form, and void."

This is a strange way to start description of a newborn Earth (whatever that means). In this chapter we analyze what is really meant by the Hebrew original words for "form" and "void." Indeed, the translated English words convey the real meaning of the Hebrew words. Yet, the latter convey "without form and void" in an extremely indirect way, so that not being familiar with the true original sense of the words may deprive one of the full context of the only biblical depiction of Earth at the moment of creation. Furthermore, how these words may be inter-related to most modern cosmological theories and most recent space observations is also lost.

The Hebrew words for "without form and void" are just *tohu*[1] and *bohu*.[2] What is meant by these words? The answer may be vague, since a combination of these words reappears only once in the whole Bible, with the words of the prophet Jeremiah: "I beheld the earth, and, lo, it was waste [*tohu*[1]] and void [*bohu*[2]]; And the heavens, and they had not their light" (Jer. 4:23). For lack of any other source to lend sense to these words, it is apparent that this translation of the *tohu*[1] and *bohu*[2] relies on what comes next in Jeremiah: "For thus says the Lord, The whole land shall be desolate; Yet will I not make a full end" (Jer. 4:27). Thus, if the

199

prophecy is about God rendering fertile land into desert, then obviously *tohu*[1] and *bohu*[2] mean "waste" and "void."

The prophet Isaiah uses *tohu*[1] and *bohu*[2] not as adjacent words, but in close proximity: "And he shall stretch out upon it the line of confusion [*kav-tohu*[3]], and the plummet of emptiness [*avnei bohu*[4]]" (Isa. 34:11). The key words here are *kav*[3] (the biblical yardstick, or measure rod) and *avnei*[4] (literally, "bricks of"). The Malbim (1809–79) explains that both words relate to a house. *Tohu*[1] refers to its external appearance, while *bohu*[2] refers to the internal build-up. Thus, the former marks "Lack of the beauty, the order and the form externally," as revealed by the yardstick which measures the house from the outside. By contrast, *bohu*[2] marks this lack in its internal composition, where "bricks of *bohu*" insinuates lack of inner strength to the house, and existence of disorder in the internal makeup oft he measured house.

Referring to *tohu*[1] and *bohu*[2] in the book of Genesis, Malbim essentially pursues the same explanation. He repeats previous interpreters, like the Ramban (1194–1270), who had regarded *tohu*[1] as the primordial matter that, lacking any form, is the source of puzzlement (hence the word *tahah*,[5] "was puzzled"). However, *bohu*[2] is the *potential* form of that primordial matter, which, since yet only in potential, is written like *bo-hu*,[6] literally meaning in Hebrew, "in it, it is." (A similar interpretation is given in Jewish tradition to the Hebrew word for "cattle," *behemah*,[7] which can be read, "bah-mah"[8]—literally, "In it—what?"—appropriately relating to the wisdom one can find in cattle.)

In this chapter, a different approach is pursued. First, we analyze the roots of *tohu*[1] and *bohu*,[2] thereby obtaining the full context of this strange combination of words. Then we analyze verbs derived from another word, which seems to deliver a sense similar to that of the *tohu*[1] and *bohu*.[2] This analysis helps clarify further the meaning of these qualifying words for the creation of the Earth. Finally, we explore how compatible are these descriptive words of the universe, at creation time, with the latest cosmology theories.

Prior to proceeding with this analysis, an important distinction needs to be made. In the first ten verses in Genesis, it becomes apparent that "the heaven" and "the earth" in Genesis 1:1–2 are not "Heaven" and "Earth" in Genesis 1:6–10. Let us read the latter (verse 7) carefully:

"And God *made* the firmament ["sky" in Hebrew], and divided the waters which were under the firmament from the waters which were above the firmament: and it was so. And God called the firmament Heaven" (Gen. 1:7–8).

This description clearly conveys two facts. First, God *made* the firmament; second, he called it "Heaven." Nothing was created when the so-called "Heaven" was made. This is significant. Both the Bible and later Jewish mysticism (Kabbalah) distinguish between the worlds of creating, forming, and doing (or making). A good demonstration of that is given by the prophet Isaiah, in one of the most strongly expressed statements about the relationship between God and the people of Israel: "Every one that is called by my name: for my glory I have created him, I have formed him; yea, I have made him" (Isa. 43:7).

In the Hebrew language, each of these verbs carries distinct and different important meaning. In particular, there is strong distinction between creating and doing. The quotation from Isaiah makes it clear that in the book of Genesis what we call "sky," which God called "Heaven," was *made* (*not* created), and it was "made" *after* "the heaven" (whatever that term means) had been "created." (Capitalization of "heaven" (and later "earth"), when it occurs, follows the traditional biblical English translation; there is no similar capitalization in the original Hebrew text.)

The same distinction extends to Earth. First, God created "the earth" (verse 1), then,

"And God said, Let the waters under the heaven be gathered together unto one place, and let the dry land appear: and it was so. And God called the dry land Earth" (Gen. 1:9, 10).

Again, God *made* "dry land" and named it "Earth," but there is no indication that this "Earth" was created. Furthermore, obviously making "Earth" (dry land) is distinct from creating "the earth," as depicted in the first two verses of Genesis. If that were not so, the Bible would then be insinuating that "Heaven" and "Earth" were created twice!

Two major qualifications thus seem to emerge on a careful reading of the text. First, "the heaven" and "the earth" were created. However there is no qualification in the text as to the nature of "the heaven," and only one qualification is given about "the earth"—namely, that it was *tohu*[1] and *bohu*.[2] Secondly, God *made* the sky, which he called just "Heaven," and the "dry land," which he called just "Earth." These were *made* after the *creation*, and one is only left to wonder, for lack of any source of information, why the Divine "chose" to call the sky by the same name as *the* created "heaven." Similarly, what are the lines of correspondence that "motivated" calling "Earth," as the term is commonly used today, by the same name as the "created earth," related to in the first verse of Genesis? We will attempt some explanation regarding "Earth" later on.

Having made the distinction between the two concepts of "Heaven" and "Earth"—one which was "created" but remains mysterious and mostly undefined, and another that in no uncertain terms is explicitly described, yet unrelated to creation—we may proceed to analyze the linguistic contents of the only description given for the creation—namely, that the created earth was *tohu*[1] and *bohu*.[2]

We start by revealing a most bizarre characteristic about the only description of the moment of creation. A "root" analysis of verbs derived from the same roots as *tohu*[1] and *bohu*[2] reveals that these verbs relate to modes of observation. How bizarre to choose that as the only qualification of the just-born Earth (whatever that term means). The root of *tohu*[1] is *T.H.H*, which gives rise to the Hebrew verb *tahah*.[5] The root of *bohu*[2] is *B.H.H*, which gives rise to the Hebrew verb *bahah*.[9] Both verbs relate to very specific modes of observing—specifically, looking at something in wonder, not really grasping its meaning (*tahah*),[3] or gazing at something purposelessly (*bahah*),[9] because there is nothing to see or because what is seen has no meaning whatsoever ... indeed, a strange way to describe a newly born Earth—in fact, the universe, as we shall see shortly.

Consider another context where Jewish tradition uses the word *tohu*.[1] The Hebrew calendar counts the number of years from creation. For example, 2005, prior to October 4 (when the new Jewish year started), was the Hebrew year 5765. Jewish tradition believes that the Messiah will come at the end of a six-thousand-year period. However, all these years, prior to the coming of the Messiah, are divided into three sets of two thousand years each, with each set bearing a different name.

The first two thousand years are called Years of *Tohu*.[1] Why? Because these were the years when paganism was prevalent, and the worship of God was secularized. This perception of the first two millennia is based, among other things, on a commonly accepted interpretation for the word *huchal*,[10] in "Then is was [*huchal*[10]] to call the name of God" (Gen. 4:26). The root of this word is *Ch.L.L*, from which such meanings are derived as "empty space," a mortally wounded person ("body without a soul"), "secular," and also defamation of God (interpretation of Rashi, one of the greatest biblical interpreters). In other words, before the emergence of Abraham (at the beginning of the second set of two thousand years), and before Abraham had started to "call the name of God" (the seed of monotheism), idolatry was the only way God was recognized. The Bible hints at the ignoring of God, or worshipping him in a secularized manner, by relating names given to children (like *Mhuyael*[11]—literally, "obliterate God"; and *Metushael*[12]—literally, short for "dead are those eager for God," Gen. 4:18).

Jewish tradition calls these years "years of *tohu*,"[1] meaning "years without meaning."

Let us refer to the common usage of the words *tohu*[1] and *bohu*[2] in other parts of the Bible—though, as alluded to earlier, the combination of these words as *toho va-vohu*[13] appears only once again, in the above quotation from the book of Jeremiah. In particular, we wish to understand from these other usages of the words in the Bible why most English translations opted, correctly, to relate to these words as meaning that "the earth" (whatever this means) was without form or contents. We start with a few examples from the Bible:

- "He found him in a desert land, and in the waste [*tohu*[1]] howling wilderness" (Deut. 32:10);

- "They trust in vanity [*tohu*[1]] and speak lies; they conceive mischief, and bring forth iniquity" (Isa. 59:4);

- "I beheld the earth, and, lo, it was waste and void [*tohu va-vohu*[13]]" (Jer. 4:23).

All these examples, and others, refer to *tohu*[1] and *bohu*[2] as nouns, which they are. However, they are used in different contexts in the various verses, which makes it hard to understand their exact meanings. So perhaps understanding the Hebrew *verbs* derived from the same roots as *tohu*[1] and *bohu*[2] may be helpful. Unfortunately, these verbs, though used in other ancient Jewish texts, do not appear as such in the Bible.

It seems more productive to consider other biblical Hebrew words with similar meanings—namely, "desert" or "wilderness." Studying verbs derived from these words, one may deduce what the exact meanings are of nonbiblical verbs associated with the roots of *tohu*[1] and *bohu*.[2] From this, one may infer the exact meanings of the latter.

One such word is *shmamah*[14] (wilderness). Learning the contents of verbs derived from *shmamah*[14] may help us break the code of what is really meant by *tohu*[1] and *bohu*.[2] Furthermore, it will confer upon the latter the same meanings as stored in the Hebrew verbs derived from the same roots.

The root of *shmamah*[14] is *S.M.M.* This root gives rise to verbs that convey wondering, feeling amazement, feeling anxiety, and being startled.

Note these examples:

- "All they that know thee among the peoples shall be appalled [*shamemu*[15]] at thee" (Ezek. 28:19);

- "And I will bring the land into desolation: and your enemies who dwell in it shall be astonished [*shamemu*[15]] at it" (Lev. 26:32);

- "And I looked and there was none to help; and I gazed astonished [*eshtomem*[16]] but there was none to uphold" (Isa. 63:5);

These examples and others describe the emotional state of a person who is in the desert: astonished, anxious, startled, overwhelmed ("and I sat where they sat, and remained there overwhelmed [*mashmim*[17]] among them for seven days," Ezek. 3:15). Rashi (1040–1105) explains *mashmim*[17] as a person who is "paralyzed to talk," while the Radak (1160–1235) explains this as "puzzled and alarmed." In modern Hebrew, another meaning was derived from the root *S.M.M*, based on an extension of the root into a four-letter root *S.A.M.M*, meaning "to be bored."

A similar fate befell verbs derived from *tohu*[1] and *bohu*[2] in the *nonbiblical* Hebrew language. Ancient written Jewish texts, as well as modern Hebrew, use verbs derived from these words to imply wondering because no sense can be made of the observed (verbs derived from *tohu*)[1] and purposeless gazing about, because there is nothing to look at (verbs derived from *bohu*).[2]

Let us explore the meanings of these verbs.

The verb *tahah*[5] means, in Hebrew (singular, masculine) "was astonished, amazed," but also "he reflected upon, trying to make sense." Thus, one may say "*Tahiti*[18] [I was wondering] what did she really mean by that." An often used idiom in Hebrew is "*Tahiti al kankano*,"[19] meaning, "I was wondering what is the essence of this man." The verb *bahah*[9] similarly means "he was surprised, amazed." But it also means, in Hebrew, "he gazed purposelessly in the air because he had nothing to look at." Thus, one may say: "I was sitting at the dentist clinic, and I gazed [*bahiti*[20]] at the wall."

It is conceivable how all these are associated with wilderness. But what does it mean that at the moment of creation, one would be wondering and amazed because it looks like desert—namely, there was no form and contents, and, in other words, "there was nothing to observe"?

14.2 Cosmological Theories of the Beginning

The bizarre coincidence is now in full view. *Tohu va-vohu*,[13] "devoid of form and contents," is exactly how modern cosmology describes the first moments of creation. In fact, if one were asked to describe the universe at the moment of creation or shortly thereafter, he or she could not have provided, in light of modern cosmology, a better depiction than the universe as in a state devoid of form and contents to such a degree that would make an observer wonder, just as in the desert, what sense can be made of the observed. Furthermore, he or she would gaze purposelessly, because "there is nothing to see."

The key word here is uniformity. Modern cosmological theories speak about lack of any information in the just created universe because of the extremely, and unexplainable, uniformity in the distribution of energy and plasma. This uniformity is supported both by theory and by experimental observations, and it is far from being intuitive.

Let us first relate to how modern cosmologists describe the first moments of creation. As we do not wish to delve into exact scientific descriptions, instead of engaging in exact time periods (like 10^{-43}, when the breaking of the ten dimensions of the just-born universe into its constituent sets of 6 and 4 dimensions was supposed to have taken place), we will mostly speak in unspecified terms like "moments" or "time intervals."

According to modern cosmology, at the time of the big bang, the universe was a soup of radiation and particles—or, in the words of Singh (2004), "The universe contained mainly protons, neutrons and electrons, all bathed in a sea of light." However, the universe was opaque, "like a thick, absorbing and impenetrable fog" (Kaku 1994, 198) since "the universe was so hot that possibly forming atoms were continually ripped apart by radiation as soon as they were formed." Shortly after the big bang, the universe had undergone an era of quick inflation, when the universe expanded by perhaps a factor of 10^{30} or more. With inflation and ever since, the universe has been cooling down. At about 380,000 years after the big bang, cooling down reached 3,000 degrees (Kaku 2005, 58), a phase where atoms could be created without being destroyed by radiation. This meant that "light could travel long distances without being scattered, and the universe suddenly became black and transparent" (Kaku 1994, 198). Electrically charged particles, like electrons and protons, which disrupt the motion of light beams, combined to form electrically neutral atoms, which then allowed light to travel freely. This light, produced in the early stages of the universe, today suffuses all of space with microwave photons (Greene 2004, 515).

Light, as we know it today, was "created" as a result of the creation of the first atoms, about 380,000 years *after* the big bang.

Remnants of this light, which were theoretically conceived to permeate the whole universe, could one day be observed. This prediction was first proposed by George Gamow, and his students Ralph Alpher and Robert Herman, soon after World War II (in 1948). It was finally detected, by accident, in 1964 by the Bell Laboratory scientists Arno Penzias and Robert Wilson—an achievement that won them the Physics Nobel Prize in 1978. This remnant from the big bang is known as cosmic microwave background (CMB) radiation.

A most interesting property of CMB is its extreme uniformity. The CMB is measured by its temperature, which is 2.73 degrees above the absolute zero (−273.15 °C). As revealed by precision satellite measurements, the temperature of the radiation in one part of the sky differs from that in another part by less than a thousandth of a degree. In fact, for many years this extreme uniformity was puzzling to scientists. If the universe was so uniform at the big bang, as revealed by the CMB radiation, where are those slight fluctuations in the uniformity of the universe that could eventually lead to the creation of galaxies and stars? After all, uniformity of the CMB radiation meant uniformity in the distribution of matter in the universe—and, consequently, no celestial objects, as we know them today, could have been created.

Something was missing.

This all changed with the launch of COBE (Cosmic Background Explorer) satellite, back in 1989. The satellite gathered highly accurate measurements throughout 1990 and 1991, and the public announcement of the results of the statistical analysis of these data was made in April 1992. The results were staggering: "The COBE satellite had found evidence that nearly 300,000 years or so after the moment of creation, there were tiny variations in CMB radiation across the universe at the level of 1 part in 100,000" (Singh 2004, 462). In other words, ripplelike variations, amounting to about ten millionths of a degree, were discovered. These were the first signs of structures emerging in the early universe. These variations grew with time and ultimately resulted in the galaxies that we see today.

The connection between modern-day cosmology and the succinct description of the universe at its infancy epoch now becomes clear: "the Earth"—namely, the universe—was at the beginning, even before observable light was created, so uniformly distributed in space that no information was conveyed. There was no sense of that which existed; everything was absolutely homogenous. An observing person would be alarmed, paralyzed, unable to speak, unable to make any sense of that which was observed—because there was nothing to observe; there was no information. Everything was uniform, like … in the desert.

The *tohu*[1] and *bohu*,[2] as their meanings were inferred from verbs associated with *shmamah*,[14] convey accurately the uniformity of the universe at the beginning, with a complete lack of information in the just-born universe. The description of the observable light in Genesis as the result of the command of God *after* the depiction of "the earth" as *toho va-vohu*[13] is also consistent with modern cosmology.

Comments

1. It is interesting to note that in modern Hebrew the meaning of *tohu*[1] and *bohu*[2] is far displaced from its original meaning as "wilderness." In modern Hebrew, *tohu va-vohu*[13] simply means "chaos, complete disorder." Although this meaning is far removed from any connotations of a desert, in a twisted way, the original sense has been revoked—but from an altogether different perspective: one is confused and cannot make sense of what is observed not because it is a "desolate wilderness," but because there is complete chaos.

    Thus, just as in biblical discourse, one is bewildered and confused in the desert because "there is nothing to observe." So in chaos, one is confused and bewildered because there are no patterns or structures to observe that would allow making sense of the observed. The desert becomes, for the Bible, the epitome of that which cannot make sense, and therefore is confusing.

The reason that we refer to the modern usage of *tohu va-vohu*[13] as somewhat twisted is because uniformity was there at the beginning, but chaos was not. The latter implies increasing entropy; the former, minimum entropy. Chaos does not imply uniformity—rather, the opposite. Uniformity in the distribution of energy and matter at the big bang and shortly thereafter is the source of all forms and structure in the universe. It is the phase of existence of the universe when the overall entropy of the universe was at its minimal level. Chaos, on the other hand, is associated with increased entropy. Thus, the *toho va-vohu*[13] of Genesis is diametrically opposite to that which is implied by the modern usage of these words.

2. Earlier, we addressed a tendency found in the Bible to take a certain word and render it an ultimate embodiment of a concept. Thus, the "womb" becomes the epitome for "mercy" (refer to subsection 2.1.1), and *shamayim*[21] (sky), the plural of "there" (*sham*),[22] is the epitome of that which is absolutely inaccessible ("the ultimate there, which can never become here," at least from an ancient-times perspective——refer to section 5.2).

   In a similar vein, the Bible relates to *tohu*[1] and *bohu*[2] as the ultimate description of a state devoid of any patterns and structures. Shadal, an acronym for a renowned Jewish interpreter of the Bible (Shmuel David Lutzato, who lived in Europe in the nineteenth century), writes this about *tohu va-vohu*:[13] "The context of these words is desolate wilderness, because in Aramaic 'Taha and Baha' relates to astonishment, as they said in Bereshit Raba (B, A): 'And that slave was sitting being "Tohae and Bohae[23]"' (present tense), meaning, being bewildered. And also in the language of the Assyrians, "Etbahbah[24]" means "becoming bored," and "Boahbah[25]" relates to wonder and bewilderment."

14.3 Summary of Main Points

- The story of creation, as given in Genesis, relates to the creation of "the heaven" (no qualification) and "the earth," which is qualified as "without form and contents."

- The *created* heaven and Earth are different from those *made* by God. The latter are not "the heaven" and "the earth," but rather "sky" and "dry land," respectively, named by the Divine as "Heaven" and "Earth" (no definite article); This would lead one to deduce that the *created* Earth refers to the universe, while the *made* Earth refers to the common usage of this word today.

- Linguistic analysis of *tohu*[1] and *bohu*,[2] the only words describing the *created* Earth, indicates an allegory with desolate wilderness, where an individual is staring amazed and startled because he or she has nothing to observe, or because no sense can be made of what is being observed. Comparison with another Hebrew word for wilderness, *shmamah*,[14] reveals a similar pattern of evolving verbs that indicate amazement and anxiety, but also boredom.

- Modern-day usage of *tohu*[1] and *bohu*[2] implies chaos, complete disorder, and lack of information. This implies growing entropy, contrary to the meaning imparted by the same words in Genesis, where *tohu va-vohu*[13] implies minimal entropy due to the overall *uniformity* (not chaos) in the distribution of matter and energy.

- The comparison in Genesis of the created Earth with desolate wilderness indicates that the main feature of the *created* universe, which the Bible conveys to the reader, is extreme uniformity—the universe being devoid of any structures or patterns, and in fact of any visible information (just as in an ultimate realization of the concept of a desert).

- Modern cosmology, as well as temperature measurements of the CMB radiation, reveal that even about 380,000 years after the big bang (however this number is deduced), the distribution of matter (in the form of plasma) and energy in the universe was so uniform that the temperature of the CMB radiation was, across space, uniform to within less than one thousandth of a degree. More recently obtained, highly accurate measurements, collected within the COBE project, detected fluctuations in the CMB radiation (which indicate the existence of spatial fluctuations in matter density in the early universe) that are of the miniscule order of 10^{-5} (one part in 100,000). These tiny fluctuations in the overall uniformity of the just-created universe ultimately gave rise to spatial structures and celestial objects as we know them today.

These are all coincidences ... maybe.

CHAPTER 15

Laban: The Case of a Lost Identity

15.1 Introduction

Laban is a biblical personality who makes first and last appearances in the book of Genesis—at 24:29 and 31:55, respectively. He is also named "Laban the Aramean" (Gen. 25:20) after his place of residence. Laban and what he represents epitomizes, in Jewish tradition, one of the gravest threats to the Jewish people and its very existence. It is therefore no coincidence that when a Jew is sitting at the table for the Seder, on Passover's eve, to read the Haggadah,[1] one of the verses relates to Laban in no uncertain negative terms: "Go and realize what Laban the Aramean wished to inflict on Jacob, our patriarch. Pharaoh decreed against the males only, however Laban wished to uproot all" (for sources to the double statements in the last sentence, refer to Exod. 1:16 and Deut. 26:5, respectively).

Why is Laban's archetype so menacing to the very existence of the Jewish people? Because Laban represents a total loss of identity, the mixing together of all. Laban wished to preserve no distinctive features, to display no particularity of personality, and no particularity of culture or of personal history. In today's speech, one would say of Laban's philosophy of life, "everything goes," or of Laban's ideal, "the global village."

What, indeed, comprises a person's own individual identity? One can assert that these minimal essentials are required to define one's own identity:

- One's own parents.
- One's own children.
- One's own religion.
- One's own language.
- One's own property.

On each of these counts, Laban is making a huge mishmash, unable to relate in an adequate fashion to any possibly identifying quality of his very existence, ultimately resulting in a display of a total loss of identity.

15.2 Mixing Laban's Parents

Laban is the brother of Rebecca, the wife of Isaac. Both Laban and Rebecca are children of Bethuel (the father) (for example, Gen. 24:15, 28:5). Their common grandmother is Milcah, and their common grandfather is Nachor, the brother of Abraham and Haran (Gen. 11:26). Both Betuel and Nachor, son and father, were idol worshippers—as can be seen, for example, by the story of how Rachel, daughter of Laban, is stealing Laban's idols (Gen. 31:19, 30). This important point will be addressed shortly. The mother of Laban is mentioned nowhere, probably because for a person whose identity has been surrendered, no reference to the mother is material. As it turns out, the identity of the father is equally of no significance. So Laban mixes together the father and the grandfather, feeling that it is of "no consequence." Not only is the identity of his parents unimportant; his parents themselves are not important.

Consider this:

- Abraham sends his chief servant, "the eldest servant of his house," to Aram-Naharayim, the city of Nachor, to take a wife for his son, Isaac. The slave first meets Rebecca as she is out to draw water from the well (Gen. 24:15). When Rebecca runs back to break the news to her "mother's home" (Gen. 24:28), the brother, Laban, takes control (not Rebecca's father, Bethuel). So Laban invites the servant to his home, though one naturally expects the servant, on a mission on behalf of Abraham, to be a guest of Rebecca's parents. Not so. Now, the narrator in Genesis details how the servant tells his story, regarding the purpose of his visit, to Rebecca's father and asks for permission to be granted for this prearranged marriage (Gen. 24:34–49). Who would one expect to respond to this request? The father? Not exactly. As the Bible tells the story, once the servant concludes his "statement," the reply starts with: "And Laban and Bethuel answered" (Gen. 24:50). First Laban, the son, is mentioned then the father, very unexpectedly. More bizarre is the qualifying word for "answered," which comes, in the Hebrew original, in the singular (*va-yan*)[2] and not, as one might expect, in the plural (*va-yanu*).[3] In other words, though two people answered, the Bible makes it abundantly clear that the "answered" was conveyed by one person only. Obviously, Laban is the only speaker (his name appeared first), and he speaks on behalf of both himself and his father. Bethuel is not speaking al all. He has no say, contrary to the likely custom in those days, when permission for an arranged marriage would be granted by the father. In short, the father is not important at all.

- Who is the real father of Laban? As one may realize by an earlier quote, Laban is definitely the son of Betuel (refer to Gen. 28:5). Yet Laban ignores that and appears in public as the son of Nachor (the grandfather). Thus, when Jacob arrives at Charan, on a mission to find a spouse for himself at the command of his parents, Isaac and Rebecca, he asks the shepherds, at a well in the field near Charan, whether they know of "Laban the son of Nachor." They answer briefly with an unfriendly "we know" (Gen. 29:5). Several verses later, the biblical narrator repeatedly reminds us that Laban is the brother of Jacob's mother, just to make sure that the reader understands that Laban cannot possibly be the son of Nachor (Gen. 29:10).

- Laban later makes a "strategic" covenant with Jacob (Gen. 31:48–55). Jacob swears to be loyal to the covenant in the name of his father, Isaac. Laban swears in the name of the Gods of Abraham and Nachor, the grandparents, again skipping the fathers (Gen. 31:53).

15.3 Mixing Laban's Children

As with parents, so with children: Laban mixes his daughters too. No remorse is expressed; many nonrelevant explanations are given. After Jacob has worked for Laban for seven years, he asks Laban to give him, as his compensation mutually agreed upon in advance, Laban's daughter, Rachel, "whom Jacob loved," for a wife (Gen. 29:20–21). Laban is making a feast, and deceptively brings Lea, his other daughter, to Jacob (instead of Rachel). Jacob unknowingly sleeps with Lea. The next morning, Laban gives a post-factum explanation that this is not the custom to let the younger marry before the firstborn (Gen. 29:25–27). Jacob has no choice but to work another seven years to fulfill his desire to take Rachel to be his wife.

The story of Laban's daughters, and how he swapped one with the other, has one common thread with the story of Laban's parents: Laban does not hesitate to confuse one with another. From his point of view, everything belongs to the same mixture; nothing is identifiable.

15.4 Mixing Religious Faiths

When Laban makes a covenant with Jacob, he excitedly exclaims, "The God of Abraham and the God of Nachor will judge between the two of us" (Gen. 31:53). The same sentence can also be read, "The gods of Abraham and the gods of Nachor will judge between the two of us" (in Hebrew, the word *Elohim* can mean both God and gods).

Let us read it again to make sure no mistake has been made: "The God of Abraham and the God of Nachor"? Did we really read this sentence in the Bible?

Previously, we have related to the fact that Nachor and Laban were both pagans—idol worshippers. Abraham had already called upon the name of God, Jehovah (Gen. 12:8). Obviously, Laban is swearing in the names of totally different perceptions of God. He is mixing together the world of paganism and the world of monotheism as if they were on the same footing—of equal validity, indistinguishable from one other. Again, Laban is incredibly nondiscerning; in his world, everything goes.

15.5 Mixing Languages

Throughout Genesis, Laban's language is always Hebrew. He never uses terms borrowed from a foreign language. Furthermore, his daughters all carry names with a Hebrew meaning (Rachel is "sheep"; Lea literally means "exhausted"). Therefore, when Laban suggests to Jacob a covenant between them, and they build a monument to serve as testimony for the covenant, Jacob properly calls this monument *Gal-Ed*,[4] which in Hebrew literally means "a testimony pile of stones." Laban has the same name in his mind, only he uses Aramaic: *Yegar Sahaduta*[5] (Gen. 31:47). *Yegar* is a pile, and *sahaduta* means "testimony." Thus, for Laban, languages can also be mixed together with no consequence.

15.6 Mixing Property

The same pattern of mixing together is revealed in how Laban relates to his property and to Jacob's. Any attempt by Jacob to separate his cattle from Laban's is responded to with deceit, and Laban does his utmost to obstruct such separation.

The story of how Laban repeatedly tries to play tricks with Jacob in order to avoid separation and discrimination between their flocks is recounted in detail in Genesis 30–31.

Rachel and Lea, Bethuel and Nachor, monotheism and paganism, Hebrew and Aramaic, Laban's property and Jacob's: Laban is devoid of any sense of identity. Parents, children, religious faiths, languages, property—they are indistinguishable and exchangeable. They can all be mixed together.

15.7 What is Laban in Hebrew?

Laban, in Hebrew, means "white."

This is indeed extraordinary. Throughout the Old Testament, and as in other cultures, "white" always carries connotations of purity, cleanliness, and celebration. White always appears with extremely positive undertones. Thus, when God calls on the people of Israel to remove the evil from their deeds, he promises: "If your sins will be like red garments—like snow will they whiten" (Isa. 1:18).

Yet Laban, the epitome of mixture, always appears in the negative. In fact, the (repeated) qualifying of Laban as "the Aramean" would yield, by permutation of the letters sequence, "the deceiver" (Laban the *Ramai*).[6] Furthermore, read in reverse, Laban yields *Naval*,[7] Hebrew for villain. This is indeed how Jewish tradition has perceived Laban over the centuries, based on the accounts of his conduct in Genesis.

A further extraordinary feature of Laban's name: it is the only one throughout the Bible that means also a name of a color.

In 1666, Isaac Newton discovered that white light is a *mixture* of all colors.

Every scientist since Aristotle had believed that white light was a basic single entity. The chromatic aberration in a telescope lens convinced Newton otherwise. When he passed a thin beam of sunlight through a glass prism, Newton noted the spectrum of colors that was formed. He therefore argued that white light is really a mixture of many different types of rays that are refracted at slightly different angles, and that each different type of ray produces a different spectral color. (Refer, for details, for example, to the BBC site at http://www.bbc.co.uk/history/historic_figures/newton_isaac.shtml.)

The Bible, in a bizarre coincidence, opted to call the champion of the "mixing of all colors" by the name of a color. And the selected color, of all possible colors, was ... white.

These are all coincidences ... maybe.

Comments

There are two pairs of biblical heroes, one epitomizing evil (or at the least indifference to evil), and the other epitomizes fight against evil (or compassion to people). The first pair is Laban and Noah. The second pair is Abraham and Jonah. Laban is a villain for all the detailed descriptions of his conduct and utterances, as conveyed in the Bible and as elaborated on by Jewish sages throughout years of Jewish scholarship. Noah is a person of a special kind. He is called Noah by his parents because "This one shall comfort us [*yenachamenu*[8]] for our work and the toil of our hands, because of the ground which the Lord has cursed" (Gen. 5:29). However, the root of Noah is not derived from "comforting," but from another root that means "to rest." In fact, in modern Hebrew, *noah* means "comfortable," which is apparently associated with the verb "to rest," rather than with the verb "to comfort." "Resting" is a good description of Noah's conduct relative to his fellow citizens. When Noah realizes that disaster is approaching, since "the earth was full of iniquity [*chamas*[9]]" (Gen. 6:11), he *comfortably* refrains from issuing warnings to his fellow citizens to mend their moral transgressions. This is why Jewish sages interprets the verse "Noah was a just man and perfect in his generations" (Gen. 6:9) to imply that Noah was "perfect," but just relative to his generation.

The story of Noah should be contrasted with the conduct of Jonah. After some futile attempts to escape the mission assigned to him by God, Jonah travels to the city of Nineveh to warn its wicked people of their immoral conduct. He is fulfilling his assignment. The people of Nineveh change their ways, and they are saved. The Bible wishes to drive home the comparison between Noah and Jonah by using in both cases the same word (*chamas*[9]) to describe what was wrong: "So the people of Nineveh believed God, and proclaimed a fast ..." and the king of Nineveh issued a decree "saying, Let neither man nor beast, herd nor flock, taste any thing ... and let them turn everyone from his evil way and from the iniquity [*chamas*[9]] that is in their hands" (Jonah 3:5, 8).

Describing how the people of Nineveh were saved because they mended their ways, following Jonah's warning, and comparing that to Noah's story, gives one a sense of the many different modes in which evil can express itself, and why Noah was only "perfect in his generations" (Gen. 6:9).

On top of these is Abraham, trying to save Sodom and Gomorra from total destruction. Abraham is arguing with God, lest he allow the righteous to perish with the wicked: "And Abraham drew near, and said, Wilt though also destroy the righteous with the wicked?" (Gen. 18:23).

That a human being should not relax and feel comfortable, either in the face of evil (as in Noah's case) or when help needs to be provided to fellow citizens, is repeatedly alluded to throughout the Bible. For example: "If thou see the ass of him that hates thee, lying under its burden, and would forbear to help him, thou shalt surely help with him" (Exod. 23:5). Jewish sages interpreted this verse in the most general context: realizing evil (even when directed to a fellow citizen who hates you), without fighting it, is like seeing an unfriendly person in distress and not lending a helping hand. Both scenarios should be obstructed.

CHAPTER 16

Special Letters in the Bible

16.1 Introduction

The Hebrew Bible carries with it a special coded language (we do not mean the Bible Code). This code, given to Moses in Sinai (according to Jewish tradition), is not explicitly explained, alluded to, or hinted at anywhere in the Bible. Therefore, it has been the subject of Jewish scholarly discourse and debate throughout many centuries, with most revered Jewish interpreters of the Bible occasionally attempting one interpretation or another.

This special code manifests itself in three modes:

- Some letters in the written text are either smaller or larger than usual. A list of all places in the Old Testament where such incidents occur is displayed in Table 16.1 (for large letters) and in Table 16.2 (for small letters).

- Some words have missing or extra letters that should or should not (respectively) have been there by standard Hebrew grammatical rules.

- Some words are differently read than written. Cases where the written is different from the read is marked by the read word given in the margin of the page, opposite the line that contains the written word; Jewish tradition enumerates ten places where a word not written should be read (sometimes because the written word is not considered "clean" language), and eight places where a written word should not be read. The Talmud mentions seven and five such cases, respectively, and determines that these cases are "given to Moses from Sinai" (Mazar 1976, entry "Kri and Ktiv").

In subsections 16.1.1–16.1.3, respectively, we explain these three forms of "coded" language. In sections 16.2 and 16.3, we expound two amazing coincidences associated with the biblical "coded" language.

16.1.1 Small and Large Letters

Examining Tables 16.1 and 16.2, we realize that there are cases in the Bible where letters are larger than usual, and there are incidents where letters appear in a smaller letter size than usual.

Various interpretations have been given to each of these incidents. We will address here two cases: one where two letters in the same verse appear larger than usual, and another where a single letter appears smaller than usual. For the latter case, there is a traditional explanation that seems to be acceptable to all. We will detail this interpretation with some extra color of our own. For the former case, we will detail our understanding of the enlarged letters (consistently with Jewish tradition), and then relate to some other explanations given by Jewish scholars.

Table 16.1. Incidents of large letters in the Bible.

English Location	Hebrew		English Location	Hebrew	
	Location	Word		Location	Word
Josh. 14:11	יע יד 11	ככחי	Gen. 1:1	בר א 1	בראשית
Isa. 56:10	יש נו 10	צפיו	Gen. 34:31	בר לד 31	הכזונה
Mal. 3:22	מל ג 22	זכרו	Gen. 50:23	בר נ 23	שלשים
Job 9:34	אב טו 34	שבטו	Exod. 11:8	שמ יא 8	צא
Song of Songs 1:1	שש א 1	שיר	Exod. 34:14	שמ לד 14	אחר
Eccles. 7:1	קה ז 1	טוב	Lev. 11:42	וי יא 42	גחון
Eccles. 12:13	קה יב 13	סוף	Lev. 13:33	וי יג 33	והתגלח
Esther 1:6	אס א 6	חור	Num. 13:30	במ יג 30	ויהס
Esther 9:9	אס ט 9	ויזתא	Num. 14:17	במ יד 17	יגדל
Esther 9:29	אס ט 29	ותכתב	Num. 27:5	במ כז 5	משפטן
Pss. 18:50	תה יח 50	על	Deut. 6:4	דם ו 4	שמע
Pss. 80:16	תה פ 16	וכנה	Deut. 6:4	דם ו 4	אחד
Pss. 84:4	תה פד 4	קן	Deut. 18:13	דם יח 13	תמים
Prov. 1:1	מש א 1	משלי	Deut. 29:27	דם כט 27	וישלכם
Dan. 6:20	דנ ו 20	בשׁפרפרא	Deut. 32:6	דם לב 6	הליהוה
1 Chron. 1:1	דא א 1	אדם			

Table 16.2. Incidents of small letters in the Bible.

English Location	Hebrew		English Location	Hebrew	
	Location	Word		Location	Word
Pss. 24:4	תה כד4	לשוא	Gen. 2:4	בר ב4	בהבראם
Prov. 16:28	מש טז28	ונרגן	Gen. 23:2	בר כג2	ולבכתה
Prov. 28:17	מש כח17	אדם	Gen. 27:46	בר כז46	קצתי
Prov. 30:15	מש ל15	הב	Exod. 32:25	שמ לב25	בקמיהם
Job 7:5	אב ז5	וגיש	Lev. 1:1	וי א1	ויקרא
Job 16:14	אב טז14	פרץ	Lev. 6:2	וי ו2	מוקדה
Job 33:9	אב לג9	חף	Num. 25:11	במ כה11	פינחס
Lam. 1:12	אה א12	לוא	Deut. 9:24	דם ט24	ממרים
Lam. 2:9	אה ב9	טבעו	Deut. 32:18	דם לב18	תשי
Lam. 3:36	אה ג36	לעות	2 Sam. 21:19	שב כא19	יערי
Esther 9:7	אס ט7	פרשנדתא	Isa. 44:14	יש מד14	ארן
Esther 9:9	אס ט9	פרמשתא	Jer. 14:2	יר יד2	וצוחת
Esther 9:9	אס ט9	ויזתא	Jer. 39:13	יר לט13	ונבושזבן
Dan. 6:20	דנ ו20	בשפרפרא	Nah. 1:3	נם א3	בסופה

Ed

Ed[1] in Hebrew is "witness." In subsection 1.3.5, we discussed at some length how Jewish tradition perceives the major assignment of the Jewish nation in the world to serve as witnesses for the existence of God. This theme is repeatedly conveyed by the Jewish prophets; some quotations supporting this fact were provided in the above subsection.

It is therefore not surprising that in the most focused expression of the mission of the Jewish people, recited in all Jewish prayers—"Hear O Israel: the Lord our God; the Lord is one"(Deut. 6:4)—two letters appear that are enlarged. The first letter is *ayin*, which appears in the word *shema*[2] (hear), and the second is *dalet*, which appears in *echad*[3] (one). Together, the two letters form the word *ed*,[1] a witness:

שמע ישראל יהוה אלהינו יהוה אחד

Some other explanations may be found with some well-known and revered Jewish interpreters, like Kli-Yakar (1550–1619), who associates the large *dalet* with the way the Tefilin is tied, or Sforno (1475–1550), who traces the large *dalet* to an indication that God is on his own in the "Fourth world" (Sforno then describes the other three worlds).

Va-Yikra[4]

The word *va-yikra*[4] appears as the first word in Leviticus: "And the Lord called unto Moses, and spoke to him out of the tabernacle, saying ..." (Lev. 1:1). However, the word "called" (*va-yikra*)[4] is written

ויקרא

namely, the last letter, the *alef*, is smaller than the other letters in the word.

We pursue here interpretations given by most Jewish scholars (like Rashi) who essentially compare the way this word is written here to the way the Bible describes how God related to the gentile prophet Balaam. However, we add our own color to this interpretation.

In section 3.5, we alluded to how randomness is perceived in the Bible. We briefly repeat this explanation here. The Bible considers the perception of incidents as happening randomly—and not as an act of the Divine—to be an abomination, a defilement of God. Various cases were detailed in which God appears to people as if by chance, and then the word used is *va-yikar*[5] ("occurred to meet," or "happened to encounter"). One such instance is God appearing to Balaam, the prophet who was requested by the king of Moab, Balak, to curse the people of Israel on their way to the Promised Land from Egypt. The translated Bible says, "And God met Balaam: and he said unto him ..." (Num. 23:4).

However, this translation misses the most important message of the verse. The original Hebrew text does not say that God met Balaam; rather, God *occurred* to Balaam. The key Hebrew word here is *va-yikar*,[5] and it is written in Hebrew:

ויקר

Note the similarity of *va-yikar*[5]—or, without the conjunctive *vav*, *yiker*,[6] to the English "occur."

Comparing this with the call of God to Moses (see the previous Hebrew word from Leviticus), one realizes how the added *aleph* at the end of the word changes the whole meaning of the encounter with God: for Moses, this was God *calling*; for Balaam, this was God *occurring* to him!

To draw our attention to this comparison, to the similarity in the structure of the words, the biblical narrator probably opted to write the *va-yikra*[4] with a small *alef.*

Comments

Some other explanations may be found at http://www.bayit02.freeserve.co.uk/html/small_letters.html, which is dedicated to the small letters in the Torah, and provides some more interpretations. In particular, this Web site refers to the explanation given by the Baal Haturim ("owner of the Turim"), a person so named after the book he had authored (Rabbi Jacob Ben Rabbi Asher, Ha-Rosh, 1269–1343). The book is dedicated to explaining words, phrases, or even entire verses of the Torah in the realm of *remez* (allusion), rather than in the realm of *peshat* (simple meaning of the verse), which is the field of the Peirush HaTur HaAruch. The Baal Haturim explains the small *alef* in this way: Moses was a very humble man, and he wanted *va-yikra*[4] written without the *aleph*, conveying a sense of chance meeting, as with Balaam. However, God insisted that this meeting was deliberate, so the right word was *va-yikra*[4] ("and the Lord called" unto Moses). The compromise is the small *aleph*.

16.1.2 *Extra and Missing Letters*

Extra and missing letters abound in the Bible, and they have been the subject of much scholarly deliberation. One example was already given in section 1.2, where we referred to the fact that maiden (*naarah*),[7] namely a woman who has not yet known a man and therefore her fertility not yet proven, is written without the final *hei*, contrary to regular Hebrew grammatical rules. Similar cases are *teomim*[8] (twins), written as *tomim*[9] (Gen. 25:24), where two letters are missing (*alef* and *yod*), and *reshit*[10] (beginning), where the letter *alef* is missing (Deut. 12:11).

Extra letters strangely implanted in a word (where they should not be) are also abundant in the Bible. We discuss these cases in the following subsection.

16.1.3 *Differently Read than Written*

Some words in the Bible are differently written than read. It is an old Jewish tradition, well rooted in Jewish mysticism, that wherever a word is read differently from the way it is written, the read word expresses the superficial meaning of the object that the word represents, while the written word expresses the inner meaning, which is sometimes hidden to the naive observer. The Gaon of Vilna (1720–97) explains that the written expresses the "internal and true meaning" of the word, while the read word expresses the "outwardly appearance."

In the Bible, the written word appears within the biblical text, while the read word appears at the page margin, opposite the line where the written word appears.

One example is in the book by prophet Isaiah: "In all their affliction he was afflicted, and the angel of his presence saved them" (Isa. 63:9). The key words in this sentence are "he was afflicted," which, translated more literally from the Hebrew text, are: "It was distressful to him" [*lo*[11] in Hebrew). However, the actual written word that appears within the text is "no" (also pronounced in Hebrew "lo").[12] This modifies completely the sense of the sentence. The new meaning is, "In all their affliction, it is not distressful."

This case is extreme, since the two words (the written *lo*[12] and the read "lo")[11] are pronounced the same, and they both confer sensible meaning on the sentence. English Bible translators, obviously familiar with Jewish tradition, ignored the written word (which means "no"), and chose the traditionally read word (which means "to him"), even though this word neither appears nor is indicated in the Hebrew text.

A less extreme case, where the written word is entirely meaningless when read in the context of the verse where it is implanted, is the subject of section 16.3.

16.2 The Case of Haman's Sons

This section has been the most difficult, and at times distressful, to write. There are two interrelated reasons for this. First, this section is related to the Holocaust. Second, my families, both on my late father's side (my father's name was Daniel, deceased 1967) and on my late mother's side (my mother's name was Havah, deceased 2005), both families perished in the Holocaust. Therefore, writing about the Holocaust, and suggesting that somehow a most bizarre coincidence in the Bible insinuates a forthcoming Holocaust, looks like an outrageous—perhaps even offensive—assertion.

After much hesitation and deliberation, I have decided to proceed with detailing this coincidence. This was done for two reasons.

First, the coincidence to be expounded in this section is not new, and it is well-known, at least in Israel. It had previously been recounted in various publications (for example, Katz 1991, 1996), and is routinely taught in seminars for nonreligious Jewish Israelis, delivered by religious not-for-profit organizations, like Arachim.[13] In discussing this coincidence, therefore, I am not introducing controversy or an as-yet-unknown coincidence.

Second, the reader was assured in the introductory chapter that we would expose Bible-related and biblical-Hebrew-related coincidences of any sort known to us, leaving the reader to decide the nature of the coincidence, whether random or otherwise (as alluded therein, the results of the statistical analyses are exempt from this characterization). Faithful to this principle of censorship-free exposure to all known curious coincidences in the Bible, the coincidence regarding Haman's sons is expounded in this section, notwithstanding the personal difficulty that I experience in detailing that coincidence.

Esther, Mordechai, and Haman are the three central figures and heroes of the book of Esther. However, there is one more hero—hidden, unspecified, not mentioned even once. But the whole book is focused about how He conducts his world, in hidden ways, as is revealed only in the name of the book. As related elsewhere in this book (chapter 20), according to Jewish tradition, the name Esther is related to the verse in Deuteronomy, where God conveys to the people of Israel that in the face of their moral transgressions, he would hide his face from them—furthermore, he would even hide the hiding. This is succinctly summarized in Hebrew in three words: "*Haster astir panai*"[14] (Deutronomy 31:18), commonly inaccurately translated as "And I will *surely hide my face*" ("… on that day for all the evils which they have perpetrated"). The root of the *haster astir* is S.T.R, which means "to conceal." This is also the root of the name Esther, and the whole book is an allegory to the Divine's ways of conduct that look random to us. How the Bible refers to the concept of randomness has been alluded to at some length in section 3.3. The reader may wish to review this section, where verses in the Bible that relate to randomness are addressed.

The coincidence of Haman and his sons is now expounded (refer to subsection 20.2.1, where the details of the story, though not the coincidence, is introduced in more detail). Haman is first mentioned in the book of Esther thus: "After these things King Ahasuerus promoted Haman, the son of Hammedatha the Agagite, and advanced him and set his seat above all the princes that were with him. And all the king's servants that were in the king's gate bowed, and reverenced Haman; for the king had so commanded concerning him. But Mordechai bowed not, nor did him reverence" (Esther 3:1–2). So we know that Haman was of an Amalekite origin (Agag was king of Amalek—1 Samuel 15:8), and that he is in a supreme position in the king's court. Then the book of Esther relates how Haman had initiated a plot to murder all Jews in the king's kingdoms: "Letters were sent by couriers to all the king's provinces, to destroy, to slay, and to annihilate all Jews, young and old, women and children, in one day, the thirteenth day of the twelfth month, which is the month of Adar … And the king and Haman sat down to drink" (Esther 3:13, 15). How very familiar …

The extermination plot, however, failed, by coincidence (or was it?). In a bizarre twist of events, the king changes his taste (perhaps following the drink he had with Haman), and both Haman and his sons are hung by the king. As the latter chain of events is recounted in Esther, "So they hanged Haman on the gallows which he had prepared for Modechai. Then the king's wrath was pacified" (Esther 7:10). And later, Haman's sons were also killed: "The ten sons of Haman the son of Hammedata, the enemy of the Jews, they slew; but they did not lay their hands on the plunder" (Esther 9:10). The king then reassures Esther, the queen: "And the king said to Esther the queen, The Jews have slain and destroyed five hundred men in Shushan the capital, and also the ten sons of Haman … now what is thy petition? and it shall be granted thee …" (Esther 9:12).

Esther's answer starts the bizarre coincidence. What does she ask the king to do? The answer is given in the next verse: "Then Esther said, If it please the king, let it be granted to the Jews who are in Shushan to do *tomorrow* also according to this day's decree, and let Haman's ten sons be hanged upon the gallows. And the king commanded it so to be done: and the decree was given at Shushan; and they hanged Haman's ten sons" (Esther 9:13–14).

The biblical narrator was very explicit to notify us that Esther knows that Haman's sons were already dead. So what is the sense in asking the king, in reply, to hang them on a tree?

Rashi (1040–1105), the most prominent Jewish interpreter of the Bible, is aware of the difficulty, and he is very succinct in explaining the hanging of Haman's sons: "those that were killed." Other interpreters are mute about it, though the Malbim (1809–79) explains that the objective of "hanging the dead" was to intimidate the enemies of the Jews who had thought that the "Jews Annihilation Decree" was still valid.

We may consider another perspective, also based upon well-established Jewish tradition. We have alluded elsewhere (chapter 20) to the fact that in the book of Esther, the name of the Divine is not mentioned. It is therefore traditionally assumed that when the king's name is explicitly mentioned—namely the king "which reigned from India even unto Ethiopia, over an hundred and seven and twenty provinces" (Esther 1:1), this implies that Ahasuerus is intended. Elsewhere, when only the word "king" appears, reference is to the King of Kings (for example, consider Esther Rabbah 3:10). Thus, the king's decree to hang Haman's sons (giving an impression of a second execution) is in fact a decree from the Divine. Furthermore, Jewish scholars lay a rule regarding the appearance in biblical text of the word "tomorrow" (a rule not relating explicitly to Esther): "There is tomorrow now and there is tomorrow after some time" (Midrash Tanchuma, Parashat BA, 13). Thus, when Esther requests of the Divine to hang Haman's sons "tomorrow" (Esther 9:13), this can be in the future and not necessarily the next day.

Hanging of Haman's sons may be interpreted, in the framework of the coincidence that we expound here, as a decree from God (Esther 9:14, where only "king" is referenced), and it may be sometime in the future, consistent with how tomorrow is sometimes used in the Bible.

Who might these ten men, to be hanged on the tree some time in the future, be—and why is this important?

We have earlier referred to the position of the Talmud that special letters in the Bible were given to Moses from Sinai. Such special letters appear in relative abundance next to the listing of the names of Haman's sons (Esther 9:7–9).

There are four such letters.

The letter *vav*, enlarged, appears in the name of Vajezatha (*Vayzata*[15] in the Hebrew text). The letter *tav* appears small in the name Parshandatha.[16] The letter *shin* appears small in the name Parmashta.[17] Finally, the letter *zayin* appears small in the name Vajezatha (*Vayzata*[15] in Hebrew).

Four letters: one large (*vav*, which has a value of 6) and the other three small letters (*tav*, *shin*, and *zayin*, in that particular order).

Rewritten together, we have (read from right to left):

$$\text{ו' תש"ז}$$

This looks amazingly similar to how a Hebrew calendar date is read. (Refer for an explanation of the Hebrew calendar to subsection 2.1.2.) For example, the Jewish year starting October 4, 2005, is

$$\text{ו' תשס"ו}$$

which in Hebrew-calendar count is 5766 (the 766th year of the sixth thousand).

Similarly, the above first letter may be perceived as implying the sixth thousand, and the other three letters give the year 707 (of the sixth thousand)—in other words, a Hebrew calendar year of 5707.

Employing the Hebrew Date Converter (http://www.hebcal.com/converter), one finds this year to correspond to the year **1946**.

On October 16, 1946, newspapers world over notified their readers that **ten** Nazi criminals were hanged after being indicted in the famous Nuremberg trials.

Were only ten charged?

Not at all. In the Nuremberg trials, twenty-three Nazi war criminals were charged. Whose verdict was it to go to the gallows? The *New York Times* headline, in a late city edition from that day, tells it all:

"Goering Ends Life By Poison, 10 Others Hanged In Nuremberg Prison For Nazi War Crimes; Doomed Men On Gallows Pray For Germany."

Out of twenty-three charged, eleven had a verdict to be executed on the gallows. However, two hours prior to execution time, Nazi criminal Goering succeeded in committing suicide. This brought down the number of men hanged to exactly **ten**, in the year **1946**, Hebrew date "תש״ז".

16.3 The Case of Pi (π)

The "pi coincidence" concerns the value of pi (π) as it may possibly be implied in the Bible. It was discovered by the eighteenth-century East European rabbi "the Gaon of Vilna" (1720–97).

The number π is a well known universal constant with the value:

$$\pi = 3.14159265358979323846 \ldots$$

Traditionally, this number is used to express the (constant) ratio of the circumference of a circle to its diameter. This number, however, also appears as a constant in formulae of various unrelated branches of science and engineering, where it has no geometrical meaning. Notable examples are the mathematical equation for the density function of the normal distribution (in statistics), or Einstein's general-relativity field equation.

The number pi was shown to be irrational (not capable of being expressed as a ratio) in 1761 by Johann Heinrich Lambert, and a stronger proof was provided in 1794 by A. M. Legendre (Blatner 1998).

An algebraic equation is defined as a polynomial with a finite number of terms, all having rational-number coefficients. A transcendental number is one that cannot be the solution to an algebraic equation. Pi is a transcendental number, as proved by Ferdinand von Lindemann in 1882 (Blatner 1998).

In a decimal form, the number pi forms an infinite series of digits after the decimal point, and no cyclic pattern of any sort has so far been detected in this series, nor any other form of regularity. In fact, increasing the number of known digits after the decimal point has been a constant challenge for many centuries, and modern-day computers even exacerbated that challenge in accelerating the competition to calculate ever larger number of digits. The latter, calculated for pi by modern-day computers, is now of the order of magnitude of many hundreds of millions.

At least two books (Beckmann 1971, Blatner 1998) had been published about pi, and there is a host of Internet sites about the number—some of them quite entertaining (for example, http://www.joyofpi.com/pilinks.html).

These sources testify to the vast interest in π, in its mysterious properties—and in how it enters, sometimes unexpectedly, into formulae of various scientific disciplines, detached altogether from its original geometrical meaning.

The history of π has been monitored in a book by Petr Beckmann (1971). An interesting reference is given in the book to a certain quotation from the Bible (1 Kings 7:23). This is the only place where the Bible relates to how the circumference is related to the diameter:

> "He made a molten sea, ten cubits from the one brim to the other; it was round all about, and its height was five cubits; and a line of thirty cubits did circle it round about" (1 Kings 7:23).
> (The same quotation is repeated in 2 Chron. 4:2, in the same context, yet without the "clue" to the real magnitude of π, as will be shortly expounded.)

Beckmann (1971) presents a photocopy of the Hebrew original quotation and some translations thereof. The interpretation Beckmann gives to these sentences and his own conclusions are as follows (ibid., 14):

> "The molten sea, we are told, is round; it measures 30 cubits round about (in circumference) and 10 cubits from brim to brim (in diameter); thus the biblical value of π is: $30/10 = 3$. The Book of Kings was edited by the ancient Jews as a religious work about 550 B.C., but its sources date back several centuries. At that time π was already known to a considerably better accuracy, but evidently not to the editors of the Bible." In the next page, Beckmann summarizes the state-of-the-art at the time: "Returning to the determination of π by direct measurement using primitive equipment, it can probably safely be said that it led to values no better than: $25/8 = 3.125 < \pi < 3.143 = 22/7$."

Blatner (1998) is relating to the same subject. In a section titled "Pi and the Bible," under the subtitle "Here are several additional dubious rationalizations," Blatner (1998) displays succinctly the coincidence that is to be addressed in this section.

While the interpretation given by Beckmann to the apparent contents of the quotation from the Bible is accurate, the conclusions he reaches about the π accuracy imparted by this quotation are probably wrong. So is Blatner's conclusion expressed by reference to "dubious rationalizations." Perhaps the importance attributed in Jewish tradition to the special letters in the Bible, as expounded in section 16.1, was unknown to both.

The "pi coincidence" regards a key word in the above quotation from 1 Kings. The word is *kav*[18] (literally, "line," but also used in the Bible for "yardstick"). This word is differently read than written. Recalling the earlier quotation from the

Gaon of Vilna that the written expresses the "internal and true meaning," while the read expresses the "outwardly appearance," we may now pursue the Gaon of Vilna, explaining why the written "line" and the read "line" differ, and how is this significant.

We start with the read "line." The Hebrew *kav*[18] is correctly written with two letters:

$$106 = (6 = \text{ו}) + (100 = \text{ק})$$

However, in the above verse in the Bible, the word *kav*[18] is written differently within the text, though still read the same (how the word should be read is written, correctly, at the margin of the page, opposite the line where the "line" appears). The written *kav*[18] is

$$111 = (5 = \text{ה}) + (6 = \text{ו}) + (100 = \text{ק})$$

This is a bizarre word of three letters that has no meaning in Hebrew (at least not in the way it is supposed to be pronounced here, as *kav*).[18] Thus, although the word is read as "line," it is misspelled in the text, having a third letter added (the letter *hei*), supposedly by mistake.

How can this be explained?
The answer is that there are places in the Bible where words appear that are traditionally differently read than written. This was alluded to in subsection 16.1.3, where several examples were given. In that subsection, the principle underlying these incidents, as explained by the Gaon of Vilna, was detailed.

Having this principle in mind, we now follow in the footsteps of the Gaon of Vilna in reference to the above quotation. Obviously, while the outward appearance is that the "line" has a length of 30 (this is what the text conveys to us), the "inner truth" is that the length is somewhat different. How much different? Knowing the importance that the Hebrew attaches to the numerical values of words, we may suspect that the unknown "true" length, denoted by X, relates to the outward appearance—namely 30—the same way that the numerical value of the written word (which represents the "internal truth") relates to the numerical value of the read word (which represents "appearances").

A simple calculation yields

Numerical value of *written* word / Numerical value of *read* word =
Numerical value of (קוה) / Numerical value of (קו)
= 111 / 106

Therefore

$$\text{(``Real'' circumference)} / \text{(``Apparent'' circumference)} =$$
$$X / 30 = 111 / 106$$

$$X = 30 \, (111 / 106) = (10)(333 / 106) = (10)(3.141509)$$

Since the diameter is 10 cubits (refer to the above quotation), this calculation implies a value for π of

$$\pi = 3.141509$$

Compared to the true value of π (3.1415926 …), we realize that the calculated pi gives accuracy to the first *four* decimal points (if rounding is ignored)! Relating again to values quoted in Beckmann's recount of the history of π, we find out that the accuracy of π in the Bible, if the above clue was correctly interpreted at the time, by far exceeds that known even in the times of Archimedes, who had given the bounds (Beckmann 1974, 66)

$$3.140845 < \pi < 3.142857$$
(*two*-decimal-point accuracy).

The first time that an accuracy of three decimal points had been achieved, according to Beckmann (1974), was only in 1220, by Fibonacci (1180–1250). In 1573, Valentinus Otho calculated π as

$$355 / 113 = 3.141593$$
(Beckmann 1974, 196)

This quotient is amazingly close to that implied in the Bible.

These are all coincidences … maybe.

CHAPTER 17

Biblical Knowledge, Good and Bad

17.1 Introduction

The Bible refers to the concept of knowledge thus:

> "And out of the ground made the Lord God to grow every tree that is pleasant to the sight, and good for food; the tree of life also in the midst of the garden, and the tree of the knowledge of good and evil" (Gen. 2:9).

This seems bizarre. Why is knowledge defined in terms of good and evil instead of truth and falsehood? This is contradictory to our modern—perhaps intuitive—notion of knowledge. It is commonly accepted that the latter implies acquaintance with truth, telling the real from the unreal, discrimination between that which is fact and that which is fantasy. So why is it that the biblical notion of knowledge is founded on moralistic grounds, on good versus evil?

The answer to that question may be surprising. The above quote from Genesis, commonly accepted in English translations, is based on an interpretation of what the Bible intends to say in this verse. It is not based on that which is indeed written in the original Hebrew. Let us read the Hebrew verse carefully. It states: "The tree of knowledge, good [*tov*[1]] and bad [*va-ra*[2]]." That is all. Both are given as adjectives, implying that the tree of knowledge allows one to tell the good from the bad. There is no necessary moral aspect to this tree ... or the moral aspect may be only one of many, embodied in the general concepts of good and bad.

As we shall realize shortly, this interpretation is appreciably more compliant with how we intuitively perceive knowledge—but also, and more importantly, with the way biblical Hebrew relates to the concepts of good, bad, knowledge, and knowing anywhere else in the Bible.

229

In unfolding this new interpretation of the tree of knowledge, a whole new biblical theory of knowledge seems to be unveiled. Furthermore, the "new" interpretation of what knowledge actually means seems to be surprisingly (that is, by coincidence) compatible with Hegel's theory of how human knowledge progressively evolves.

In the next section, 17.2, we explore how the Bible relates to the concepts of good (*tov*)[1] and bad (*ra*).[3] In section 17.3, we further explore the concepts of knowing and knowledge in the Bible, as materialized in their various usages. Section 17.4 outlines briefly Hegel's theory of knowledge. The last section, 17.5, summarizes, based on the previous sections, biblical perception of the theory of knowledge and its relationship to Hegel's theory about the development of human knowledge.

17.2 "Good" and "Bad"

A useful departure point for a discussion of what "good" and "bad" may possibly mean in relation to knowledge in the Bible might be to borrow these very same concepts from modern quality engineering (of which the author perceives himself to be somewhat knowledgeable, a perception hopefully shared by a few others).

In modern quality engineering, the quality of a product is judged to be good or bad according to one criterion: conformance to requirements. The requirements are determined by the end-user of the product, and if the latter meets the requirements of the former, then the product is classified as being of high quality, or good. Conversely, if requirements are not met (however these requirements are defined), then the product is judged to be of low quality, or bad. In the prehistory of quality engineering (that is, about fifty years ago), when the market was a producers' market, conformance to requirements had only one meaning: conformance to specifications. The *design* of the product was solely determined by the manufacturer and translated into technological specifications, which determined the "laws" that the *manufacturing* of the product needed to comply with.

With the quality revolution in the mid-eighties of the last century, and the gradual change of market into a consumers' market, the rules of the game have changed. No longer does the product's manufacturer alone determine what the requirements are; now, the product has to fulfill the true requirements of the end-user. This has enormous ramifications. For example, the product could be perfectly consistent with the defined specifications, yet be considered of low quality (bad), because the true requirements of the end-user were not adequately translated into proper specifications in the design of the product. Conversely, a product could be inconsistent with, or not fully conforming to, all specifications, and yet fulfill the requirements of some customers. For these customers, the product was of sufficiently high quality (good). For example, the product label could have been placed in a wrong position, in violation of a written specification, but with no material consequences to the customer.

With this framework for "good" and "bad" in mind, four possible scenarios may be conceived:

- Product conforms to all specifications and to all of the end-user requirements: product is good and of high quality.

- Product conforms to all specifications but not to all of the end-user requirements: product may be good or bad, dependent on which end-user requirements are not met.

- Product does not conform to all specifications, but still meets the requirements of the end-user: product may be good or bad, dependent on which end-user requirements are not met.

- Product does not conform to all specifications and also does not meet most end-user requirements: product is bad.

With these definitions of "good" and "bad," taken from modern quality engineering, it is indeed surprising to realize how consistent the Bible is with these definitions, as one observes biblical usages of the combination of "good" and "bad," or just "good," or just "bad."

Let us start with the very first usage of "good" in the Bible. The sentence "And God saw that it was good [or very good]" repeats itself seven times in the depiction of creation (Gen. 1). It is apparent that "good" here means that what was created complied with the Creator's design, or requirements—namely, it was conforming to specifications (the latter are obviously identical to the requirements; in earth-bound human experience, this is not always so). One realizes that in "God saw that it was good" there is no human moral element to the qualification "good" for that which was just created.

When we search the Bible for combinations of "good" and "bad," we find out that these combinations refer mainly to two possible meanings:

- Nondeparture (or, conversely, departure) from specifications;
- Compliance (or lack thereof) with requirements—that is, with *moral* requirements of God.

The "good" and "bad" combination appears in the Bible, in its various forms, thirty-two times. These are all enumerated below:

> Genesis 2:9, 17; 3:5, 22; 24:50; 31:24, 29
>
> Numbers 13:19
>
> Leviticus 27:10, 12, 14, 33
>
> Deuteronomy 1:39
>
> 2 Samuel 13:22; 14:17; 19:36 1 Kings 3:9
>
> Isaiah 5:20
>
> Jeremiah 42:6
>
> Amos 5:14, 15
>
> Micah 3:2
>
> Psalms 31:12; 34:15; 37:27; 52:5
>
> Proverbs 15:3; 31:12
>
> Job 30:26
>
> Lamentations 3:38
>
> Ecclesiastes 12:14
>
> 2 Chronicles 18:17

Close examination of the various usages of "good" and "bad" reveals surprising correspondence with modern-day usage of "good" and "bad," in the sense pursued in quality engineering.

To understand this correspondence, let us recall how monotheism relates to God. There are two logically unrelated references to God:

- Creator of heaven and earth—that is, the Supreme Divine who laid down the laws of nature, the world's design, the world's specifications.
- The source of human morality, who has definite requirements regarding human moral conduct.

Thus, monotheism perceives God's requirements as embodied on two different planes:

- **In God's realized requirements,** reflected by God's design and specifications for the world (the laws of nature). These requirements are imposed on all living creatures. The human race has no choice, or free will, whether to comply with these requirements or otherwise. The design is already there, engraved in the "product" (the universe). Furthermore, no scientific argument can possibly explain the existence of the laws of nature, let alone why these can so successfully be formulated in terms of mathematical expressions. There is no logical necessity that enforces the existence of the laws of nature.

- **In God's yet-unrealized requirements**, expressed by moral code that had been conveyed to humanity by such scriptures as the Ten Commandments and derivatives (like "Before the blind do not place a stumbling block"). Fulfillment of these requirements awaits implementation by humankind, as the Bible conveys in no uncertain terms: "And God blessed the seventh day, and sanctified it: because in it he rested from all his work which God had created to do" (Genesis 2:3). This peculiar description of what God had created ("work") and the destiny of that work ("to do") attests that some part of the design is yet awaiting humanity "to be done." There are unfulfilled divine requirements that need fulfilling. The prophet Micah explicitly uses the word "require": "He has told thee, O man, what is good and what does the Lord *require* of thee, but to do justice, and to love true loyalty, and to walk humbly with thy God" (Micah 6:8).

All allusions in the Bible to "good" and "bad" may be easily traced to either one or the other of these two categories: conformance to specifications (consistent with the perception of God as the source of the laws of nature), or fulfilling God's moral requirements (those not yet engraved in the world's design).

Examples:

- "And the Lord God said, It is not good [*tov*[1]] that the man should be alone" (Gen. 2:18)—meaning "It is against man's nature to be alone; we need conformance to specifications. A madam has to be created."

- "And God came to Laban the Aramean in a dream by night, and said to him, Take heed that thou speak not to Jacob either good or bad" (Gen. 31:24)—meaning, "Behave yourself; show moral conduct."

- "And if it be a beast, of which men bring an offering to the Lord, all that any man gives of such to the Lord shall be holy. He shall not alter it, nor change it, a good for a bad, or a bad for a good: and if he shall at all change beast for beast, then it and its substitute shall be holy" (Lev. 27:9–10)—meaning, "'Good' and 'bad' relate only to judging quality of the offering in terms of conformance to specifications."

- "And your little ones, concerning whom you said they should be a prey, and your children who in that day had no knowledge of good [*tov*¹] and evil [*ra*²], they shall go in there, and to them will I give it" (Deut. 1:39) — meaning, "Kids have no knowledge of God's moral requirements."

- "Woe to them that call evil [*ra*²] good [*tov*¹] and good evil" (Isa. 5:20)— meaning, "Woe to those not meeting, out of free will, God's moral requirements."

- "Hate the evil [*ra*²] and love the good [*tov*¹], and establish justice in the gate: it may be that the Lord God of hosts will be gracious to the remnant of Joseph" (Amos 5:15).

- "But when I hoped for good [*tov*¹] then the bad came" (Job 30:26)— meaning, "Nonconformance to my expectations has taken place," with no moral element insinuated.

- "For God shall bring every work into judgment, with every secret thing, whether it be good, or whether it be evil" (Eccles. 11:14).

The terms "good" and "bad"—which the eating of the tree of knowledge is supposed to help discriminate between—now assume an altogether different interpretation.

Knowledge implies acquaintance with God's requirements. This may assume two different modes, corresponding to how God is perceived: as the creator of the world, or as the origin of the human moral code.

According to the first mode, telling the good from the bad implies distinguishing the world's specifications from nonspecifications. In other words, since God is the creator, knowing his design means to know how the world really is: revealing the laws of nature. Amassing knowledge is thus tantamount to separating truth from falsehood, separating the real from the unreal, putting it all in order, and identifying the design embedded in the world around us.

This is the regular sense of knowledge, as commonly used today. This is what science is about—revealing the world's specifications.

The second mode of being able to tell the good from the bad as a result of eating from the tree of knowledge regards the perception of God as the source of sovereignty of the human moral code. The thirteen features of divine conduct, as enumerated by Moses (Exod. 34:6–7), indeed present the requirements of God from humankind, within the realm of the latter's free will. This type of knowledge, thence, refers to the other kind of divine requirements, those not reflected in the world's perceived specifications (laws of nature), but rather those awaiting us, humans, to be fulfilled on earth.

As a final comment, it is important to note that although, according to all monotheistic faiths, God has laid down "ordinances of heaven and earth" (Jer. 33:25), he is still capable of generating departures from the world's specifications (laws of nature). Not all is predetermined by these laws alone. The Bible repeatedly warns of the punishments awaiting violations of the divine moral requirements, either when these punishments can be traced to the moral transgressions that have brought them about, or otherwise (*haster astir panai*,[4] "I will hide my hiding").

17.3 Biblical Knowledge

The biblical reference to knowledge is bizarre. Usages of the concept of knowledge, or "knowing," appear in so disparate allusions that one struggles to identify the underlying concept that binds together words that convey such unrelated meanings while carrying the same Hebrew root.

Some examples:

- "Tree of the *knowledge* of good and evil" (Gen. 2:9).

- "And the man *knew* Eve his wife; and she conceived, and bore Cain" (Gen. 4:1).

- "And there arose not a prophet since in Israel like Moses, whom the Lord *knew* face to face" (Deut. 34:10).

- "For they proceed from evil to evil, and they *know* me not, says the Lord" (Jer. 9:2).

Two meanings are apparent: knowing in the sense of acquaintance (with God's requirements, with people, with certain bits of information), and knowing in the sense of a sexual encounter between man and woman.

How can these possibly be combined by a shared logic?

One can only make sense of this marriage of such disparate senses by recalling how the Hebrew language generates epitomes to demonstrate a concept. We have already encountered two such examples: that of the concept of "there" (realized by *shamayim*,[5] "sky"), and that of the concept of compassion or mercy (refer to sections 5.2 and 2.1.1, respectively).

Biblical Hebrew seems to go here one step further in generating a most general epitome, a meta-knowledge concept. This epitome explains the process of the acquisition of knowledge—how the thought processes of humanity progress (or, simply, how one becomes knowledgeable). The allegory embedded in this epitome is created by equating the act of acquiring knowledge and the end product of this process, to the act of sexual encounter (with the resulting offspring). The latter is essential. The Bible invariably refers to "man knowing a woman" while explicitly specifying an offspring, most commonly by name. Sometimes, an explanation for the name is also given.

Why is a sexual encounter that breeds offspring always referred to in the Bible as "knowing"? What is it in the offspring-producing encounter of two opposites, male and female, thesis and antithesis forming a synthesis, that leads one to denote this as "knowing"?

One can hardly avoid relating to the philosopher Hegel and his theory of knowledge, better known as the "Dialectical logic". It seems as though the latter reflects, in a highly precise fashion, the epitome that the Bible tries to produce— namely, a concept that succinctly describes the process of the evolution of human thought, or the act of knowing.

17.4 Hegel's Theory of Knowledge

Georg Wilhelm Friedrich Hegel (1770–1831) was a German philosopher. He was educated in theology at Tübingen and was a private tutor at Bern and Frankfurt. In 1805, he became professor at the University of Jena. While considered a follower of Schelling, he developed his own system, which he first presented in *The Phenomenology of Mind* (1807). Hegel's interests were wide, and they were all incorporated into his unified philosophy, which is generally termed "the Hegelian dialectic."

According to Hegel, the world develops and acquires knowledge via the dialectical logic. In this development (which progresses according to the Hegelian dialectic), one concept, the thesis, inevitably generates its opposite, the antithesis. The interaction of the two leads to a new concept: synthesis. This in turn becomes the thesis of a new triad. The evolution of human thought thus proceeds in ever more developed cycles, where the end result of a previous cycle (the synthesis) becomes the trigger (a new thesis) for a new cycle. (A graphical demonstration of the Hegelian dialectic is given in Figure 17.1.)

An example for this thought process is given in the way Hegel regarded Immanuel Kant's theory of categories. He thought that the categories were incomplete in Kant's formulation. Kant's idea of "being" is fundamental, but it evokes its antithesis, "not being." These two are not mutually exclusive, for they necessarily produce the synthesis "becoming." Hence, activity is basic, progress is rational, and logic is the basis of the world progress.

In Hegel's perspective of reality, the dialectic logic is the tool to describe how thoughts, or ideas, develop.

The Hegelian dialectic served a fundamental cornerstone for Karl Marx in developing his theory and worldview of Marxism.

The surprising match between the Hegelian dialectic and the biblical reference to all sexual encounters (which ultimately result in offspring) as acts of "knowing" is one of the most bizarre coincidences found in biblical Hebrew and in this book.

17.5 Synthesis of "Good," "Bad," and "Knowledge"

The Bible describes the "tree of knowledge, of good and bad" (Gen. 2:9). Each of these three concepts has been addressed separately. It is time for a synthesis.

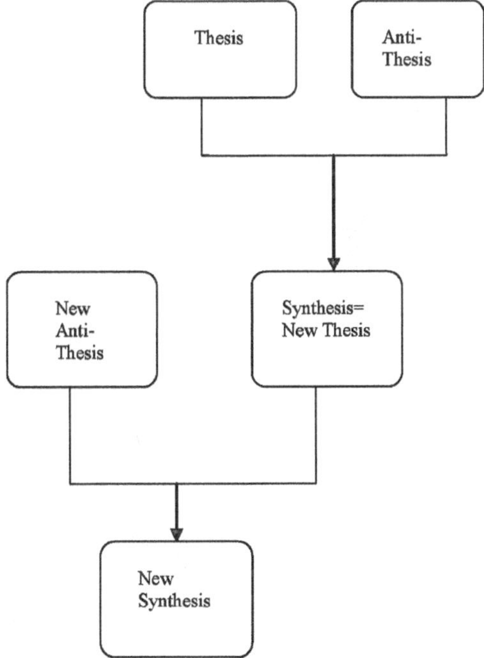

Figure 17.1. A graphical demo of the Hegelian Dialectic.

"Good" and "bad" both refer to God's requirements: Is this (whatever "this" entails) true or false? Is this good or evil? Studying the two options clarify their meanings and their implications. Knowledge is gained. The thesis and the antithesis are identified and distinguished. They are both part of creation, because God created them both: "Consider the work of God: For who can make that straight, which he has made crooked? In the day of prosperity [*tovah*[6]] be joyful [*tov*[1]—literally, "be well"], but in the day of adversity [*raah*[7]] consider: God has made the one as well as the other" (Eccles. 7:13–14).

Once the two aspects of reality—fact and fantasy, truth and lie, the good and the evil—are told apart, a synthesis may be created, and existence on a higher level—the level of the new synthesis, the offspring of the Hegelian dialectic—may be reached.

"Good," "bad, "sexual intercourse," the Hegelian dialectic, the biblical theory of knowledge ...

These are all coincidences ... maybe.

PART IV

Supplementary Coincidences

CHAPTER 18

The Secret of *Ibur*

The Hebrew word *ibur*[1] refers to the act of impregnating—namely, conception. In the Hebrew language, one common sense of the term *ibur*[1] is associated with the Hebrew calendar and its unique structure. Since this calendar is based on the lunar month, however most Jewish festivities in Israel are associated with the annual seasons, there was a necessity to coordinate the moon-based Hebrew calendar with the solar (tropical) year.

To achieve this goal, the Hebrew calendar adds a month to the calendar, called Adar B (which naturally follows Adar A), and this is done seven times in a cycle of nineteen years. A year when an extra month is added is called Shanah Meuberet.

Some details of how the Hebrew calendar is structured are given in section 2.1.2 and the references therein.

The subject of this chapter is to explain how ancient Jewish sages came to the conclusion that the lunar month is **29.53059** days (with exactly that precision).

That Jewish sages have been aware of this figure, and how it is anchored in Jewish oral and written sources, is the subject of this chapter.

But how close is this estimate to the precise figure, obtained by modern precision measurements?

According to current measurements, the synodic month (the duration of the lunar month which is the mean interval between conjunctions of the moon and the sun, corresponding to the cycle of lunar phases) is **29.53058888531** days.

(Refer, for example, to the Wolfram Research Company Web sites:
http://scienceworld.wolfram.com/astronomy/Month.html;
http://scienceworld.wolfram.com/astronomy/SynodicMonth.html.

Also refer to the Web site by the Institute for Dynamic Educational Advancement, or IDEA:
http://webexhibits.org/calendars/credits.html.)

How had Jewish sages reached such an accurate estimate of the lunar month?

We start with two quotes from the Bible and how these were interpreted by Jewish sages.

"See, I have taught you statutes and judgments as the Lord my God commanded me, that you should do thus in the land where you are entering to possess it. Keep therefore and do them, for this is your wisdom and your understanding in the sight of the nations, which will hear all these statutes and say, Surely this great nation is a wise and understanding people" (Deut. 4:5–6).

Jewish rabbis and scholars traditionally attribute "This is your wisdom" to the secret of *ibur*.[1]

A similar explanation is clearly manifested by how the following verse is traditionally interpreted:

"My hand shall be against the prophets who see false visions and utter lying divinations. *They shall not belong to the council of my people,* or be listed in the records of the house of Israel, nor will they enter into the land of Israel" (Ezek. 13:9).

The literal Hebrew is, "They shall not be in the secret of my people." A Jewish sage explains this to mean the secret of the *ibur*[1] (Talmud, Massechet Ketubot, 112).

How was the duration of the lunar month, the secret of the *ibur*,[1] passed on from one generation of Jewish scholars to the next?

Rabban Gamliel (90 CE), who headed the Sanhedrin (the Jewish ancient Supreme Court), is quoted as saying: "It is so acceptable from the house of the father of my father: The renewal of the moon is not less than 29 days and a half, and two thirds of an hour, and 73 parts" (Talmud, Rosh Hashanah, 25 [71]). The 73 parts refer to the division of the hour into 1,080 parts, which will be addressed shortly in the quote from Rambam.

Rambam (1135–1204) similarly states, "The hour is divided into 1080 parts. And why have they so divided the hour? Because according to this counting you have halves, and quarters, and eighths, and thirds, and ninths, and fifths and tenths ... Twenty nine days and twelve hours of the thirtieth day, from the beginning of its night, and 793 parts from the thirteenth hour. This is the time between one renewal and the next, and this is the moon month" (Hilchot Kidush Hachodesh 5:2).

Let's calculate the lunar month according to both sources.

Rabban Gamliel (recall that an hour has 1080 parts):

$$29.5 + \{[(2/3)1080 + 73] / 1080\} / 24 = 29.53059 \text{ days}$$

Rambam:

$$29.5 + (793 / 1080) / 24 = 29.53059 \text{ days}$$

Note that the number of parts in an hour may be factored, expressed by prime numbers, as

$$1080 = (2^3) (3^3) (5^1)$$

The versatility of that number, alluded to above in the quote from Rambam, is apparent.

How is it that the secret of the *ibur*,[1] known to Jewish sages in ancient times, gave the duration of the synodic month accurate to the fifth decimal point?

The following is an explanation, based on my best knowledge and capability to explain the above quoted numbers, and their origin in Jewish tradition and in the Bible.

The departure point is the calculation of the exact time when the first lunar month started.

According to Jewish tradition, this happened at the moment of the creation of the first man, which marks the beginning of the Jewish year (Rosh Hashanah).[2] The Bible tells us that man was created on the sixth day of creation (Gen. 1:27). However, Jewish tradition, according to the Oral Torah (*Torah she-Be-Al Peh*),[3] gives a more exact time: Friday, after the fourteenth hour (since sunset of the previous day), which is the beginning of the third hour into the day of Friday. Recall that the Jewish day starts at sunset of the previous day, and there are twelve hours for nighttime and twelve hours for daytime. Therefore, after fourteen hours of Friday is the beginning of the fifteenth hour, which is the third hour (15 − 12 = 3) into daytime of Friday.

This is symbolized in Hebrew by the Hebrew letters *vav*, *yod*, and *dalet*,

$$14 = (4 = ד) + (10 = י), (6 = ו)$$

where the 6 stands for the day (Friday) and 14 stands for the number of hours at the end of which man was created—and, according to Jewish tradition, the moon started its first cycle.

The first lunar month is called Molad ve-Yad[4] ("the renewal *V.I.D*"), and it is referenced several times in various Jewish sources (for example, refer to the Rambam source quoted earlier).

Next we look for some clues in the written Torah (remember, the "6, 14" was based on Jewish oral tradition). To do this, we roll back twelve months from the first lunar month (which, we remember, was on Friday). This rolling back twelve months prior to the first lunar month (when man was created), generates an imaginary year (since the world was created just five days earlier, and not a complete year earlier). The first lunar renewal in this imaginary year—namely, the imaginary first renewal of the moon—is called Molad of Tohu[5] (the Renewal of Vanity, if you wish).

According to Jewish tradition, the exact time *in the week* of the Molad of Tohu[5] may be read from the Bible as follows:

1. Take the first letter in Genesis; you get the letter *bet*.

2. Now count forty-two letters, to arrive at the letter *hei* (in the word *va-vohu*).[6]

3. Count another forty-two letters, and you pick up the letter *resh* (in the word *va-yomer*).[7]

4. Finally, you similarly pick up the letter *dalet* (in the word *va-yavdel*).[8]

These four letters, called *baharad*[9]—which, according to Jewish mysticism, is related to one of the forty-two-letter names of God—provide the final series of letters, interpreted as follows:

(*bet* = 2) = second day of the week

(*hei* = 5) = five hours

(*resh* = 200, *dalet* = 4) = 204 parts of the hour

(Remember that an hour has 1,080 parts.)

This is the exact time of the beginning of the Molad Tohu,[5] the imaginary first moon renewal, exactly one year prior to the creation of man (when the actual first moon renewal took place, according to Jewish tradition).

The rest of the calculation is peanuts … well, almost.

Let the true duration of the lunar month (in days) be denoted X.

Assume that there are four weeks (twenty-eight days) per month. The difference between the actual lunar year and the calculated duration according to the number of weeks is

$$12*X - 12*28 = 12\,(X - 28) \text{ days} = (7k) + A \text{ days}$$

where k is an integer (the number of whole weeks in the difference calculated on the left-hand side), and A is the remaining part of the week (expressed in days).

Suppose that the actual lunar year were an integer number of weeks (A = 0). Then, the Jewish reported time of the creation of man (given in terms of the time in the week) would be the same as that of the beginning of the Molad Tohu[4]— namely, Monday (the second day of the week, according to the Jewish calendar), at the 5+204 / 1080 = 5.188889 hour.

However, this is not the case. There is a difference. As "reported" in Genesis and complemented by Jewish oral tradition, the first man was created on Friday, at the end of the fourteenth hour.

This difference in the time of week may now be easily calculated.
From Monday, at the 5.188889 hour, to the exact same hour on Friday: 4 days.
From the 5.188889 hour on Friday to the end of the fourteenth hour:

$$14.0000 - 5.188889 = 8.81111$$

The total difference, in days, is

$$4 \text{ days} + 8.81111 \text{ hours} = 4 + 8.81111 / 24 = 4.36713 \text{ days.}$$

This is the value of A given above, and all that is left is try a few values of k that let X fall between 29 days and 30 days (note that the actual length of the Hebrew month alternates between these two numbers).

The fundamental equation is (from the earlier expression with A = 4.36713):

$$12\,(X - 28) \text{ days} = (7k) + 4.36713 \text{ days}$$

Trying a few values of k, working with ten-digit precision, we obtain

$$\text{For } k = 1: X = 28.947261$$

$$\text{For } k = 2: X = 29.530594$$

$$\text{For } k = 3: X = 30.113927$$

Only k = 2 delivers a value for X in the required range. Therefore, the true length of the synodic month is, according to Jewish tradition, equal to 29.530594 days. This value departs from the actual duration, as reported by NASA, by

$$\textbf{29.530594} - \textbf{29.530589} = \textbf{0.000005 days}$$

(The difference is five parts in a million.)

These are all coincidences ... maybe.

CHAPTER 19

Non-Hebrew Names of Self-Proclaimed Foes of the People of Israel

19.1 Introduction

The Jewish nation had, and still has, enemies posing grave threats to its survival over the centuries, either when Jews were scattered in Diaspora or when they entertained sovereignty in their own ancestral homeland, the land of Israel. These enemies had names that originated in various sources unrelated to the Hebrew language. Yet, by still another bizarre coincidence, an improbable proportion of these names turn out to have extremely negative meaning in the Hebrew language, which at times expresses very precisely the character of the threat that these enemies have posed to the very existence of Jews, as a nation or as individuals.

In this chapter, we present some of these names. Not all names that fall into this category of coincidences are given here; some might be perceived as politically incorrect and were therefore omitted. We feel that although the excluded names define, in the Hebrew sense, the essence of the enemy and the nature of the threat posed to the Jewish people, some readers may find these examples offensive. They were therefore removed.

The author apologizes to those readers who might still take offense to any names in the set of remaining examples given. I wish to assure you that offense or controversy is not the intention here. Only self-proclaimed enemies of the Jewish people are included, and no judgmental or evaluative statements are intended. Our sole purpose in this chapter is to demonstrate the bizarre phenomenon (coincidence) that in numerous cases people and organizations who had declared themselves, at one period or another, enemies of the Jewish people, by deed and by talk, turned out to own names of non-Hebrew origin that in Hebrew possess extremely negative meanings.

The sheer number of examples in the set given below (and those excluded) has justified producing this chapter, which examines another interesting coincidence, this time by combining Jewish history with the Hebrew language.

19.2 The Nazis

The adjective "Nazi" is derived from the name of the Nazi party, established by Hitler prior to World War II (the National Socialist Party). The Nazi party constituted the political basis for Hitler's lawful grab of power in Germany in the 1930s.

It was the dominant party throughout World War II and the implementation of the "Final Solution" by Hitler and his willing executioners. Six million Jews were murdered in the Holocaust.

In the Hebrew language, the root of "Nazi" (pronounced "natzi") has a very clear and defined sense.

The root *N. A. Z* in Hebrew = curse.

Examples:

neatzah[1] = a curse

le-naetz[2] = to curse

19.3 Hamas

Hamas is a terrorist organization which has, in recent years, claimed the lives of hundreds of Jews, in Israel and elsewhere. Its main claim for existence is its desire to liberate Palestine (meaning, all territories where Jews are now living) and to return these territories to Muslim control.

The roots of this organization are in the Muslim Brotherhood, which was founded in 1928 in Egypt. For many years, the latter was one of the principal Islamic revivalist movements in the Middle East. They were primarily a social and religious group, although in Egypt four of their members were the assassins who killed Egyptian President Anwar Sadat for his peace treaty with Israel. In 1987, after years of concentrating on social and educational activity within the Palestinian population in Arab areas, the Muslim Brotherhood was confronted with fundamental challenges in the wake of the intifada in Gaza and the West Bank. As the uprising became the main focus of the Palestinian Arab population, the Muslim Brotherhood's leaders found themselves detached from the events led by Islamic Jihad and the Palestine Liberation Organization (PLO) from their headquarters in exile in Tunisia. The Arab population's response was a new organization, founded December 14, 1987, at the beginning of the intifada: Hamas (Harakat Muqawama Islamiyya—the Islamic Resistance Movement).

The Hamas Covenant was drawn up in 1988, explaining the organization's Islamic ideological sources, its ideas on the Israeli-Palestinian conflict, its approach as a Muslim-Palestinian movement, and its attitude toward the PLO. Hamas recognized the contributions of the PLO in creating the idea of a Palestinian nation and in leading the political and military struggle against Israel. But Hamas did not regard the PLO as superior or primary in representing the Palestinian Arabs, especially regarding Islam. For Hamas, the one true path to liberating the land is armed struggle (jihad), and negotiations with Israel have no role. The Hamas Covenant says it plainly: "There is no other solution for the Palestinian problem other than jihad. All the initiatives and international conferences are a waste of time and a futile game."

In the democratic elections that took place in January of 2006, Hamas had won majority of seats in the parliament, and thus became the dominant faction in the Palestinian political arena.

What is the Hebrew meaning of Hamas (*Chamas*[3] in Hebrew and in Arabic)?

Chamas = act of unjustly seizing somebody else's property (plundering, extortion, property seized unjustly)

The first mentioning of the word *chamas*[3] in the Bible is at the opening paragraph describing why God has brought about the deluge (*mabul*):[4]

> "The earth was corrupt before God, and the earth was filled with [*chamas*[3]]. And God looked upon the earth, and, behold, it was corrupt; for all flesh had corrupted his way upon the earth. And God said to Noah, The end of all flesh is come before me; for the earth is filled with [*chamas*] because of them; and, behold, I will destroy them with the earth" (Gen. 6:11–13).

Further biblical referral to this word and its derivatives always addresses the immoral aspects of acts associated with *chamas*.[3] It recurs abundantly in the prophets' reproach for the people of Israel, and in Proverbs and Psalms, where the injustice of the act of plundering is the focus of the morality assertions.

Some examples:

- "Their acts are acts of iniquity and the spoils of [*chamas*^{3}] is in their hands" (Isa. 59:6).

- "Thus said the Lord God; Enough now, presidents of Israel, remove [*chamas*^{3}] and robbery and do judgment and justice ..." (Ezek. 45:9).

- "A man of [*chamas*^{3}] would entice his friend and lead him astray" (Prov. 16:19).

- "saying let neither man nor beast, herd nor flock, taste any thing ... and let them turn everyone from his evil way and from the [*chamas*^{3}] that is in their hands" (Jon. 3:5, 8).

19.4 Arafat

Arafat is considered by many to be the founding father of the nation of the Palestinians. Throughout his life, his relationships with the state of Israel have undergone ups and downs. These relationships comprised mainly three periods. The first period started in 1959, when a group of about twenty Palestinians met in Kuwait and secretly formed Fatah (or al-Fatah, which is an acronym standing for Harakat Al-Tahrir Al-Watani Al-Filastini—the Movement for the National Liberation of Palestine), an organization that became the principal component of the PLO under the leadership of Yasser Arafat.

The actual date of founding of the PLO is controversial; sources give various dates in the 1950s or early sixties. Backed by Syria, Fatah began carrying out terrorist raids against Israeli targets in 1965—launched from Jordan, Lebanon, and Egyptian-occupied Gaza (so as not to draw reprisals against Syria). Dozens of raids were carried out each year, exclusively against civilian targets.

Fatah's original covenant called for the destruction of pre-1967 Israel and disavowed interest in the West Bank and Gaza Strip (by then held by Jordan and Egypt, respectively). Only in 1968, in the aftermath of the Six-Day War, did the PLO alter the covenant to demand the establishment of a Palestinian state on the entire territory of the land of Israel. Thus, Fatah and the PLO were built around the refugees of 1948–49, and, more than a generation later, these refugees still constitute the core of the organizations' leadership and support cadres.

Fatah was originally opposed to the founding of the PLO, which it viewed as a political opponent. Fatah's popularity among Palestinians grew until it took control of the PLO in 1968. Since then, it has been the PLO's most prominent faction, under the direct control (until his death) of PLO Chairman Yasser Arafat. In the following years, acts of violence by members of PLO have killed and maimed hundreds of Israelis and Jews.

This first period, as just described, was followed by a period of reconciliation that started with the Oslo Accords, formally signed between the PLO, headed by Arafat, and the state of Israel, in 1993. This was a period that was characterized by a series of interim accords, as both parties to the Oslo Accords attempted to move forward toward a settlement of their historic dispute. Although acts of terrorism against Israelis did not stop at this era, they were relatively subdued relative to the more recent period, started in 2000, that was initiated with the breakout of the intifada, while Arafat was the president of the Palestinian Authority. The last period was characterized by hundreds of suicide bombings, which have killed and maimed thousands of Israelis, Jews, and non-Jews. This intifada continued until the death of Arafat in 2004.

In Hebrew, the root of the name Arafat is: *A.R.F*[5]

This root has only extremely unfavorable meanings in Hebrew, and it is source to such negatively tilted words in at least six different places in the Bible.

19.5 The Philistines (Biblical Times)

The Bible relates to the Philistines no fewer than 253 times. In biblical times, the Philistines occupied the region of Philistia (*Pleshet*,[6] roughly today's Gaza Strip). As conveyed in the Bible, the Philistines were sworn enemies of the children of Israel, fought them in countless wars, and have caused them trouble for many centuries. In fact, even the prophets relate to them when they detail prophecies for days to come.

The first encounter between the Jews and the Philistines is related in Genesis. As the story is told, "Abraham reproved Abimelech" (the ruler of the Philistines) "because of the well of water, which Abimelech's servants had violently taken away;

And Abimelech said, I know not who has done this thing, neither did thou tell me, neither yet heard I of it, but today" (Gen. 21:26). Such encounters persisted with Isaac, and more violent encounters that involved wars are related in the book of Judges, the first and second books of Samuel, and the first and second books of Kings. King David was the first to conquer the land of the Philistines, *Pleshet*,[6] in a series of wars and combats that have begun with the famous story of David, the youngster, striking Goliath with a stone. Later wars involved various kings of Israel and Judah, like Hezekiah, the son of Ahaz, king of Judah, who "smote the

Philistines, even unto Gaza" (2 Kings 18:8), and king of Judah, Uzziah, who also built cities among the Philistines (2 Chron. 26:6).

In Hebrew, the root *P.L.S* = "invade," "invasion,"
"entering land which is not yours"

19.6 Pharaoh, King of Egypt (Biblical Times)

As demonstrated by the story of Laban (chapter 15), names in the Bible nearly always convey the inner essence of the named. "Pharaoh" is one more example where a name conveys catastrophe for the children of Israel, yet the name probably originated elsewhere, because it was found inscribed in various excavations in Egypt.

The term "pharaoh" was originally used for the place where the king resided, and it is to be translated as "great house." Gradually the term came to be used for the king himself, which probably happened somewhere between 1400–900 BCE.

During a period historians call the New Kingdom, there was a clear distinction between divine kingship and the pharaoh himself. Through long periods of Egyptian history, the pharaoh is described as an institution, not as an individual. The ideal image of the pharaoh was presented. There are a good number of exceptions from this, often connected to pharaohs that were successful in a military sense.

Of the pharaohs in the Bible, Shishak is Sheshonk I, Neco or Necoh is Necho, and Hophra is Apries. Many scholars believe that the pharaoh who oppressed the Jews (Exodus, chapters 1–14) was Seti I, and that his son Ramses II was the pharaoh of the Exodus.

The Hebrew root of the "pharaoh" is *P.R.A.*[7] This root has multiple meanings in Hebrew. However, actual linguistic usages of this root in the spoken Hebrew language, as well as in biblical discourse, often imply acts of violence against Jews. For example, the word *praot*[8] is routinely used in Hebrew for pogroms—namely, unrestrained maiming and killings conducted against the Jewish people as individuals or against Jewish communities, both during the expulsion from the land of Israel (the *Galut*)[9] or earlier or later.

The first usage in this sense appears in the book of Judges: "In time of tumultuous strife [*befroa praot*[10]] in Israel ..." (Judges 5:2). The same root is also used earlier in Deuteronomy 32:42. Other related senses are contained in different usages of this root, scattered all over the Bible.

Comments

1. "Arafat" and "Pharaoh" share the same letters in their respective roots (as the names are written in Hebrew). The meanings of various words, derived from the respective roots, differ. However they all have adverse meanings in the Hebrew language.

2. One could alternatively assert that Hebrew words with root *P.R.A*,[7] having the negative meaning expounded earlier, in fact evolved from the name "Pharaoh" (and the related adversive experience that the Israelites had with the ancient Egyptian kings). Obviously, this alternative explanation cannot be ruled out unless one demonstrated that the Hebrew language, with the above root, had preceded the time of the pharaohs.

These are all coincidences … maybe.

CHAPTER 20

Coincidences in Jewish History and Beyond

20.1 Introduction

There are three issues addressed in this chapter. The first two relate to Jewish history, both representing extremely bizarre coincidences. They are detailed in the two sections that follow this one.

In the last section, 20.4, we ponder the meaning of coincidences in daily life and address a public coincidence of recent years, marked by a clue ignored by all.

Section 20.3 addresses the Hebrew month of Iyar and what this month symbolizes in Jewish tradition and mysticism. We then demonstrate how, via a strange succession of historical events centuries apart, the month of Iyar has become, over centuries of Jewish history, the most crucial month in the buildup of Jewish nationality. The bizarre correspondence between what the month of Iyar symbolizes in Jewish tradition, and its actual role as host to historical events that constituted defining moments in shaping Jewish nationality, is discussed.

In the next section 20.2, we recount two chains of unfolding events that have taken place in recent years in the Middle East. The timing of these two chains of events is unrelated to the Jewish calendar. Yet, by a bizarre twist of unexplained coincidence, the Jewish calendar seems to be tightly correlated with these events.

The contents of this section were originally submitted to an English newspaper, published in Israel, in February of 2004—a time of anguish for the people of Israel due to the frequent suicide bombers that had killed and maimed many Israelis. The submitted paper was rejected and not published. That submission is replicated here (section 20.2) almost verbatim.

20.2 Two Events of Recent History

The coincidence that I am about to unfold in this comment is the strangest I have ever encountered. I am carrying this coincidence with me for the last year [that is, back in 2003], amazed by it, and yet unable to tell of it because it is, well … a coincidence. Yet, it is so extremely strange that a feeling has been steadily growing within me, in recent months, that if I had not made this coincidence public, it be unfair to those of us who may consider this more than a coincidence. So, for those in Israel who have experienced in recent years loss, personal injuries, pain, and despair because of "the situation" (a recently introduced Israeli term relating to, well … the situation), here is an extremely strange coincidence, for anyone to read, shape her or his own judgment, and perhaps draw some personal solace.

20.2.1 *Two Jewish Festivities: Commemorating a Disaster and a Rescue from One*

Two festivities in Jewish tradition signify two events of contrary symbolism. The first is Tishah B'Av[1] (the ninth of the Hebrew month of Av,[2] corresponding, roughly, to the month of August); the other is Purim[3] (which usually occurs at the end of February or the beginning of March).

Tishah B'Av[1] is the traditional date of the destruction of the first and the second Jewish temples in Jerusalem (destroyed at 586 BC and 70 CE, respectively). Tishah B'Av[1] has come to symbolize the worst catastrophes that befell the Jewish people throughout history. On this day, religious Jews fast to mourn the destruction of the temple, the exile of the Jewish people, and the calamities that befell Jews over the centuries as a result of the exile (*Galut*).[4]

Purim[3] is the polar opposite of Tishah B'av.[1] This festivity signifies Jewish salvation from disaster and celebrates redemption. While Passover celebrates transition from slavery in Egypt to freedom, Purim[3] commemorates the deliverance of the Jewish people from a malicious plan to exterminate all Jews living in the Persian Empire. As the story is told in the book of Esther (3:13, 15): "Letters were sent by couriers to all the king's provinces, to destroy, to slay, and to annihilate all Jews, young and old, women and children, in one day, the thirteenth day of the twelfth month, which is the month of Adar … And the king and Haman sat down to drink."

The book of Esther recounts how the Jews were miraculously saved from the plot to annihilate them. This book, by itself, is ridden with bizarre coincidences, one of which is described in section 16.2. Suffice it to say that even the name of the book, which is the name of the heroine and central figure in the story, is indicative of the contents and message of the whole book. The root of the name

Esther means, in Hebrew, "to hide." This immediately brings to mind how the catastrophes that would befall the Jewish people are depicted in the Bible:

- "Then my anger will be kindled against them on that day, and I will forsake them and *hide* [*histarti*[5]] my face from them, and they will be devoured, and many evils and troubles will come upon them; so that they will say in that day, Have not these evils come upon us because our God is not among us? And I will surely *hide* [*haster astir*[6]] my face in that day" (Deut. 31:17–18).

- "I dealt with them according to their uncleanness and their transgressions, and *hid* my face from them ... and I will not *hide* my face any more from them, when I pour out my spirit upon the House of Israel, says the Lord God" (Ezek. 39:24, 29).

Thus the book of Esther, perceived by many to be devoid of any religious significance because the name of God is not mentioned, turns out to be the story of the realization of God's will.

Summing up, Tishah B'Av[1] stands in the collective memory of the Jewish people as an epitome and a landmark for disasters that descended upon the Jewish people throughout history (some of these in fact took place on exactly that Hebrew calendar day). By contrast, Purim[3] symbolizes the rescue of Jews from such calamities.

Given this background with respect to the significance of the two festivities, Tishah B'Av[1] and Purim,[3] can one recall a recent historic event that

- A. posed the greatest threat to the physical survival of Jews as a collective since the Holocaust?

- B. contrary to most pessimistic expectations, ended with relatively few casualties to Jews?

- C. started on the last hours of Tishah B'Av[1] and ended ("prematurely," so it was told at the time) on the first day of Purim[3] the same (Hebrew) year?

20.2.2 A Gathering Threat and the Rescue: Two Recent Historical Events

It is time to be more particular. To detail the extremely strange coincidence, the subject of this section, major events that took place in the Middle East in the last dozen years or so (as of the time of authoring this book) are enumerated.

- Saddam Hussein invaded Kuwait. This invasion triggered the Gulf War. **Date: August 1, 1990** (in fact, on the night between the first and the second of August).

- A cease-fire was declared in the Gulf (end of hostilities in Iraq), and the end of the emergency state in Israel was declared. **Date: February 28, 1991**.

- Restarting the war in Iraq by American bombings over Baghdad. **Date: March 19, 2003** (in fact, on the night between March 19 and March 20).

Let us recheck the dates.

In 1990, Tishah B'Av was on July 31. On the night between August 1 and 2, Iraq invaded Kuwait. This was the beginning of a chain of events, during which missiles were launched against the Jewish state. Anxiety about the possibility of chemical war-heads falling on Israeli population triggered distribution of gas masks.

Purim[3] in the Hebrew calendar is always on the fourteenth of the Hebrew month of Adar, and Shoshan Purim[7] (second day of Purim) is on the fifteenth of Adar. On February 28, 1991, the United States declared a cease-fire in the Gulf. This was on the fourteenth of Adar, the first of the two days of the festivity of Purim,[1] the Jewish festivity celebrating the Jews' rescue from disaster.

The following is an imaginary dialogue:

"What about the third event, the beginning of the bombings in Iraq in 2003?"

"Well, this happened the next day."

"What do you mean by the next day? Twelve years have elapsed since!"

"I mean 'next day' according to the calendar."

"Still, this needs explanation. The cease-fire in the Gulf was declared on February 28; bombings in Iraq started on the night between the nineteenth and the twentieth of March, twelve years later. So even according to the calendar, this is more than two weeks later (ignoring the year), rather than the next day."

"Well, not according to the Hebrew calendar. The war in Iraq 2003 started on the fifteenth of Adar—March 19, 2003. According to the Hebrew calendar, that's 'a day' after cease-fire was declared there, on the fourteenth of Adar, twelve years earlier …"

A summary of these dates, in both calendars, is given in Table 20.1.

20.2.3 A Personal Comment

I conclude this section with a personal comment. Back in 1990, when I realized that invasion of Kuwait had taken place so near Tishah B'Av[1] (in fact, the following day), I was puzzled. As missiles fell on Israel, and anxiety built up with each passing day, and with Purim approaching, I wondered whether all this mayhem might come to an end at Purim.[3] I told my close family and friends that I believed the war would most probably end in Purim.[3] I was ridiculed. I was right.

Prior to the start of the second Gulf war in 2003, as American and allied forces amassed in the Gulf, and Israelis anxiously awaited the start of yet another war in Iraq, expecting the worst and carrying around personal gas masks, my graduate students in one of the courses I delivered at the time asked when I believed the war would start. I guessed, "Probably on Purim." In hindsight, I could have been more precise. Obviously, by the Hebrew calendar, the war would start where it left off (prematurely)—namely, a Hebrew-calendar day after the cessation of the incomplete war back in 1991!

And so it was. How else could it be?

Table 20.1. Summary of major dates in the two Gulf wars
(Hebrew and general calendar).

Event	General Calendar	Hebrew Calendar
Tisha B'av	July, 31, 1990	9th of Av
Invasion of Kuwait	August, 1, 1990	10th of Av
Cease-Fire (1st Gulf War)	February, 28, 1991	14th of Adar
First day of Purim (same year)	February, 28, 1991	14th of Adar
Start of Coalition Bombings in Iraq (2nd Gulf War)	March, 19, 2003	15th of Adar
Second Day of Purim (same year)	March, 19, 2003	15th of Adar

20.3 The Month of Iyar

According to biblical counting, the month of Iyar[8] is the second month in the Hebrew calendar. It comes after the first month of Nisan,[9] the month that marks the exodus from Egypt ("This month shall be to you the beginning of months: it shall be the first month of the year to you"—Exod. 12:2). In modern days, the first month in the Hebrew calendar is the month of Tishrei,[10] which starts with the two-day festivity of Rosh Hashanah[11] (literally, the Head of the Year).

What characterizes the month of Iyar, and what is unique about it?
In over three thousand years of existence, the Jewish people asserted and gained nationhood through very brief transition periods, when profound transformation in the Jewish people's mode of existence had taken place. These transformations could be realized by a transition from slavery to freedom, by building temples to God, or by the conquering of territory by force in the Promised Land.

There are six such defining eras in the history of the Jewish people, when Jews declared themselves a free nation, entitled to manifest their own nationhood in their ancestral *Eretz*—Israel.

20.3.1   *Exodus*

The first historical event is the exodus from Egypt. On the fourteenth of Nisan, the first day of the festivity of Passover, the Israelites left Egypt, transforming themselves from being slaves into being a free nation. Shortly thereafter, "And all the congregation of the children of Israel came unto the wilderness of Sin, which is between Elim and Sinai, on the fifteenth day of the second month after their departing out of the land of Egypt" (Exod. 16:1). It is not in vain that the Bible marks only this day. This is the day when the Israelites "officially" started their wandering in the desert, leaving Egypt "for good" on their way to the Promised Land. Thus, it is the second month, the month of Iyar, that marks the first month the Israelites became a free nation, coming out of the bondage of Egypt.

20.3.2   *Entering the Promised Land*

The second defining moment in Jewish history, when Jews exercised their right for sovereignty in the land of Israel, is their entrance into the Promised Land after forty years of wandering in the Sinai desert. On the tenth of the month of Nisan, the Israelites crossed the Jordan River (Josh. 4:19), entering the land of Israel. This entrance is marked by the Bible by a seemingly insignificant comment: "And the manna ceased on the morrow when they ate of the corn of the land; neither had the children of Israel manna any more; but they did eat of the produce of the land of Canaan that year" (Josh. 5:12). The manna was the food miraculously provided by God throughout the wandering in the Sinai desert. The cessation of the manna signaled the transition from an existence of miracles (under the provision of God, in the desert) to a phase of existence as a people that have to earn their own living by toil, like any other nation.

When was the first battle of the Israelites waged to conquer territory in the land of Israel, once they crossed the Jordan River? That battle was over Jericho. The Bible does not specify the exact date. However, the Israelites celebrated their first Passover in the Promised Land for seven days, from the fourteenth of Nisan to the twenty-first of the same month. The battle over Jericho was launched after the Israelites had first encircled the city, with no combat operations, for seven consecutive days (a single encirclement every day for the first six days, and then seven times on the seventh day—Josh. 6:3–4). Thus, the battle over Jericho, the first in the Israelite's wars to conquer the land, which was launched on the seventh consecutive day of their encircling the city, could not have started prior to the twenty-eighth of the month of Nisan. Most likely, it was launched well into the second month—the month of Iyar.

With certainty, one can assert that the start of the war to gain sovereignty over a land of their own, exercising their right for nationhood in the Holy Land, was started by the Israelites in the second month of the biblical calendar, on the month of Iyar.

20.3.3 Building the First Temple

The third cycle, when Jews manifested their nationhood in the Holy Land, involved the building of the first Jewish temple. As the story is recounted in the Bible regarding King Solomon's building of the temple, "And it came to pass in the four hundred and eightieth year after the children of Israel were come out of the land of Egypt, in the fourth year of Solomon's reign over Israel, in the month Ziv, which is the second month, that he began to build the house of Jehovah" (1 Kings 6:1).

The event of the beginning of construction of the first temple took place in the month of Ziv (month of Light), the second month in the Hebrew biblical calendar—the month of Iyar.

20.3.4 Building the Second Temple

The fourth defining moment for the Jews as they exercised their right for nationhood came about after Cyrus, king of Persia, called upon the Jews to immigrate to Israel, proclaiming that "The Lord God of heaven has given me all the kingdoms of the earth; and He has charged me to build him a house at Jerusalem, which in Judah" (Ezra 1:2). This time, many Jews immigrated to the Holy Land, with the specific permission of the ruler of that region. No wars had to be waged, so the only signature of sovereignty for the Jews was the start of the building of the second temple.

When did the construction of the second temple begin? The book of Ezra specifies it:

> "Now in the second year of their coming to the house of God at Jerusalem, *in the second month*, began Zerubbabel the son of Shealtiel, and Jeshua the son of Jozadak, and the remnant of their brethren the priests and the Levites, and all they that were come out of the captivity unto Jerusalem; and appointed the Levites, from twenty years old and upwards, to superintend the work of the house of the Lord" (Ezra 3:8).

In other words, on the month of Iyar, the construction of the second temple had started (just as with the first temple), this time as a sign of sovereignty for the Israelites returning back from exile to the Promised Land, under the auspices of the ruler of the country (Cyrus, king of Persia).

20.3.5 *Declaration of Independence*

The fifth defining moment in Jewish history as the Jews proclaimed sovereignty over the land of Israel was with the Declaration of Independence on the fifteenth of May, 1948. The Hebrew date was the fifth of Iyar. This date was not pre-planned by the Israelis; it was determined elsewhere, by the British, who had ended their mandate over Palestine the following day (see below, in a list of major historical events that took place in the month of Iyar, which were significant for Jewish history and nationhood).

Thus, the fifth cycle, when Jews proclaimed their right for sovereignty in *Eretz* Israel, started once again in Iyar, and then was followed by a bloody war with Arab armies invading the country. This war left 6,373 Israelis dead—about 1% of the Jewish population at the time (about 600,000 people).

20.3.6 *The Six-Day War*

The sixth cycle in bringing parts of the land of Israel under Jewish control, including the old city of Jerusalem (where the Wailing Wall, a remnant of the second Jewish temple, has withstood the ravages of nearly two thousand years since the temple destruction at 70 CE) took place with the outbreak of the Six-Day

War, on June 6, 1967. This war started as a result of a series of misunderstandings, when Arab armies amassed at the borders of Israel, forcing Israel to launch pre-emptive military strikes that ended six days later, with all of the land of Israel, west of Jordan River, under Jewish control, including the old city of Jerusalem.

The Six-Day War started on the twenty-sixth of the Hebrew month of Iyar.

These six eras in Jewish history are all significant; three of them represent the Jewish people returning from exile to re-inhabit the Holy Land, and all represent major events where Jews proclaimed nationhood—either by exiting from slavery, or by building temples, or by conquering pieces of the Promised Land. All these events started in the same month … the second month of the Jewish biblical calendar … the month of Ziv … the month of Iyar.

20.3.7 The Month of Iyar in Jewish Tradition

The name "Iyar" is, like others in the Hebrew calendar, of Babylonian origin. The zodiac sign of Iyar is an ox eating grass. This may be explained by the fact that this month corresponds to the first month in the warm season in *Eretz* Israel, when the ox can still find enough grass to satisfy its appetite from the grass of the field.

Yet, there is more symbolism to the ox. The ox eating grass reminds one of how the people of Israel are described in the Bible when they pass through territories of various peoples prior to their entry into the Promised Land. One of these peoples is the Moab, and the Bible describes the anxiety of this people after learning of the victories of the Israelites in combats waged against Moab's neighboring countries: "And Moab was distressed because of the children of Israel. And Moab said to the elderly of Midyan, Now shall this company lick up all that are round about us, as the ox licks up the grass of the field" (Num. 22:3–4).

The month of Iyar is regarded in Jewish mysticism (Kabbalah) as the month associated with the Sefirah of *Gevura*,[12] the fifth of the ten Sefirot. There are various interpretations and implications to this concept.

According to the Kabbalah, *gevurah*[12] is associated in the soul with the power to restrain one's innate urge to bestow goodness upon others, when the recipient of that good is judged to be unworthy and liable to misuse it. As the force that measures and assesses the worthiness of creation, *gevurah*[12] is also referred to in the Kabbalah as *midat ha-din*[13] ("the attribute of judgment"), as contrasted with *chesed*,[14] which is *midat ha-rachamim*[15] ("the attribute of compassion and mercifulness"). It is the restraining might of *gevurah*[12] that allows one to overcome his enemies, be they from without or from within (his evil inclination).

Chesed[14] and *gevurah*[12] act together to create an inner balance in the soul's approach to the outside world. While the right arm of *chesed*[14] operates to draw others near, the left arm of *gevurah*[12] reserves the option of repelling those deemed undeserving. (Even toward those to whom one's initial relation is that of "the left arm repels," one must subsequently apply the complementary principle of "the right arm draws near.")

However, there is more to *gevurah*[12] than implied by Sefirot of the Kabbalah.

Gevurah[12] in Hebrew means, literally, heroism. For example, a soldier in the IDF (Israel Defense Forces), who had performed an act of heroism during combat, may get the military Ot Ha-Gevurah[16] (the Medal of Heroism).

According to Jewish tradition, the month of Iyar is associated, with regard to the zodiac (astrological) signs, with planet Mars, known in many cultures (like the ancient Greek and Roman) to be associated with wars. In fact, the Kabbalistic associations of this month—both with the ox and with planet Mars—are indications that in Jewish mysticism this sign assumes the same interpretation. Furthermore, one of the many manifestations of the divine conduct, often related to in the Bible, is *gevurah*,[12] with all its implications.

It is indeed extraordinary—a bizarre coincidence—that most Jewish manifestations of establishing nationhood in the land of Israel (we have expounded six) all started in the month of Iyar, the same month that in Jewish calendar and mysticism signifies wars and periods of transition.

20.3.8   Some Major Iyar Events

Following is a list of major events regarding Jewish renewed presence in the ancient land of Israel, and the struggle to preserve this presence. The dates for these events were taken from the Web site
http://www.ou.org/about/judaism/bhyom/hebrew/iyar.htm.

While the exact dates for ancient-time events may be debatable, the fact that these happened on the month of Iyar remains unchallenged.

Fifth Iyar

- Joseph Rivlin laid the cornerstone of the first private home to be erected outside the walls of the Old City of Jerusalem, marking the beginning of the modern Yishuv (the presovereignty community of Jews in Israel), 1869.

- Israel was proclaimed an independent state in 1948. The first legislative act of the provisional government of the state of Israel provided for the repeal of the British White Paper of 1939, which had restricted Jewish immigration and the acquisition of land in *Eretz* Israel.

Sixth Iyar

- The British mandate over *Eretz* Israel went into effect in 1920. This date became known as San Remo Day.

- The British mandate over *Eretz* Israel came to an end in 1948, exactly twenty-eight years after it began.

- The armies of Egypt, Jordan, Syria, Iraq, and Lebanon invaded Israel in 1948.

Seventh Iyar

- The new walls built by Nechemya around Jerusalem were dedicated in 443 BCE (refer to the book of Nehemiah, 12:27). This date was observed as a holiday in ancient times. A little over five hundred years later, the Jews surrendered the wall, on the same day, to the Roman Empire.

Fourteenth Iyar

- Adolf Eichmann, key to implementation of the "Final Solution" by Nazi Germany, was captured in Buenos Aires by Israeli agents in 1960. He was in charge of sending all Jews to the extermination camps.

Eighteenth Iyar

- Tzahal (Israel Defense Forces) was established in 1948.

Twenty-Third Iyar

- Shimon Ha-Chashmona'i, leader of the Jewish revolt in *Eretz* Israel, drove the Syrians and their allies, the Hellenized Jews, out of the Citadel, their last stronghold in Jerusalem, in 142 BCE. The date was observed as a holiday in ancient times.

- The Arab states and Israel agreed to a cease-fire in 1948. By the time of the first truce, Israel had already scored substantial victories over the Syrian and Egyptian armies.

Twenty-Fourth Iyar

- Germany surrendered unconditionally to the Allies in 1945.

Twenty-Sixth Iyar

- War broke out between Israel and the Arab nations on June 6, 1967.

Twenty-Eighth Iyar

- Israel captured the old city of Jerusalem and united it (for the first time since the establishment of the state) in 1967.

- Hostilities between Israel and Jordan came to an end upon their acceptance of the cease-fire demanded by the Security Council of the UN in 1967.

Twenty-Ninth Iyar

- Israel, Egypt, and Syria accepted the cease-fire ordered by the Security Council, 1967;

This list, though not exhaustive, is bizarrely coincidental due to the disproportional number of major military incidents that have taken place in that month.

20.4 Everyday Coincidences and Their Lessons

Coincidences happen to us all, all the time. The truth is that we are constantly bombarded by bizarre coincidences, each one with a message, frequently of a moral nature. Furthermore, clues are constantly sent to us to observe the messages. Yet, we are blind to them—and most of the time, we ignore them, because they go against the way we have been brought up. We were taught to perceive the natural world around us as ruled by visible, logical, and controllable regularities.

The subject of coincidences is not new to human culture. Indeed, it has been the focus and central theme in most cultures and countless number of books. For example, the two best-sellers, *The Celestine Prophecy* and *The Tenth Insight*, by James Redfield (1995 and 1996, respectively) focus, first and foremost, on coincidences and their messages.

Jewish tradition also accepts coincidences. The only difference is that it refuses to acknowledge them as such. In Jewish culture, all coincidences are acts of God, intended to help us avoid "missing the target" (refer to section 2.1). One can quote numerous verses in the Bible where this theme is raised, and there is emphasis on the "error of judgment" in any acceptance of a bizarre coincidence as random. In fact, as discussed in chapter 3, the sheer concept of randomness is an abomination to Jewish thought. When God warns the children of Israel to obey his statues, he warns them: "If you will walk with me in [*kerri*[17]]; then I will walk with you with the fury of [*kerri*[17]]" (Lev. 26:27–28; also see 26, 21, 23, 24, 27, 40, 41). *Kerri,*[17] of course, implies randomness, and the verse implies that if one behaves randomly in his or her personal conduct, not obeying moral code, then the reaction—the punishment—will also be administered randomly, as though it were completely dissociated from the very conduct of the recipient of the punishment. This nature of random punishment is revealed in God's "hiding the hiding" of his face (*haster astir panai*,[18] Deut. 31:18).

Another realization of this attitude of Jewish thought is revealed in a quote from Jewish sages: "Measure against measure [*midah ke-neged midah*[19]]. By the same measure that a person conducts his or her ways, they [meaning heaven] measure to him." In fact, this same attitude lies at the core of Jewish law. The much misinterpreted, misused, and abused biblical "an eye for an eye" was not intended to be read literally (and this can be shown easily by properly interpreting the pursuing verses). Rather, it was meant to serve as an epitome for the fundamental tenet that underlies Jewish law, and indeed most legal systems in today's democratic nations: "Punishment should be proportional to the consequences of the deed of iniquity—of the transgression."

Here are two examples for this philosophy of justice, assumed to be inherent in the very nature and structure of the world, as conveyed by the Bible. When God speaks to King David, delivering the message that his son will build the temple, God describes his future relationship with David's yet-unspecified son: "I will be to him like a father, and he will be to me like a son, so that when he distorts his ways [*be-haavoto*[20]] I would reproach him by the rod of man and with the afflictions of human beings" (2 Samuel 7:14; my translation). In the same vein, the author of Proverbs teaches the same lesson, succinctly and beautifully: "In all thy ways know him, and he will straighten your walkways" (Prov. 3:6).

To help gain insight as to what the nature of coincidences is in everyday life, and demonstrate our potential blindness to the messages in these coincidences— and how we practically turn a blind eye to clues that are supposed to draw our attention to these messages—let us address two scandals of recent times. They are known by the names Watergate (named after a hotel in Washington DC) and Whitewater (named after Whitewater Development Corporation, founded 1978). How strange that such two unrelated scandals are called by so similar names.

Is it possible that they are yet interrelated?

I conducted a comprehensive search of the Internet and other written public sources to find out whether there is any allusion to the moral lesson of these two similarly named, but seemingly unrelated scandals, yet I found none.

Is it possible that a certain individual was involved in both scandals, displaying overenthusiasm to indict a president in one scandal, only to be, some years later, on the receiving end of overkill accusations in the other scandal? Was there a moral lesson here, intended to teach, with a loudly shouting clue (similar names), which nobody was attentive to?

I do not know. This may as well be just a coincidence.

CHAPTER 21

How probable are the results?
—A simulation study

Nineteen statistical analyses were introduced in earlier chapters and results displayed with respect to nine subjects:

- Diameters of the three celestial objects: the moon, Earth and the sun (M, E, S), chapter 8;
- Diameters of the planets, chapter 8;
- Water specific heat capacity (SHC) for the three phases of water: ice, liquid, and steam, chapter 9;
- Light wave frequencies, perceived by receptors in the human eye, chapter 10;
- Color wave frequencies, chapter 12;
- Time-period frequencies, chapter 12;
- Various cyclic phenomena frequencies, chapter 12;
- Transition metals' atomic weights, chapter 13;
- Other materials' atomic weights, chapter 13.

Each of the nine separate categories of analysis was based on different and statistically independent samples of observations. Each resulted in statistically significant results (one was bordering significance). For all nineteen analyses F-ratio values, significance values (p values) and scatter plots, together with the fitted linear regression lines, were provided.

While statistical significance had been achieved for almost all analyses, one may claim that the small sample size used in many of these analyses (three data points) undermines any attempt to attribute meaning to them. One way to circumvent this criticism is to ask: How probable are these results? Put differently:

What is the probability of three data points, as defined in the various analyses, aligning themselves on a straight line (or thereabout) by chance alone?

To examine this question we display in this chapter results from a simulation study, where data points, similar in a certain way to the data points used in the various analyses, are generated randomly by the computer. While values of the physical property, used in a certain analysis, remain the same (as in the original analysis), "Hebrew words" that represent the various objects are generated randomly by the computer, and the experiment is repeated many times. The central question posed with respect to the results of the simulation is: What percentage of the trios of "Hebrew words", generated artificially by the computer, align themselves on a straight line or thereabouts (as in the original trio of biblical Hebrew words)?

In the next section 21.1 we expound in detail a single example, related to the relationship between values of Hebrew biblical words for colors and their respective wave frequencies. In section 21.2 we display results related to all nine categories of analysis, as described above.

21.1 A detailed example: Colors wave frequencies (WF)

In Table 12.1 the seven elementary colors of the human visible spectrum were enumerated with their wavelength and frequency intervals. In section 12.3.2 we have identified four elementary colors which "were deemed as having clear non-debatable Hebrew meanings" in the Bible: Red, yellow, green and blue. Each of these has its own interval of wave frequency (WF), and in Table 12.3 we have selected (somewhat arbitrarily) the mid-point to represent the WF of the respective color. This may be justified for the last three colors (namely, yellow, green and blue), whose WF intervals lie within the human visible spectrum. It is different for "red", which lie at the lower boundary of the visible spectrum (infra-red is by definition non-visible). Furthermore, color "orange" (one of the seven elementary colors; refer to Tables 12.1 or 12.3) is not recognized in the Bible. Finally, the human receptor for "red" achieves its maximum sensitivity at WF=517.2 (Section 10.3.3), far from the formal definition of the WF for red as an elementary color (Tables 12.1 and 12.3). We take this value (517.2) as the WF for red in the pursuing analysis.

Taking account of these considerations, the analysis in this section proceeds in two stages as expounded below.

Stage I: Using the two data points associated with yellow and blue, an equation of a line is derived, which expresses the WF of a color in terms of the color numerical value (CNV) of the respective biblical Hebrew name. To examine how well the model predicts the WF of colors not partaking in its mathematical derivation, we then introduce into this equation CNVs associated with biblical names of three other colors: elementary colors "red" and "green", and the non-elementary color magenta (*argaman* in Hebrew). The latter is produced by equal proportions of red and blue and it has an *equivalent* WF of 546.5THz (find details in Comment 2 of section 12.3.3).

For yellow and blue:

- Yellow: CNV= 97; WF = 520 THz;
- Blue: CNV=850; WF=650.

Introducing these two data points into the equation of a line: $WF = \beta_0 + \beta_1(CNV)$, we obtain: $\beta_0 = 503.2$; $\beta_1 = 0.1726$ (these values are close to the values obtained by linear regression applied to all four colors in the basic set; find details in Analysis III of section 12.3.3).

Introducing into this equation CNV values of the other colors, we obtain:

- Green (CNV=366, actual WF=**565**): WF (predicted from the model) = **566.4**;
- Red (CNV=51, actual WF=**517.2**): WF (predicted) = **512.1**;
- Magenta (*argaman*; CNV=294, actual WF=**546.5**): WF (predicted) = **554.0**.

Actual data-points for (yellow, green, blue) are displayed in Table 21.1 (Example 4) and in Figure 21.4.

Stage II: At this stage we use computer simulation to generate artificially trios of three-letter "biblical Hebrew" words in order to examine the likelihood of their alignment on a straight line, similarly to the configuration observed for the original true Hebrew words (refer, for example, to Figure 12.7). To guarantee both randomness and adherence to the natural structure of biblical Hebrew words, three-letter words are first generated randomly, where each letter is selected with probability equal to its actual appearance in the Hebrew Bible. Thus, the second letter in the Hebrew alphabet, the letter *bet*, appears 5.448% of the times and therefore it is selected randomly with this probability (or sampling weight). Also, generated words with same *three* letters are discarded as well as trios having any two words with identical numerical values. The last rejection criterion was pursued assuming that two Hebrew words representing two different objects (like Earth and sun) do not share same numerical values. Also, all generated words had *three* letters, even when actual (true) trios of words occasionally included four-letter words. For example, the Hebrew for blue, *Tchelet*, is a four-letter word. We have assumed that integrating this particular information would bias the results and therefore all computer-generated trios comprised only three-letter words (as do the majority of actual Hebrew words taking part in this analysis).

The response variable (the metric subjected to statistical analysis) is the ratio of the slopes (SR) of the two lines that connect two adjacent points, namely:

$$SR = \frac{SR^{23}}{SR_{12}} = \frac{(Y_3 - Y_2)/(X_3 - X_2)}{(Y_2 - Y_1)/(X_2 - X_1)},$$

where Y_j (j=1,2,3) is the value on the vertical axis (the physical property) of the j-th point, Xj is the respective value on the horizontal axis (Hebrew numerical value) and the words in the trio are sorted (for the analysis) according to values of the physical property (the Y values). Obviously for three points that are arranged exactly on a single line (whether the line has positive or negative slope) we expect (ideally) SR=1. For three-point sets that are arranged near a straight line we expect SR values around 1.

Continuing with same example as in Stage I, it can be easily established from Table 1.1 and Table 21.1 that for the set {yellow, green, blue}, the SR values are (refer to section 12.3.2):

SR_{12} = 0.1673; SR_{23} = 0.1756; SR = (0.1756) / (0.1673) = 1.0498.

Simulating by the computer N=50000 trios of words and randomly selecting from that body of data a sample of n=5000 trios, a value of SR was calculated for each. The sample of 5000 SR values delivered mean and standard deviation equal to, respectively (Example 4 in Table 21.1):

$$\mu_{SR} = -1.35; \ \sigma_{SR} = 42.9.$$

Using these estimates and assuming normality of SR values (refer to Figure 21.4), we may calculate the probability of SR randomly falling in the interval ±5% around SR=1 (as happened with the actual trio of words):

$$\Pr[0.95 < SR \le 1.05] = 0.00093.$$

We realize that there is extremely small probability for SR to occur so near 1. Figure 21.4 shows a histogram of the artificially generated SR values. The figure clearly shows that the simulated SR values are indeed normally distributed and that they have a large span of variation.

21.2 The complete simulation study

To learn whether the implausibility, found in the previous section, for a trio of biblical Hebrew words to align themselves in a linear configuration (or near to one) extends to other examples the analysis above was implemented to nine more examples (some of which are enumerated at the beginning of this chapter). Actual data-points and other relevant information are given in Table 21.1. Table 21.2 displays actual SR values, means and standard deviations obtained from the simulation experiments and the respective probability values (rightmost column).

Table 21.1. Examples of trios of biblical Hebrew words bound by a common physical property. HNV-Hebrew numerical value; MU-measurement unit (MU) on original scale; PP= Value of physical property used in analysis; "Figure" relates to relevant figures in this book. All examples are also shown in Figs. 21.1-21.10.

Ex.	Trio of words (HNV)	Physical property (MU) (PP)	Figure	Relevant book section
1	{moon, Earth, sun} (218, 291, 640)	Log-diameter (km) (8.153, 9.454, 14.145)	8.2	8.3.2
2	{Earth, Jupiter, Sun} (291, 508, 640)	Log-diameter (km) (9.454, 11.848, 14.145)	8.5	8.3.5
3	{ice, water, steam} (308, 90, 319)	Specific heat capacity (2050, 4181, 1970)	9.1	9.4
4	{yellow, green, blue} (97, 366, 850)	Wave frequency (THz) (520, 565, 650)	12.3	12.3.3
5	{day, month, year} (56, 218, 355)	Log-frequency (Hz) (-11.37, -14.75, -17.24)	12.6	12.4.1
6	{day, sound, light} (56, 130, 207)	Log-frequency (Hz) (-11.37, 5.991, 33.97)	21.6	12.4.2
7	{day, thunder, lightening} (56, 310, 800)	Log-frequency (Hz) (-11.367, 5.9915, 33.968) Log-	12.7	12.4.2
8	{ standstill, sound, ,light} (89, 130, 207)	velocity (km/sec.) (0, 5.840, 19.52)	21.8	23.3
9	{silence, thunder, lightening} (89, 310, 800)	Log-velocity (km/sec.) (0, 5.840, 19.52)	21.9	23.3
10	{gold, silver, copper} (14, 160, 363)	Recip. atomic weight (5.077E-3, 9.270E-3, 15.74E-3)	13.2	13.4.1

Table 21.2. Examples of trios of Hebrew words bound by a common physical trait (Table 21.1) and their probability to be aligned by chance on a straight line (or thereabouts) (n=5000 three-letter trios of "Hebrew words" sampled from a body of artificially generated N=50,000 trios). SR - Slopes ratio;

STD—Standard deviation

Ex.	trio of Hebrew words	Physical property	Relevant Figure	$SR_{ac.}$ (Actual SR)	{Mean, STD} (of SR)	Probability of $(1-\Delta<SR<1+\Delta)$ $\Delta = \mid SR_{ac.}-1\mid$
1	{moon, Earth, sun}	Log-diameter	8.2	0.755	{-.775, 98.3}	0.00203
2	{Earth,Jupiter, Sun}	Log-diameter	21.3	1.58	{.188, 23.0}	0.0208
3	{ice, water, steam}	Specific heat capacity (SHC)	9.10.744		{-.020, 1.06}	0.118
4	{yellow, green, blue}	Wave frequency (WF, THz)	21.1	1.05	{-1.35, 42.9}	0.000927
5	{day, month, year}	Log-frequency12.6 (freq. in Hz)		0.868	{-.553, 23.2}	0.00514
6	{ day, sound, light}	Log-frequency (freq. in Hz)	12.7	1.55	{-.703, 43.1}	0.0102
7	{day, thunder, lightening}	Log-frequency (freq. in Hz)	21.7	0.835	{-.575, 38.2}	0.00333
8	{ standstill, sound, ,light}	Log-velocity	21.8	1.25	{-3.26, 56.9}	0.00769
9	{ silence, thunder, lightening}	Log-velocity	21.9	1.05	{-1.28, 61.2}	0.000781
10	{gold, silver, copper}	Reciprocal atomic weight	13.2	1.11	{-1.36, 47.8}	0.00167

The latter clearly indicate that it is highly unlikely for a trio of Hebrew words to be aligned along a straight line by chance, irrespective of the values of the physical property described on the vertical axis. Figures 21.1-21.10 display plots of actual data points and histograms of the artificially generated SR values.

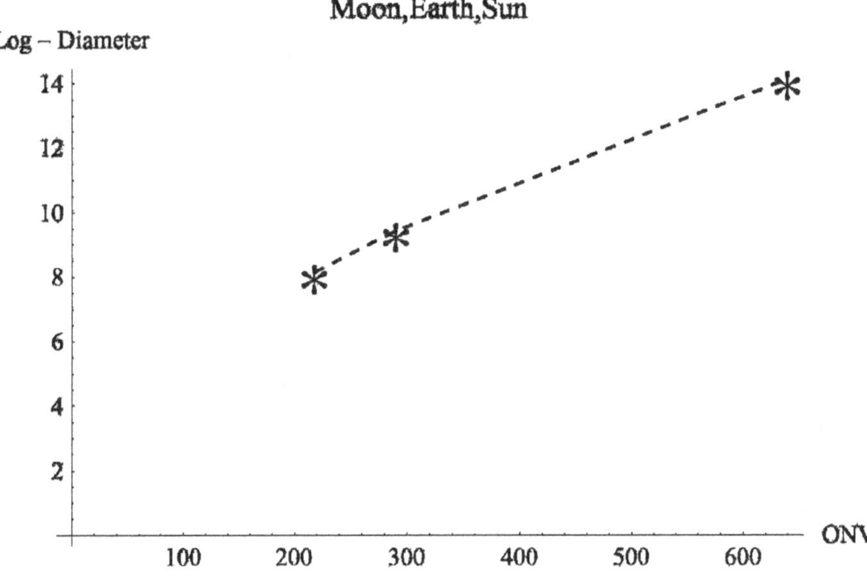

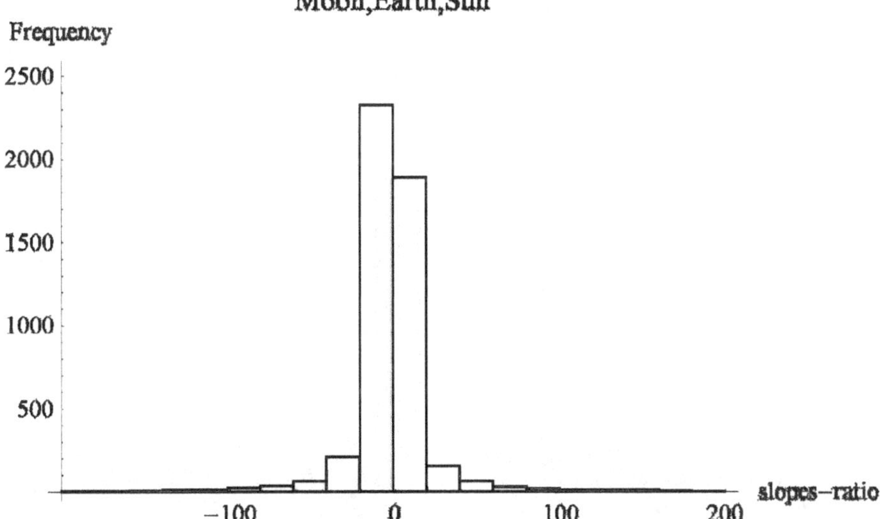

Figure 21.1. Example 1: Plot of data-points (upper figure) and a histogram of slopes-ratio for n=5000 trios of artificially generated Hebrew words. Celestial ONV (Object numerical value) is numerical value of the Hebrew word.

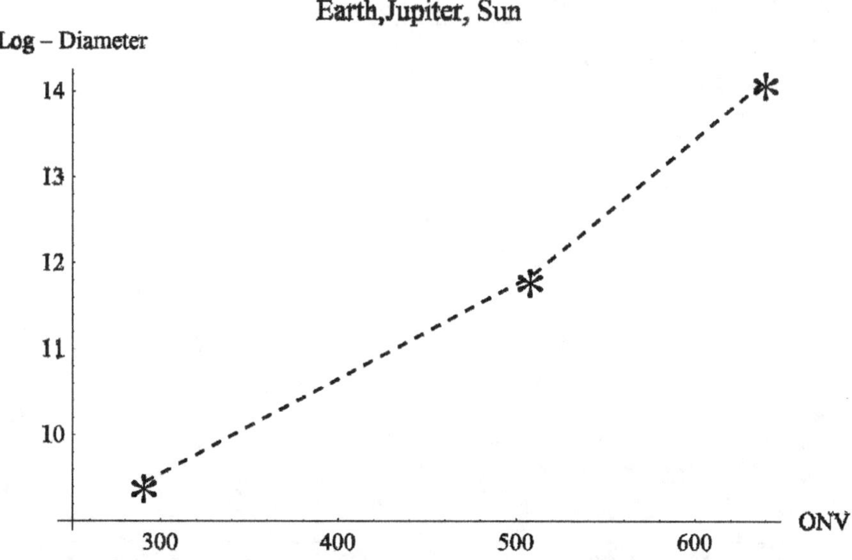

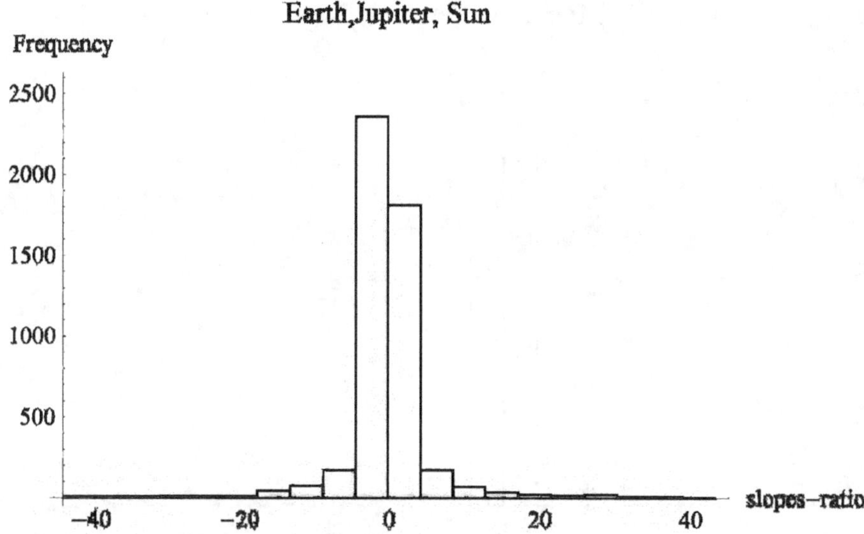

Figure 21.2. Example 2: Plot of data-points (upper figure) and a histogram of slopes-ratio for n=5000 trios of artificially generated Hebrew words. Celestial ONV (Object numerical value) is numerical value of the Hebrew word.

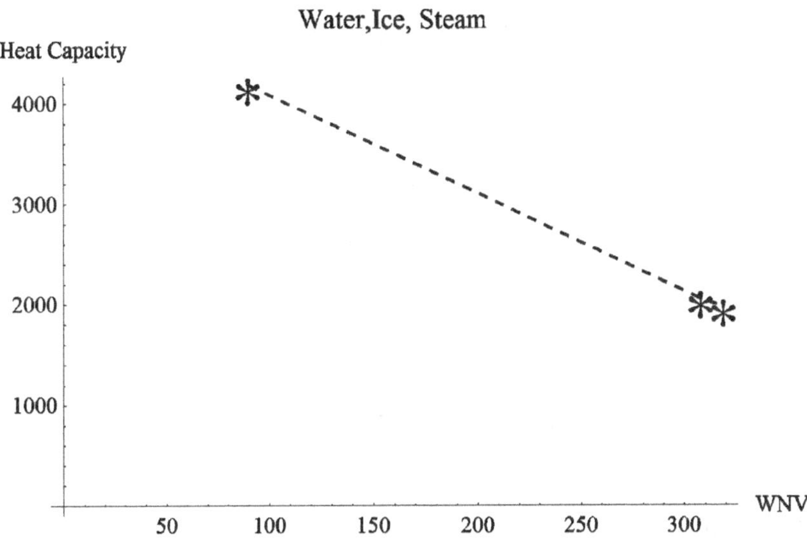

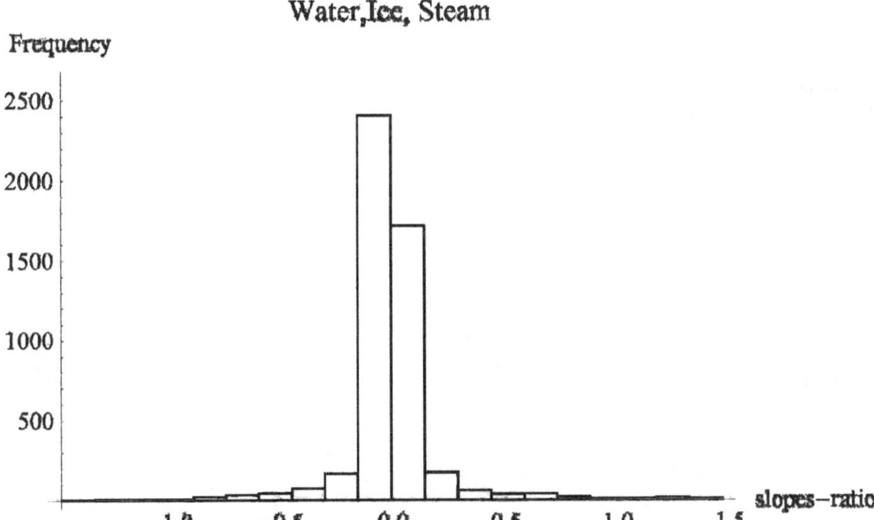

Figure 21.3. Example 3: Plot of data-points (upper figure) and a histogram of slopes-ratio for n=5000 trios of artificially generated Hebrew words. WNV (Water numerical value) is numerical value of the Hebrew word.

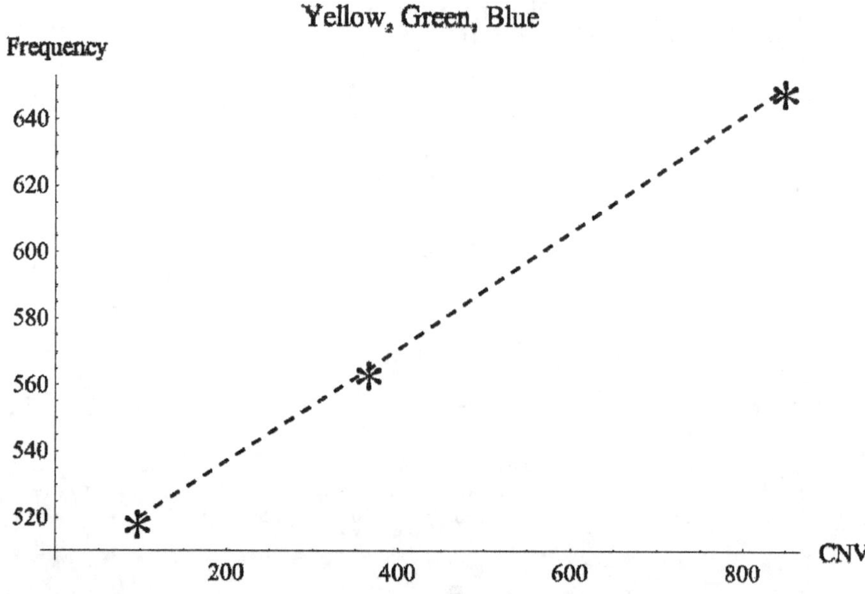

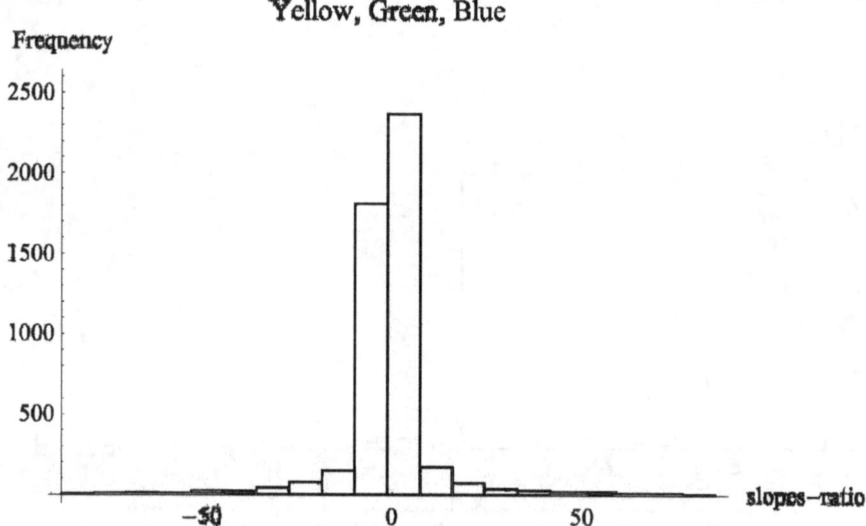

Figure 21.4. Example 4: Plot of data-points (upper figure) and a histogram of slopes-ratio for n=5000 trios of artificially generated Hebrew words. CNV (Color numerical value) is numerical value of the Hebrew word.

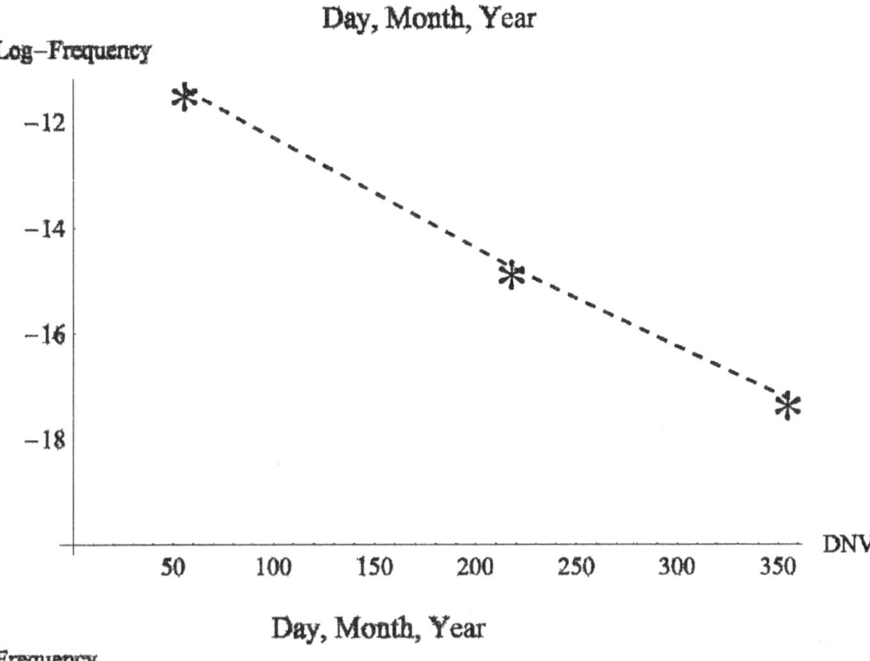

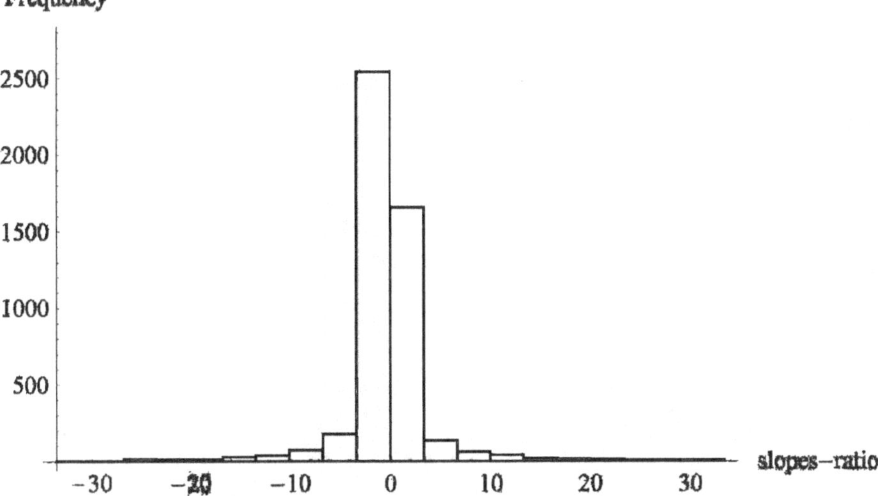

Figure 21.5. Example 5: Plot of data-points (upper figure) and a histogram of slopes-ratio for n=5000 trios of artificially generated Hebrew words. DNV (Duration numerical value) is numerical value of the Hebrew word.

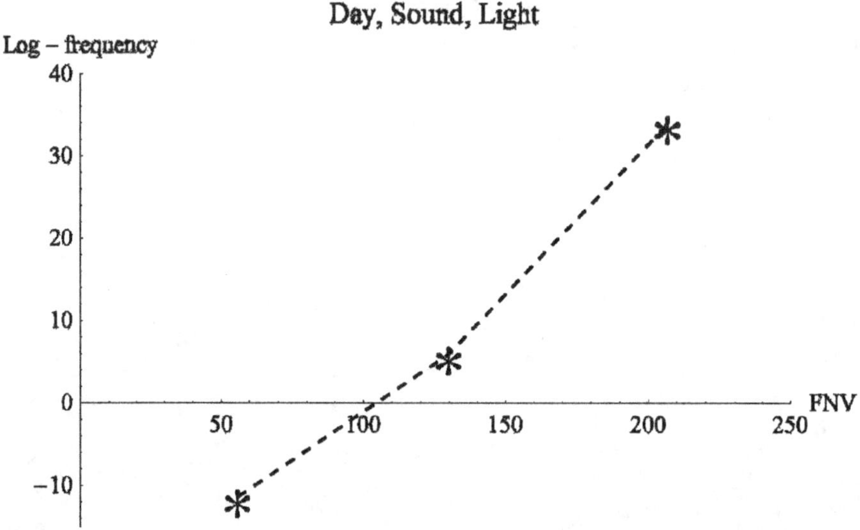

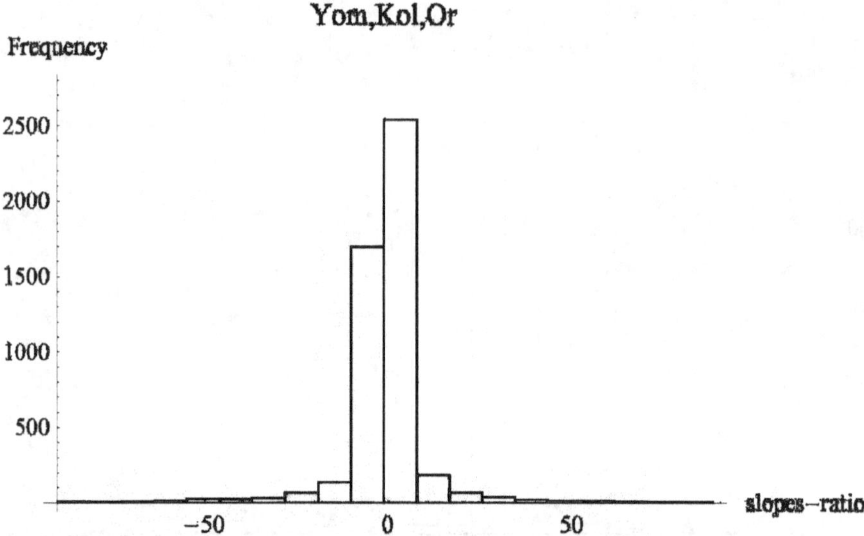

Figure 21.6. Example 6: Plot of data-points (upper figure) and a histogram of slopes-ratio for n=5000 trios of artificially generated Hebrew words. FNV (Frequency numerical value) is numerical value of the Hebrew word.

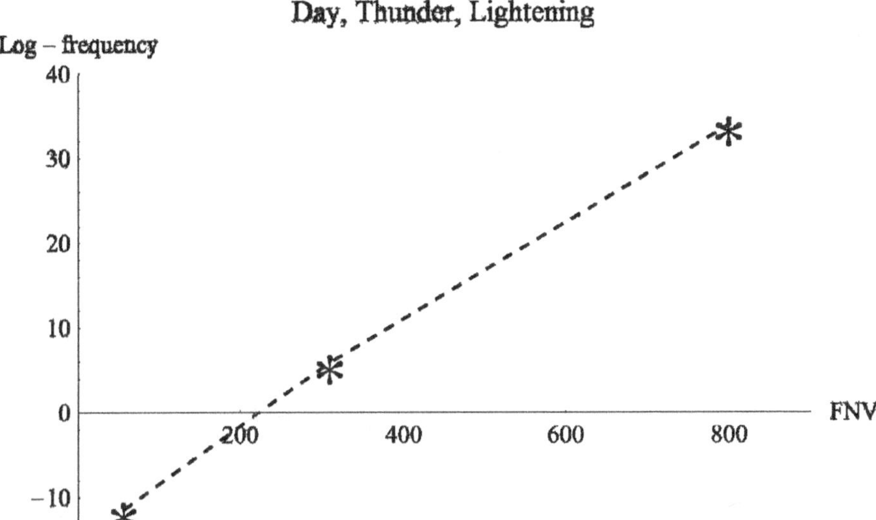

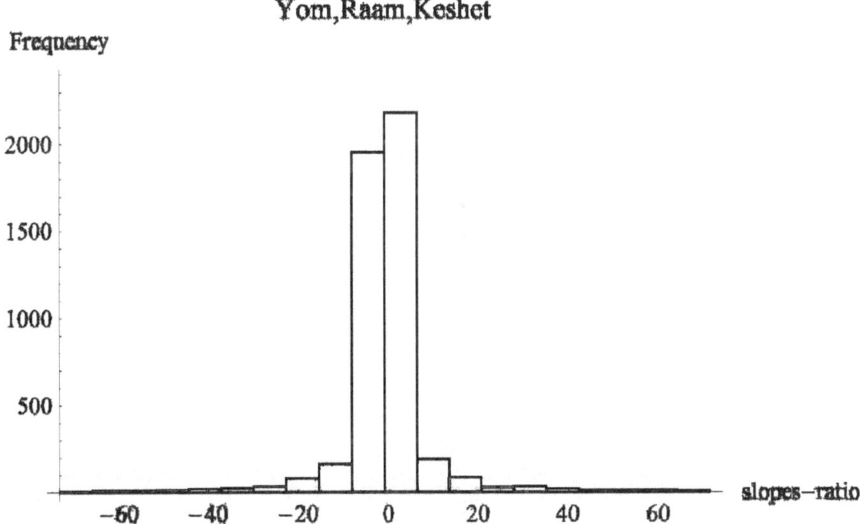

Figure 21.7. Example 7: Plot of data-points (upper figure) and a histogram of slopes-ratio for n=5000 trios of artificially generated Hebrew words. FNV (Frequency numerical value) is numerical value of the Hebrew word.

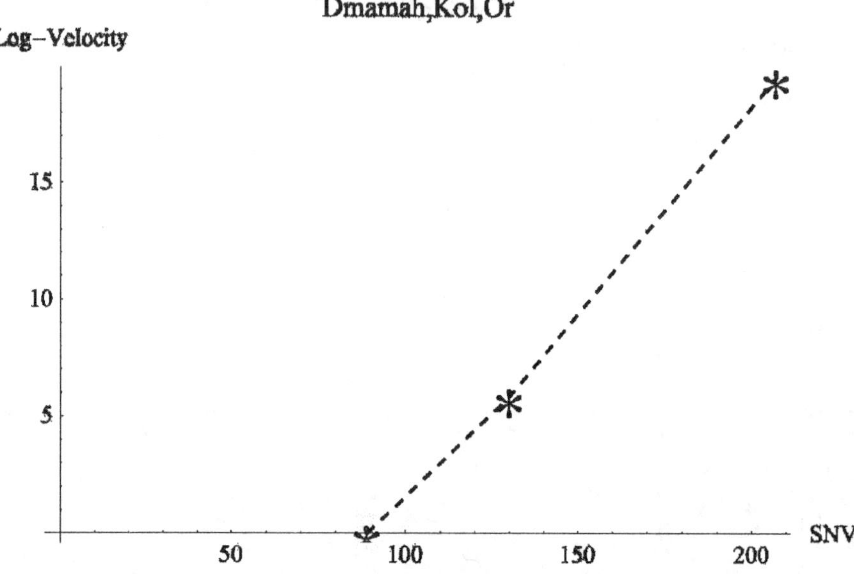

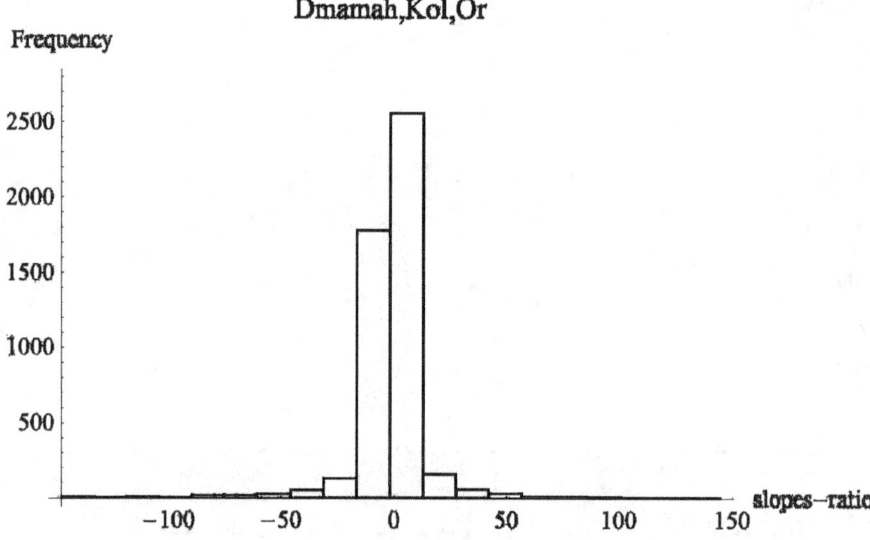

Figure 21.8. Example 8: Plot of data-points (upper figure) and a histogram of slopes-ratio for n=5000 trios of artificially generated Hebrew words. SNV (Speed numerical value) is numerical value of the Hebrew word.

Dmamah,Raam,Keshet

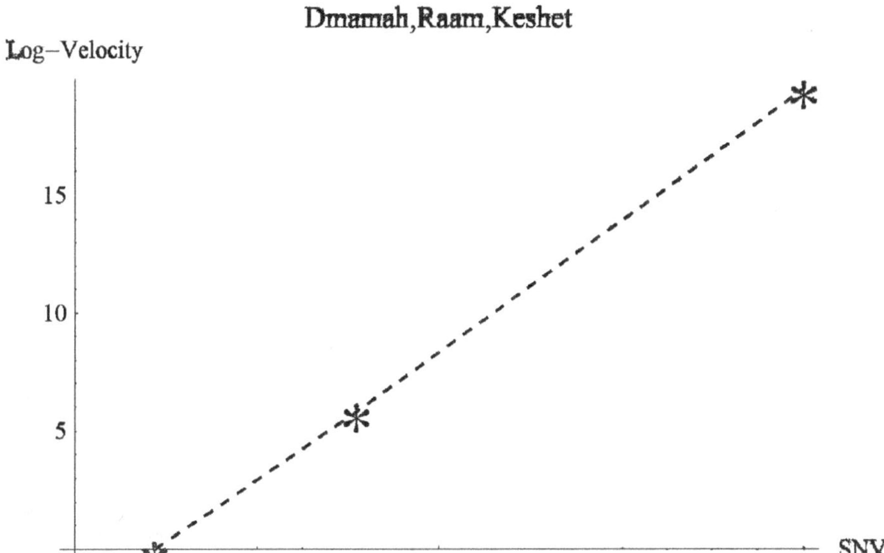

Dmamah,Raam,Keshet

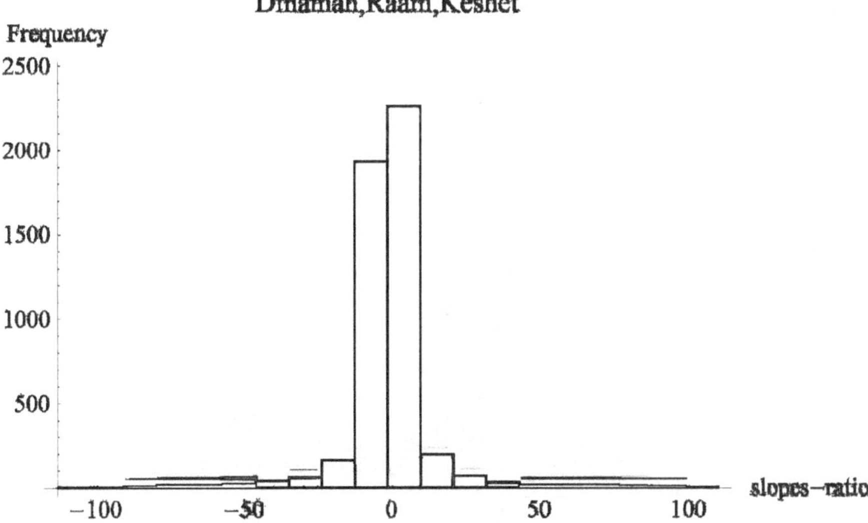

Figure 21.9. Example 9: Plot of data-points (upper figure) and a histogram of slopes-ratio for n=5000 trios of artificially generated Hebrew words. SNV (Speed numerical value) is numerical value of the Hebrew word.

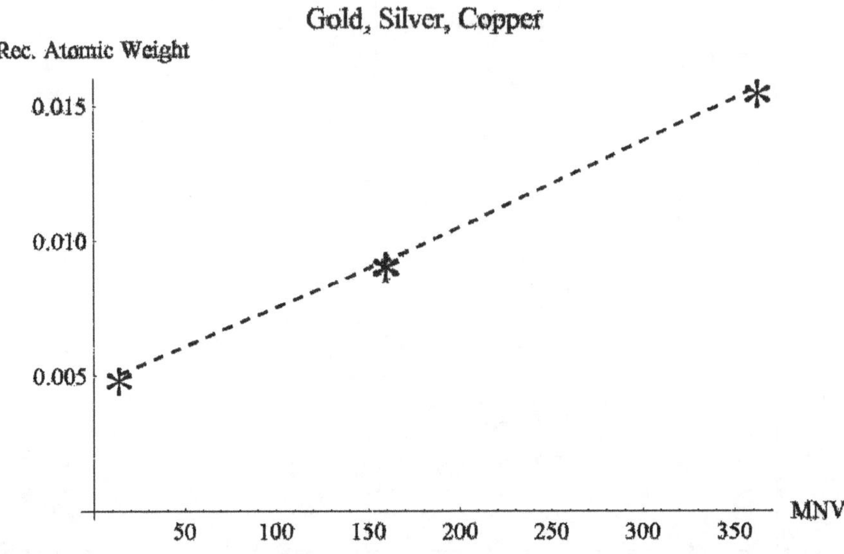

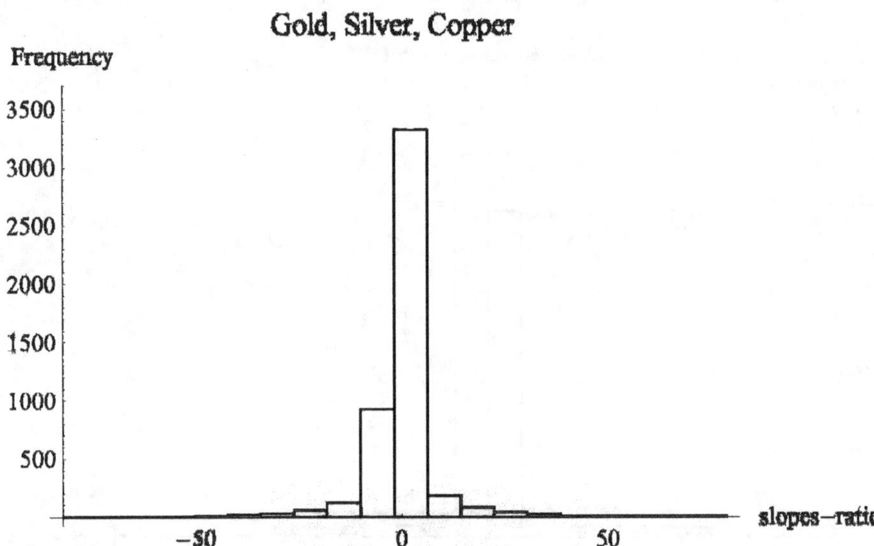

Figure 21.10. Example 10: Plot of data-points (upper figure) and a histogram of slopes-ratio for n=5000 trios of artificially generated Hebrew words. MNV (Metal numerical value) is numerical value of the Hebrew word.

CHAPTER **22**

Genesis Creation Story and Recent Cosmological Findings—A Statistical Evaluation

22.1 Abstract and Structure of the Chapter

Evolution of the universe is depicted in our civilization on two different time-scales: in Genesis story, where the universe evolution is described in "Days," and in modern day cosmology, described in billions of years (Giga-years; Gyrs). While the latter scale is scientifically validated by both theory and observation, the former scale is considered an article of faith, incompatible with the scientific scale. In this chapter, we relate to most recent findings regarding dating of significant cosmological events and pinpoint corresponding events in the biblical time-scale. We then apply statistical analysis to establish possible correspondence between the two time-scales.

The structure of this chapter is as follows: in section 22.2 we describe the nature of the analyses conducted. In section 22.3, data sources and data used in the pursuing statistical analyses are expounded. Section 22.4 delivers results from the statistical analyses with some predictions, as implied by the derived data-driven statistical models. Section 22.5 addresses some methodological issues associated with current and former analyses, and section 22.6 delivers some conclusions.

22.2 Introduction

The story of the creation of the universe and its evolution has been, for the better part of humankind existence on Earth, an article of faith belonging in the sphere of religion. In the Judeo-Christian religious culture, the "history" of the universe is unfolding in the first chapter of Genesis, where the universe evolution is described in terms of six time phases. Each of these phases, denoted "Day,"

285

has characteristic momentous events, which had taken place either via Divine utterance or by Divine actual creating (or making). Thus, light was created, on the first day, by utterance: "And God said, Let there be light: and there was light" (Gen.1:3). By contrast, on the sixth day: "And God *made* the beasts of the Earth after their kind, and cattle after their kind, and everything that creeps on the Earth after its kind." (Gen.1:25). Similarly, for humankind: "So God *created* Mankind in his own image, in the image of God he created him; male and female he created them" (Gen. 2:27). (Author's italics are for emphasis).

According to Genesis, the story of creation is unfolding in six days. However, there is also the seventh day, about which the Bible is mute, except for saying in no obscure terms that on that day the act of creation had ceased: "And by the seventh day God ended his work which he had done; and he rested on the seventh day from all his work which he had done" (Gen. 2:2). Thus, while the evolution of the universe from the moment of creation of "the heaven and the earth" to creation of humankind is depicted as unfolding in six "Days," the "destiny" of the seventh day, and what had "occurred" on that day (or perhaps might happen in the future according to Jewish faith, as will be shortly expounded) remains largely undefined.

Biblical story of creation constitutes one time-scale, which had been the subject of much scholarly discourse, Jewish and non-Jewish, from ancient times to present day.

A second time-scale is provided by the Jewish calendar. The latter "measures" the time that has elapsed since the creation of mankind, as depicted in the first chapter of Genesis. Jewish tradition asserts that mankind was created on the sixth day, in fact the same instant, when the first lunar month started. Thus, the Jewish calendar is supposed to deliver the time-scale of mankind existence on Earth (find details and references in chapter 18). However, Jewish tradition goes farther than that. As expressed by "Moses the man of God": "For a thousand years in thy sight are but like yesterday" (Psalms 90:4), Jewish tradition believes that humankind evolution is a repetition of Genesis story of creation. Just as God had rested on the seventh day, so would peace prevail and the Divine would bring forth his kingdom, with the coming of the messiah, at the end of six thousand years (for example, the Jewish year, which had started September, 22nd, 2006, was the 5767th in the Hebrew calendar year).

The Jewish calendar time-scale is not the subject of this chapter, and will not be referred to any further here.

A third time-scale is provided by modern day cosmology. With the ever-developing and more sophisticated measurement and observational techniques at their disposal, science and technology have been able to pinpoint with ever-increasing accuracy occurrence times of various momentous events in the evolution of the universe. Fortunately, some of these events are described in non-ambiguous terms in Genesis creation story. For example, no one doubts that according to the Bible "light" was created on the first day, or that "the two great lights; the greater light to rule the day, and the lesser light to rule the night" (Gen.1:16) relates to the creation, on the fourth day, of the sun and the moon, respectively. Other events may be less clear-cut, yet they may still reasonably correlate with known cosmological events, aided by how the best of Jewish interpreters had perceived these events over thousands of years of Jewish scholarship.

In this chapter, we analyze dating of six cosmological events, as they are depicted in biblical time-scale and in modern-cosmology time-scale. We then attempt to establish, by means of rigorous statistical analysis, whether a statistically significant relationship exists between the two time-scales. Two principles guide us in conducting this study:

(1) We do not manipulate numbers; neither do we provide data unsubstantiated by credible and well-recognized sources;

(2) We do not manipulate the techniques used in the statistical analysis; only well known and widely accepted statistical techniques are employed.

With this general characterization of the study to be strictly adhered to, this research is conducted in two parts. The first part, expounded in section 22.3, describes how the data for this study were obtained. The second part, in section 22.4, analyzes the data, with the explicit intent of establishing whether a statistically significant relationship exists between the two time-scales.

22.3 The Data

22.3.1 Definition of Events

In this section we relate to six events, well recognized by modern science and probably related to in Genesis story:

(1) Creation of light; section 22.3.2;

(2) Creation of first large-scale celestial structures (galaxies, nebulae); section 22.3.3;

(3) Creation of the sun; section 22.3.4;

(4) Creation of the moon; section 22.3.4;

(5) Creation of multi-cellular and sexually reproducible life on Earth; section 22.3.5;

(6) Creation of mankind; section 22.3.6.

These events will be addressed as they are depicted on two time-scales:

- **Cosmologic time-scale:** Dates or ages in this time-scale will be measured from the moment of the big bang. The measurement unit is billion of years, or Gyrs (giga-years, where giga means 10^9). Values in this time-scale will be referred to as "response values." In regular statistical-modeling parlance, a "response" is the variable whose variation we attempt to explain (via the mathematical-statistical relationship). The response is also commonly denoted the "dependent variable."

- **Biblical time-scale:** Dates or ages in this time-scale will be expressed in "Days" (from time zero, whatever that might mean in biblical discourse). Values in this time-scale will be referred to as "regressor values." In statistical modeling, the "explanatory" variable, namely, the variable whose variation explains most variation in the response (via the mathematical relationship) is called regressor variable, or, simply, regressor. The latter is also often referred to as the "independent variable."

The two time-scales, the cosmologic and the biblical, will henceforth be denoted by variables "Y" and "X", respectively. In this section, we assign values to the two variables with respect to the six events defined earlier. The sample of six observations will later be used to statistically evaluate whether a significant relationship exists between X and Y.

Note, that the six points in the sample are not of equal reliability, as far as scientific dating is concerned. While cosmologic dating of the source for the cosmic microwave background (CMB) radiation (creation of light, as we know it today; observation point 1), for the creation of the sun and the moon (points 3 and 4) and for the appearance of Homo Sapiens (point 6) are of relatively small margins of error (relative to the order of magnitude of the cosmologic time-scale), this cannot be extended to the other two observations in the sample. A main reason is that the other points describe events that may have stretched over extended periods of time, which are meaningful even on the cosmologic time-scale. For example, it is difficult to date the appearance of large-scale structures in the universe with errors much smaller than, say, $\pm(1/2)$ Gyr, a meaningful error even in the cosmic time-scale.

Accordingly, two separate analyses will be conducted in section 22.4, with the controversial observations (section 22.4.1) and with their exclusion (section 22.4.2). It is emphasized, though, that we have done our utmost to provide the most acceptable current mainstream estimates for all sample points, including the two hard-to-estimate points.

22.3.2 *Light*

Cosmologic value (Y1)

At the time of the big bang, the universe was so hot that no atoms could be created, and therefore no light, as we know it today, was visible. Only when the universe cooled down to such a degree that atoms could have formed did light become tangible. As described elsewhere in the book (section 14.2), according   to modern cosmologies, at the time of the big bang, the universe was a soup of radiation and particles—or, in the words of Singh (2004), "The universe contained mainly protons, neutrons and electrons, all bathed in a sea of light." The universe was so hot that possibly forming atoms were continually ripped apart by radiation as soon as they were formed. Therefore, the universe was opaque, and "any light beam moving in this super-hot universe would be absorbed after traveling a short distance, so the universe looked cloudy." (Kaku, 2005, 58). Shortly after the big bang, the universe had undergone an era of quick inflation, when the universe expanded by perhaps a factor of 10^{30} or more. With inflation and ever since, the universe has been cooling down. "After 380,000 years, however, the temperature dropped to 3000 degrees. Below that temperature, atoms were no longer ripped apart by collision. As a result stable atoms could form, and light beams could now travel for light years without being absorbed." (Kaku, 2005, 58). A similar description is given by Greene (2004): "Electrically charged particles, like electrons and protons, which disrupt the motion of light beams, combined to form electrically neutral atoms, which then allowed light to travel freely. Ever since, such ancient light—produced in the early stages of the universe—has traveled unimpeded, and today suffuses all of space with microwave photons." (Greene, 2004, 515).

Light, as it is known to us today, was "created" as a result of the creation of the first hydrogen and helium atoms, about 380,000 years *after* the big bang, in an event called *recombination*. This event produced what is now known as the cosmic microwave background (CMB) radiation that spread all over the universe.

In terms of the cosmologic time-scale, and expressed by its unit, we have for the first data point:

$$Y_1 = 380,000(10^{-9}) = 0.00038 \text{ Gyr}$$

Biblical Value (X1)

According to Genesis creation story, light was created by the utterance of the Divine "let there be light," on the first day of creation. Therefore:

$$X_1 = 1 \text{ day}$$

22.3.3 Formation of First Large-scale Celestial Structures

Cosmologic value (Y2)

The question of when were first celestial structures been formed has drawn the attention and research efforts of astronomers and cosmologists for the better part of the twentieth century and to this day. We base our estimate on various sources that seem to converge.

In the abstract of their paper, Gratton *et al.* (1997) present as their fifth result that "The age of the bona fide old globular clusters (Oosterhoff II and BHB), based on the absolute magnitude of the turnoff (a theoretically robust indicator) is:

$$\text{Age} = 11.8 \text{ Gyr}$$

with errors +2.1 and -2.5 Gyr as the 95% confidence range."

A references-based account is a web-site maintained by Wright of UCLA (at http://www.astro.ucla.edu/~wright/age.html). Regarding the age of the oldest globular clusters, Wright writes: "Chaboyer *et al.* (1998) give 11.5 ± 1.3 Gyr for the *mean* age." Regarding the age of the oldest white dwarfs, Wright writes: "In 2004 Hansen *et al.* gave an age for globular cluster M4 of 12.1 ± 0.9 Gyr, which is very consistent with the age of globular clusters from the main sequence turnoff." Inspection of the quoted paper reveals that in fact the number given is 12.1 Gyr, with a 95% *lower* limit of 10.3 Gyr.

In a paper from 2005, Peloso *et al.* report the determination of the age of the Galactic thin disk by means of Th/Eu nucleo-cosmo-chronology. They claim that "This method is only weakly dependent on stellar evolutions models, therefore allowing an important verification of the most used dating techniques, which are the fitting of isochrones to the oldest Galactic open clusters, and the calculation of white dwarf cooling sequences." Furthermore, their result, "(8.8 ± 1.7) Gyr, corroborates the most recent white dwarf ages determined via cooling sequence calculations."

Another source is NASA web-page from January, 2006 (http://www.nasa.gov/vision/universe/starsgalaxies/fuse_fossil_galaxies.html). This page states: "After the creation flash, the lights went out, because there were no stars or any other bright objects—they had not yet formed. This long night is known as the cosmic dark ages, when no stars existed. The present universe is mostly ionized, and astronomers generally agree that this re-ionization occurred at the end of the dark ages, between 12.5 and 13 billion years ago, when the first large-scale structures (galaxies, galaxy clusters) were forming." Note that the rough estimate given by NASA is consistent with the more precise estimates quoted by Wright earlier.

"Dark Ages" are also described in a relatively recent web-page at http://asia.spaceref.com/news/viewpr.html?pid=20827 (source: National Astronomical Observatory of Japan, press release from September, 2006). According to this source, as the dark ages came to conclusion, first large-scale structures appeared in the universe. This happened as a result of the re-ionization of the universe, and "In this case, most of the re-ionization would have taken place earlier than 12.88 billion years ago".

Kaku (2005, 11) estimates the ages of oldest stars as 12 billon years. Given the conflicting values reported in most recent publications, it is hard to arrive at a value that seems to be acceptable to all. We therefore opted to relate to the two numbers reported in Wright's account (and quoted earlier), which deliver dating ages of *actual* observable large-scale structures. Averaging these numbers, we obtain a value of 11.8 Gyr (average of 11.5 and 12.1).

Therefore:

$$Y_2 = 13.7 - 11.8 = 1.9 \text{ Gyr}$$

(The most updated current age of the universe, from the big bang, is 13.7 ± 0.2 Gyr)

Comments

The value of Y_2, as defined here, is currently a subject of intensive research effort, attempting to identify a timeline for the formation of first large-scale structures in the universe. It is therefore open to debate, and requires special attention in the pursuing statistical analysis. Deleting this observation from the analysis, however, would not fundamentally alter the conclusions obtained. As related earlier, an additional analysis, excluding this observation and another, is conducted in section 22.4.2.

Biblical Value (X2)

Genesis story of creation does not relate specifically to the formation of stars or galaxies (obviously the latter were unknown in biblical times), but rather to the formation of the sky: "And God said, "Let there be an expanse between the waters to separate water from water". So God made the expanse and separated the water under the expanse from the water above it. And it was so. God called the expanse "sky". And there was evening, and there was morning—the second day" (Gen.1:6-8).

Therefore:

$$X_2 = 2 \text{ day}$$

22.3.4 Creation of Sun and Moon

Cosmologic Values (Y3, Y4)

The ages of the sun and the moon are:

- The Sun: 4.57 ± 0.02 Gyr (Source: http://en.wikipedia.org/wiki/Sun)
- The Moon: 4.53 ± 0.01 Gyr (Source: http://en.wikipedia.org/wiki/Moon#Formation)

Time of creation of the sun (Y_3) and the moon (Y_4) in the cosmologic time-scale:

$$Y_3 = 13.7 - 4.57 = 9.13 \text{ Gyr (Sun)}$$

$$Y_4 = 13.7 - 4.53 = 9.17 \text{ Gyr (Moon)}$$

Biblical Values (X3, X4)

No controversy exists among biblical interpreters that the Bible refers to the sun and the moon as created on the fourth day. Therefore:

$$X_3 = 4 \text{ day}; X_4 = 4 \text{ day}$$

22.3.5 Creation of Life on Earth

Cosmologic Value (Y5)

Since the sun and the moon were created on the fourth day (section 22.3.4), one has to assume that the description of life on Earth as created on the fifth day relates to the first appearance of life. This is emphasized since the Bible describes appearance of life on Earth (in the form of grass and trees) already on the third day, when the sun was not yet. Jewish scholars have addressed this challenging mystery, and gave it various interpretations (mostly symbolic and allegoric). We would ignore this day (the only day which is inconsistent with the *order* mandated by the scientific timeline), and assume that the biblical description for the fifth day, regarding generation of life in the water and "above the Earth," relates to first formation of life on Earth.

It is extremely difficult to provide dating for first appearance of most forms of life on Earth. We assume here that two ingredients are essential for all forms of life as now known: living organisms are multi-cellular and sexually reproduced. An excerpt from Wikepedia, the free encyclopedia, representative of other sources, summarizes first signs of life, as just characterized, and their timeline (Source: Wikipedia, the free encyclopedia, at http://en.wikipedia.org/wiki/Timeline_of_ evolution; MA means "million years ago"):

- 1200 Ma: Sexual reproduction evolves, leading to faster evolution. While most life still exists in oceans and lakes, some cyano-bacteria may already live in moist soil by this time.

- 1000 Ma: Multi-cellular organisms appear, initially colonial algae, and later seaweeds, living in the oceans.

Both these time-dating estimates rely on references from 2005 (see details in the afore-cited source).

A related source for the *former* dating (sexual reproduction) is an article from Wikipedia, the free encyclopedia (http://en.wikipedia.org/wiki/Sexual_ reproduction#Origin of Reproduction):

"The evolution of sex is a major puzzle. The first fossilized evidence of sexually reproducing organisms is from eukaryotes of the Stenian period, about 1.2 to 1 billion years ago. Sexual reproduction is the primary method of reproduction for the vast majority of visible organisms, including almost all animals and plants. Bacterial conjugation, the transfer of DNA between two bacteria, is often mistakenly confused with sexual reproduction, because the mechanics are similar."

A related source for the *latter* dating (multi-cellular life), yet from the same source (http://en.wikipedia.org/wiki/Multicellular organism):

"The oldest known taxonomically resolved multi-cellular organism is a red algae, Bangiomorpha pubescens, found fossilized in 1.2 billion year old rock from the Ectasian period of the Mesoproterozoic era." This figure is also quoted by White (2007), in a table reporting "Significant dates in the history of the universe".

Crystal (1993, 19) dates earliest marine life and fossils to the Precambrian Riphean period. This period had stretched from 1.6 Gyr ago to 0.65 Gyr ago, with mid-value of 1.125 Gyr ago.

Given these sources, and assuming that Genesis story, relating to the fifth day, rightly depicts first signs of life as originating in water, we assign for the origin-of-life dating (averaging 1.2 and 1.0 Gyr, from the first source quoted above, and consistent with Crystal, 1993):

$$Y_5 = 13.7 - 1.1 = 12.6 \text{ Gyr}$$

Biblical Value (X5)

Ignoring the mysterious and unexplainable description for the creation of life on the third day (*before* the sun was "made"), Genesis story of life on Earth is depicted succinctly as originating on the fifth day: "And God said, "Let the water teem with living creatures, and let birds fly above the Earth across the expanse of the sky." So God created the great creatures of the sea and every living and moving thing with which the water teems, according to their kinds, and every winged bird according to its kind. And God saw that it was good … And there was evening and there was morning—the fifth day" (Gen. 1:20-21, 23). Accordingly:

$$X_5 = 5 \text{ day}$$

22.3.6 Creation of Mankind

Cosmologic Value (Y6)

How old is the human race? Controversy exists and is ongoing. It is difficult to pinpoint time reference for the first appearance of humans on the surface of Earth, not least because scientists are divided on what constitutes a species that can be defined human. Since there is no controversy that the "age" of currently existing human species is measurable in hundreds of thousands of years (not in millions of years), high precision is not essential to estimate Y_6.

As reported in Wikipedia, the free encyclopedia, "Anatomically modern humans—Homo sapiens—are believed to have originated somewhere around 200,000 years ago or earlier in Africa;" (http://en.wikipedia.org/wiki/History_of_ Earth; Also: http://en.wikipedia.org/wiki/Human).

Other sources roughly corroborate this estimate for the age of Homo sapiens. Therefore:

$$Y_6 = 13.7 - 200,000(10^{-9}) = 13.6998 \text{ Gyr}$$

Note, that since Y_6 is measured in Gyr the admissible margin of error for this estimate, which would still be inconsequential for the pursuing statistical analysis, is quite large.

Biblical Value (X6)

Biblical story of the creation of mankind specifies that it has taken place on the sixth day (Gen. 1:27). This is the only detail given. However, Jewish tradition, according to Oral Torah ("Torah She-Be-Al-Peh"), gives a more exact timing: Friday, after the fourteenth hour (since sunset of the previous day), which is the beginning of the third hour into the day of Friday (the Jewish day starts at sunset of the previous day, supposedly taking place at 6PM of the previous day). In fact, this very detail, known in Hebrew by the concept of "Molad Ve-Yad", is fundamental for calculating the average lunar month duration, which, according to Jewish tradition, is 29.530594 days (vs. 29.530589, the value reported in NASA site). In turn, this ancient Jewish value for the duration of the lunar month is cornerstone for the Hebrew calendar, and for the adaptations needed to render it compatible with the solar year. Find further details and references in chapter 18.

Adopting this date from established and often quoted traditional Jewish interpretations for biblical dating of the creation of man (as told in Gen.1:27), we obtain for X_6:

$$X_6 = 5 + 14/24 = 5.5833 \text{ day}$$

Table 22.1 displays all values, derived in this section. This table serves for the statistical analyses in section 22.4.

Table 22.1. Dating of cosmic events in the evolution of the universe and Earth, according to Genesis (Ch. 1), X, and according to recent cosmologic findings, Y.

Event #	Event Description (Creation of)	X (Biblical, "Day")	Y (Cosmic, Gyr)	Model's Residuals (Obs. – Pred., Gyr) (Fig. 22.1)
1	"Light"	1	0.0003	0.479866
2	"Cosmic Large-Scale Structures"	2	1.9	-0.789095
3–4	"Sun"	4	9.13	0.103745
	"Moon"	4	9.17	0.143745
5	"Multi-cellular sexually-reproduced life"	5	12.6	0.405165
6	"Humans"	5.5833	13.6998	-0.343425

22.4 Statistical Analysis and Predictions

Table 22.1 displays six observations, as currently available with respect to two time-scales: the scientific cosmic time-scale, measured in Gyr, and biblical time-scale, measured in days. For the latter scale, we have been assisted by oral Jewish tradition, going back at least two thousands years, to determine the value of a single observation (X_6). For the former scale, it has been emphasized that with regard to two observations, there seems to be scientific controversy whether estimates can be given for the Y values to any reasonable accuracy. One observation regards approximate dating for the appearance of first large-scale structures (at the end of the dark ages and the re-ionization of the universe). The other observation regards the beginning of life on Earth as we know it (namely, characterized by first appearance of multi-cellular and sexually reproducing life). Accordingly, the statistical analysis is divided into two parts:

- Section 22.4.1: statistical analysis applied to the complete sample (six observations);
- Section 22.4.2: statistical analysis applied to a reduced sample (four observations only; two possibly controversial observations removed).

22.4.1 Statistical Analysis of the Complete Sample

In this section, we statistically test two mutually exclusive hypotheses:

- H_0: There is no relationship between the two time-scales;
- H_1: The two time-scales are linearly related (implying that the two time-scales measure the same "thing", only in different units).

To test these hypotheses, linear regression analysis was applied to the complete sample, with biblical time-scale serving as the independent variable (the horizontal axis), and the cosmic scientific time-scale as the dependent variable (the vertical axis). For n=6, linear regression analysis yields linear correlation of 0.9963, with adjusted R^2 of 0.9907. For 1 and 4 degrees of freedom, the sample F-ratio value is 534.8, which is statistically significant (p=0.000021). In other words, the probability of the observations aligning themselves on a straight line, the way they did, by chance alone (that is, if H_0 was true), is less than 0.0021%.

Figure 22.1 displays the results with the associated 95% confidence limits. All observations are within these limits. The linear regression equation is given in the figure caption (atop the plot). Note, that the results of this analysis would

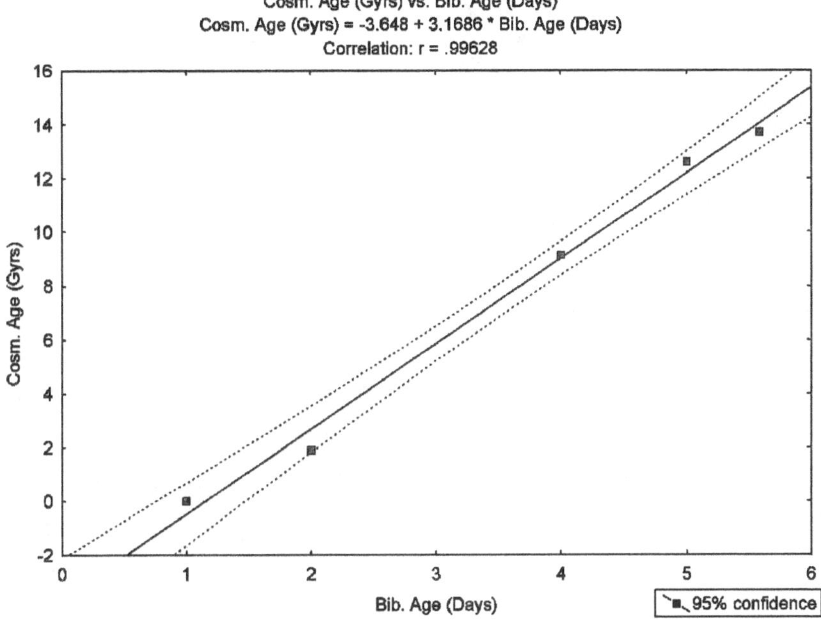

Figure 22.1. Linear regression analysis for the complete sample (n=6)

have been greatly altered if dating of the creation of mankind, according to biblical scale, ignored traditional Jewish Oral Torah (namely, if X_6 would have been assigned a different value).

22.4.2   *Statistical Analysis of the Reduced Sample (observations 2 and 5 excluded)*

For reasons detailed earlier, two observations, with debatable response values, have been removed from the sample. These are observation 2 (appearance of first large-scale structures in the universe; "sky" created) and observation 5 (first appearance of life on Earth).

With the remaining four observations in the sample, the statistical analysis was repeated. For n=4, linear correlation of 0.9998 was obtained, with adjusted R^2 of 0.9995. For 1 and 2 degrees of freedom, the sample F-ratio value is 6064.8 with p=0.000165. In other words, the probability of the four observations aligning themselves on a straight line, the way they did, by chance alone (that is, were H_0 true) is less than 0.0165%.

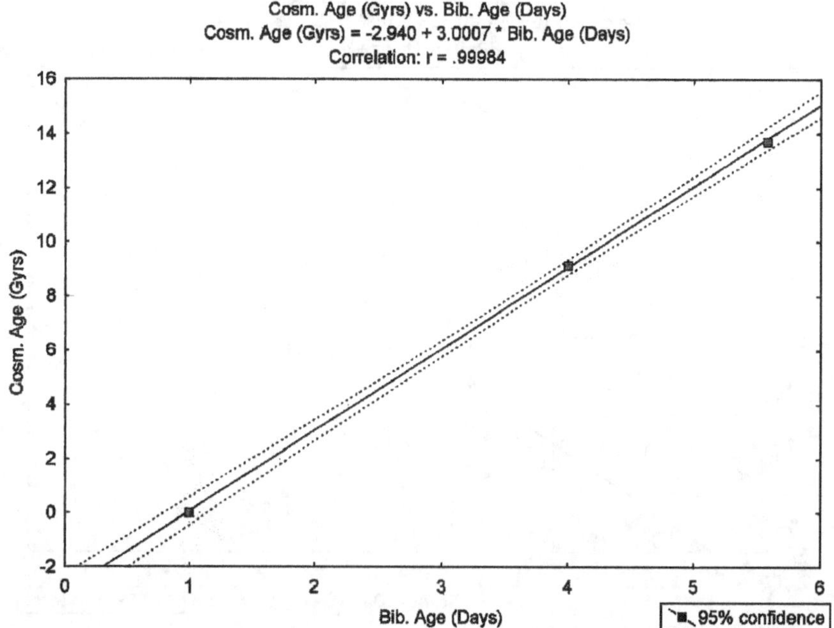

Figure 22.2. Linear regression analysis for the reduced sample (n=4).

Figure 22.2 displays the results with the associated 95% confidence limits. All observations are within these limits. Note that the confidence limits are so close to the linear regression line that they are hardly distinguishable from one another.

22.4.3 Scientific Prediction???

A peculiar feature of both linear regression models, derived in sections 22.4.1 and 22.4.2, is that time zero does not coincide with the instant of the big bang— time zero is roughly 3 Gyr earlier (insert zero into the right-hand side of either equation).

Given the peculiar new concepts of "Dark energy" and "Dark matter", now widely entertained by modern cosmology, is it possible that cosmologists, at some future point in time, would update their estimates to claim that only the visible universe was created at the big bang, however the "Dark" constituents of our universe preceded the estimated instant of the big bang by approximately 3 Gyr???

22.5 Methodological Aspects—Some Comments

In this section we address some methodological aspects pertaining to the statistical analyses of this chapter. We also respond to some comments, of a more general character, regarding the statistical analyses in this composition, which we have encountered in public presentations delivered since publication of the first edition of the book.

22.5.1   Selection of X Values (Genesis creation story)

A legitimate concern may be raised regarding dating of various cosmological events described in Genesis creation story. For example, light was created by utterance of the Divine on the first day; therefore we have assigned $X_1=1$. However, nowhere in scripture is there indication at what point of time, in the first "Day," was light created. One may therefore wonder why not assign $X_1=0.5$ (namely, light created at the *middle* of the first "Day," whatever "Day" means), or $X_1=0$ (namely, light created at the *start* of the first "Day")?

There are two sorts of justifications for this legitimate question. The first is that by Jewish tradition any instant given in terms of time units refers to the end of the specified time unit. Relate, for example, to Molad ve-Yad (chapter 18). This term, part and parcel of Jewish Oral Torah, embodies Jewish credo that first man was created at the *end* of the fourteenth hour of Genesis "Friday", and that this is also the instant when the moon started its first cycle. However, "ve-Yad" only symbolizes "14" in terms of numerical values of Hebrew letters (refer to chapter 18). Nowhere in Jewish tradition does it say at what instant in the fourteenth hour (whatever "Hour" means) was the first human being created. Although this looks marginal and inconsequential, the ramifications of this assertion cannot be discounted: Jewish calendar is based on the moon, and according to Jewish tradition the average lunar month is 29.53059 days (refer to chapter 18). As the reader may realize on reading that chapter, obtaining the correct value for the lunar month duration requires the assumption that man was created at the *end* of the fourteenth hour. The high accuracy, achieved in calculating the duration of the lunar month, could not have been obtained had we assumed another value for the instant of man creation (and the beginning of the first lunar cycle). Asserting that Adam was created at the *end* of the fourteenth hour of Friday thus becomes crucial for the calculation of lunar month duration according to Jewish tradition.

In a similar vein, we have assumed in our analyses that if, for example, Genesis story asserts that light was created on the first day of creation, this implies $X_1=1$, namely, the *end* of the first day. Same rule had been applied throughout the data collection process, as described earlier.

A second argument, pertaining to why we were justified in selecting integer values for events mentioned in Genesis creation story, relates to a more general argument regarding the nature of explorative scientific research. This is addressed in the next section.

22.5.2 *The Nature of Scientific Empirical Modeling*

Scientific enquiries typically progress in a two-phase process. In the first phase, patterns in noisy data are searched for in order to detect those that may eventually prove to contain valid information. In the second phase, hypotheses are generated and tested, very often by means of statistical hypotheses testing. The first phase is that of exploration, and it represents the induction part of the research. The second phase is the deduction part of the research, when newly generated hypotheses are put to statistical testing in order to establish the general validity of the pattern, formerly detected in the sample.

A risk that often accompanies a genuine scientific enquiry is that the investigator may have innocently manipulated the data collection process to fit his or her preconceived hypotheses. For example, the search for patterns may have been directed to detect a certain category of patterns, ignoring others. Thus, one may argue, when statistical testing is eventually implemented there is no wonder that statistically significant results are obtained. While this is obviously a valid point, there is no escape from the fact that the very nature of scientific exploration requires probing the data until possibly meaningful patterns were revealed. Therefore, one cannot blame a scientist that data were manipulated if he or she had made several attempts to arrive at possibly meaningful patterns. After all, this is what scientific enquiry is all about. One can only hope that manipulation of the data mining process, in order to arrive at statistically-proven valid patterns of nature, remains within allowable, acceptable and legitimate parameters.

To learn of the relevance of these arguments to the statistical analyses presented in this book (and particularly for the results of this chapter), consider the claim that the numerical values of the triad of Hebrew words for "moon, Earth, sun" delivers information about the relative size of these celestial bodies (section 8.3). One of the arguments I have encountered in my oral presentations on the subject was that same rule should apply to all Hebrew words for this triad, and, furthermore, that this rule would be accepted as valid only if found to apply to other features of the same celestial bodies, for example, their mass density.

I consider such severe requirements for acceptance of the scientific validity of the statistical analyses in this book outrageous and unfair. Such demands are never put on any other scientific enquiry of nature. For example, suppose that we investigate the relationship between the level of cholesterol in the human blood (X, the independent variable) and the level of a certain other ingredient (Y, the response). If a significant relationship was found, say, via regression analysis, however no significant relationship was found with other ingredients in the blood, this does not imply that the statistical analysis was invalid. It is understood that "nature" was so designed that cholesterol is correlated with the investigated ingredient, but not with others. Likewise, if numerical values of a certain triad of Hebrew words for certain celestial bodies are correlated with the diameters of these bodies, and the relationship has been proven to be statistically significant, no further corroboration is required for the validity of this analysis. One does not need to prove that other similar Hebrew words maintain the same relationship, neither that same relationship should hold with regard to other features of the respective celestial bodies.

Summing up, scientific research progresses by empirically detecting possibly information-carrying patterns, and then statistically testing these patterns to establish that their occurrence randomly in the sample is improbable. If a certain pattern proves to be statistically insignificant, then a search for other patterns begins. This is an iterative process, and it remains legitimate so long as all tested patterns are within the parameters of the investigation.

Same reasoning may be applied to the analyses in this chapter. If statistical analysis shows that results are significant only for integer values of X (apart from X_6, as explained earlier), however same analyses result in insignificant outcomes if other values are assigned to X (like $X_1=0.5$), this does not imply that the analyses are not valid. Rather, it implies the existence of a certain "state-of-nature," according to which only integer values deliver significant results. This is how Genesis creation story, with its hidden story, was probably intended to be delivered in the first place. No further tests are required.

This same approach has been implemented throughout the statistical analyses presented in this book. These analyses, it is our conviction, should withstand any unbiased scientific scrutiny.

22.5.3   *Why Not Publish in Recognized Scientific Journals?*

The reader may wonder why the statistical analyses in this book, including those in the current chapter, have not been submitted for publication in recognized and highly-esteemed scientific journals, like Science or Nature. The answer may be easily guessed: no journal was willing to even consider reviewing (let alone publish) papers with claims, as displayed in this book. Open-mindedness to all facts of nature, source of pride for many highly-revered journals, ended when claims of religious flavor, no matter how scientifically corroborated, were involved. Therefore, as a result of responses received to preliminary enquiries, none of the statistical analyses displayed in this book have ever been submitted for review in peer-reviewed journals

I can hardly blame editors who have refused even seeing a first draft of a paper. I might have decided likewise, have I not known better.

22.6 Conclusions

This study is an attempt to relate in a serious and scientifically rigorous fashion to two time-scales, whose compatibility with one another had plagued Western Civilization with endless and often overheated debate for many years. Obviously, this debate has become ever more heated with recent scientific findings, commonly perceived to provide final "victory" to the scientific time-scale over the biblical time-scale.

The statistical analyses, provided in this chapter, seem to suggest that these two time-scales are in fact one and the same, with one time-scale derivable from the other by a simple linear transformation. Furthermore, the latter conclusion is not shaken by the removal of possibly controversial observations, since the rest of the observations in the sample, of more reliable nature, still deliver highly statistically significant results.

How could such different time-scales, derived from two so different modes of human observation upon the world, be yet so compatible with one another? This indeed remains a mystery.

Chapter 23

New results
(an update, November, 2012)

On December, 4, 2009, the Israeli daily, the Jerusalem Post, published an interview with me about the findings of this book. The interview was posted on the Internet and translated to other languages. Following this interview, numerous communications were received and articles about the methodology used in the book published in various Jewish local newspapers (for example, Benazra, 2010ab). Some writers provided me with findings of their own. Concurrently, I continued with my own research and found some new relationships (not yet made public).

The purpose of this new chapter (added to the 2012 revision of the book) is to deliver an update that reflects these endeavors and expound their results. It opens (section 23.1) with an introduction of the Jewish roots of the approach pursued in this book, namely, the belief that there exist hidden linkages between physical properties of "entities" of the real world and respective biblical verses or biblical Hebrew words that relate to these entities. Some results (not all new), which demonstrate realizations of this belief, are displayed in Table 23.1. No statistical analysis is attempted to establish the validity of these findings. Section 23.2 is a "Parable (all facts imaginary; conclusions valid)". I have found this parable useful in explaining why a linear relationship between two sets of observations, collected by two measuring devices possibly operating on different scales, indicates that the two sets of observations deliver identical information. While this may seem self-evident and redundant to readers trained in the exact sciences, it may not be so for other readers. Therefore a numerical example is introduced, given in the form of a parable. In section 23.3 a simple new detailed example is introduced, which relates to velocity as the physical trait associated with various Hebrew words. Its purpose is to demonstrate (once again) the significance of a linear relationship.

303

A unique (and significant) feature of this example is that two sets of biblical Hebrew words that are analyzed share a common word. The two sets are represented by two lines that indeed intersect at the shared word (Figure 23.2). This example appears as separate Examples 8 and 9 in Table 21.1. Section 23.4 addresses the main theme of this chapter, namely, the planets and their physical properties. This analysis is a continuation and extension of earlier analyses (chapter 8). It is especially important due to the large number of observations (large sample size) involved in the analyses. Section 23.5 delivers some further numerical examples, received from a reader of the Jerusalem Post interview. The last section 23.6 relates to a new finding regarding species names in the Bible.

23.1 Introduction

An ancient Jewish tradition assumes the existence of hidden linkages between physical traits of "entities" of the real world and respective biblical verses or biblical Hebrew words. This conviction is expressed not merely by general assertions, like "Bezaleel knew how to assemble letters with which heaven and Earth had been created" (Talmud, Berachot, 55a), but also in various detailed examples, often reflecting efforts to extract real (often useful) information about the physical world from analysis of the structure and the numerical values of related words, or verses, that appear in the Hebrew old-testament Bible. For example, the numerical value of *Heraion* (pregnancy; Hoshea 9:11) represents the expected duration of human pregnancy (271 days; Midrash Rabbah, Bereshit, 20). Also therein, Rabbi Shmuel relates to a verse from the Bible: *"Harbeh arbeh itzvonech ve-heronech"* ("I will greatly multiply the pain of thy child bearing", Gen. 2:16). Since *harbeh* ("greatly") is numerically equivalent to 212, an embryo surviving 212 days, thus Rabbi Shmuel, will probably survive the whole pregnancy.

Further examples, relating to "counts" data, are given in Table 23.1 (some repeat examples given earlier in the book).

Table 23.1. Numerical examples (with "counts" data) for matches between numerical values of biblical Hebrew words and corresponding values of related major physical traits

Biblical Hebrew word (English)	Num. value of Hebrew word	Associated physical trait	Num. Value of physical Trait	Source	Example quoted in:
"שנ.ה" (*Shanah*, Year)	355	Duration (number of days) of lunar-based year	29.530589X12= 354.3671	Average lunar month (from NASA site)	(Here, ch. 18)
"י.ד" (*Yad*, hand)	14	Number of bones in human hand	14	Common knowledge	(Here, 10.3.6)
"הר.י.ו.ן" (*Heraion*, pregnancy)	271	Duration (number of days) of Human Pregnancy	273 or 271.5	Common knowledge	Midrash Rabbah (here, 2.1.2)
"א.ד.ם" (*Adam*, human being)	45	Number of chromosomes common to all human beings	45 (23 pairs, one sex chrom. different for male and female)	Common knowledge	No prior reference
"ג.מ.ל" (*Gamal*, camel)	73*	Number of chromosomes common to all camels	73 (37 pairs, one sex chrom. different for male and female)	Site: Answer.com	No prior reference
"ח.ל.ד" (*Choled*, rat)	42*	Number of chromosomes	42 (21 pairs)	Site: wikipedia.org	No prior reference

* These examples are a small subset from a larger sample; not all animal names in biblical Hebrew succumb to this linkage; possible reasons: only rarely does a single number of chromosomes characterizes all branches of a given species; also, not all species names in the Bible have interpretations agreed by all.

While these examples and many others may be perceived as a collection of anecdotes ("cherry picking", in statistical parlance), statistical analyses detailed earlier in this book, which refer to data measured on continuous scales, seem to suggest that the Hebrew tradition may have deeper roots in reality than initially and intuitively suggested by documented Jewish oral and written tradition. Some further analyses are expounded in this chapter. All analyses attempt to establish that there is a linear relationship between the numerical values of Hebrew words, representing entities with a common physical trait, and respective values of this trait (measured on a shared measuring scale). For example, later in this chapter (section 23.3) we analyze "velocity" (physical trait) of light, sound and silence (or standstill) in relation to respective Biblical Hebrew words. Linear relationships are found. Why is this important? The following parable explains it all.

23.2 A Parable (all facts imaginary; conclusions valid)

At the beginning of the twentieth century, an archeological excavating expedition arrived to the Holy Land to carry out some research in the vicinity of the city of Jericho. A while into the excavation, a papyrus was exposed that contained a series of twenty numbers. These are given in Table 23.2a (denoted "First set").

Table 23.2. Two sets of measurements reported
by the excavation delegation (Section 23.2).

a. First set

1	2	3	4	5	6	7	8	9	10
80.6	87.8	68	57.2	62.6	78.8	50	57.2	80.6	55.4

11	12	13	14	15	16	17	18	19	20
62.6	71.6	80.6	93.2	59	53.6	62.6	71.6	86	91.4

b. Second set

Temperatures measured at this site for 20 days in the year 150 BC										
No.	1	2	3	4	5	6	7	8	9	10
Tem.	27	31	20	14	17	26	10	14	27	13
No.	11	12	13	14	15	16	17	18	19	20
Tem.	17	22	27	31	15	12	17	22	31	33

No caption explained what the numbers meant so the mysterious papyrus was stored in a secured place and excavation continued. A while later, a second papyrus was revealed, with a second list of numbers (of same size as before; refer to Table 23.2b).

However, this time the caption gave exact details of the nature of these numbers and when these numbers were collected. It read: "Temperatures measured at this site for 20 days in the year 150 BC". Researchers were delighted and they had no doubt that this was an authentic document; however they were still at loss explaining the numbers in the first document, even after consulting the best available statisticians of the time. Several months later, a young archeologist from the expedition came up with a brilliant idea: Perhaps the numbers in the first document are measurements of same temperatures as specified in the second document. After some scholarly arguments and mutual persuasions, the team decided to test this hypothesis statistically.

How could the new hypothesis be tested?

Figure 23.1 plots the two sets.

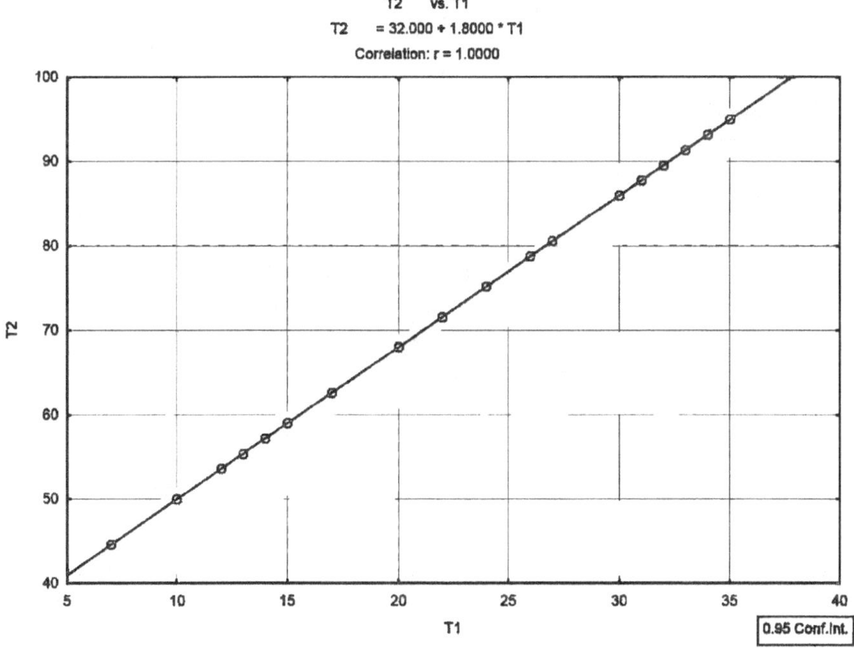

Figure 23.1. Temperature measurements in F° (T2) as function of C° (T1)

A linear relationship is obvious. Linear regression analysis gave the following equation:

$$T_2 = 32 + 1.8\, T_1$$

Data analysis indeed validated the young archeologist's choice of method to resolve the mystery surrounding the first set of numbers. Her conjecture was indeed validated.

23.3 An Introductory Example

This example is a modification of examples given in this book (section 12.4.2) and in Benazra (2010b). We have already alluded to this example in section 23.1. Therein we referred to the trio of words (light, sound, silence) and their shared physical trait—speed. We now elaborate further on this example and expand it. Light may be represented in Hebrew by *keshet* (rainbow) or . . . *or* (light). Sound may be represented by *raam* (thunder) or . . . *kol* (sound or voice). What Hebrew word should represent "silence"? Interestingly, two different phenomena associated with zero speed, namely, "silence" and "standstill", share in Hebrew a common root: D.M.M. Thus, *domem* denotes in Hebrew all non-living objects (assuming "living" is associated with self mobility) but also objects that do not produce sound (silent). We have elected to use in this example *dmamah*, a Hebrew word derived from the above root (D.M.M.) that has (surprisingly!) the double meaning of silence and stillness. Table 23.3 displays the two trios of Hebrew words, which share a common word, with their respective numerical values, denoted SNV (Speed Numerical Values). Also given are the respective speeds of light and sound (the latter's speed is measured at air temperature of 20°C).

Table 23.3. Data for analysis of velocities (light, sound, zero-speed)
SNV - Speed numerical value. Sound speed in air at 20°C.

Hebrew	SNV	Speed (m/s)	Log Speed
Or (*light*)	207 (1+6+200)	299 792 458	19.52
Keshet (rainbow)	800 (100+300+400)	299 792 458	19.52
Kol (*sound, voice*)	136 (100+6+30)	343.26	5.84
Raam (thunder)	310 (200+70+40)	343.26	5.84
Dmamah (silence, stillness)	89 (4+40+40+5)	1	0

Note that since temperature and air pressure both affect the speed of sound the value selected is somewhat arbitrary. However, selecting another temperature and pressure would not alter the general result (given the log-speed scale used in the analysis). The natural log scale is necessary, as in some earlier analyses in this book, due to differences in order of magnitude of the different speeds taking part in the analysis. Also, the "speed" of silence (or stillness) on the log scale was chosen to be zero (on the original scale this represents a near-zero speed of 1 meter per second (m/s), about a third of a percent of the speed of sound). Figure 23.2 is a plot of the data in Table 23.3 (speed is in m/s, given on a log scale on the vertical axis).

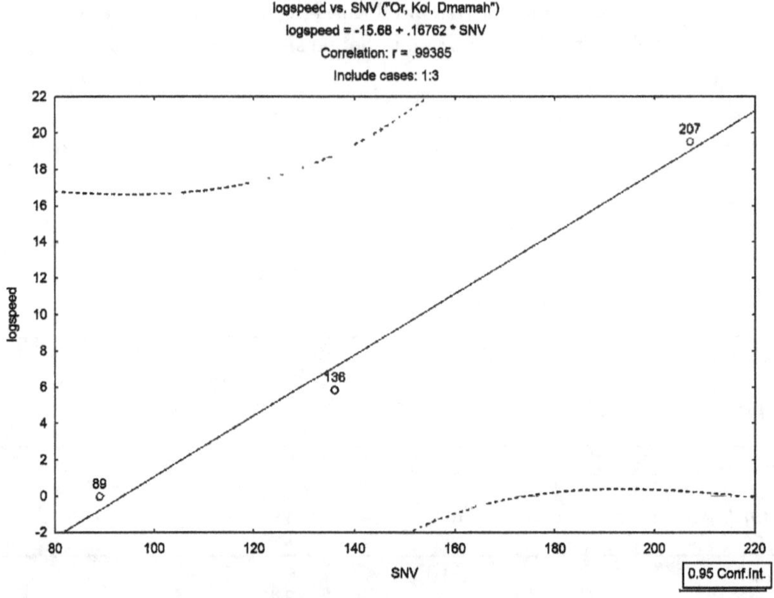

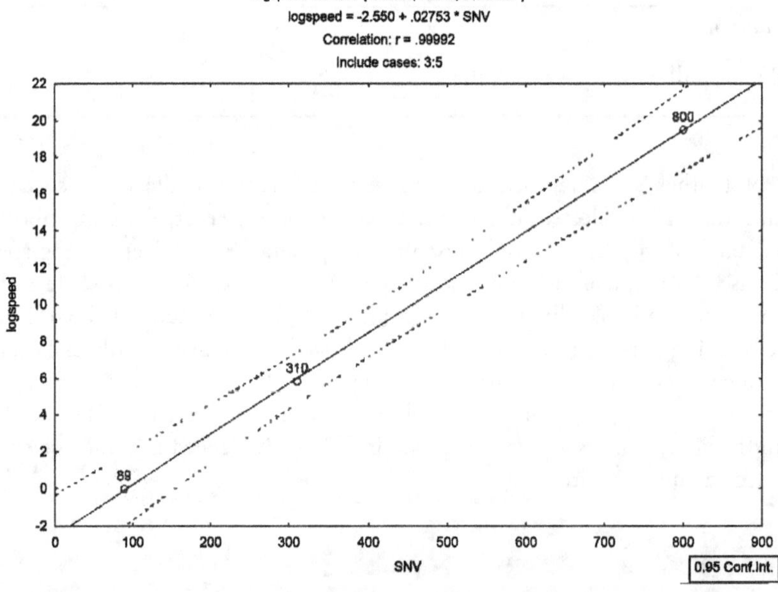

Figure 23.2. Two sets of intra-related Hebrew words and their relationship to speed (on a log scale). SNV—Speed Numerical Value.

We realize that the two trios of words, (*Keshet, Raam, Dmamah*) and (*Or, Kol, Dmamah*), are represented, with the allied speed values, by two lines with significance levels of .0081 and .0706, respectively. The lines converge (intersect) at a point with SNV (x-value) nearly equal to that of *Dmamah* (silence, standstill). Table 21.1 (Examples 8 and 9) and Figures 21.8 and 21.9 display additional computer-simulation results associated with these examples.

23.4 Primary Example—The Planets

23.4.1   *Planetary Diameters*

This example examines a possible link between names for celestial objects that appear in the Hebrew Bible and known physical properties of the planets. This is an extension of the analysis in Section 8.3, which related only to the planets' diameters. As related therein, we are unaware of any scholarly interpretation that attributes celestial biblical names to specific planets. However, certain names are traditionally interpreted to be associated with groups of stars or just representing a planet (no attribution attempted). We discard these traditional interpretations, and assume that all references to celestial objects in biblical Hebrew (excluding the sun and the moon) relate to planets. There are five such names: *Kimah* (Amos 5:8; Job 9:9, 38:31), *Ksil* (Isa.13:10; Amos 5:8; Job 9:9, 38:31), *Ash* (Job 9:9), *Aish* (Job 38:32) and *Teman* (Job 9:9). The latter means in biblical Hebrew also south, but from the general context of the verse where it appears *Teman* obviously relates to a celestial object (and so is it interpreted by Jewish biblical scholars). We add to this set *Kochav,* which in biblical Hebrew simply means star. *Kochav* is assumed here to relate also to an unknown planet, though in the Bible it most often appears in the plural to signify all stars. Two other names added to the set are *Mazar* (only the plural, *Mazarot* or *Mezarim,* appear in the Bible, at Job 38:32 and Job 38:9, respectively), and *Shachar*. The first (*Mazar*) is interpreted in Even-Shoshan (1988) the same as *Mazal* (a planet, in both ancient and modern Hebrew). The second is often interpreted by Jewish scholars as "a morning star" (relate, for example, to SofS. 6:10, and how Jewish commentators interpret it). As elaborated on at some length in Section 8.3, these names probably represented originally the two most luminary stars in the sky, after the sun and the moon, namely, Venus (probably named *Mazar* in Hebrew) and Jupiter (probably named *Shachar* in Hebrew; refer to 8.3). As we shall see, statistical analysis indeed corroborates this attribution of meanings to the two words.

We now have nine biblical names for celestial objects (including Earth). Apart from the latter, which planets do these names possibly allude to?

For no obvious alternative method to assign names to planets, we sort in an ascending order the numerical values of the biblical Hebrew names (denoted ONV for celestial "Object Numerical Values"), and likewise for the equatorial diameters (as given at NASA site, including also Pluto that had recently been omitted from the list of planets). Table 23.4 displays the results.

Table 23.4. Data for equatorial diameters and mass densities of planets with their assumed biblical names and their Object Numerical Values (ONV)

Name	Hebrew name	ONV	Equatorial Diameter* (km)	Log(diameter)	Mass Density* (g/cm^3)
Pluto	*Kochav*	48	2302	7.7415	2.00
Mercury	*Kimah*	75	4879	8.4928	5.43
Mars	*Ksil*	120	6794	8.8238	3.94
Venus	*Mazar*	247	12104	9.4013	5.24
Earth	*Eretz*	291	12756	9.4538	5.51
Neptune	*Ash*	370	49528	10.8103	1.76
Uranus	*Aish*	380	51118	10.8419	1.30
Saturn	*Teman*	490	120536	11.6997	0.70
Jupiter	*Shachar*	508	142984	11.8705	1.33

* Source: http://solarsystem.jpl.nasa.gov/planets/charchart.cfm

The most surprising finding in this table is that the words *Mazar* and *Shachar* indeed occupies in the sorted list same ordinal positions as the very same planets that these names have been attributed to from altogether non-statistical arguments (Sections 8.3.4 and 8.3.5). Also Earth occupies same positions in both sorted lists. We conclude that this convergence of three planets to identical ordinal positions in the two separately sorted lists add to the validity of the pursuing analyses.

Plotting the planets' diameters on the vertical axis and ONV on the horizontal axis results in Figure 23.3.

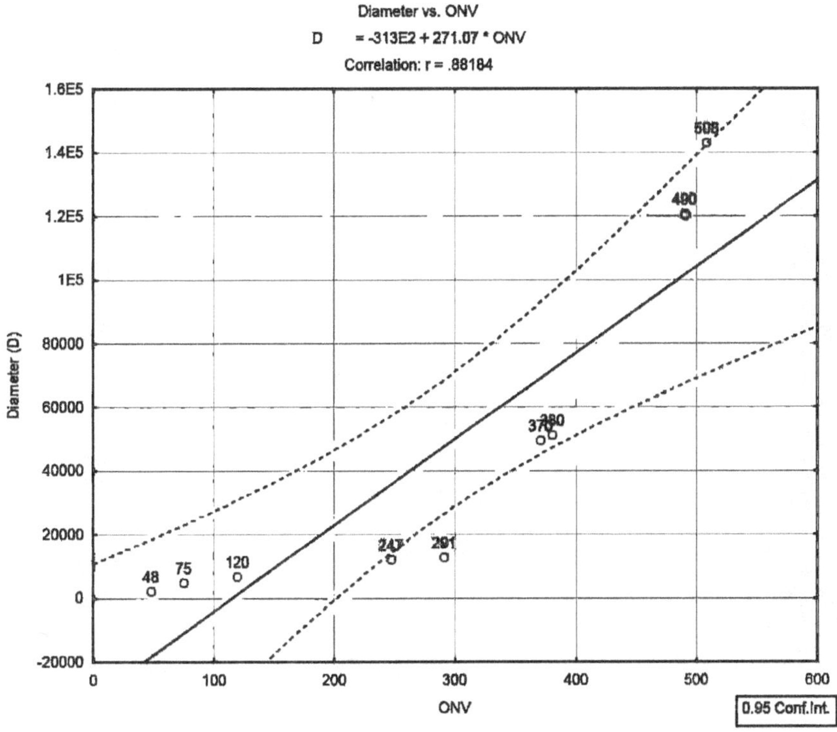

Figure 23.3. Data points for the planets (n=9) on original scale (D).

A nonlinear relationship is evidenced by the plotted points. Proceeding as in the previous example (namely, plotting diameters on a log scale) we obtain Figure 23.4.

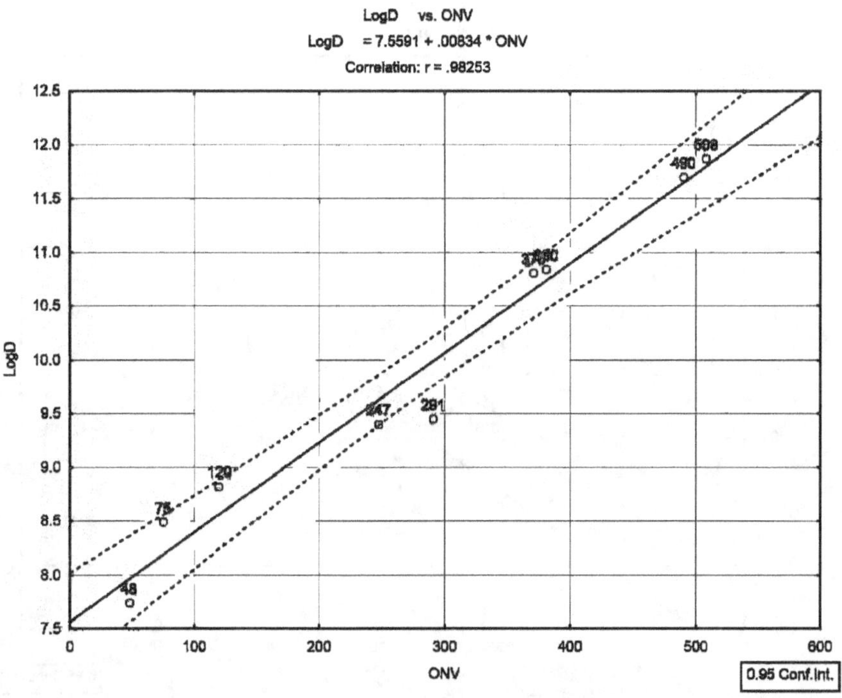

Figure 23.4. Log-diameter ("LogD") of the planets (n=9) as function of their Object Numerical Values (ONV). All planets' names are biblical. Earth (ONV=291) is somewhat deviant.

A linear relationship surfaces, unexpectedly and with no logical explanation. Statistical linear regression analysis was applied to the entire sample of nine points to ascertain whether the linear relationship is significant. With n=9, a correlation (ρ) of 0.9825 is obtained, with model F-ratio of 195.2, which is highly significant (p<0.000002). Confidence interval limits (95% confidence) are also plotted in Figure 23.4. Since Earth (ONV=291) lies somewhat below the lower confidence limit, the previous analysis is re-run, excluding Earth. Results are plotted in Figure 23.5.

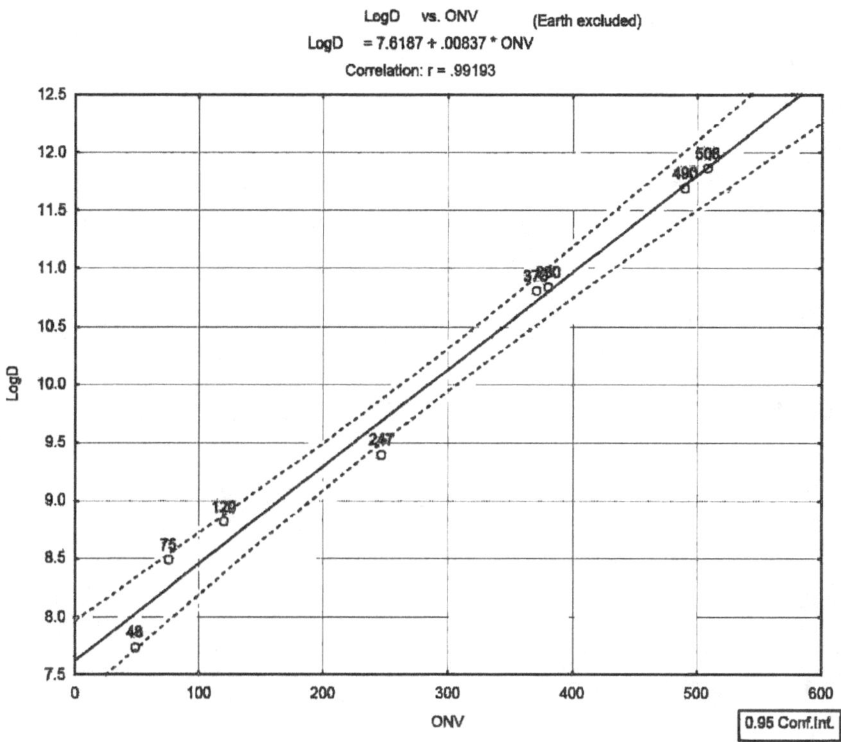

Figure 23.5. Log-diameter ("LogD") of the planets as function of their ONV (n=8, excluding Earth)

With n=8, ρ is now 0.9919, and model F-ratio has jumped to 367 (formerly 195.2), a highly significant result (p<0.000001).

23.4.2   *Planetary Orbital Angular Momentums (OAM)*

The idea for this analysis was forwarded to me by Dr. Howard Sharpe from Canada. Assembly of data sets and all analyses presented herewith are the author's.

One of the most significant characteristics of a planet's orbit is its orbital angular momentum (OAM). The latter is defined as the product of the planet's mass (M; kg) times the planet's average distance from the sun (R, average orbital radius; meters) times the planet's average orbital speed (V; meters per second):

$$OAM = M*R*V = M(2\pi R^2) / T,$$

where T is orbital period (in seconds). Table 23.5 displays Hebrew words' numerical values (ONVs, as in Table 23.4) together with planets' OAM values (kg*m²/sec; m is "meter"), both in their original and log values.

Table 23.5. Data for planetary orbital angular momentum (OAM) with assumed biblical names and their Object Numerical Values (ONV). E3 means 10^3.

Name	Hebrew name	Object Numerical Value (ONV)	Angular Orbital Momentum (OAM; kg*m/sec)	Log(OAM)	Mass (M; kg)	Log(M)
Pluto	*Kochav*	43	3.6E38	88.78	1.310E22	50.896
Mercury	*Kimah*	75	9.1E38	89.71	3.302E23	54.153
Mars	*Ksil*	120	3.5E39	91.05	6.418E23	54.819
Venus	*Mazar*	247	1.8E40	92.69	4.868E24	56.845
Earth	*Eretz*	291	2.7E40	93.10	5.974E24	57.049
Neptune*	*Ash*	370	2.5E42	97.62	1.024E26	59.887
Uranus*	*Aish*	380	1.7E42	97.24	8.685E25	59.726
Saturn	*Teman*	490	7.8E42	98.76	5.685E26	61.604
Jupiter	*Shachar*	508	1.9E43	99.65	1.899E27	62.812

* Ordinal positions of these two planets were determined in Table 23.4 according to their equatorial diameters; these positions are preserved here even though sorting according to OAM or M should lead to swapping of these positions.

On comparison of Tables 23.4 and 23.5 we realize that when sorted according to their OAM values, only Neptune and Uranius could not have maintained their original ordinal positions (as given in Table 23.4). The mass density of Neptune (1.76 g/cm³) is larger than that of Uranius (1.30 g/cm³), however the equatorial radius of the latter (25,559 km) is larger than that of the former (24,764 km). Both equatorial radius and mass density affect OAM (as evidenced by the formula above). It is therefore not necessary that nearly all planets in Table 23.5 (with Uranius and Neptune excepted) should have preserved their sorted positions both with respect to equatorial diameter and to OAM. Yet they do. Due to the proximity in both size and OAM of Neptune and Uranius we have decided to preserve in Table 23.5 same ordinal positions for all planets as given in Table 23.4.

Figure 23.6 presents the results (the vertical axis presents log-OAM).

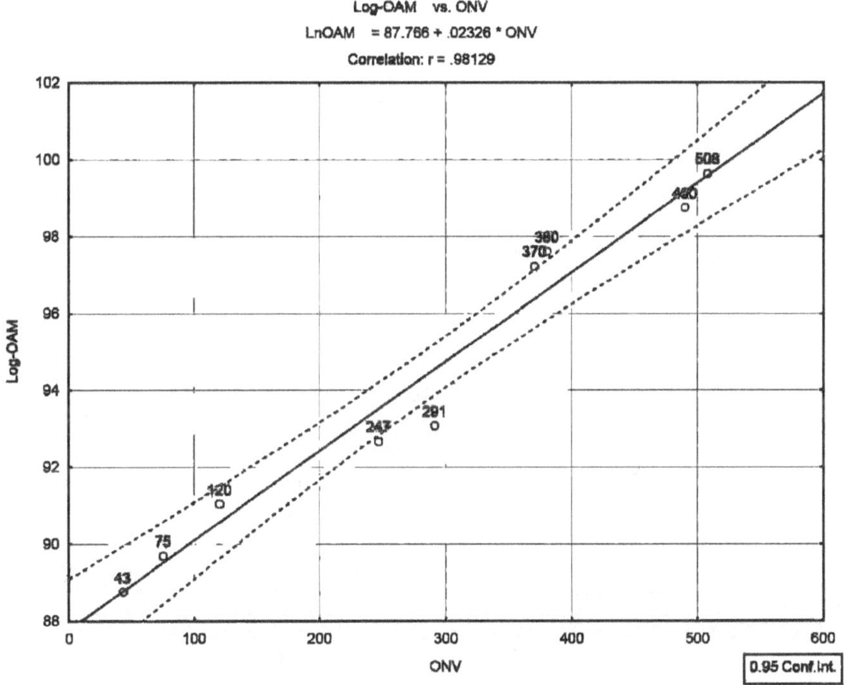

Figure 23.6. Planetary log-OAM (log orbital angular momentum, n=9) as function of Object Numerical Value (ONV)

We realize that all nine points align themselves near a straight line. The adjusted ρ-squared (ρ is correlation) is 0.958. Model F-ratio is 181.8, which, for n=9, is highly significant (p<0.000003). Since Earth data-point is somewhat deviant (below the lower confidence limit) it is removed from the sample, and linear regression analysis re-run for a sample of n=8. The adjusted ρ-squared is 0.977. The model F-ratio is now 294.3, which, for n=8, is highly significant

318

(p<0.000003). The results are presented (with Earth excluded) in Figure 23.7.

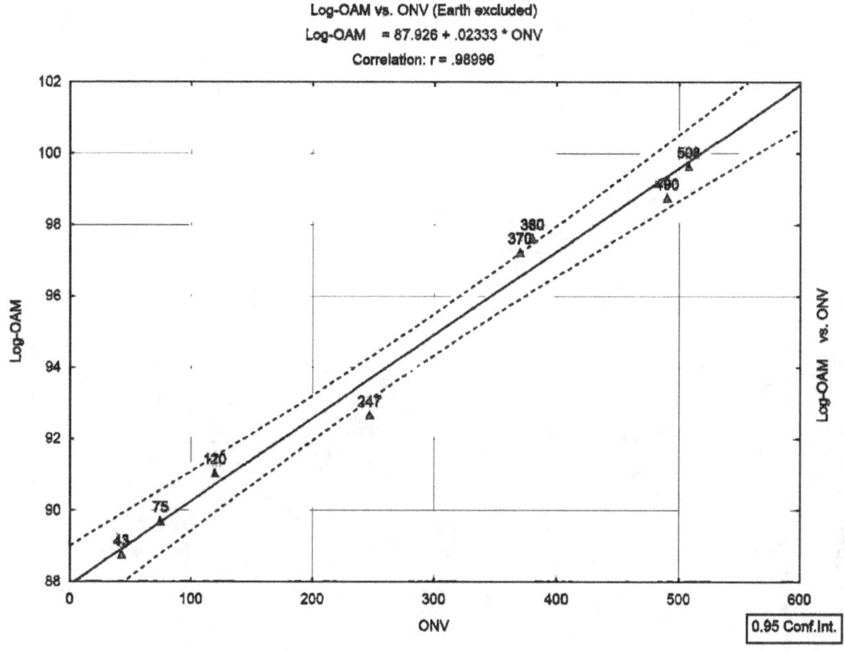

Figure 23.7. Planetary log-OAM (log orbital angular momentum)
as function of ONV (n=8, Earth excluded)

23.4.3 *Planetary Masses*

Planets' diameters and planets' masses, both measured on a *log* scale, should be linearly inter-related if they shared equal mass densities. However, we know that average mass densities of planets differ (relate to Table 23.4). Therefore, values of planets' masses are added to Table 23.5, and we explore the relationship between ONV and respective planetary mass for all nine planets.

Figure 23.8 displays the results.

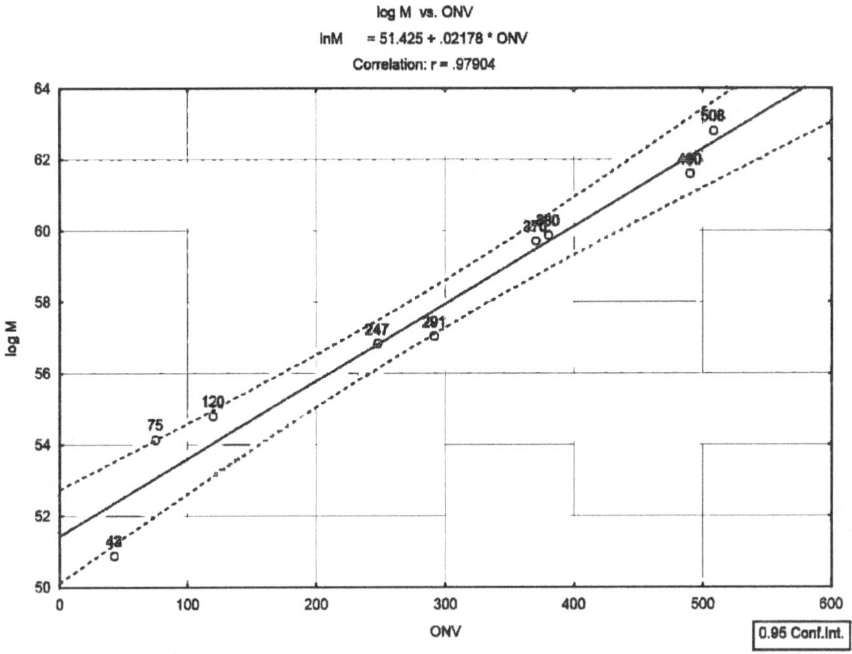

Figure 23.8. Planetary log-M (Mass, in kg; n=9) as function of ONV

A linear relationship is evidenced by the plot. From linear regression analysis with n=9, the adjusted ρ-squared is 0.953 and model F-ratio is 161.8, which is highly significant (p<0.000004).

23.5 Some Further Numerical Examples

Examples in this section, though numerical, are not accompanied by statistical analysis. They were forwarded to me by an American Obstetrician/ Gynecologist, living and working in Mali, West Africa. He preferred to remain anonymous and therefore we will refer to him as Dr. X. Permission was granted to publicize excerpts from his e-mails, as given below.

23.5.1 *How Long is Human Pregnancy?*

In his e-mail to me, Dr. X regards the duration of human pregnancy. Earlier in the book, I have quoted the numerical value of 271 days for "Herayon" (pregnancy) as indicative of expected duration of human pregnancy (sub-section 2.1.2). However I quote two commonly accepted methods to calculate duration of human pregnancy: "One method is to measure human pregnancy from fertilization time, which is commonly accepted to be, on average, 266 days. Another method is to measure human pregnancy from the last menstrual period, which is commonly accepted as 280 days. The simple average (midpoint) between these two figures is 273 days (about nine months)."

Thus Dr. X in his e-mail:

"Dr Nagele, a physician in the 1850's or so, created a rule for estimating the due date of a human pregnancy based on the first day of the last menstrual period. At this point, no one even knew that ovulation and therefore conception was taking place at approximately day 14 of the ovulatory cycle, so the only fixed point was the first day of the last menstrual cycle, and of course, one is not pregnant at this point, as one is actively sloughing the endometrial contents. Nevertheless, this is the one fixed point by which to date a pregnancy, and in his study of patients, he determined that the due date is 280 days after the first day of the woman's last menstrual cycle. He invented a rule by which to estimate this for patients. It is still used today—Nagele's rule (information available on Wikipedia under this heading): Take the first day of the last cycle and then subtract three calendar months and add 7 days—the resulting day (about 280 days later) will be the patient's approximate due date.

Later, in the 1930's or 40's it was determined (O'Dowd and Phillip, 1994) that ovulation, and therefore conception, was taking place approximately 14 days after the first day of the last menstrual period. Thus the classic length of human gestation of 266 days after ovulation (and therefore conception, plus or minus one day, as both the sperm and the egg can live in the female genital tract for about one day in the unfertilized state, before dying) was established.

These two numbers have been used ever since, and you refer to them in your book. However, Dr Robert Mittendorf *et al.* (1990) published a comprehensive study of estimated delivery dates of American women. As far as I know, this is the most recent scholarship done on this question. Interestingly the research found that for women who had never had a child before, the average length of pregnancy was 274 days after conception, while for women who have had at least one baby before, the average length of gestation was 269 days. I find it fascinating that the average of these two is 271.5!! It is remarkable to me that 271 is found to be so near the center of the distribution by the most recent scholarship.

Thus Dr Mittendorf's data show average gestation to be about 5 days longer on average than Dr Nagele's data, and this only serves to further tighten the biblical evidence for 271. I suspect a true picture of the data would show a bell shaped curve centered directly on 271."

23.5.2   *What Percentage of Human Blood is Cellular?*

In the same message, Dr. X relates to the fact that blood in Hebrew ("Dam") is numerically equivalent to 44. This is referred to in section 10.3.4 and also in section 2.1.3, where I draw attention that whenever a numerical value of a biblical Hebrew word amounts to a repeated appearance of a single digit (like "Sheleg", snow, equaling 333), this digit indicates a major physical property of the object that the word is associated with. Relating to human blood, I have interpreted the repeated "4" as signaling the number of human blood varieties. Dr. X believes that the number "44" conveys an even deeper meaning, signaling the proportion of cellular blood (all the rest is liquid) in the human blood:

"One other thing that strengthens your case is the fact that one standard measure of human blood is called the hematocrit. This is the percentage of blood that is cellular (the rest being liquid—the plasma). The hematocrit normal values vary between males and females, but normally they are cited to be 42-50% for men and 35-47% for women. Consult any laboratory manual and you will see that the norms cited for male and female hemoglobins always contain the number 44 for both, and a simple average of the male and female norms will always center around 44!!! I looked at several different limits of normal according to different texts and sites, and found my averages to always be between 42.5 and 45. So . . . this is astounding, eh?? 44 is definitely a key number for human blood."

23.6 Species Biblical Names

Biblical names of species belonging to the *plant* or the *animal* kingdoms abound in the Bible. The meanings of these names (namely, which currently known species they allude to) are not always clear. The Bible refers to Adam as the absolute name-giver (Gen. 2: 19-20), and some biblical scholars have attempted to attach significance to specific names by relating to known qualities of the species. For example, "dog" in Hebrew may also be read "Like heart", referring to qualities commonly attributed to domesticated dogs. In this section, we relate to a newly found feature that we believe is common to an unexplainably high proportion of biblical species names. We present a large sample of names that share this characteristic, and perform a certain probability calculation that seems to suggest that this unique property is probably too common in the Hebrew Bible to be considered as sheer coincidence (actual frequency of occurrence of the phenomenon far exceeds the calculated probability, assuming randomness). We provide no explanation for this phenomenon, however suggest possible explanations for its significance.

Let the numerical value (NV) of a Hebrew letter, as given in Table 1.1 of this book, be registered by the following formula:

$$NV = k*10^m \ (m=0,1,2)$$

For example, the eleventh letter, *Kaf* ("כ"), has NV = 20 = $2(10)^1$ (k=2, m=1). Note that k delivers the "value" of the letter while m denotes its order of magnitude. Table 23.6 displays all Hebrew letters classified (uniquely) according to their (k, m) values.

The phenomenon we refer to may be articulated as follows: For most species names in biblical Hebrew, at least two letters share the same k. For example, in *Adam*, both the second letter in the name, *Dalet*, and the third letter, *Mem*, are associated with k=4. In *Tamar* (palm tree) both the first letter (*Tav*, value of 400) and the second letter (*Mem*, value of 40) share same k=4. In *Kelev* (dog) both the first letter (*Kaf*, value of 20) and the last letter (*Bet*, value of 2) share the same k=2.

To learn how probable is that configuration (how likely it is to happen by chance), we have calculated the probability that in a species name of three letters, at least two letters share the same k. We assume that all letters have equal probability to appear in each of the three positions of the name, and denote by Pk the probability that any letter selected randomly will have the given value of k. Table 23.6 displays these probabilities.

Table 23.6. Hebrew letters classified according
to their numerical values (NV) registered as:

$$NV = k * 10^m.$$

For example, the eleventh letter, Kaf ("כ"), has NV= 20 = 2(10)^1 (k=2, m=1)

k	m			k occurrence (P_k, %)
	0	1	2	
1	א	י	ק	3 (13.6364%)
2	ב	כ	ר	3 (13.6364%)
3	ג	ל	ש	3 (13.6364%)
4	ד	מ	ת	3 (13.6364%)
5	ה	נ		2 (9.0909%)
6	ו	ס		2 (9.0909%)
7	ז	ע		2 (9.0909%)
8	ח	פ		2 (9.0909%)
9	ט	צ		2 (9.0909%)
Total				22 (100%)

Let us define the following:

A (a random event) = In a Hebrew name of three letters same k appears in at least two letters.

P_k = Probability that a Hebrew letter selected at random has a value of k (according to the formula NV = k(10)^m; Relate to Table 23.6);

Given k, the (conditional) probability of A, according to the binomial probability model, is:

$$P(A \mid k) = \sum_{j=2}^{3} \binom{3}{j} P_k \, (1 - P_k)^{3-j}$$

The (unconditional) probability of A is, according to the formula of total probability:

$$P(A) = \sum_{k=1}^{9} P_k \sum_{j=2}^{3} \binom{3}{j} P_k \, (1 - P_k)^{3-j}$$

Using the probabilities, {Pk}, in Table 23.6, we find:

$$P(A) = \frac{560}{14641} = 3.825\%$$

In other words, we expect this phenomenon to occur by chance in about 3.8% of species names in the Bible. We currently do not have count of the total number of biblical species names (either of three letters or otherwise). Table 23.7 presents a sample of species names in biblical Hebrew that conform to the above characterization (namely, a common k shared by at least two letters in the name), together with the associated k.

Table 23.7. Biblical Hebrew species names with at least two letters sharing same k. Names with two different k's having this characterization are classified twice (once for each k) and are starred. Altogether there are 69 *different* names in this list.

k	Biblical species names (in Hebrew)
1	איל, ארי, איה, ילק, קאת, לביא, אנקה*, לילית*, קשוא
2	כלב, כבש, בקר, כר, דבר, רהב, ברוד, ארבה, ערב, ברוש, בור, כפיר, זבוב, עכבר, זרזיר*, דבורה, דרדר*, ערער*, ברקן, כרכם
3	ליש, שלו, שחל, שועל, גמל, שלך, לילית*, חרגל, אשל
4	אדם, רותם, תמר, עתוד, תחמס, תנשמת, שממית, תולעת, דוכיפת, דרדר*, תדהר
5	יונה, תאנה, נמלה, יענה, קנה, עזניה, תנין, אנקה*, אנפה, לבנה, קנמון, לבונה, סנה
6	סוס, סוף, כוס
7	עז, עזניה, זרזיר*, ערער*
8	שחף, אפרח, שפיפן, צפצפה*, חוח
9	צפצפה*

The number of different names in the table (69, of which 27 are three-letter names) is large. It is hard to believe that this number (27) comprises only 3.8% (probability of occurring randomly) of all three-letter species names that appear in the Bible.

A natural question arises: If based on the probability calculation listed above one cannot perceive this phenomenon as coincidence, then . . . what is its significance?

We have no definite answer but can offer two possible responses. First, if a certain structure (pattern) is found in biblical species names that occurs with frequency that defies randomness, obviously it has significance. Secondly, referring to the substance of this phenomenon we may contemplate two possible frameworks for discussion. First, earlier in the book we have related to the fact that the word "life" in Hebrew, *Chaim,* implies double in a symmetrical way (section 5.5). Does the same hold true for the *double* appearance of same k in two different letters?

A more outrageous framework for discussion may have to do with the double helix in cell chromosomes of every sexually multiplying living creature. Since occasionally numerical values of Hebrew biblical species names correspond to their number of chromosomes (refer to three examples in Table 23.1), does the common k convey information related in any way to the genetics of that species ("and whatever the man called every living creature, that was its *name*"; Gen. 2:19)?

REFERENCES

[1] Benazra, R. 2010a. Information cachées dans l'hébreu biblique. *A.C.I St-Fons La Voix de la Communauté* 62 (March-April): 41-45.

[2] Benazra, R. 2010b. Information cachées dans l'hébreu biblique (suite). *A.C.I St-Fons La Voix de la Communauté* 63 (September-October): 27-35.

[3] Even-Shoshan, A. *New Concordance for Torah, Neviim, and Ketuvim*. Revised edition. Jerusalem: Kiriat-Sefer, 1988.

[4] Mittendorf R, Williams MA, Berkey CS, Cotter PF 1990. The Length of Uncomplicated Human Gestation. *Obstet Gyneco* 75:929-32. PMID 2342739.

[5] O'Dowd M, Phillip E. *The History of Obstetrics and Gynecology*. Parthenon Publishing Group 1994, p. 259

[6] Shore, H. 2009. Author's interview with interviewer Yocheved Miriam Russo. The Jerusalem Post, Dec., 4th, 2009; Accessible via this book's USA Amazon site and elsewhere (several languages).

PART V

New Coincidences

CHAPTER 24

Kavod — Most Peculiar Word in Biblical Hebrew

24.1   Introduction

Kavod in modern Hebrew means honor, respect or glory. A person may show *Kavod* to his fellow human being, and a military medal of honor, bestowed unto a military service person, is a medal of *Kavod* (*Ot Kavod*).

The word appears in the Jewish Bible no less than 199 times. Numerous times it appears therein in the same sense as in modern spoken Hebrew. Examples:

"Akhan, My son, give, I pray thee, respect to Jehovah, God of Israel..." (Joshua 7:19);

"And on that day it shall come to pass that the glory of Jacob shall fade..." (Isaiah 17:4);

"The Heavens declare the glory of God..." (Psalms 19:2).

Yet, this is only one sense with which *Kavod* appears in the Bible and it is not the most frequent one. A more frequent usage does not relate at all to the created giving glory to the Creator. Rather, it relates to *Kavod* as intrinsically linked to the Divine. And here we encounter the impossible combination of words:

Jehovah's Kavod.

What does that mean? The Significant Hidden Information (and Message) that Jewish bible interpreters have attempted, throughout the ages, to impart plausible meaning to this bizarre idiom; however, they have always relied on the traditional sense of "honor" or "respect" or "glory". In most Bible translations (from biblical Hebrew), "Jehovah's *Kavod*" translates into "Jehovah's glory".

As we shall soon realize, all those interpretations fall short of satisfactorily explaining most usages of this combination of words in the Jewish Hebrew Bible. Thus, we are left helpless figuring out and imparting any sensible meaning to this bizarre expression; That is, until we scrutinize instances where it appears, and try to integrate these with scientific knowledge we currently possess about the universe. Once we do that, stunning amazement and deep appreciation for Jehovah's *Kavod* follows.

Let us start with a few examples:

When Moses expresses desire to learn of Jehovah's ways in leading His world, he asks: "Please show me *Kevodcha*" ("Your *Kavod*"). The Divine response: "...I will make all my goodness pass before thee, and I will proclaim the name of the Lord before thee; and will be gracious to whom I will be gracious, and show mercy on whom I will show mercy. And He said, thou cannot see my face for no man shall see me and live" (Exodus 33:18-20);

Prophet Isaiah explains why the world exists (seemingly the only time the Bible relates so explicitly to this question): "All that can be named, by My Name and for my *Kavod* I have created it, I have formed it, I have even made it" (Isaiah 43:7);

Prophet Isaiah delivers an account of his vision, hearing the Seraphim crying to each other, saying: "...Holy, Holy, Holy is the Lord of hosts, the whole earth is full of his *Kavod*" (Isaiah 6:3).

How can we settle the first example with the last, while they seem so much at odds and unrelated to one another?

In the first example, Moses obviously requests to learn how the Divine is leading His world. While the response Moses gets is unsatisfactory ("I will be gracious to whom I will be gracious"), the

Divine response affirms that what Moses really desired in his request ("Show me your *Kavod*") is to learn the ways by which God is leading His world. No reference whatsoever to God's glory, as the latter is seemingly implied by the last example!!

Jewish tradition makes a reasonable distinction between two types of Divine leadership of the universe: By Law-of-Nature and by Divine Intervention (often explicitly expressed on a personal level as Divine Providence, or *Hashgachah Pratit*).

The former, Law-of-Nature, relates to the Ten Divine "sayings" of Genesis Creation narrative (Genesis 1). Later, after Noah's flood, God re-assures humankind that Law-of-Nature exists and that it is ever-lasting: "While the earth remains, seed time and harvest, and cold and heat, and summer and winter, and day and night would not cease" (Genesis 8:22).

The latter, Divine Intervention, relates to divine intervention in the world to exercise a system of justice: "...Would not the Judge of all the earth do Justice?" (Gen. 18:25). However, this Divine intervention is mitigated by Divine graciousness and mercy, as the former quote of God's response to Moses has shown. Furthermore, leadership by Divine intervention is not restricted to the confines of Law-of-Nature; Occasionally, it operates contrary to Law-of-Nature, as the Ten plagues of Egypt (Exodus 7:20-12:30) testify.

Let us assume that indeed Jehovah's *Kavod* is an overall term for the two basic Divine leaderships of the universe: By Law-of-Nature and by Divine intervention.

Is there indication for Law-of-Nature in Jehovah's *Kavod*?

Is there indication for Divine intervention (or Divine moral code) in Jehovah's *Kavod*?

Expressed differently: Can one find evidence, within the term itself, that Jehovah's *Kavod* indeed represents the double-faceted Divine leadership of the world?

Surprisingly, the answer is a resounding YES.

Let us address the former first. As quoted earlier, prophet Isaiah describes his vision of Seraphim crying to each other, saying: "the whole

Eretz is full of his *Kavod*." (Isaiah 6:3). However, as addressed in my book (Section 14.1, p. 201), *Eretz* (earth in biblical Hebrew) implies either "world" or "Earth". Given current scientific knowledge, we may therefore re-translate Isaiah thus: "...Holy, Holy, Holy is the Lord of hosts, the whole universe is permeated with his *Kavod*." (Isaiah 6:3).

Is there any hint in Jehovah's *Kavod* for Law-of-Nature, something that, by modern science, permeates the whole universe?

We can think of one answer only:

The gravitation force!! (in modern spoken Hebrew, force of *Kevidah*).

By Einstein's general theory of relativity, the gravitation field, generated by any celestial mass (like galaxies and stars), determines the most fundamental properties of the four-dimensional space-time, as we experience it in daily life and as we observe throughout the universe via astronomy, aided by scientific theory (Einstein's General Theory of Relativity, with succeeding derivatives up to the present Super-string theory). There is indeed nothing else that we can state permeates the whole universe.

And how do we, mere Earth-bound mortals, experience gravitation force?

By feeling that every physical object, large and small, is heavy, carries weight. We nowadays are aware that this sensation of physical articles being heavy is due to gravitation force. That is how we experience it in our every-day life. Additionally, by modern science, we have learned that the gravitation force (indeed gravitational field) determines the fundamental properties of the four-dimensional space-time continuum, in which we live, and the gravitational field indeed permeates the whole universe.

So:

If Jehovah's *Kavod* expresses modes of Divine leadership of the universe (as Moses used the term in his request to God, "Show me thy *Kavod*");

And if one of the two modes of leadership, by Jewish tradition, is Law-of-Nature;

And if per modern science, the most central and fundamental force-of-nature to determine the basic properties of the space-time continuum, permeating the whole universe, is the gravitation force;

Given all that, does Jehovah's *Kavod* in any way points to the gravitational force???

Amazingly, Biblical Hebrew makes the impossible and implausible link between two utterly non-related concepts: Jehovah's presence in the world via Law-of-Nature, and the most basic force of the universe, the most influential on observed Law-of-Nature, only known by modern science — the gravitation force.

Heavy, in biblical Hebrew, is Kaved (same root as *Kavod*, implausible as this may sound). Examples (altogether 41 instances of *Kaved* in the Bible imply heavy):

"Behold, tomorrow about this time I will rain heavy hail, the like of which has not been in Egypt since its foundation until now" (Exodus 9:18,24);

"And now my father had burdened you with a heavy yoke and I will add to your yoke..." (1 Kings 12:11).

We finally address the second question, put forward earlier:

Is Jehovah's *Kavod* also indicative of Jehovah's leadership via Divine intervention, imposing the set of moral Divine commandments via a system of justice operatingwithin the confines of free-will?

The answer is similar to that for the previous question: As Jehovah's *Kavod* indicates a major Law-of-Nature (Gravitation Law), so it hints at a major Divine commandment, the fifth commandment, which starts with *Kabed* (meaning honor):

"*Kabed* thy father and thy mother" (Exodus 20:12; Deuteronomy 5:16).

24.2   Summary

Jehovah's *Kavod*, mostly wrongly interpreted to-date as Jehovah's glory, has been shown in this post to really mean, consistent with Jewish tradition, Jehovah's double-faceted leadership of the universe;

It is completely incomprehensible why biblical Hebrew should link "glory" with… "heavy" (as both derive from same linguistic root);

Aided by modern science, and pursuing the new interpretation of Jehovah's *Kavod*, an incredible link has been established between *Kavod* and *Kaved* (both emanating from same biblical Hebrew root);

Consistent with the new interpretation, Jehovah's *Kavod* is appropriately indicative of both force of gravity (leadership by Law-of-Nature) and of the Ten Commandments (leadership by Divine intervention).

Personal confession: Mind boggling…

Comments:

Comment [1]: The three-letter Hebrew root of *Kavod* (and related words) is "כ.ב.ד" (K.B.D). The gematria value of this root is the same as Jehovah (26). This is perhaps further evidence that *Kavod* in biblical Hebrew is indeed a general term for all modes by which the Divine manifests its presence in the world.

Comment [2]: The Coronavirus pandemic, denoted by WHO (World Health Organization)—COVID-19 (COronaVIrus Disease-2019), is indicative of, sounds like—*Kavod* (a stunning insight by Avinoam Ben-Mordechai);

Comment [3]: In the most prominent biblical demonstration of Divine intervention in the affairs of humankind (Divine leadership, *Kavod*), the Ten Plagues of Egypt, the word *Kavod*, with variations, appears Ten Times (within only three chapters!). Five times the word describes, as adjective, four of the plagues ("natural" disasters), stating that they were "heavy"; the other five times, *Kavod* describes Pharaoh's "heavy" heart, refusing "Let My People Go". Here is the list in Exodus (Chapter:Verse):

{(8:11), (8:20), (8:28), (9:3), (9:7), (9:18), (9:24), (9:34), (10:1), (10:14)}.

CHAPTER 25

"There was Evening and There was Morning" (Gen. 1) — A Different Interpretation

25.1　Introduction

The known verse from the first chapter of Genesis appears therein, not surprisingly, six times. The two central words of the verse, which confer on it its meaning, are *Boker* (morning in biblical Hebrew) and *Erev* (evening). However, their order of appearance in the verse is bizarre:

"…and there was evening and there was morning one day" (Genesis 1:5).

This is logically flawed (and same applies to all other five variations of the verse). The correct articulation should be:

"…and there was morning and there was evening one day".

Perhaps the verse is misconstrued by us? Is there an alternative interpretation that may remove the logical flaw, inherent to current interpretation?

In this post (and the allied podcast), we offer a new interpretation. The latter integrates well with the creation narrative, as unfolding in

Genesis 1, and, astoundingly, it also comports well with current scientific knowledge of the Big-Bang and its aftermath.

Ultimately, the new interpretation also explains why the same two words, *Erev* and *Boker*, stand for "evening" and "morning", respectively, in traditional interpretations of the verse.

25.2   *"Erev"* and *"Boker"* — New Interpretation

We base the new interpretation on a basic root analysis of the two words, and support it with numerous other verses in the Jewish Bible, where same roots appear in a context utterly divorced from the traditional meaning as "evening" and "morning"; yet, in context that is consistent with the new interpretation. Therefore, both *Erev* and *Boker*, and their respective roots, are hence forth discussed with no relationship whatsoever to their acceptable meanings as evening and morning, respectively.

We start with *Erev*.

This word, and other words of same root, appear over 150 times in the Bible. The Hebrew root of *Erev* corresponds to E.R.B, in English. Most times, the root is associated with "evening", but not uniquely so. Another common usage relates to mixing, or mixture. Thus, *Erev-Rav* (literally, "much mixture") stands for a mixture of tribes; *Arov* stands for a mixture of animals (one of the Ten Plights of Egypt); *Le-itarev* means to mix together.

In other words, *Erev*, in biblical Hebrew, simply means mixture. Not surprisingly, the time of day when darkness starts crawling over earth, is also called *Erev* in Hebrew.

Let us next consider *Boker*.

Traditionally, the word means morning. We might be astonished to learn that its root is tightly linked to *Erev*, when the latter is interpreted as mixture. Furthermore, as we shall soon realize, the root of *Boker* diametrically represents the opposite of *Erev*, when the latter is interpreted as mixture.

Let us analyze usage of the root of *Boker* (B.K.R) in various biblical Hebrew words.

The grammatical structure of *Boker* is the same as *Chodesh* (month, in Hebrew). The verb associated with *Chodesh* is *Le-Chadesh*, meaning to renew. One may understand why month in Hebrew implies renewal, since the Hebrew calendar is based on the lunar (moon-based) month, with some periodical adjustments to keep it in tune with the solar calendar (sun-based calendar).

Similarly, the respective verb, associated with *Boker*, is *Le-Vaker*. Among other related meanings, *Le-Vaker* in biblical Hebrew means to seek out, namely, to make something that is mixed distinct and separate. For example (from Collins Concise Dictionary): "She sought out her friend from among the crowd".

A typical example for the use of *Le-Vaker*, sharing same root with *Boker*, is found in Leviticus. The verse describes donation of an animal to be sacrificed to Jehovah. The verse addresses the donor and relates to his animal donation (Leviticus 27:33):

"He must not seek out (*Lo Ye-Vaker*) the good from the bad or make any substitution. If he does make a substitution, both the animal and its substitute become holy and cannot be redeemed."

In other words, if the donated animal is defective, impaired in some sense, the donor must not distinguish the good from the bad, or make substitution, so that the sacrifice includes only good parts of the animal. The latter must be sacrificed in its totality.

Similarly, refer to Leviticus 13:36, or Ezekiel 34:11-12.

We realize that, according to the new interpretation based on root analysis, *Erev* and *Boker* are inherently connected, diametrically representing two opposite states. *Erev* describes a state of mixture; *Boker* describes a state that is the outcome of sorting out the mixture into its individual constituents, rendering them distinct, "separate from the crowd" (the mixture). In short, *Boker* describes a new state, where constituents of the mixture stand each on its own, materializing to full fruition as a result of the act of *bakarah* (seeking out the ingredients of the mixture).

With this new insight, based on root analysis of the two words *Erev* and *Boker*, the well-known verse, "and there was evening and there was morning", acquires a completely new meaning. It may more precisely be re-articulated as follows:

"There was mixture (*Erev*), and then there was non-mixture (*Boker*)", a new state where the mixture is dissolved, sorted out into its individual constituents.

We again note that the traditional interpretation, "And there was evening and there was morning one day" (and other versions of same verse) are logically flawed. The morning appears before the evening (to define a day), not the other way around. With the new interpretation, this logical flaw disappears since time is appropriately preserved.

Is the new interpretation consistent with the general description of creation, as unfolding in Genesis creation narrative?

Indeed, very much so.

In Genesis creation narrative, as unfolding in the first chapter of Genesis, the word "create" (*Bara*), appears not six times, as might be expected, but only thrice. It first appears in Genesis 1:1 as an overall statement of all that have been created:

"In the beginning Elohim created the Heavens and the Earth" (Genesis 1:1).

The third time creation is mentioned in Genesis creation narrative relates to the human species (Genesis 1:27):

"So Elohim created Mankind, in His own image, in the image of Elohim created He him, male and female He created them".

One may wonder: If creation had happened "In the Beginning" (Genesis 1:1), and then on the sixth day (Genesis 1:27), what was the Divine engaged in the rest of the six days, where creation is not at all mentioned?

The surprising answer is embedded in the two words, *Erev* and *Boker*, based on their new interpretation, based on their root analysis.

In the other days, when no creation is specified, Genesis creation narrative describes, individually for each day, how Elohim, by Divine utterance, has turned *Erev* (a state of mixture) into *Boker* (a state of non-mixture, individual parts sorted out from the mixture).

In other words, in most of the creation narrative of Genesis 1, the Divine separates the mixture, created "in the beginning", into its distinct individual elements, materializing them from the uniform mixture, into which they were initially embedded.

How does this interpretation comport with modern science?

Indeed, surprisingly well. The two words, *Erev* and *Boker*, as newly interpreted, are extremely consistent with how the Big-Bang and its aftermath, in the first few seconds of existence, are currently described by science.

A central element in this description is the Cosmic Microwave Background Radiation (CMBR). This radiation is a relic of the Big-Bang and its immediate aftermath. The uniformity of the radiation across the universe testifies that in the "Beginning" the universe was extremely uniform.

This uniformity is echoed in the Bible, describing the just created physical world ("The Earth"; Genesis 1:2):

"And The Earth was without form and void (*Tohu Va-Vohu*)..".

Using root analysis of the two Hebrew words, *Tohu* and *Vohu*, let us make sense of this verse and find out what it really conveys.

Science describes the first few seconds after the Big-Bang as extremely uniform. Nothing is yet distinct, there is no information to observe. This scientific description is reflected in *Tohu* and *Bohu*. The Bible describes the just created world as being in a state that whatever an observer at the time would observe, he or she will be bewildered (*Li-Tehot*, to wonder; Hebrew verb linked to *Tohu*). Also, the imaginary observer would look around purposelessly (*Li-vehot*; Hebrew verb linked to *Bohu*). Both descriptions allude to an observer, bewildered and looking around purposelessly. Why? because there is no information, nothing to observe that might help making sense of the observed (just as in a desert).

We have come to the end of our exploration journey regarding creation of The Earth, as alluded to in Genesis 1. We realized that in most days of creation, the Divine sorted out, by uttering a Divine command, that which was created "In the beginning".

We address the second creation, that of humankind (on the sixth day of creation; Genesis 1:27).

Humankind was not created when God created "The Heavens and the Earth" (Genesis 1:1), or the word "created" would not be repeated describing creation of Mankind (Genesis 1:27).

Since creation first alludes to "The Heavens and the Earth", and only later to Humankind, we, human beings, are doomed to repeat, in our own life, the same process, as described regarding The Earth in the first five days of Genesis creation (and some also on the sixth day) .

According to the creation narrative, the physical world (The Earth) has moved, from one day to the next, from a vague mixture (*Erev, Tohu Va-Vohu*) into its visible distinct constituents (*Boker*), turning the potential into observable reality.

We, human beings, who were separately created, are doomed to repeat the same process as The Earth:

Exercising free will, we are doomed to sort out the hidden faceless mixture, residing within us from infancy, into observable, distinct and separate personality and character.

Once we do that, transforming the potential, lurking within us in a mixture form, into the "I", or "Me", which we have grown up to become;

Once we do that, then, and only then, may we offer our own creation, our own non-mixed unique self, to the world, to be of benefit to the rest of humanity, and to all other creatures living on the surface of Planet Earth.

Comment:

What is "control" in modern Hebrew — *Bakarah*; and "controller" — *MeVaker*; and SPC (Statistical Process Control) — "*Bakarat…*"; All from same root as *Boker*; All implying the same: Achieving a state of "*Boker*", namely, separation of the mixture into its individual constituents!!!

CHAPTER 26

The Three Pillars of Truth (Lessons from the Hebrew Alphabet)

Truth is a sublime concept. But what does it stand on? What are the required ingredients for something to be "Truth"?

The Hebrew Alphabet delivers us three pillars to tell truth from falsehood. Observing the two words *Emeth* (Truth) and *Sheker* (Falsehood/lie), as their letters appear in an orderly sequence of the Hebrew Alphabet, teaches us powerful lessons on what constitute "Truth":

Emeth is written in Hebrew: אמת

Sheker is written in Hebrew: שקר

The letters of these words appear emphasized in the sequence of orderly Hebrew Alphabet below (read from right to left; letters in parentheses are "final letters", appearing only as last letters of words):

Emeth:

א ב ג ד ה ו ז ח ט י כ(ך) ל **מ(ם)** נ(ן) ס ע פ(ף) צ(ץ) ק ר ש ת

Sheker:

א ב ג ד ה ו ז ח ט י כ(ך) ל מ(ם) נ(ן) ס ע פ(ף) צ(ץ) ק ר **ש** ת

Based on these two sequences, three observations are called for that define the three pillars of "Truth":

Pillar 1: Completeness

The letters of *Emeth* (Truth) "scan" the whole spectrum, from first to last of the Hebrew Alphabet, with the middle letter appearing exactly as a middle term in the sequence. By contrast, the Hebrew letters for "Falsehood" are **concentrated** together in a small segment of the sequence, conveying an impression of "Half-truth", of an incomplete picture.

The tendency to make judgements or general assertions based on partial truths produces the worst form of falsehood. Partial truths contain seeds of truth, thus conveying an impression of truth when such is non-existent. This renders it difficult, at times impossible, to tell truth from non-truth. We judge a person based on a single wrong deed or utterance, ignoring a lifetime of righteous and fruitful deeds. We take part of a sentence, or paragraph, to slander someone ignoring the context and the true meaning of the complete pronouncement.

The book of Psalms regards "Completeness" as main feature of truth, which we have to account for observing and attempting to understand Divine righteous intervention in the world:

"Judgments of Jehovah are *Emeth*, they are righteous **altogether**" (Psalms 19:10).

Only in its totality may one appreciate Divine judgement as righteous. Components of that judgment, on their own, do not constitute righteousness; and only when taken **altogether** may these components be regarded as *Emeth*.

Pillar 2: Correct Order

The letters of *Sheker* appear in a perverted order in the sequence above, unlike the correct order of appearance of *Emeth*.

Falsehood is often generated, and truth violated, by placing "things" not in their correct order. Violating correct order can appear in all forms and shapes. When two warring parties are engaged in war, and we ignore the correct order of events that have "rolled" the parties into a state of war, or at times portraying real events, however in a perverted order of occurrence – we create falsehood (lie). Interchanging cause and effect, calling cause effect and calling effect cause, displaying thereby an incorrect cause-effect relationship, also obscure truth and generate falsehood. When a person blames his business partner for a certain adverse reaction to his own conduct, portraying his own conduct as reacting to that reaction (rather than as a trigger for the latter), he is engaged in creating falsehood. Preserving correct order is an essential ingredient for preserving truth.

Pillar 3: Supportive Evidence

Observing the two sets of Hebrew letters that constitute *Emeth* and *Sheker*, one discerns a major characteristic that tells them apart: The letters of *Emeth* look stable, well rooted in the ground (as shown by two "legs" or by a horizontal base, as in the middle letter). Conversely, all letters of *Sheker* seem shaky, not well rooted in the ground, two standing on one leg and a third (the first letter) "prone" to swing from one side to the other. Observing these letters an impression is conveyed of instability, as though the letters do not really have anything to support them. One is led to the conclusion that lack of evidence, grounded in reality, is main feature that distinguishes "truth" from "falsehood", *Emeth* from lack thereof.

In conclusion: The Hebrew Alphabet teaches us that to tell truth from falsehood one needs only examine and confirm to what degree do the three essential ingredients of truth prevail; to what degree do **Completeness, Correct order** and **Evidence** permeate given descriptions of world affairs.

Epilogue: Some Personal Reflections

A central concept of the Jewish faith is *hashgacha pratit* (divine Providence—literally, divine "personal caretaking".) What this implies is that everything that occurs in one's life is accounted for, registered somewhere, and that you are guided by God to do the right things. This occasionally materializes in "bad things happening to good people." The fundamental Jewish tenet of *hashgacha pratit* perhaps finds its most sublime expression in the words of God to King David, after the latter has expressed his wish to build the temple. God's reply: "Are you the one to build me a house to dwell in?" (2 Samuel 7:5). "I will raise up your offspring to succeed you ... He is the one who will build a house for my Name ... I will be his father, and he shall be my son. When he does wrong, I will chasten him with the rod of men, and with such plagues as befall the sons of Adam" (2 Samuel 7:12–14).

Similar believes are often shared by nonreligious individuals, however spiritually inclined, who hold the conviction that each of us has guardian angels to guide us throughout our life journey.

I believe that each of us is constantly bombarded with clues that point to the right things to do. Being trained in the statistical mode of thinking, and therefore sensitized to improbable coincidences, I have encountered in my own life experience countless episodes, where wrong decisions were made ... yet, in hindsight, seemingly meaningless random events, improbable in nature, could have saved me from the wrong decisions; if only had I been attentive enough at the time. Regrettably, most of us have been raised in a culture that does not traditionally train us to look for such clues. Consequently, these clues are most often wasted as a result of ignorance and ignoring.

All of the above has been found to be extremely relevant with regard to the initial hesitation I experienced with regard to publishing this book, as alluded to in the preface. This hesitation persevered throughout the authoring process. Yet, as happens to us all, clues rained down in abundance in various forms and ways that at times were indeed stunning. These clues were expressed in different fashions. Countless times, books opened exactly to where a desired subject could be researched. There were other ways these clues presented themselves as well, and they were no less unlikely or amazing. Gradually, as this book progressed toward its final form, my initial reluctance to write this book gradually diminished. Enthusiasm took its place.

I conclude this epilogue on a personal note.
In the last four years, I have lost all of those most dear to me, people who have nourished me intellectually and emotionally—some of them for many years.

First the news came about Professor Yehuda T. Radday's death. I was attending a conference at a hotel in Tel-Aviv when a colleague notified me about Yehuda passing away. I first met Yehuda when I was still a young teaching assistant at Haifa University, back in the 1970s. I researched with Yehuda, a biblical scholar affiliated with the Technion, doing statistical analysis of biblical texts. The objective was to statistically detect possible multiple authorship in various books of the Bible. A few published papers were the result of this shared effort. In 1985, our coauthored book was published by the Biblical Institute Press (E Pontificio Instituto Biblico) in Rome. The book presented results of the statistical analysis of the book of Genesis, and as in earlier research endeavors, attempted to establish possible multiple authorship, this time in relation to the well-known documentary hypothesis, which claims multiple authorship for the book of Genesis (there was none). Since that time, Yehuda and I had maintained close friendship, notwithstanding the huge age difference. We used to meet periodically and enjoy each other's tales about the fruits of our respective sources of creativity. Yehuda died on September 11, 2001. I was at that time in Canada, attending a conference, giving some lectures and canceling others where needed flights were unavailable. I was not aware of Yehuda's death until that day at the conference. I have until today a deep sense of sorrow that I was not in Israel prior to his passing away.

Hugh and Judy Sinclair lived in Toronto, Canada. Hugh was family-related to Ruth, and when I decided to spend my sabbatical at McMaster University in 2002–2003, Hugh and his wife were our hosts in Toronto every single weekend. Hugh, like Judy, was an artist. Hugh was the most uncritical person I have ever met. He knew how to express his mind, but he was always infinitely warm and open and forthcoming. At times, I wondered whether such a man really existed. A few days after the twin towers collapsed in New York, we attended the synagogue together, for the Rosh Hashanah morning prayer. The mood was subdued. On the evening of that day, we were supposed to take our flight back to Israel. The prayer was moving; the choir was touching. I could not restrain my tears.

Then a stranger approached me and handed me a piece of paper. It read: "Congratulations! You have been designated to open the Ark … Please go up to the Bimah [the raised stage] when we reach page 173, and be prepared to follow the instructions you will be given." I was surprised, because apart from Hugh and Judy, I knew nobody in the audience, no one in the audience knew me. Hugh explained what the note handed to me meant. He asked if he could join me. So I was standing there with Hugh, in front of a huge audience, and together we opened the doors of the Ark before the Blessing of the Cohanim (the priests), then closed it together as the public blessing was over. Less than a year later, when we were still in Canada, Hugh passed away of a heart failure. It happened one week before the end of the summer semester at McMaster University, where I delivered a statistics course at the time, and two weeks before my flight back to Israel for an interim visit.

I have felt since that the shared public service Hugh and I were coincidentally required to deliver at that awesome Rosh Hashanah, in September 2001, at that synagogue in front of a large audience of prayers, was a symbolic prelude for his later untimely departure.

And then my mother departed, at ninety-four, a week before the conclusion of the winter semester at Ben-Gurion University, on January 7, 2005.

Let this book be dedicated to them and to my father (deceased in September 1967), who have nourished my soul with so much wisdom, care, and love while it was still possible.

Appendix

Hebrew Words in Latin Letters

No.	CHAPTER 1	
1	yeled	ילד
2	midah	מידה
3	Elohim	אלוהים
4	aluf	אלוף
5	yaldah	ילדה
6	ish	איש
7	ishah	אישה
8	chacham	חכם
9	chachamah	חכמה
10	naarah	נערה
11	naara	נער
12	rosh	ראש
13	peh	פה
14	*P.R.H*	פ.ר.ה.
15	*P.R.XX*	פ.ר.ע
16	*P.R.Tz*	פ.ר.ץ
17	*P.R.S*	פ.ר.ש
18	chamor	חמור
19	chomer	חומר
20	chomrani	חומרני
21	chomranut	חומרנות
22	ve-yekhu li	וייקחו לי
23	ed	עד
24	kehilah	קהילה

25	tzibur	ציבור
26	kahal	קהל
27	agudah	אגודה
28	hammon	המון
29	edah	עדה
30	le-emor	לאמור
31	el	אל
32	ha-teva	הטבע
	CHAPTER 2	
1	yadid	ידיד
2	yad	יד
3	olam	עולם
4	healem	העלם
5	taaluma	תעלומה
6	le-halim	להעלים
7	le-hitalem	להתעלם
8	averah	עבירה
9	pesha	פשע
10	chatah[1]	חטא
11	chatat	חטאת
12	avon	עוון
13	aven	אוון
14	chamas	חמס
15	avel	עוול
16	maal	מעל
17	oshek	עושק
18	avlah	עוולה
19	nevalah	נבלה
20	raah	רעה
21	rishah	רשעה
22	gezel	גזל
23	lo taturu	לא תתורו
24	chet	חטא
25	rechem	רחם
26	le-rachem	לרחם
27	me-rachem	מרחם

28	ani	אני
29	anochi	אנוכי
30	who	הוא
31	anah	אנה
32	yehuna	יאונה
33	oniah	אניה
34	ain	אין
35	chalal	חלל
36	chiloni	חילוני
37	le-chalel	לחלל
38	mit-chalel	מתחלל
39	midah	מידה
40	li-mdod	למדוד
41	bi-mesura	במשורה
42	le-hodot	להודות
43	shanah	שנה
44	shnayim	שניים
45	mishnah	מישנה
46	shanah meuberet	שנה מעוברת
47	shavua	שבוע
48	sheva	שבע
49	chodesh	חודש
50	yerach	ירח
51	yom	יום
52	lail, lailah	ליל, לילה
53	tzoharaim	צהרים
54	neshef	נשף
55	erev	ערב
56	boker	בוקר
57	le-arev	לערב
58	erev-rav	ערב-רב
59	le-vaker	לבקר
60	heraion	הריון
61	le-harot	להרות
62	heron	הרון
63	heronech	הרונך
64	harbeh arbeh etzvonech	הרבה ארבה עצבונך

65	alef	אלף
66	bechor	בכור
67	sheleg	שלג
68	dam	דם
69	ishah	אישה
70	ish	איש
71	adamah	אדמה
72	adam	אדם
73	av	אב
74	ben	בן
75	neched	נכד
76	dor reviei	דור רביעי
77	neen	נין
78	geza	גזע
79	anaf	ענף
80	perach	פרח
81	pri	פרי
82	purah	פורה
83	etz	עץ
84	tzel	צל
85	tzameret	צמרת
86	tehom	תהום
87	tehomot	תהומות
88	maayan	מעיין
89	nahar	נהר
90	nachal	נחל
91	midbar	מידבר
92	le-daber	לדבר
93	mispar	מספר
94	sepher	ספר
95	sippur	סיפור
96	sepharim	ספרים
97	sephar	ספר
98	yada	ידע
99	yadoa	ידוע
100	zachar	זכר
101	bassar	בשר

102	le-vaser	לבשר
103	bessorah	בשורה
104	briah	בריאה
105	briut	בריאות
106	ot	אות
107	oti	אותי
108	oto	אותו
109	otam	אותם
110	otan	אותן
111	laban	לבן
112	naval	נבל
113	hashem	השם
114	sneh	סנה
115	hannes	הנס
116	roa	רוע
117	iver	עור
118	osher	עשר
119	resha	רשע
120	mavet	מות
121	tom	תום
122	be-tumo	בתומו
123	aluf	אלוף
124	peleh	פלא
125	chen	חן
	CHAPTER 3	
1	haster astir	הסתר אסתיר
2	le-hechavae	להיחבא
3	olam	עולם
4	keri	קרי
5	nikro nikreti	נקרא נקריתי
6	asher karcha	אשר קרך
7	nikrah	נקרה
8	va-yikar	ויקר
9	karah	קרה
10	mikreh	מקרה

11	kor	קור
12	kar	קר
	CHAPTER 4	
1	adon	אדון
2	el	אל
3	el shadai	אל שדי
4	elohim	אלוהים
5	eheyeh	אהיה
6	hashem	השם
7	hashem elohenu	השם אלוהינו
8	hashem hamephorash	השם המפורש
9	Yehovah	יהוה
10	eheyeh asher eheyeh	אהיה אשר אהיה
11	Yom Kippur	יום כיפור
12	hayah,[12a] havah[12b]	היה, הווה
13	oveh	הווה
14	yehiyeh	יהיה
	CHAPTER 5	
1	gever	גבר
2	gevarim	גברים
3	achot	אחות
4	achayot	אחיות
5	yeled	ילד
6	yeladim	ילדים
7	yaldah	ילדה
8	yeladot	ילדות
9	shnayim	שניים
10	shtayim	שתיים
11	yad	יד
12	yadayim	ידיים
13	regel	רגל
14	raglayim	רגליים
15	shvuot	שבועות
16	shvuayim	שבועיים
17	yamim	ימים

18	yomayim	יומיים
19	shen	שן
20	shinayim	שיניים
21	Yerushalayim shel malah	ירושלים של מעלה
22	Yerushalayim shel matah	ירושלים של מטה
23	rakia	רקיע
24	shamayim	שמיים
25	sham	שם
26	mayim	מיים
27	chayim	חיים
28	chai	חי
29	chaiyah	חייה
30	kol	כל
31	kol chai	כל חי
32	mi kol ha chai	מכל החי
33	ve kol ha chaiyah	וכל החייה
34	em kol chai	אם כל חי
35	chaiot	חיות
36	hineni	הנני
37	hasneh	הסנה
	CHAPTER 6	
1	el	אל
2	li-lmod	ללמוד
3	kniyat daat	קניית דעת
4	limud	לימוד
5	lo tuchal	לא תוכל
6	melamdecha	מלמדך
7	melachah	מלאכה
8	melachot	מלאכות
9	malach	מלאך
	CHAPTER 7	
1	elohenu	אלוהינו
2	Elohim[2]	אלוהים
3	el, eloha	אל, אלוה
4	bara	ברא

5	elohecha	אלוהיך
6	koach	כוח
7	oz	עוז
8	otzmah	עצמה
9	vav	וו
10	ve-hayah	והיה
11	hayah	היה
12	ve-nissa	ונישא
13	yomer	יאמר
14	yehi	יהי
15	yehiyeh	יהיה
16	hoveh	הווה
17	hayah	היה
18	anah	אנה
19	an	אן
20	ad-anah	עד-אנה
21	ad an	עד-אן
22	anah ve-anah	אנה ואנה
23	olam	עולם
	Chapter 8	
1	eretz	ארץ
2	yareach	ירח
3	yerach	ירח
4	sahar	סהר
5	levanah	לבנה
6	lavan	לבן
7	shemesh	שמש
8	cheres	חרס
9	beterem bo charsah	בטרם בוא חרסה
10	chamah	חמה
11	kochav	כוכב
12	tzedek	צדק
13	shabtai	שבתי
14	nogah	נוגה
15	maadim	מאדים
16	mazalot	מזלות

17	mazarot	מזרות
18	mazal	מזל
19	mazar	מזר
20	mapik	מפיק
21	zayin	זיין
22	nezer	נזר
23	shachar	שחר
24	kimah	כימה
25	ksil	כסיל
26	ash[26a], aish[26b]	עש, עיש
27	teman	תמן
	CHAPTER 9	
1	mayim	מים
2	bechor	בכור
3	sheleg	שלג
4	kerach	קרח
5	kitor	קיטור
6	ayin	עיין
7	anan	ענן
8	av	עב
9	arafel	ערפל
10	arifim	עריפים
11	aveh	עבה
12	ed	אד
13	kerach	קרח
14	kitor	קיטור
	CHAPTER 10	
1	yad	יד
2	kaf	כף
3	ayin	עיין
4	peh	פה
5	rosh	ראש
6	shen	שן
7	yerech	ירך
8	berech	ברך

9	sehar	שיער
10	safa	שפה
11	metzach	מצח
12	panim	פנים
13	leshad	לשד
14	shad	שד
15	dad	דד
16	panim	פנים
17	ozen	אוזן
18	moznayim	מאזניים
19	ve-izen	ואיזן
20	anan	ענן
21	arafel	ערפל'
22	av	עב
23	dam	דם
24	dat	דת
25	kiliah	כליה
26	le-chalot	לכלות
27	chalah	כלה
28	chalu hamayim	כלו המים
	CHAPTER 11	
1	nahar	נהר
2	naharah	נהרה
3	ve-nahart	ונהרת
4	ve-naharu	ונהרו
5	choshech	חושך
6	chasuch marpe	חשוך מרפא
7	aphelah	אפילה
8	shachor	שחור
9	sachar	שחר
10	chor	חור
11	chavar	חוור
12	yachaviru	יחוויַרו
13	chur	חור
14	atzilut	אצילות
15	keri	קרי

	CHAPTER 12	
1	lavan	לבן
2	chivar	חיוור
3	shesh	שש
4	yashish	ישיש
5	shoshan	שושן
6	shaish	שייש
7	shachor	שחור
8	kachol	כחול
9	tchelet	תכלת
10	adom	אדום
11	dam	דם
12	admoni	אדמוני
13	adamdam	אדמדם
14	shashar	ששר
15	chachlili	חכלילי
16	sharok	שרוק
17	argaman	ארגמן
18	shani	שני
19	chum	חום
20	tzhaov	צהוב
21	zahav	זהב
22	zahov	זהוב
23	sagol	סגול
24	yerakon	ירקון
25	yarok	ירוק
26	yerakrak	ירקרק
27	barod	ברוד
28	chamutz	אמוץ
29	afel	אפל
30	kasuf	כסוף
31	chachalt	כחלת
32	yerek	ירק
33	chivaron	חיוורון
34	admon	אדמון
35	sered	שרד

36	yom	יום
37	yerach	ירח
38	shanah	שנה
39	keshet	קשת
40	raam	רעם
41	shaon	שאון
	CHAPTER 13	
1	zahav	זהב
2	kessef	כסף
3	bdil	בדיל
4	oferet	עופרת
5	nechoshet	נחושת
6	nechushah	נחושה
7	barzel	ברזל
8	pladot	פלדת
9	afar	עפר
10	melach	מלח
11	geer	גיר
12	zechuchit	זכוכית
13	neter	נתר
14	gofrit	גפרית
15	etzem	עצם
16	chometz	חומץ
	CHAPTER 14	
1	tohu	תהו
2	bohu	בהו
3	kav-tohu	קו תהו
4	avnei bohu	אבני בהו
5	tahah	תהה
6	bo-hu	בו-הוא
7	behemah	בהמה
8	bah-mah	בה-מה
9	bahah	בהה
10	huchal	הוחל
11	mechuyael	מחויאל

12	metushael	מתושאל
13	toho va-vohu	תהו ובהו
14	shmamah	שממה
15	shamemu	שממו
16	eshtomem	אשתומם
17	mashmim	משמים
18	tahiti	תהיתי
19	tahiti al kankano	תהיתי על קנקנו
20	bahiti	בהיתי
21	shamayim	שמיים
22	sham	שם
23	tohae and bohae	תוהה ובוהה
24	etbahbah	אתבהבה
25	boahbah	בוהבה
	CHAPTER 15	
1	haggadah	הגדה
2	va-yan	ויען
3	va-yanu	ויענו
4	gal-ed	גל-עד
5	yegar sahaduta	יגר שהדותא
6	ramai	רמאי
7	naval	נבל
8	yenachamenu	ינחמנו
9	chamas	חמס
	CHAPTER 16	
1	ed	עד
2	shema	שמע
3	echad	אחד
4	va-yikra	ויקרא
5	va-yiker	ויקר
6	yiker	יקר
7	naarah	נערה
8	teomim	תאומים
9	tomim	תומם
10	reshit	רשית

11	lo	לוֹ
12	lo	לֹא
13	arachim	ערכים
14	haster astir panai	הסתר אסתיר פני
15	vayzata	ויזתא
16	parshandatha	פרשנדתא
17	parmashta	פרמשתא
18	kav	קו
	CHAPTER 17	
1	tov	טוב
2	va-ra	ורע
3	ra	רע
4	haster astir panai	הסתר אסתיר פני
5	shamayim	שמים
6	tovah	טובה
7	raah	רעה
	CHAPTER 18	
1	ibur	עיבור
2	Rosh Hashanah	ראש השנה
3	torah she-be-al peh	תורה שבע"פ
4	molad ve-yad	מולד וי"ד
5	molad shel tohu	מולד של תוהו
6	va-vohu	ובהו
7	va-yomer	ויאמר
8	va-yavdel	ויבדל
9	baharad	בהר"ד
	CHAPTER 19	
1	neatzah	נאצה
2	le-naetz	לנאץ
3	chamas	חמס
4	mabul	מבול
5	*A.R.F*	ע.ר.ף
6	pleshet	פלשת
7	*P.R.A*	פ.ר.ע

8	praot	פרעות
9	galut	גלות
10	be-froa praot	בפרוע פרעות
	CHAPTER 20	
1	Tishah B'Av	תשעה באב
2	Av	אב
3	Purim	פורים
4	galut	גלות
5	histarti	הסתרתי
6	haster astir	הסתר אסתיר
7	Shoshan Purim	שושן פורים
8	Iyar	אייר
9	Nisan	ניסן
10	Tishrei	תשרי
11	Rosh Hashanah	ראש השנה
12	gevurah	גבורה
13	midat ha-din	מידת הדין
14	chesed	חסד
15	midat ha-rachamim	מידת הרחמים
16	ot ha-gevurah	אות הגבורה
17	keri	קרי
18	haster astir panai	הסתר אסתיר פני
19	midah ke-neged midah	מידה כנגד מידה
20	be-haavoto	בהעוותו

References

Bible Translations Used in This Book

[I]   *The Jerusalem Bible*. Jerusalem: Koren Publishers Jerusalem Ltd., 2000. (major source for quotations in this book.)

[II] *Holy Bible: New International Version Anglicised, compact edition*. International Bible Society. London: Hodder & Stoughton Publishers, 1984. (few quotations)

[III] *The Holy Bible: New American Standard*. UltraThin Reference Edition. Nashville: Broadman & Holman Publishers, 1985. (few quotations)

[IV] *The Bible: Authorized King James Version/edited with an introduction and notes by Robert Carroll and Stephen Prickett*. Oxford World's Classics. Oxford, New York: Oxford University Press, 1997. (rare quotations)

Other References

[1] Aczel, A. D. *God's Equation: Einstein, Relativity, and the Expanding Universe*. New York: Dell Publishing, 1999.

[2] Ayto, John. *Arcade Dictionary of Word Origins*. New York: Arcade Publishing, 1990.

[3] Beckmann, P. *A History of* π (Pi). St. Martin's Press, 1971.

[4] Blatner, D. *The Joy of* π.. Middlesex, England: Penguin Books, 1998.

[5] Benner, J. A. *The Ancient Hebrew Language and Alphabet: Understanding the Ancient Hebrew Language of the Bible Based on Ancient Hebrew Culture and Thought*. Virtualbookworm.com Publishing, 2004.

[6] Chaboyer, B., Demarque, P., Kernan, P. J., Krauss, L. M. 1998. The age of globular clusters in light of Hipparcos: Resolving the Age Problem? *The Astrophysical Journal*. 494: 96.

[7]   Crystal, D. *The Cambridge Factfinder*. Cambridge University Press, 1993. [8] Even-Shoshan, A. *New Concordance for Torah, Neviim, and Ketuvim*. Revised edition. Jerusalem: Kiriat-Sefer, 1988.

[9]   Gratton, R. G., Pecci, F. F., Carretta, E., Clementini, G., Corsi, C. E., Lattanzi, M. 1997. Ages of globular clusters from Hipparcos parallaxes of local subdwarfs. *The Astrophysical Journal*. 491:749-771.

[10]   Greene, B. *The Fabric of the Cosmos*. Random House, 2004.

[11]   Guth, A. H. *The Inflationary Universe: The Quest for a New Theory of Cosmic Origins*. Addison-Wesley Longman Inc., 1997.

[12]   Hanks, P. (chief editor), McLeod, W. T., Makins, M. (managing editors). *The Collins Concise Dictionary of the English Language*. London: William Collins Sons & Co., 1988.

[13]   Hansen, B., Richer, H., Fahlman, G., Stetson, P., Brewer, J., Currie, T., Gibson, B., Ibata, R., Rich, R. M., Shara, M. 12/2004. Hubble Space Telescope Observations of the White Dwarf Cooling Sequence of M4. *The Astrophysical Journal Supplement Series*. 155(2): 551-576.

[14]   Helpern, P. *The Great Beyond: Higher Dimensions, Parallel Universes, and the Extraordinary Search for a Theory of Everything*. John Wiley & Sons: 2004.

[15]   Jaynes, E. T. 1957. Information theory and statistical mechanics. *Phys. Rev.A*, 106: 620.

[16]   Kaku, M. *Hyperspace: A Scientific Odyssey Through Parallel Universes, Time Warps, and the Tenth Dimension*. New York: Oxford University Press, 1994.

[17]   Kaku, M. *Parallel Worlds: A Journey Through Creation, Higher Dimensions, and the Future of the Cosmos*. Doubleday: 2005.

[18]   Kaku, M. 2005a. Testing string theory. *Discovery*, August, 30–37.

[19]   Kaplan, A. *Sefer Yetzirah: The Book of Creation*. Revised edition. Boston: Weiser Books, 1997.

[20]   Katz, M. *CompuTorah: Hidden Codes in the Torah*. CompuTorah: 1996. Hebrew version published 1991.

[21]   Lederman, L. M., and C. T. Hill. *Symmetry and the Beautiful Universe*. New York: Prometheus Books, 2004.

[22]   Leibowitz, N. *Studies in Vayikra (Leviticus)*. Jerusalem: World Zionist Organization, 1983.

[23]   Leibush, Meir (Malbim). 1892. "Yair Or." Available for free downloading at: http://www.halachabrura.org/library3.htm#דקדוק.

[24] Lipiner, E. *The Metaphysics of the Hebrew Alphabet*. 2d ed. Jerusalem: the Hebrew University Magnes Press, 2003 (originally printed in 1989).

[25] Mazar, B., and H. Tadmor, and S. Ahituv (eds.) *Biblical Encyclopedia*. Jerusalem: the Bialik Institute, 1976.

[26] Mitton, J. *The Penguin Dictionary of Astronomy*. 3d ed. Penguin Books Ltd., 2000.

[27] Peloso, E., Silva, L., Gustavo, F., Arany-Prado, L. I. 2005. *The age of the Galactic thin disk from Th/Eu nucleocosmochronology: extended sample*. Proceedings of the International Astronomical Union, 1: 485-486. Cambridge University Press.

[28] Penrose, R. *The Road to Reality: A Complete Guide to the Laws of the Universe*. New York: Knopf, 2004.

[29] Redfield, J. *The Celestine Prophecy*. Warner Books, 1995.

[30] Redfield, J. *The Tenth Insight: Holding the Vision (Celestine Prophecy)*. Warner Books, 1996.

[31] Shannon, C. E. 1948. A mathematical theory of communication. *The Bell System Technical Journal*. 27: 379–423 and 623–656, July and October.

[32] Shannon, C. E., and W. Weaver. *Mathematical Theory of Communication*. Urbana, IL: University of Illinois Press, Chicago: 1949, 1963.

[33] Shinan, A., and Y. Zakovitch. *That's Not What the Good Book Says*. Hebrew. Tel-Aviv: Miskal-Yedioth Ahronoth Books and Chemed Books, 2005.

[34] Shore, H. *Response Modeling Methodology: Empirical Modeling for Engineering and Science*. Singapore: World Scientific Publishing, 2005.

[35] Singh, S. *Big Bang: The Origin of the Universe*. HarperCollins Publishers Inc., 2004.

[36] Watson, A. 1999. Exploring the proton sea. *Science*. 283: 472–474.

[37] Weinberg, S. *Dreams of a Final Theory*. New York: Pantheon, 1992.

[38] White, R. S. 2007. The age of the Earth. Faraday Paper No. 8. *The Faraday Institute for Science and Religion*, St Edmund's College, Cambridge, U.K. Available at: www.faraday-institute.org.

Index

www.ingramcontent.com/pod-product-compliance
Lightning Source LLC
Chambersburg PA
CBHW051806150726
47998CB00001B/55